21 世纪英语专业系列教材

本书针对《语言学教程》第
深度剖析，全方位自我检测
助您零障碍挑战《语言学教程》

主编 赵永青 姚振军

编者 赵永青 姚振军 李春姬 康卉
王卉 罗英 史艳 刘雪莲

Highlights and Practice for
Linguistics: A course book

《语言学教程》纲要与实践

北京大学出版社
PEKING UNIVERSITY PRESS

图书在版编目(CIP)数据

《语言学教程》纲要与实践/赵永青,姚振军主编. —北京:北京大学出版社,2011.9
(21世纪英语专业系列教材)
ISBN 978-7-301-19274-0

Ⅰ.①语… Ⅱ.①赵…②姚… Ⅲ.①语言学－高等学校－教学参考资料 Ⅳ.①H0

中国版本图书馆CIP数据核字(2011)第145757号

书 名:《语言学教程》纲要与实践
著作责任者:赵永青 姚振军 主编
责 任 编 辑:孙 莹
标 准 书 号:ISBN 978-7-301-19274-0/H·2905
出 版 发 行:北京大学出版社
地 址:北京市海淀区成府路205号 100871
网 址:http://www.pup.cn 电子信箱:zbing@pup.pku.edu.cn
电 话:邮购部 62752015 发行部 62750672 编辑部 62754382 出版部 62754962
印 刷 者:三河市富华印装厂
经 销 者:新华书店
　　　　　　 730毫米×980毫米 16开本 20.25印张 420千字
　　　　　　 2011年9月第1版 2011年9月第1次印刷
定　　 价:42.00元

未经许可,不得以任何方式复制或抄袭本书之部分或全部内容。
版权所有,侵权必究
举报电话:(010)62752024 电子信箱:fd@pup.pku.edu.cn

序

  2010年初，大连外国语学院的《外语与外语教学》改版和编委会换届，我从所赠予的刊物上看到赵永青教授的名字，对这位新主编有了良好的印象。其实2005年前，在北京大学出版社召开的一次制定"十一五"规划的《英语综合教程》修订审稿会上，永青教授作为大连外国语学院英语学院院长与会，我们早已经见过面了。2007年在山东大学召开的学术会上，她送过我一本她根据《语言学教程》（第二版）编的练习册。2010年夏北京大学出版社在北大召开全国教师暑期培训班，我们都作了大会主题发言，不过其余时间各就各位，听其他专家发言，我们没有机会多做交谈。看来我们两人在性格上好似有共同的缺陷，不善言谈。这次北京大学出版社外语部张冰主任和永青教授请我为她和姚振军老师合编的《〈语言学教程〉纲要与实践》一书写序时，才发现永青教授长期从事语言学教学工作，原是同行，相见恨晚。本书的另一主编姚振军博士曾是永青教授的研究生，现在东北财经大学任教。

  使我惊奇和欣慰的是本书是为我、姜望琪教授和钱军教授合编的《语言学教程》（第四版）配套的练习教材，而且主编和参与编写的各位老师在大连外国语学院已开设"语言学概论"课程多年，长期选用从第一版到第四版《语言学教程》作为教材。这次，又根据第四版作了增补。坦率地说，我们这些《教程》的原作者在练习编写上花的工夫不多。《纲要与实践》一书的出版正好弥补了这点不足。

  不尽如此，《纲要与实践》有很多特色。正如永青教授在前言中所言，它把《教程》中的许多基本概念和理论梳理了，把一些重要术语和讲解不到位的内容增补了，并为学生查阅方便对有关词语进行了合理编排。在练习方面，区分基本练习和高级练习，以满足不同需要。我对高级练习特感兴趣，因为我一直告诫我的学生，不要死背术语和定义，而应吃透每一个术语或理论的基本概念，用自己的话说出来，按死背的方法学习语言学实在太累了。本书的第二个特色是提供了十套综合试题，使读者能考查自己对语言学知识深入理解的程度和灵活运用的能力。所有的项目都附有参考答案和解释。我谨代表《教程》的全体作者向《纲要与实践》的编者和作者表示衷心的感谢，并希望各位老师今后对《教程》继续提供宝贵的意见。

  自80年代末开始，我国在教材编写方面奉行从"统编教材"的模式走向"一纲多本"的模式，从此出现了适用于不同地区、不同高校、不同培养目标、不同学生程度的多种语言学教材，百花盛开。语言学概论的授课教师一定会有这样的体会：不论各种教材的难易和厚薄，将语言学作为一门学科来看，总有一些最基本的概念和内容是共同的。在这个意义上,《纲要与实践》对使用其他语言学教材的老师和同学也是适用的。这是因为参与编写的作者在教学实践中积累了长期经验和大量资料,既了解课程的要求,也了解学习者的困难。当然,永青教授和其他作者也会在本书的使用过程中认真听取各地院校的授课教师和学生的意见和要求,不断完善本书。

  愿永青教授学术青春永驻!也祝愿姚振军博士和本书的其他作者将语言学的教学和研究事业在新世纪大放异彩!

胡壮麟
北京大学外国语学院
外国语言学和应用语言学研究所
2011 年 4 月 14 日

前　　言

本书是为胡壮麟先生主编的《语言学教程》(第四版)所配套的系列丛书之一。全书分两大部分:一是依据《语言学教程》的章节划分,对每章的内容进行详细的整理和适度的扩展,共有十二章。二是综合测试,共有十套试卷。

第一部分各章分为以下几个部分:

- 基本概念和理论(Concepts and Theories)。编者详细地梳理和提炼了各章涉及的主要理论和概念,给学生提供了一个各章内容的纲要。
- 相关术语(Related Terms)。编者就各章出现并解释的重要术语、提到但没有详细解释的,却又涉及各章内容的术语,根据字母顺序进行了排列整理和解释,以便学生在学习时查阅和核对。
- 基本练习(Practice)。这部分目的是让学生对各章的重要内容有个初步掌握。练习的内容仅限于重要的基本概念和知识,练习后附有参考答案。
- 高级练习(Further Practice)。这部分主要是对各章内容进行扩展练习。其中包括对重要术语的识别、知识的理解和灵活应用。练习后附有参考答案和解释。

第二部分的十套综合测试题达到了英语专业研究生入学考试的难度。测试题对《语言学教程》所涉及的知识从点到面有着全方位的覆盖,并且能灵活考查学生对语言学知识的理解和运用。测试题后附有参考答案和解释。

胡先生的《语言学教程》多年来一直是我国高校英语专业本科生的通用教材,还是多数学校研究生入学考试的指定参考教材。《语言学教程》几经修订,不仅内容覆盖面广了,而且尽可能地反映了语言学新的发展状况。

本书的编者在学生时期都学习过胡先生的《语言学教程》,当了教师后又有了使用《语言学教程》教授"语言学概论"这门课程的经历。这本书是编者在教授"语言学概论"课程过程中所积累的资料的总结。编者衷心希望本书不仅能成为学生学习《语言学教程》的助手,同时也能有助于同行教师平日的教学。

本书在编写过程中参阅了多位学者的教材,编者对他们表示由衷的敬仰和感谢。

本书的出版得到北京大学出版社的大力支持,编者在此表示衷心的感谢。

由于编者的水平所限,疏漏和错误不可避免,敬请同行批评指正。

编　者
2010 年 8 月

目　　录

Chapter 1　Invitations to Linguistics ……………………………………… (1)

Chapter 2　Speech Sounds ………………………………………………… (24)

Chapter 3　From Morpheme to Phrase …………………………………… (46)

Chapter 4　From Word to Text …………………………………………… (68)

Chapter 5　Meaning ………………………………………………………… (97)

Chapter 6　Language and Cognition ……………………………………… (121)

Chapter 7　Language, Culture and Society ……………………………… (150)

Chapter 8　Language in Use ……………………………………………… (163)

Chapter 9　Language and Literature ……………………………………… (176)

Chapter 10　Language and Computer …………………………………… (200)

Chapter 11　Language and Foreign Language Teaching ……………… (216)

Chapter 12　Theories and Schools of Modern Linguistics …………… (245)

综合测试 ……………………………………………………………………… (263)

Chapter 1 Invitations to Linguistics

Concepts & Theories

I. Some Fundamental Views about Language
1. Children learn their native language swiftly, efficiently and without instruction.
2. Language operates by rules.
3. All languages have three major components: a sound system, a system of lexicogrammar and a system of semantics.
4. Everyone speaks a dialect.
5. Language slowly changes.
6. Speakers of all languages employ a range of styles and a set of jargons.
7. Languages are intimately related to the societies and individuals who use them.
8. Writing is derivative of speech.
9. Through studying language, we can have a better understanding of our human race.

II. Definition and Design Features of Language
1. **The definition of language**

    Language is the system of human communication which consists of the structured arrangement of sounds (or their written representation) into larger units, e.g. morphemes, words, sentences, utterances.

2. **Design features of language**

    The features that define our human languages can be called design features which can distinguish human language from any animal system of communication. There are four design features of language:

    (1) Arbitrariness
    - ☆ Saussure holds the idea that the forms of linguistic signs bear no natural relationship to their meaning.
    - ☆ Arbitrariness exists at the morpheme level and at the syntactic level.
    - ☆ The link between a linguistic sign and its meaning is a matter of convention.

    (2) Duality
    - ☆ Duality refers to the property of having two levels of structures, such that units of the primary level are composed of elements of the secondary level and each of the two levels has its own principles of organization.
    - ☆ Duality exists on different levels of language, namely, on the level of words, sentences and texts.
    - ☆ Duality contributes to the productivity of human language.

    (3) Creativity

    Creativity means that language is resourceful because of its duality and its recursiveness. Recursive rule refers to the rule which can be applied repeatedly without any definite limit.

(4) Displacement

Displacement means that human languages enable their users to symbolize objects, events and concepts which are not present (in time and space) at the moment of language use.

III. Origin of Language

There are some popular views about the origin of language.
1. The bow-wow theory
2. The pooh-pooh theory
3. The *yo-he-ho* theory

IV. Functions of Language

1. As is proposed by **Jacobson**, language has six functions:
   (1) Referential function: people use language to convey message and information;
   (2) Poetic function: people use language to indulge in language for its own sake;
   (3) Emotive function: people use language to express attitudes, feelings and emotions;
   (4) Conative function: people use language to persuade and influence others through commands and entreaties;
   (5) Phatic function: people use language to establish communion with others;
   (6) Metalingual function: people use language to clear up intentions, words and meanings.

2. **Halliday** (1994) proposes a theory of metafunctions of language. It means that language has three metafunctions:
   (1) Ideational function: people use language to convey new information, to communicate a content that is unknown to the hearer;
   (2) Interpersonal function: it embodies all use of language to express social and personal relationships;
   (3) Textual function: it refers to the fact that language has mechanisms to make any stretch of spoken and written discourse into a coherent and unified text and make a living passage different from a random list of sentences.

3. According to the textbook, language has at least seven functions:
   (1) Informative function

   The informative function means language is the instrument of thought and people often use it to communicate new information. It is also called ideational function in functional grammar.

   (2) Interpersonal function

   The interpersonal function means people can use language to establish and maintain their status in a society.

   (3) Performative function

   The performative function of language is primarily to change the social status of persons. It can extend to the control of reality as on some magical or religious occasions.

   (4) Emotive function

   The emotive function is one of the most powerful uses of language because it is so crucial in changing the emotional status of the audience.

   (5) Phatic communion

Chapter 1

Invitations to Linguistics

The phatic communion means people always use some small, seemingly meaningless expressions such as *Good morning*, *God bless you*, *Nice day*, etc., to maintain a comfortable relationship between people.

(6) Recreational function

The recreational function means people use language for the sheer joy of using it, such as a baby's babbling or a chanter's chanting.

(7) Metalingual function

The metalingual function means people can use language to talk about itself.

V. Linguistics

1. The definition of linguistics

Linguistics is the scientific study of language. It studies not just one language of any one community, but the language of all human beings.

2. Main branches of linguistics

(1) Phonetics

Phonetics is the study of speech sounds. It covers three main areas: articulatory phonetics, acoustic phonetics, and auditory phonetics.

(2) Phonology

Phonology studies the rules governing the structure, distribution, and sequencing of speech sounds and the form of syllables.

(3) Morphology

Morphology studies the minimal units of meaning-morphemes and word-formation processes.

(4) Syntax

Syntax refers to the rules governing the way words are combined to form sentences in a language, or simply, the study of the formation of sentences.

(5) Semantics

Semantics examines how meaning is encoded in a language.

(6) Pragmatics

Pragmatics is the study of meaning in context.

3. Macrolinguistics

(1) The definition of Macrolinguistics

Macrolinguistics is the study of language in all aspects.

(2) Main branches of Macrolinguistics

☆ Psycholinguistics
☆ Sociolinguistics
☆ Anthropological linguistics
☆ Computational linguistics

4. Important distinctions in linguistics

(1) Descriptive vs. prescriptive

To say that linguistics is a descriptive science is to say that the linguist tries to discover and record the rules to which the members of a language community actually conform and does not seek to impose upon them other rules or norms of correctness.

However, prescriptive linguistics aims to lay down rules for the correct use of language and settle the disputes over usage once and for all.

(2) Synchronic vs. diachronic

Synchronic study takes a fixed instant (usually at present) as its point of observation.

Saussure's diachronic description is the study of a language through the course of its history.

(3) Langue & parole

According to Saussure, langue is relatively stable and systematic, parole is subject to personal and situational constraints; langue is not spoken by an individual, parole is always a naturally occurring event.

(4) Competence & performance

According to Chomsky, a language user's underlying knowledge about the system of rules is called the linguistic competence, and the actual use of language in concrete situations is called performance.

Related Terms

acoustic phonetics
Acoustic phonetics refers to the study of the properties of the sound waves.

anthropological linguistics
Anthropological linguistics uses the theories and methods of anthropology to study language variation and language use in relation to the actual patterns and beliefs of man.

applied linguistics
Applied linguistics is a term covering several linguistic subjects as well as certain interdisciplinary areas that use linguistic methods, like psycholinguistics, computational linguistics, sociolinguistics, etc. to study the nature of language teaching.

arbitrariness
Arbitrariness refers to the fact that the forms of linguistic signs bear no natural relationship to their meanings. Language is arbitrary on the morpheme level, yet it is not arbitrary on the syntax level.

articulatory phonetics
Articulatory phonetics refers to the study of articulatory organs and the investigation of the speech sounds produced by these organs by identifying and classifying the individual sounds.

auditory phonetics
Auditory phonetics focuses on the way in which a listener analyses or processes a sound wave.

bow-wow theory
Bow-wow theory is a theory about the origin of language. In this theory language developed from the people imitating the sounds of the animal calls in the wild environment they lived in.

competence
Competence is the ideal language user's knowledge of the rules of his language according to Chomsky.

computational linguistics
Computational linguistics is an approach to linguistics which uses mathematical techniques, often with the aid of a computer. Computational linguistics includes the

analysis of language data, e.g. in order to establish the order in which learners acquire various grammatical rules or the frequency of occurrence of some particular item. It also includes research on automatic translation, electronic production of artificial speech and the automatic recognition of human speech.

convention

Convention refers to a regularity in the behavior of members of a given group who repeatedly find themselves confronted by a problem of co-ordination, who solve this problem in one of several possible ways, and in return expect the response by others in the group.

The arbitrariness of the linguistic sign arises from the conventionality of language.

creativity

By creativity we mean language is resourceful because of its duality and its recursiveness.

descriptive study

Descriptive study refers to the study of language in which the rules to which the members of a language community actually conform are just described.

design features

Design features are the features that define our human languages. The frequently discussed design features are arbitrariness, duality, creativity and replacement.

diachronic linguistics

Diachronic linguistics is the study of language through the course of its history. E.g. a study of the changes English has undergone since then would be a diachronic study of language.

dialect

Dialect refers to a variety of a language, spoken in one part of a country (regional dialect), or by people belonging to a particular social class (social dialect or sociolect), which is different in some words, grammar, and/or pronunciation from other forms of the same language.

displacement

Displacement means that human languages enable their users to symbolize objects, events and concepts which are not present (in time and space) at the moment of communication.

duality

Duality is the property of having two levels of structures, such that units of the primary level are composed of elements of the secondary level and each of the two levels has its own principles of organization.

Duality is a distinctive characteristic of language which refers to the fact that language are organized in terms of two levels. At one level, language consists of sequences of segments or units which do not themselves carry meaning (such as the letters *g*, *d* and *o*). however, when these units are combined in certain sequences, they form larger units and carry meaning (such as *god*, *dog*).

emotive function

Emotive function refers to the function of language by which people express attitudes, feelings and emotions.

informative function

Informative function refers to the function of language by which people tell what the

speaker believes, give information about facts or reason things out. One important feature of this function that the speaker commits himself to the truth that something is or is not the case.

interpersonal function

Interpersonal function refers to the function of language by which people make sociological use of language to establish and maintain their status in a society.

language

Language is the system of human communication which consists of the structured arrangement of sounds (or their written representation) into larger units, e.g. morphemes, words, sentences, utterances.

langue

Langue refers to the abstract linguistic system shared by all the members of a speech community according to Saussure.

linguistics

Linguistics is the scientific study of language. It studies not just one language of any one community, but the language of all human beings.

macrolinguistics

Macrolinguistics is the scientific investigation of all related disciplines such as sociology, psychology and philosophy.

metalingual function

Metalingual function is the function of language by which people discuss language by itself. For example, you can explain your words by telling *what I really want to say is* ...

morpheme

Morpheme is the minimal unit of meaning.

morphology

Morphology is concerned with the internal organization of words. It studies the minimal units of meaning-morphemes and word-formation processes.

onomatopoetic word

Onomatopoetic word is the word which is formed through the imitation of sounds from nature.

parole

Parole refers to the actualized language, or realization of language according to Saussure.

performance

Performance is the actual realization of the ideal language user's knowledge of the rules of his language in linguistic communication according to Chomsky.

performative function

Performative function refers to the function of language by which people use language to *do things*, to perform actions.

The performative function of language is primarily to change the social status of persons. It can extend to the control of reality as on some magical or religious occasions.

phatic communion

Phatic communion refers to the social interaction of language.

phoneme

Phoneme is the basic unit in phonology. It is a unit that is of distinctive value. But it is an abstract unit. To be exact, a phoneme is not a sound, but a collection of distinctive phonetic features such as /p/ and /b/.

phonetics

   Phonetics studies speech sounds, including the production of speech, that is how speech sounds are actually made, transmitted and received, the sound of speech, the description and classification of speech sounds, words and connected speech, etc.

phonology

   Phonology studies the rules governing the structure, distribution and sequencing of speech sounds and the shape of syllables.

pooh-pooh theory

   Pooh-pooh theory is about the origin of language. In this theory, language is developed through our primitive ancestors uttering instinctive sounds of pain, anger and joy in their hard life.

pragmatics

   Pragmatics is the study of meaning in context. It deals with particular utterances in particular situations and is especially concerned with the various ways in which the many social contexts of language performance can influence interpretation. In other words, pragmatics is concerned with the way language is used to communicate rather than with the way language is structured.

prescriptive study

   Prescriptive study is the study of language in which rules are laid down for *correct* behaviors.

psycholinguistics

   Psycholinguistics investigates the interrelation of language and mind, in processing and producing utterances and in language acquisition for example.

recreational function

   Recreational function refers to the function of language which will bring joy to people for its own sake.

recursiveness

   Recursiveness is a term borrowed from mathematics and used in linguistics for the formal properties of grammars, which use a finite inventory of elements and a finite group of rules to produce an infinite number of sentences.

semantics

   Semantics is a branch of linguistics which examines how meaning is encoded in a language. It is not only concerned with meaning of words as lexical items, but also with levels of language below the word and above it, e.g. meaning of morphemes and sentences.

sociolinguistics

   Sociolinguistics is a term which covers a variety of different interests in language and society, including the language and the social characteristics of its users.

   Sociolinguistics is the study of the characteristics of language varieties, the characteristics of their functions, and the characteristics of their speakers as these three constantly interact and change within a speech community.

synchronic study

   Synchronic study is the study of language by taking a fixed instant (usually, but not necessarily, present) as its point of observation. E.g. a study of the features of the English used in Shakespeare's time would be a synchronic study of language.

syntax

   Syntax is about principles of forming and understanding correct English sentences.

yo-he-ho theory

Yo-he-ho theory is a theory about the origin of language. In this theory language is developed from some rhythmic grunts that are produced by primitive people when they work together.

Practice

I. Mark the choice that best completes the statement. (20%)

1. All languages have three major components: a sound system, a system of _____ and a system of semantics.
   A. morphology   B. lexicogrammar   C. syntax   D. meaning
2. Which of the following words is entirely arbitrary?
   A. tree   B. typewriter   C. bowwow   D. bang
3. The function of the sentence *Water boils at 100 degrees Centigrade* is _____.
   A. interpersonal   B. emotive
   C. informative   D. performative
4. In Chinese when someone breaks a bowl or a plate the host or the people present are likely to say 碎碎(岁岁)平安 as a means of controlling the forces which they believe might affect their lives. Which function does it perform?
   A. Interpersonal   B. Emotive
   C. Informative   D. Performative
5. Which of the following property of language enables language users to overcome the barriers caused by time and place of speaking (due to this feature of language, speakers of a language are free to talk about anything in any situation)?
   A. Transferability   B. Duality
   C. Displacement   D. Arbitrariness
6. What language function does the following conversation play? (The two chatters just met and were starting their conversation by the following dialogue.)
   A: *A nice day, isn't it?*
   B: *Right! I really enjoy the sunlight.*
   A. Emotive   B. Phatic
   C. Performative   D. Interpersonal
7. _____ refers to the actual realization of the ideal language user's knowledge of the rules of his language in utterances.
   A. Performance   B. Competence
   C. Langue   D. Parole
8. When a dog is barking, you assume it is barking for something or at someone that exists here and now. It couldn't be sorrowful for some lost love or lost bone. This indicates that dog's *language* does not have the feature of _____.
   A. reference   B. productivity
   C. displacement   D. duality
9. _____ answers such questions as how we as infants acquire our first language.
   A. Psycholinguistics   B. Anthropological linguistics
   C. Sociolinguistics   D. Applied linguistics
10. _____ deals with the study of dialects in different social classes in a particular region.
    A. Linguistic theory   B. Practical linguistics

Chapter 1
Invitations to Linguistics

C. Sociolinguistics   D. Comparative linguistics

II. Mark the following statements with "T" if they are true or "F" if they are false. (10%)

1. The widely accepted meaning of arbitrariness was discussed by Chomsky first.
2. For learners of a foreign language, it is arbitrariness that is more worth noticing than its conventionality.
3. Displacement benefits human beings by giving them the power to handle generalizations and abstractions.
4. For Jakobson and the Prague school structuralists, the purpose of communication is to refer.
5. Interpersonal function is also called ideational function in the framework of functional grammar.
6. Emotive function is also discussed under the term *expressive* function.
7. The relationship between competence and performance in Chomsky's theory is that between a language community and an individual language user.
8. A study of the features of the English used in Shakespeare's time is an example of the diachronic study of language.
9. Articulatory phonetics investigates the properties of the sound waves.
10. The nature of linguistics as a science determines its preoccupation with prescription instead of description.

III. Fill in each of the following blanks with an appropriate word. The first letter of the word is already given. (10%)

1. Nowadays, two kinds of research methods co-exist in linguistic studies, namely, qualitative and q_____ research approaches.
2. In any language words can be used in new ways to mean new things and can be combined into innumerable sentences based on limited rules. This feature is usually termed as p_____.
3. Language has many functions. We can use language to talk about language. This function is m_____ function.
4. The claim that language originated by primitive man involuntary making vocal noises while performing heavy work has been called the y_____ theory.
5. P_____ is often said to be concerned with the organization of speech within specific languages, or with the systems and patterns of sounds that occur in particular languages.
6. Modern linguistics is d_____ in the sense that the linguist tries to discover what language is rather than lay down some rules for people to observe.
7. One general principle of linguistic analysis is the primacy of s_____ over writing.
8. The description of a language as it changes through time is a d_____ linguistic study.
9. Saussure put forward the concept l_____ to refer to the abstract linguistic system shared by all members of a speech community.
10. *Linguistic potential* is similar to Saussure's langue and Chomsky's c_____.

IV. **Explain the following concepts or theories.** (20%)
1. Design features
2. Displacement
3. Competence
4. Synchronic linguistics

V. **Answer the following questions briefly.** (10%)
1. Why do people take duality as one of the important design features of human language? Can you tell us what language would be like if it had no such design features?
2. How can we use language to *do things*? Please give two examples to show this point.

VI. **Match each term in Column A with one relevant item in Column B.** (10%)

A	B
(1) language varieties	a. phonetics
(2) information retrieval	b. phonology
(3) shape of syllables	c. morphology
(4) emergence of language	d. syntax
(5) word formation	e. semantics
(6) production of speech	f. pragmatics
(7) immediate constituents	g. psycholinguistics
(8) reference, force and effect	h. sociolinguistics
(9) denotation of words	i. anthropological linguistics
(10) cognition	j. computational linguistics

VII. **Essay questions.** (20%)
1. Explain Jakobson's views of communication and the functions of language.
2. Describe the differences between Saussure's *langue and parole* and chomsky's *competence and performance*.

参考答案

I.
1. B 2. A 3. C 4. D 5. C 6. B 7. A 8. C 9. A 10. C

II.
1. F 2. F 3. T 4. F 5. F 6. T 7. F 8. F 9. F 10. F

III.
1. quantitative 2. productivity 3. metalingual 4. *yo-he-ho* 5. Phonology
6. descriptive 7. speech 8. diachronic 9. langue 10. competence

IV.
1. Design features: It refers to the defining properties of human language that tell the difference between human language and any system of animal communication.
2. Displacement: It means that human languages enable their users to symbolize objects,

events and concepts, which are not present (in time and space) at the moment of communication.
3. Competence: It is a term brought about by Chomsky. It is the speaker's knowledge of his or her language; that is, of its sound structure, its words, and its grammatical rules. Competence is, in a way, an encyclopedia of language. Moreover, the knowledge involved in competence is generally unconscious.
4. Synchronic linguistics: It refers to the study of a language at a given point in time. The time studied may be either the present or a particular point in the past; synchronic analysis can also be made of dead languages, such as Latin. Synchronic linguistics is contrasted with diachronic linguistics, the study of a language over a period of time.

V.
1. Duality makes our language productive. A large number of different units can be formed out of a small number of elements. For instance, tens of thousands of words out of a small set of sounds, around 48 in the case of the English language. And out of the huge number of words, there can be astronomical number of possible sentences and phrases, which in turn can combine to form unlimited number of texts. Animal communication systems do not have this design feature of human language. If language had no such design feature, then it would be like animal communicational system which would be highly limited. It cannot produce a very large number of sound combinations, e.g. words, which are distinct in meaning.
2. We can use language to do things because language has the performative function. For example, a judge can imprison a criminal by sentencing him in court. We can also say *It is too cold in here* to make someone close the window or door, or turn on the heater, etc.

VI.
(1) h   (2) j   (3) b   (4) i   (5) c   (6) a   (7) d   (8) f   (9) e   (10) g

VII.
1. Jakobson's model of the functions of language distinguishes six elements, or factors of communication, that are necessary for communication to occur: (1) context, (2) addresser (sender), (3) addressee (receiver), (4) contact, (5) common code and (6) message. Each factor is the focal point of a relation, or function, that operates between the message and the factor. The functions are the following, in order: (1) referential (*The Earth is round*), (2) emotive (*Yuck!*), (3) conative (*Come here*), (4) phatic (*Hello!*), (5) metalingual (*What do you mean by saying that?*), and (6) poetic (*poetry*). When we analyze the functions of language for a given unit (such as a word, a text or an image), we specify to which class or type it belongs (e.g., a textual or pictorial genre), which functions are present/absent, and the characteristics of these functions, including the hierarchical relations and any other relations that may operate between them.
2. Saussure distinguished the linguistic competence of the speaker and the actual phenomena or data of linguistics as langue and parole. Langue is relatively stable and systematic, while parole is subject to personal and situational constraints; langue is not spoken by an individual, while parole is always a naturally occurring event. What a linguist should do, according to Saussure, is to draw rules from a mass of confused facts, i.e. to discover the regularities governing all instances of parole and make them

the subject of linguistics. According to Chomsky, a language user's underlying knowledge about the system of rules is called the linguistic competence, and the actual use of language in concrete situations is called performance. Competence enables a speaker to produce and understand and indefinite number of sentences and to recognize grammatical mistakes and ambiguities. A speaker's competence is stable while his performance is often influenced by psychological and social factors. So a speaker's performance does not always match his supposed competence. Chomsky believes that linguists ought to study competence, rather than performance. Chomsky's competence-performance distinction is not exactly the same as, though similar to, Saussure's langue-parole distinction. Langue is a social product and a set of conventions of a community, while competence is deemed as a property of mind of each individual. Saussure looks at language more from a sociological or sociolinguistic point of view than Chomsky since the latter deals with his issues psychologically or psycholinguistically.

Further Practice

I. Mark the following statements with "T" if they are true or "F" if they are false. Provide explanations for the false statements.

1. Linguistics is generally defined as the scientific study of a particular language.
2. If a linguistic study describes and analyzes the language people actually use, it is said to be descriptive.
3. Design features refer to the defining properties of human language that distinguish it from any other system of communication.
4. No animal communication system has duality or even comes near to processing it.
5. Animal communication systems can be used to refer things which are present or not present.
6. The unique function of language is to exchange information.
7. Language we use today has a form-meaning correspondence.
8. Children learn their native language swiftly, efficiently and without instruction.
9. Arbitrariness is one of the design features of language, so language is totally arbitrary.
10. Language operates by rules.
11. Language is instrumental, social and conventional.
12. The properties of the words uttered by human beings and calls that animals make are the same.
13. Every person speaks a dialect.
14. Language slowly changes.
15. Any system of communication is a kind of language.
16. The honeybee's dance can refer to a source of food, which is remote in time and space when it reports it. So we say that the dance has the property of replacement and is a kind of language.
17. The fact that we can understand some abstract terms like *joy* and *hatred* shows that language has the property of creativity.
18. Speakers of all languages employ a range of styles and a set of jargons.
19. Languages are intimately related to the societies and individuals who use them.
20. Writing is derivative of speech.
21. According to Jakobson, *Context* is related to the referential function of language.

Chapter 1
Invitations to Linguistics

22. According to Jakobson, the phatic function of language corresponds to the communication element of addressee.
23. Phonetics is part of phonology.
24. Word is the basic meaningful element of a language.
25. Morphology describes principles of forming and understanding correct sentences.
26. Linguistics is usually defined as the science of language or the scientific study of language. So language is only studied in the field of linguistics.
27. If description is better than prescription, then we should completely avoid prescription in language study.
28. A book that concerns Latin grammar in the 16th century is a study of grammar in history, so we say that the book is of diachronic study in nature.
29. People usually speak with sign language like gestures and facial expressions, so we can say that Sign language is also part of our language.
30. People from different speech communities have different underlying grammar rules in their brain.
31. According to sociolinguists, your dialect shows who you are.
32. Most linguistic analysis owes more to intelligent guesswork than scientific method.
33. Knowing the relevant language's grammar and sounds is not enough to make a person a fully functioning member of a speech community.
34. A human language is a formal system for relating meanings and sounds.
35. The diversity of languages is testament to the success of the design features of human language.
36. The discipline of linguistics would be little different if there had only been one language in the world.
37. It is the utterance in context rather than the idealized sentence that should be the focus of linguists' research.

II. Fill in each of the following blanks with (an) appropriate word(s).

1. Language is _____ in that communicating by speaking or writing is a purposeful act.
2. Language is _____ and _____ in that language is a social semiotic and communication can only take place effectively if all the users share a broad understanding of human interaction.
3. The features that define our human languages can be called _____, which include _____, _____, _____, _____.
4. _____ is the opposite side of arbitrariness.
5. The fact that in the system of spoken language, we have the primary units as words and secondary units as sound shows that language has the property of _____.
6. Language is resourceful because of its _____ and its _____, which contributes to the _____ of language.
7. _____ benefits human beings by giving them the power to handle generalization and abstractions.
8. In Jakobson's version, there are six functions of language, namely, _____, _____, _____, _____, _____ and metalingual function.
9. When people use language to express attitudes, feelings and emotions, people are using the _____ function of language in Jakobson's version.

10. In functional grammar, language has three metafunctions, namely, _____, _____, _____.
11. Among Halliday's three metafunctions, _____ creates relevance to context.
12. The _____ function of language is primary to change the social status of persons.
13. Please name five main branches of linguistics: _____, _____, _____, _____ and _____.
14. In _____ phonetics, we study the speech sounds produced by articulatory organs by identifying and classifying the individual sounds.
15. In _____ phonetics, we focus on the way in which a listener analyzes or processes a sound wave.
16. _____ is the minimal unit of meaning.
17. The study of sounds used in linguistic communication is called _____.
18. The study of how sounds are put together and used to convey meaning in communication is called _____.
19. The study of the way in which symbols that represent sounds in linguistic communicate are arranged to form words has constituted the branch of study called _____.
20. The study of rules which governs the combinations of words to form permissible sentences constitutes a major branch of linguistic studies that is _____.
21. The fact that we have *alliteration* in poems is probably because of the _____ function of language.

III. Mark the choice that best completes the statement.

1. The description of a language at some point in time is a _____ study.
   A. descriptive B. prescriptive C. synchronic D. diachronic
2. According to Chomsky, a speaker can produce and understand an infinitely large number of sentence because _____.
   A. he has come across all of them in his life
   B. he has internalized a set of rules about his language
   C. he has acquired the ability through the act of communicating with others
   D. he has learned all the rules of his language
3. Saussure's distinction between langue and parole is very similar to Chomsky's distinction between competence and performance, but Saussure takes a _____ view of language and Chomsky looks at language from a _____ point of view.
   A. sociological, psychological   B. psychological, sociological
   C. biological, psychological   D. psychological, biological
4. The fact that there is no intrinsic connection between the word *pen* and the thing we write with indicates language is _____.
   A. arbitrary B. rule-governed C. applied D. illogical
5. We can understand and produce an infinitely large number of sentence including sentences we never heard before, because language is _____.
   A. creative B. arbitrary C. limitless D. resourceful
6. _____ means language can be used to refer to contexts removed from the immediate situations of the speaker.
   A. Duality   B. Displacement

C. Productivity   D. Arbitrariness
7. _____ examines how meaning is encoded in a language.
   A. Phonetics   B. Syntax   C. Semantics   D. Pragmatics
8. _____ is concerned with the internal organization of words.
   A. Morphology   B. Syntax   C. Semantics   D. Phonology
9. _____ refers to the fact that the forms of linguistic signs bear no natural relationship to their meaning.
   A. Duality   B. Arbitrariness   C. Replacement   D. Creativity
10. _____ of language makes it potentially creative, and _____ of language makes learning a language laborious.
    A. Conventionality, arbitrariness   B. Arbitrariness, replacement
    C. Arbitrariness, conventionality   D. Conventionality, arbitrariness
11. When people use language to indulge in itself for its own sake, people are using the _____ function of language.
    A. poetic   B. creative   C. phatic   D. metalingual
12. _____ proposes a theory of metafunctions of language.
    A. Chomsky   B. Saussure   C. Jacobson   D. Halliday
13. _____ function constructs a model of experience and constructs logical relations.
    A. Interpersonal B. Textual   C. Logical   D. Ideational
14. Interpersonal function enacts _____ relationship.
    A. social   B. experiential C. textual   D. personal
15. By _____ function people establish and maintain their status in society.
    A. experiential   B. referential
    C. metalingual   D. Interpersonal
16. The study of the description and classification of speech sounds, words and connected speech belongs to the study of _____.
    A. phonology   B. phonetics   C. morphology   D. syntax
17. In _____ phonetics, we investigate the properties of the sound waves.
    A. articulatory B. acoustic   C. auditory   D. sound
18. French distinguishes between nouns like *GARE* (station) which is feminine and nouns like *TRAIN* which is masculine. This shows that French is a language which _____.
    A. is illogical   B. has grammatical gender
    C. has biological gender   D. has two cases
19. *Competence*, in the linguistic sense of the word, is _____.
    A. pragmatic skill   B. intuitive knowledge of language
    C. perfect knowledge of language skill D. communicative ability
20. French has *Tu* (means: you) *aimera* (means: will love) *Jean* and English has *You will love Jean*. This shows us that _____.
    A. both languages are alike in expressing future time
    B. both languages have a future tense but English requires more words
    C. English is loose while French is compact
    D. French forms its future tense by adding a special suffix
21. Knowing how to say something appropriate in a given situation and with exactly the effect you intend is a question of the _____.
    A. lexis   B. syntax   C. semantics   D. pragmatics
22. A(n) _____ is a speaker/listener who is a member of a homogeneous speech

community, who knows language perfectly and is not affected by memory limitations or distractions.
   A. perfect language user   B. ideal language user
   C. proficient user   D. native language user

IV. **Analyze the following with your linguistic knowledge.**
1. Use the following two examples to support the idea that language is not all arbitrary.
   a. *They married and had a baby.*
   b. *They had a baby and married.*
2. Examine the way the following words are separated. Comment on the way of separation in relation to Bloomfield's idea that word is the minimal unit of meaning.
   a • typical, success • ful • ly, organiz • ation, hard • ly, wind • y, word
3. What is the difference between the following two statements in terms of attitude to grammar? What kind of linguistic concepts do they represent?
   a. *Never put an a before an uncountable noun.*
   b. *People usually do not put an a before an uncountable noun.*
4. How do you understand the sentence *Music is a universal language*?
5. What are the two interpretations of the sentence *They are hunting dogs*? What is the linguistic knowledge that enables you to distinguish the meanings of this sentence?

V. **Match each term in Column A with one relevant item in Column B.**
1. Match the linguistic items in Column B with the relevant terms in Column A.

A	B
(1) Emotive function	a. contact (of communication element)
(2) Context (of communication element)	b. imperatives and vocatives
(3) Conative function	c. metalingual function
(4) Phatic function	d. intonation showing anger
(5) Message (of communication function)	e. referential function
(6) Code (of communication element)	

2. Match the sentences in Column B with the language functions in Column A.

A	B
(1) informative function	a. We have 15 people here.
(2) interpersonal function	b. Pass me the salt please.
(3) performative function	c. *God! Damn it!*
(4) emotive function	d. *Dear sir ; Johnny*

3. Match the linguistic items in Column B with the linguistic branches in Column A.

A	B
(1) Phonology	a. morphology
(2) Phonetics	b. phoneme

Chapter 1
Invitations to Linguistics

continued

A	B
(3) Morphology	c. entailment
(4) Semantics	d. speech act
(5) Syntax	e. synonymy
(6) Pragmatics	f. word order in a sentence
	g. word formation
	h. conversational implicature
	i. speech organs
	j. sound waves

4. Match the linguistic items in Column B with the linguistic branches in Column A.

A	B
(1) Psycholinguistics	a. language acquisition
(2) Sociolinguistics	b. dialect
(3) Anthropological linguistics	c. corpus
(4) Computational linguistics	d. emergence of language
	e. language and cognition
	f. computer translating
	g. biological foundation of language
	h. the divergence of languages over thousands of years
	i. gender and language

VI. Answer the following questions as comprehensively as possible, giving examples if necessary.

1. Why do we say that language distinguishes human beings from animals?
2. What is language?
3. Do you think that language is completely arbitrary? Give examples to support your idea.
4. Why is our language resourceful?
5. Name at least two theories about the origin of language and explain them.
6. What is the difference between phonology and phonetics?
7. Because of its duality and recursiveness, language could be creative. Yet we seldom produce extremely long and ever-running sentences. Could you explain the reasons?
8. Answer the following questions based on the extract from the Chinese essay *Peach Blossom Springs*. Please pay attention to the underlined parts.

　　既出，得其船，便扶向路，处处志之。及郡下，诣太守，说如此。太守即遣人随其往，寻向所志，遂迷，不复得路。

(1) What changes have taken place through the years in Chinese in the aspects

meaning and grammar?

(2) Is this kind of comparative study of language change synchronic or diachronic?

9. Identify five different language functions (poetic function, interpersonal function, textual function, performative function and emotive function) in addition to the ideational function in the following extract from Obama's Inaugural Address. Pay attention to the underlined parts.

<u>Today</u> I say to <u>you</u> that the challenges <u>we</u> face are real. They are serious and they are many. They will not be met easily or in a short span of time. But know this, America-they will be met.

<u>On this day</u>, <u>we</u> gather because <u>we</u> have chosen hope over fear, unity of purpose over conflict and discord.

<u>On this day</u>, <u>we</u> come to <u>proclaim</u> an end to the petty grievances and false promises, the recriminations and worn out dogmas, that for far too long have strangled our politics.

10. Observe the following Japanese sentences and use your linguistic knowledge to describe the Japanese grammar concerning the underlined part and the word order in each sentence.

山田さんは　彼のお父さんに　本を<u>あげました</u>。（山田 gives his father a book.）

山田さんのお父さんは 山田さんに　本を<u>くれました</u>。（山田's father gives him a book.）

山田さんは　彼のお先生に　りんごを<u>あげました</u>。（山田 gives his father an apple.）

山田さんのお先生は 山田さんに　りんごを<u>くれました</u>。（山田's father gives him an apple.）

（りんご means *apple* or *apples*；先生 means *teacher*；山田 is the name of someone；彼の means *his*；の means *someone's*）

参考答案

I.

1. F. Linguistics investigates not any particular language, but languages in general.
2. T　3. T　4. T
5. F. No animal communication system possesses the feature of displacement. Animal calls mainly uttered in response to immediate change of situation. In bee's language, food sources are the only kind of messages that can be sent through the bee dance; yet bees do not *talk* about themselves, the hives, or wind, let alone about hopes or desires. Most animals can not talk about things that are not present.
6. F. Besides the exchanging of information, language has many other functions, like performative function, emotive function, recreational function, etc.
7. T. Language is arbitrary by nature. That is, the forms of linguistic signs bear no natural relationship to their meaning. It is even true with the onomatopoetic words. Yet through language development the meanings and the word forms that bear them have formed a steady corresponding relationship. In another word, convention has made word forms correspond to their meanings.
8. T
9. F. Arbitrariness is one of the design features of language, but language is not totally

Chapter 1
Invitations to Linguistics

arbitrary. Arbitrariness refers to the fact that the forms of linguistic signs bear no natural relationship to their meaning. On the sentential level, the words are not arbitrarily arranged, in certain places we should fill in certain words. For example, to fill in the slot of subject, we should not use verbs or adjectives but simply nouns.

10. T   11. T
12. F. The properties of the words by human beings and calls that animals make are not totally the same. They are the same in the sense that both words in human language and animal calls have some corresponding meanings. They are different in the sense that words in human language can be divided into sounds because of the duality of human language, but animal calls can not be further divided.
13. T   14. T
15. F. Animals can communicate with each other with their calls, yet their communication systems are not languages, because they do not have the four design features of human language. The design features are arbitrariness, creativity, replacement and duality.
16. F. In the honeybee's dance, it is only the food source that is conveyed. Bees can not communicate with each other about the complex things like the weather, wind, not mention the abstract terms like beauty or joy. So the honeybee dance has not the design feature of replacement and it is not a language.
17. F. The fact that we can understand some abstract terms like joy and hatred shows that language has the property of displacement. Displacement means that human languages enable their users to symbolize objects, events and concepts which are not present (in time and space) at the moment of communication. Displacement can not only refer to things in the physical world but also the abstract things. In a word, the intellectual benefits of displacement to us are that it makes it possible for us to talk and think in abstract terms.
18. T   19. T   20. T   21. T
22. F. People use the phatic function of language to contact with each other, so the phatic function of language corresponds to the communication element of contact. On the other hand, people use conative function of language to persuade and influence others through commands and entreaties, so it is the conative function of language that corresponds to the communication element of addressee.
23. F. Phonetics studies speech sounds, including the production of speech, that is how speech sounds are actually made, transmitted and received, the sound of speech, the description and classification of speech sounds, words and connected speech, etc.
   Phonology studies the rules governing the structure, distribution and sequencing of speech sounds and the shape of syllables.
   Phonetics is the study of speech sounds that the human voice is capable of creating whereas phonology is the study of the subset of those sounds that constitute language and meaning. The first focuses on chaos while the second focuses on order. They do not belong to each other but have different focuses.
24. F. Word is not the basic meaningful element of a language. Some word can be broken down into still smaller units called morphemes.
25. F. Morphology is not the principles of forming and understanding correct sentences. It is the syntax that is about principles of forming and understanding correct sentences.
26. F. Linguistics is usually defined as the science of language or the scientific study of language, but language is only studied in the field of linguistics. Other disciplines

such as psychology, sociology, ethnography, etc. are also preoccupied with language.
27. F. Though the nature of linguistics as a science determines its preoccupation with description instead of prescription, we should not completely avoid prescription.

In some particular fields we still need prescription. For example, in the field of second language acquisition and the field of standardizing the principal dialect that is employed within a particular country or region, etc., description should still be put in a dominant place.
28. F. The book is a synchronic description of Latin grammar.

A synchronic description takes a fixed instant as its point of observation, while a diachronic study is the study of a language through the course of its history.

The book takes a fixed instant of the 16th century as its point of observation, so we say that the book is a synchronic study.
29. F. Those signs as gestures and facial expressions are a part of our speech, which help to deliver the meaning of the speech. They do not have the four design features that human language has.
30. T 31. T
32. F. Scientific guess is based on the daily observation. Usually, it should be tested by scientific research and proof.
33. T. The person should also have the knowledge of using it in the community. That is to say he has to understand the functions of language in the speech community.
34. F. A language should also serve the purpose of communicating, and it should have four design features.
35. T 36. T
37. F. The study of utterances in the real context belongs to the domain of descriptive study, from which we can get find rules in people's linguistic performance. The study of the idealized sentences belong to the domain of prescriptive study, from which linguists can form rules and find an ideal speaker/listener's linguistic competence. Both are very important in linguistics, the first being the foundation of the second.

II.

1. instrumental
2. social; conventional
3. design features; arbitrariness; duality; creativity; displacement
4. Convention
5. duality
6. duality; recursiveness; creativity
7. Displacement
8. referential; emotive; conative; poetic; phatic
9. emotive
10. ideational function; interpersonal function; textual function
11. textual function
12. performative
13. phonology; morphology; syntax; semantics; pragmatics
14. articulatory
15. auditory
16. morpheme
17. phonetics
18. phonology
19. morphology
20. syntax
21. poetic/ recreational

III.

1. C 2. B 3. A 4. A 5. A 6. B 7. C 8. A 9. B 10. C
11. A 12. D 13. D 14. A 15. D 16. B 17. B 18. B 19. B 20. D

Chapter 1
Invitations to Linguistics

21. D 22. B

IV.
1. Arbitrariness: Arbitrariness refers to the fact that the forms of linguistic signs bear no natural relationship to their meaning. For example there is no natural relationship between the word form *pen* and the object it really refers to. However, language is not completely arbitrary. On the level of sentence, we must arrange words according to grammatical rules. We could not use a noun as a predicate verb. The same is true with word order. The word order in the two sentences affects the meaning of the sentence. That is to say different components in a meaningful sentence should not be arranged arbitrarily. In this sense language is not arbitrary.
2. The minimal unit of meaning is morpheme. A morpheme can make up a new word either by itself, like *word*, or together with other morpheme, like *a • typical*, *wind • y* • etc.
    From the words above we can also see that word is not the minimal unit of meaning.
3. *Not to put an a before an uncountable noun* is a piece of English grammar. The first sentence presents it in a prescriptive command, while the second presents the grammar in a descriptive sense. To be prescriptive is to prescribe how language ought to be, while to be descriptive is simply to describe what language is. The nature of linguistics as a science determines its preoccupation with description instead of prescription. However prescription is also important in some particular fields, e.g. in second language learning and in the process of standardizing a dialect in a particular region or country.
4. This is a metaphor. This sentence compares music to language which means that music can create a common feeling in its audience from different places in the world. However, the word *language* in the sentence is not *language* in its real sense, although *musical language* is arbitrary and it has, to some degree, duality and creativity in nature. Music can only describe what happened to a musician or what one particular musician really wants to express. But to other language users there is not a systematic correspondence between the meaning and the sound form of music. Music is perceived differently by people.
5. That is an ambiguous sentence which has two meanings: *They are dogs used in hunting* and *They are chasing and hunting some dogs*. The knowledge of syntax (and semantics) is needed especially to understand the meaning and structure of the sentence.

V.
1. (1) d   (2) e   (3) b   (4) a   (5) 空   (6) c
2. (1) a   (2) d   (3) b   (4) c
3. (1) b   (2) i; j   (3) a; g   (4) c; e   (5) f   (6) d; h
4. (1) a; e; g (2) b; i   (3) d; h   (4) c; f

VI.
1. Language distinguishes us from animals because of four design features. The four design features are as follows:
    (1) Arbitrariness: Arbitrariness refers to the fact that the forms of linguistic signs bear no natural relationship to their meaning. A good example is the fact that different sounds are used to refer to the same object in different languages. Language is

arbitrary by nature, but it is not entirely arbitrary. e.g. It is not arbitrary on the sentence level.

(2) Creativity: By creativity we mean language is resourceful because of its duality and its repulsiveness. Creativity is unique to human language. Most animal communication systems appear to be highly restricted with respect to the number of different signals that their users can send and receive.

(3) Duality: By duality is meant the property of having two levels of structures, such that units of the primary level are composed of elements of the secondary level and each of the two levels has its own principles of organization.

(4) Displacement: Displacement means that human languages enable their users to symbolize objects, events and concepts which are not present (in time and space) at the moment of communication. These four design features stated above do not appear in any other king of animal communicating system, so we say that language distinguishes us from animals.

2. Language is a system of arbitrary vocal symbols used for human communication. It distinguishes us from animals because of four design features. Language is instrumental in that communicating by speaking or writing is a purposeful act. It is social and conventional in that language is a social semiotic and communication can only take place effectively if all the users share a broad understanding of human interaction.

3. Language is not completely arbitrary. Arbitrariness refers to the fact that the forms of linguistic signs bear no natural relationship to their meanings. On the sentential level, the words are not arbitrarily arranged, in certain places we should fill in certain words. For example, to fill in the slot of subject, we should not use verbs or adjectives but simply nouns.

4. Language is resourceful because of its duality and its recursiveness. By duality is meant the property of having two levels of structures, such that units of the primary level are composed of elements of the secondary level and each of the two levels has its own principles of organization. Recursiveness is a term from mathematics used in linguistics for the formal properties of grammars, which use a finite inventory of elements and a finite group of rules to produce an infinite number of sentences. Because language has the feature of duality and also because language is recursive, we can use words to make up infinite sentences and expressions, so we say that language is resourceful.

5. Bow-wow theory: This theory claims language is developed from the people imitating the sounds of the animal calls in the wild environment they lived. Pooh-pooh theory: This theory claims language is developed through our primitive ancestors uttering instinctive sounds of pain, anger and joy in their hard life. *Yo-he-ho* theory claims that language is developed from some rhythmic grunts that are produced by primitive people when they work together.

6. Phonetics studies speech sounds, including the production of speech, that is how speech sounds are actually made, transmitted and received, the sound of speech, the description and classification of speech sounds, words and connected speech, etc. Phonology studies the rules governing the structure, distribution and sequencing of speech sounds and the shape of syllables. Phonetics is the study of speech sounds that the human voice is capable of creating whereas phonology is the study of the subset of those sounds that constitute language and meaning. The first focuses on chaos while the second focuses on order.

Chapter 1
Invitations to Linguistics

7. Language has the function of communication. Thus we should speak understandable and acceptable sentences. Yet if we produce ever-running senteces, it is very hard for listeners to understand. On the other side, according to Chomsky, we have in our brain a set of underlying grammar that governs our language performance. This set of grammar determines that we never create ever-running sentences. As a result, although language could be creative, we never create extremely long and ever-running sentences.

8. (1) There are several changes in the development of Chinese. a. In ancient Chinese a subject would usually be omitted, as in 既出,得其船,便扶向路,处处志之。及郡下.... In modern Chinese we tend to have a subject in one sentence even though we sometimes omit subjects. This is the change in syntax. b. The part of speech of some words has changed. For example, 志 in the quoted passage in ancient Chinese is a verb. Yet in modern Chinese it becomes a noun. This is the change in semantics. c. The meanings of some of the words have changed. For example, 扶 in this passage has the meaning of *following, and taking some route*, but in modern Chinese, it has changed as *assist someone* or *have something as assistance*. This is also the change in semantics. d. The word order in the sentences has also changed. For example, 寻向所志 in modern Chinese has been changed into 向所志寻. It is the change in syntax.

    (2) The study of this kind belongs to the diachronic study of Chinese language.

9. (1) The poetic function can be carried out by employing the structure of *Today ... on this day, ... on this day ...* . By using the three similar expressions at the very beginning of each paragraph, we feel that the passage is beautiful and with rhythm. (2) The interpersonal function can be carried out by the expression of *we* that is frequently employed in the passage, which has made the relationship between the president and the public deeper. (3) The textual function is carried out by the repeatedly used *on this day*, by which the passage is well organized. (4) The performative function is carried out by using the sentence *we come to proclaim an end to the petty grievances* ... . Saying that, Obama is actually changing the government's work. (5) The emotive function is carried out by the sentence *They will not be met easily or in a short span of time. But know this, America—they will be met* and those *we* and the parataxis sentence. Through these ways the president has expressed a confident and ambitious emotion.

10. These four sentences describe the giving-receiving relationship between 山田 and his father and his teacher. Through the four Japanese sentences we can find: (1) The object is put before the predicate verbs. The order of the Japanese sentences with objects and predicate verbs would be like subject + object + predicate verb. (2) We can discover the social relationship in Japanese sentences. When a person of a lower class gives something to a person of a higher class, he uses one form of the verb. When a person of a higher social class gives something to a person of a lower class, the same verb would take another form.

Chapter 2 Speech Sounds

Concepts & Theories

I. Phonetics
Phonetics is the study of speech sounds. It includes three main areas:
1. articulatory phonetics—the study of the production of speech sounds
2. acoustic phonetics—the study of the physical properties of the sounds produced in speech
3. auditory phonetics—the study of perception of speech sounds

Most phoneticians are interested in articulatory phonetics.

II. How speech sounds are made?
1. **Speech organs**

   Speech organs are those parts of the human body involved in the production of speech. The speech organs can be considered as consisting of three parts: the initiator of the air stream, the producer of voice and the resonating cavities.

2. **The IPA**
   (1) In 1886, the Phonetic Teachers' Association was inaugurated by a small group of language teachers in France who had found the practice of phonetics useful in their teaching and wished to popularize their methods.
   (2) It was changed to its present title of the International Phonetic Association (IPA) in 1897.
   (3) The idea of establishing a phonetic alphabet was first proposed by the Danish grammarian and phonetician Otto Jespersen (1860-1943) in 1886.
   (4) The first version of the International Phonetic Alphabet (the IPA chart) was published in August 1888.
   (5) Its main principles were that there should be a separate letter for each distinctive sound, and that the same symbol should be used for that sound in any language in which it appears. The alphabet was to consist of as many Roman alphabet letters as possible, using new letters and diacritics only when absolutely necessary. These principles continue to be followed today.

III. Consonants and vowels
1. **Consonants**

   A consonant is produced by constricting or obstructing the vocal tract at some places to divert, impede, or completely shut off the flow of air in the oral cavity.

   A vowel is produced without obstruction so no turbulence or a total stopping of the air can be perceived.

   The categories of consonant are established on the basis of several factors. The most important of these factors are:
   ☆ the actual relationship between the articulators and thus the way in which the

air passes through certain parts of the vocal tract (manner of articulation);
- ☆ where in the vocal tract there is approximation, narrowing, or the obstruction of the air (place of articulation).

(1) Classification of consonants: manners of articulation
- ☆ Stop/plosive: A speech sound which is produced by stopping the air stream from the lungs and then suddenly releasing it.
- ☆ Fricative: A speech sound which is produced by allowing the air stream from the lungs to escape with friction. This is caused by bringing the two articulators, e.g. the upper teeth and the lower lip, close together but not closes enough to stop the airstreams completely.
- ☆ (Median) approximant: An articulation in which one articulator is close to another, but without the vocal tract being narrowed to such an extent that a turbulent airstream is produced.
- ☆ Lateral (approximant): A speech sound which is produced by partially blocking the airstream from the lungs, usually by the tongue, but letting it escape at one or both sides of the blockage.

Other consonantal articulations include trill, tap or flap, and affricate.

(2) Classification of consonants: places of articulation
- ☆ Bilabial: A speech sound which is made with the two lips.
- ☆ Labiodental: A speech sound which is made with the lower lip and the upper front teeth.
- ☆ Dental: A speech sound which is made by the tongue tip or blade and the upper front teeth.
- ☆ Alveolar: A speech sound which is made with the tongue tip or blade and the alveolar ridge.
- ☆ Postalveolar: A speech sound which is made with the tongue tip and the back of the alveolar ridge.
- ☆ Retroflex: A speech sound which is made with the tongue tip or blade curled back so that the underside of the tongue tip or blade forms a stricture with the back of the alveolar ridge or the hard palate.
- ☆ Palatal: A speech sound which is made with the front of the tongue and the hard palate.
- ☆ Velar: A speech sound which is made with the back of the tongue and the soft palate.
- ☆ Uvular: A speech sound which is made with the back of the tongue and the uvula, the short projection of the soft tissue and muscle at the posterior end of the velum.
- ☆ Pharyngeal: A speech sound which is made with the root of the tongue and the walls of the pharynx.
- ☆ Glottal: A speech sound which is made with the two pieces of vocal folds pushed towards each other.

2. Vowels

(1) The theory of cardinal vowels
- ☆ Cardinal vowels are a set of vowel qualities arbitrarily defined, fixed and unchanging, intending to provide a frame of reference for the description of the actual vowels of existing languages.

☆ By convention, the eight primary cardinal vowels are numbered from one to eight.

☆ A set of secondary cardinal vowels is obtained by reversing the lip-rounding for a given position: CV9-CV16.

(2) The criteria of vowel description

☆ The part of the tongue that is raised—front, center, or back.

☆ The extent to which the tongue rises in the direction of the palate. Normally, three or four degrees are recognized: high, mid (often divided into mid-high and mid-low) and low.

☆ The kind of opening made at the lips—various degrees of lip rounding or spreading.

☆ The position of the soft palate-raised for oral vowels, and lowered for vowels which have been nasalized.

(3) Vowel glides

☆ Pure (monophthong) vowels: vowels which are produced without any noticeable change in vowel quality.

☆ Vowel glides: Vowels where there is an audible change of quality.

☆ Diphthong: A vowel which is usually considered as one distinctive vowel of a particular language but really involves two vowels, with one vowel gliding to the other.

☆ A double movement produces a triphthong, which is *a glide from one vowel to another and then to a third, all produced rapidly and without interruption*.

☆ They are really diphthongs followed by the schwa [ə], found in English words like wire [waɪə] and tower [taʊə].

3. **The sounds of English**

Received Pronunciation (RP): The type of British Standard English pronunciation which has been regarded as the prestige variety and which shows no regional variation. It has often been popularly referred to as *BBC English* or *Oxford English* because it is widely used in the private sector of the education system and spoken by most newsreaders of the BBC network.

(1) The consonants of English can be described in the following way:

[p] voiceless bilabial stop
[b] voiced bilabial stop
[s] voiceless alveolar fricative
[z] voiced alveolar fricative
[m] bilabial nasal
[n] alveolar nasal
[l] alveolar lateral
[j] palatal approximant
[h] glottal fricative
[r] alveolar approximant

(2) The vowels of RP

high front tense unrounded vowel
high back lax rounded vowel
central lax unrounded vowel
low back lax rounded vowel

Chapter 2
Speech Sounds

IV. From phonetics to phonology
1. Coarticulation and phonetic transcription
☆ Coarticulation: The simultaneous or overlapping articulation of two successive phonological units.
☆ Anticipatory coarticulation: If the sound becomes more like the following sound, as in the case of *lamp*, it is known as anticipatory coarticulation.
☆ Perseverative coarticulation: If the sound displays the influence of the preceding sound, as in the case of *map*, it is perseverative coarticulation.
☆ Nasalization: Change or process by which vowels or consonants become nasal.
☆ Diacritics: Any mark in writing additional to a letter or other basic elements.
(1) Broad and narrow transcriptions
   The use of a simple set of symbols in our transcription is called a *broad transcription*. The use of more specific symbols to show more phonetic detail is referred to as a *narrow transcription*. The former was meant to indicate only those sounds capable of distinguishing one word from another in a given language while the latter was meant to symbolize all the possible speech sounds, including even the minutest shades of pronunciation.

2. Phonemes
A phoneme is the smallest linguistic unit of sound that can signal a difference in meaning.
(1) Minimal pairs
   Minimal pairs are two words in a language which differ from each other by only one distinctive sound and which also differ in meaning. E.g. the English words tie and die are minimal pairs as they differ in meaning and in their initial phonemes /t/ and /d/. The word *phoneme* simply refers to *a unit of explicit sound contrast*: the existence of a minimal pair automatically grants phonemic status to the sounds responsible for the contrasts.
   By convention, phonemic transcriptions are placed between slant lines / / while phonetic transcriptions are placed between square brackets [ ]. In phonetic terms, phonemic transcriptions represent the *broad* transcriptions.
(2) Allophones
   A phoneme is the smallest linguistic unit of sound that can signal a difference in meaning. Any of the different forms of a phoneme is called its allophones.
(3) Phonetic similarity: the allophones of a phoneme must bear some phonetic resemblance.
(4) Free variants and free variation

V. Phonological processes, phonological rules and distinctive features
1. Assimilation
(1) Assimilation: A process by which one sound takes on some or all the characteristics of a neighboring sound.
(2) Regressive assimilation: If a following sound is influencing a preceding sound, we call it regressive assimilation.
(3) Progressive assimilation: If a preceding sound is influencing a following sound, we call it progressive assimilation.
(4) Devoicing: A process by which voiced sounds become voiceless. Devoicing of voiced consonants often occurs in English when they are at the end of a word.

2. Phonological processes and phonological rules

The changes in assimilation, nasalization, dentalization, and velarization are all phonological processes in which a target or affected segment undergoes a structural change in certain environments or contexts. In each process the change is conditioned or triggered by a following sound or, in the case of progressive assimilation, a preceding sound. Consequently, we can say that any phonological process must have three aspects to it: a set of sounds to undergo the process; a set of sounds produced by the process; a set of situations in which the process applies.

We can represent the process by means of an arrow: voiced fricative → voiceless / _____ voiceless. This is a phonological rule. The slash (/) specifies the environment in which the change takes place. The bar (called the focus bar) indicates the position of the target segment. So the rule reads: A voiced fricative is transformed into the corresponding voiceless sound when it appears before a voiceless sound.

3. Epenthesis, rule ordering and the elsewhere condition

We treat the change *a* to *an* as an insertion of nasal sound. Technically, this process of insertion is known as Epenthesis.

4. Distinctive features

The idea of Distinctive Features was first developed by Roman Jacobson.
(1) Distinctive feature: A particular characteristic which distinguishes one distinctive sound unit of a language from another or one group of sounds from another group.
(2) Binary feature: A property of a phoneme or a word which can be used to describe the phoneme or word. A binary feature is either present or absent. Binary features are also used to describe the semantic properties of words.

VI. Suprasegmentals

Suprasegmental features are those aspects of speech that involve more than single sound segments. The principal suprasegmental features are syllables, stress, tone, and intonation.

1. Syllable structure
(1) Syllable: A unit in speech which is often longer than one sound and smaller than a whole word.
(2) Open syllable: A syllable which ends in a vowel.
(3) Closed syllable: A syllable which ends in a consonant.
(4) Open syllable: bar, tie
(5) Closed syllable: bard, tied
(6) English syllable: (((C)C)C)V((((C)C)C)C)
(7) Chinese syllable: (C)V(C)
(8) Maximal onset principle: When there is a choice as to where to place a consonant, it is put into the onset rather than the coda.

2. Stress
Stress refers to the degree of force used in producing a syllable. In transcription, a raised vertical line is used just before the syllable it relates to.

3. Intonation
Intonation involves the occurrence of recurring fall-rise patterns, each of which is used with a set of relatively consistent meanings, either on single words or on groups of words of varying length.

4. Tone language
Languages like Chinese are known as Tone Languages.

Related Terms

acoustic phonetics
It is the study of the physical properties of the sounds produced in speech.
articulatory phonetics
It is the study of the production of speech sounds.
assimilation
It is a process by which one sound takes on some or all the characteristics of a neighboring sound. Nasalization, dentalization and velarization are all types of assimilation. There are two possibilities of assimilation: *regressive assimilation* and *progressive assimilation*.
auditory phonetics
It is concerned with the perception of speech sounds.
binary features
Many phonemes can be grouped into two categories: one with certain features and the other without. These features are binary features and they have two values or specifications detonated by " + " and " - ".
broad transcription
Broad transcription refers to the phonetic transcription omitting details that are judged to be inessential; hence identical with, or close to a representation of phonemes.
cardinal vowels
Cardinal vowels are a set of vowels established and recorded by Daniel Jones, to serve as fixed reference points for the description of vowels in any language. Together they define the limits of a space within which vowels can be articulated and within which a phonetician who has been trained to do so can place any particular vowel that is heard.
closed syllable
A syllable with coda is called a closed syllable.
coarticulation
Speech is a continuous process, so sounds continually show the influence of their neighbors, e.g. when [æ] is followed by [m], as in *lamb*, the velum will begin to lower itself during the articulation of [æ] so that it is ready for the following nasal sound. When such simultaneously overlapping articulations are involved, we call the process coarticulation. If the sound becomes more like the following sound, as in the case of *lamb*, it is known as *anticipatory coarticulation*. If the sound displays the influence of the preceding sound, it is *perseverative coarticulation*. Coarticulation can bring about all types of assimilation.
complementary distribution
The allophones of the same phoneme which occur in different environments and never form a contrast are said to be in complementary distribution. For example [p^h] and [p^t]
consonants
The sounds in the production of which there is an obstruction of the airstream at some point of the vocal tract are called consonants.
diacritic
A graphemic addition to a written symbol is used to create a new symbol from a pre-

existing symbol. Economically, diacritics help keep the inventory of basic phonetic signs as small and as comprehensive as possible.

distinctive features

Distinctive features are a class of phonetically defined components of phonemes that function to distinguish meaning. In contrast to redundant features, distinctive features constitute relevant phonological features.

epenthesis

Epenthesis refers to insertion of transitional sounds without etymological motivation, e.g. the [p] in *Thompson*.

free variation

If two sounds occurring in the same environment do not contrast, that is, the substitution of one for the other does not produce a different word form, but merely a different pronunciation of the same word, then the two sounds are in free variation.

IPA

The IPA, International Phonetic Alphabet, was devised by International Phonetic Association to solve the problem of divergence between spelling and pronunciation and recording the sounds that made by languages without writing system of their own. Its main principles were that there should be a separate letter for each distinctive sound, and that the same symbol should be used to represent that sound in any language in which it appears. The alphabet was to consist of as many Roman alphabet letters as possible, using new letters and diacritics only when absolutely necessary.

intonation

Intonation involves the occurrence of recurring fall-rise patterns, each of which is used with a set of relatively consistent meanings, either on single words or on groups of words of varying length.

manner of articulation

The way in which the airstream is modified during the articulation of a consonant: (oral or nasal) stop, fricative (both median and lateral), affricate, approximant, flap, or trill.

maximal onset principle

The principle states that when there is a choice as to where to place a consonant, it is put into the onset rather than the coda.

minimal pairs

When two different forms are identical in every way except for one sound segment which occurs in the same place in the strings, the two words are said to form a minimal pair. So *pill* and *bill* are a minimal pair and so are *pill* and *bill*, *till* and *kill*, *kill* and *dill*.

narrow transcription

Narrow transcription is meant to symbolize all the possible speech sounds including the minute shades. E.g. [pʰiːk]

open syllable

A syllable that has no coda is called an open syllable.

phone, phoneme and allophone

A phone is a phonetic unit or segment. It does not necessarily distinguish meaning; some do; some don't. For example /s/ and /t/ do; while /t/ and /tʰ/ don't.

Phoneme is the basic unit in phonology. It is a unit that is of distinctive value. But it is an abstract unit. To be exact a phoneme is not a sound, but a collection of distinctive phonetic features. The different phones which can represent a phoneme in different phonetic environments are called the allophones of that phoneme. For example, the phoneme / 1 /in English can be realized as dark /ɫ/, and clear / l /, which are allophones of the phoneme / l /.

phonetic similarity

It means that the allophones of a phoneme must bear some phonetic resemblance, for instance, the clear and dark /l/ are sufficiently alike to be treated as variant realizations of the same phoneme.

phonetic transcription

Any written representation of successive speech sounds, in a notation such as the alphabet of the International Phonetic Association, designed to be used universally for this purpose. E. g. [siˈgɑː] is a phonetic transcription in one version of this alphabet in use for English of *cigar*. Phonetic transcriptions may show varying degrees of detail: broad transcription and narrow transcription.

phonetics

Phonetics is defined as the study of the phonetic medium of language; it is concerned with all the sounds that occur in the world's languages. The three branches of phonetics are labeled articulator phonetics, auditory phonetics and acoustic phonetics.

phonological rule

In generative phonology, phonological rule refers to the type of transformational rule that transfers the phonological representation of sentences into the phonetic transcription. Phonological rules are in the form of: A → B/ X ____ Y, i. e. *replace segment A with element B in the environment of immediately following X and immediately preceding Y*.

phonology

Phonology is a study of speech sounds. It is interested in the system of sounds of a particular language; it aims to discover how speech sounds in a language form patterns and how these sounds are used to convey meaning in linguistic communication.

RP

It is a shortened form of *Received Pronunciation* (RP), and many people call it BBC English or Oxford English. RP originates historically in the southeast of England and is spoken by the upper-middle and upper classes throughout England. It is widely used in the private sector of the education system and spoken by most newsreaders of the BBC network.

stress

The degree of force used in producing a syllable is called stress.

suprasegmental features

Suprasegmental features are those aspects of speech that involve more than single sound segments. The principal suprasegmental features are syllable, stress, tone, and intonation.

voicing and voiceless

Vibration of the vocal cords results in a quality of speech sounds called *voicing*, which is a feature of all vowels and some consonants, such as [b],[z] and [m]. When the vocal cords are drawn wide apart, letting air go through without causing vibration, the sounds produced in such a condition are not voiced; they are voiceless. Some consonants in English such as [t],[f] are voiceless.

vowels

The sounds in the production of which no articulators come very close together and the airstream passes through the vocal tract without obstruction are called vowels.

Practice

I. Mark the choice that best completes the statement. (20%)

1. In a syllable, a vowel often serves as _____.
   A. Peak or Nucleus   B. Onset
   C. Coda   D. Rhyme
2. Conventionally a _____ is put in slashes //.
   A. allophone   B. phone   C. phoneme   D. morpheme
3. An aspirated [pʰ], an unaspirated [p°] and an unreleased [p˺] are _____ of the /p/ phoneme.
   A. analogues   B. tagmemes
   C. morphemes   D. allophones
4. The opening between the vocal cords is sometimes referred to as _____.
   A. glottis   B. vocal cavity
   C. pharynx   D. uvula
5. The diphthongs that are made with a movement of the tongue towards the center are known as _____ diphthongs.
   A. wide   B. closing   C. narrow   D. centering
6. A phoneme is a group of similar sounds called _____.
   A. minimal pairs   B. allomorphs
   C. phones   D. allophones
7. Which of the following sounds is a voiceless bilabial stop?
   A. [p]   B. [m]   C. [b]   D. [t]
8. Which one is different from the others according to places of articulation?
   A. [n]   B. [m]   C. [b]   D. [p]
9. Which vowel is different from the others according to the characteristics of vowels?
   A. [i:]   B. [u]   C. [e]   D. [i]
10. What kind of sounds can we make when the vocal cords are vibrating?
    A. Voiceless   B. Voiced   C. Glottal stop   D. Consonant

II. Mark the following statements with "T" if they are true or "F" if they are false. (15%)

1. [f] is a dental consonant.
2. Phonology is a branch of linguistics which studies the sentence patterns of a language.
3. The different members of a phoneme, sounds which are phonetically different but do not make a different word, are phones.
4. [p] is a voiced bilabial stop.
5. The speech sounds which are in complementary distribution are not always allophones of the same phoneme.
6. The last sound of *cut* can be articulated as an unreleased or released plosive. These different realizations of the same phoneme are NOT in complementary distribution
7. Phonology is language specific but phonetics is not.
8. Distinctive features can show phonological contrasts or oppositions of language sounds.
9. Received Pronunciation is the pronunciation accepted by most people.
10. The maximal onset principle states that when there is a choice as to where to place a

consonant. It is put into the coda rather than the onset.
11. When the vocal folds are apart, the air can pass through easily and the sound produced is said to be voiced.
12. The sound segments are grouped into consonants and vowels.
13. Uvular is made with the back of the tongue and the uvula.
14. Phonetic similarity means that the allophones of a phoneme must bear some morphological resemblance.
15. A syllable can be divided into two parts, the NUCLEUS and the CODA.

III. Fill in each of the following blanks with an appropriate word. (10%)
1. V_____ is made with the back of the tongue and the soft palate. An example in English is [k] as in *cat*.
2. Consonant sounds can also be made when two organs of speech in the mouth are brought close together so that the air is pushed out between them, causing f_____.
3. The qualities of vowels depend upon the position of the t_____ and the lips.
4. One element in the description of vowels is the part of the tongue which is at the highest point in the mouth. A second element is the h_____ to which that part of the tongue is raised.
5. Consonants differ from vowels in that the latter are produced without o_____.
6. In phonological analysis the words *fail / veil* are distinguishable simply because of the two phonemes /f/—/v/. This is an example for illustrating m_____ pairs.
7. In English there are a number of d_____, which are produced by moving from one vowel position to another through intervening positions.
8. C_____ refers to the phenomenon of sounds continually show the influence of their neighbors.
9. P_____ is the smallest linguistic unit.
10. Speech takes place when the organs of speech move to produce patterns of sound. These movements have an effect on the a_____ coming from the lungs.

IV. Explain the following concepts or theories. (20%)
1. Assimilation
2. Suprasegmental feature
3. Complementary distribution
4. Distinctive features

V. Answer the following questions. (10%)
1. What is acoustic phonetics?
2. What are the differences between voiced sounds and voiceless sounds in terms of articulation?

VI. Match each term in Column A with one relevant item in Column B. (10%)

A	B
(1) Approximant	a. tool and stool
(2) Labiodental	b. tool and pool
(3) Aspirated and unaspirated	c. produced by pushing air out
(4) English syllable	d. (C)V(C)

continued

A	B
(5) Chinese syllable	e. [v]
(6) minimal pair	f. Roman Jacobson
(7) pulmonic	g. (((C)C)C)V((((C)C)C)C)
(8) non- pulmonic	h. Otto Jespersen
(9) distinctive features	i. [w]
(10) IPA	j. produced by sucking air in

VII. Essay questions. (15%)
1. Illustrate phonological processes and phonological rules. (8%)
2. Illustrate the differences between phonetics and phonology. (7%)

参考答案

I.
1. A 2. C 3. D 4. A 5. A 6. D 7. A 8. A 9. B 10. B

II.
1. F 2. F 3. F 4. F 5. T 6. T 7. T 8. T 9. F 10. F
11. F 12. T 13. T 14. F 15. F

III.
1. Velar   2. friction   3. tongue   4. height   5. obstruction
6. minimal   7. diphthongs   8. Co-articulation   9. Phonemes   10. air-stream

IV.
1. Sound assimilation: Speech sounds seldom occur in isolation. In connected speech, under the influence of their neighbors, are replaced by other sounds. Sometimes two neighboring sounds influence each other and are replaced by a third sound which is different from both original sounds. This process is called sound assimilation.
2. Suprasegmental feature: The phonetic features that occur above the level of the segments are called suprasegmental features; these are the phonological properties of such units as the syllable, the word, and the sentence. The main suprasegmental features include stress, intonation, and tone.
3. Complementary distribution: The different allophones of the same phoneme never occur in the same phonetic context. When two or more allophones of one phoneme never occur in the same linguistic environment they are said to be in complementary distribution.
4. Distinctive features: It refers to the features that can distinguish one phoneme from another. If we can group the phonemes into two categories: one with this feature and the other without, this feature is called a distinctive feature.

V.
1. Acoustic phonetics deals with the transmission of speech sounds through the air. When a

speech sound is produced it causes minor air disturbances (sound waves). Various instruments are used to measure the characteristics of these sound waves.
2. When the vocal cords are spread apart, the air from the lungs passes between them unimpeded. Sounds produced in this way are described as voiceless; consonants [p, s, t] are produced in this way. But when the vocal cords are drawn together, the air from the lungs repeatedly pushes them apart as it passes through, creating a vibration effect. Sounds produced in this way are described as voiced. [b, z, d] are voiced consonants.

VI.
(1) i (2) e (3) a (4) g (5) d (6) b (7) c (8) j (9) f (10) h

VII.
1. The changes in assimilation, nasalization, dentalization, and velarization are all phonological processes in which a target or affected segment undergoes a structural change in certain environments or contexts. In each process the change is conditioned or triggered by a following sound or, in the case of progressive assimilation, a preceding sound. Consequently, we can say that any phonological process must have three aspects to it: a set of sounds to undergo the process; a set of sounds produced by the process; a set of situations in which the process applies.

   We can represent the process by mans of an arrow: voiced fricative → voiceless / _____ voiceless. This is a phonological rule. The slash (/) specifies the environment in which the change takes place. The bar (called the focus bar) indicates the position of the target segment. So the rule reads: a voiced fricative is transformed into the corresponding voiceless sound when it appears before a voiceless sound.

2. Phonetics is the study of speech sounds. It includes three main areas: articulatory phonetics, acoustic phonetics, and auditory phonetics. On the other hand, phonology studies the rules governing the structure, distribution, and sequencing of speech sounds and the shape of syllables. There is a fair degree of overlap in what concerns the two subjects, so sometimes it is hard to draw the boundary between them. Phonetics is the study of all possible speech sounds while phonology studies the way in which speakers of a language systematically use a selection of these sounds in order to express meaning. That is to say, phonology is concerned with the linguistic patterning of sounds in human languages, with its primary aim being to discover the principles that govern the way sounds are organized in languages, and to explain the variations that occur.

✵ Further Practice ✵

I. Mark the following statements with "T" if they are true or "F" if they are false. Provide explanations for the false statements.
1. Speech organs are also known as vocal organs.
2. Linguists are concerned with all the sounds that are produced by the human speech organs.
3. Most of the repetitious of what might be heard as the same utterance are physically different, even though they sound identical to our ears.
4. In terms of phonetics, any segment must be either a vowel or a consonant.
5. There is only one lateral in English, and it is [l].
6. Phoneticians often use the term stop to indicate a nasal stop.

7. In English, the sound [tʃ] as in church and the sound [dʒ] as in jet are both fricatives.
8. Stops, fricatives and affricates are called obstruents because the production obstructs airflow.
9. [ŋ] in the word *sing* is a velar nasal.
10. RP is the short form for Received Pronunciation, and it is one of the most common model accents in the teaching English as a foreign language.
11. The sounds [f] and [v] are made with the lower lip and the upper front teeth, so they are labiodental.
12. The basic principle of IPA is using a different letter for each distinguishable speech sound.
13. Broad transcription is the one normally used in dictionaries and teaching textbooks.
14. In broad transcription, the pronunciation of the word *build* should be represented as [biɫd].
15. In terms of place, of articulator, [p] and [b] can be classified into the category of stops.
16. [m] is both a labiodental and a nasal.
17. [iː] is a front vowel, while [i] is a back one.
18. The hard roof of mouth is called hard palate.
19. [n] is one of syllabic consonants.
20. The mouth, also termed the pharyngeal cavity, is one of the three important areas of the human articulatory apparatus.
21. A basic way to determine the phonemes of a language is to see if substituting one sound for another results in a change of meaning.
22. To nasalize a vowel when it is followed by a nasal sound is assimilation rule.
23. Cardinal vowels are not all monophthongs and their quality may change during their production.
24. The distinction between vowels and consonants lies in the manners of articulation.
25. In the IPA chart, a set of diacritics are used for the purpose of transcribing the minute difference between variations of the same sound.
26. The sound [p] is unaspirated in the word *peak*, and aspirated in the word *speak*.
27. Phonology is the study of all possible speech sounds, while phonetics studies the way in which speakers of a language systematically produce the sounds.
28. Sounds in free variation should be assigned to different phonemes.
29. All vowels are voiced.
30. In English, the word *please* is monosyllabic.
31. A syllable must have a nucleus or peak, which is often the task of a consonant.
32. According to the sonority scale, the least sonorous sounds are vowels.
33. In English, the stress of words may fall on any syllable in principle, and it also changes over history and exhibits regional or dialectal differences.
34. It was Daniel Jones who put forward the most famous system about cardinal vowels.
35. When stops are articulated, incomplete closure of the articulators are involved so that the airstream can escape through the mouth.
36. Suprasegmental features cannot distinguish meaning.
37. The location of stress in English sentences sometimes distinguishes meaning.
38. Different ways to divide intonation units can give the same sentence different meanings.
39. The reason for the divergence between sound and symbol in English is simply that there are more sounds than its letters can represent, so each letter must represent more

than one sound.
40. In Chinese and English, the vowels whose quality remains throughout the articulation are known as *pure* or *monophthong vowels*.
41. [h] is described as a glottal fricative.
42. Suprasegmental phonology refers to the study of phonological properties of units larger than the segment-phoneme, such as syllable, word and sentence.
43. The air stream provided by the lungs has to undergo a number of modification to acquire the quality of a speech sound.
44. Two sounds are in free variation when they occur in the same environment and do not contrast, namely, the substitution of one for the other does not produce a different word, but merely a different pronunciation.
45. Acoustic phonetics is concerned with the perception of speech sounds.
46. All syllables must have a nucleus but not all syllables contain an onset and a coda.
47. When pure vowels or monophthongs are pronounced, no vowel glides take place.
48. According to the length or tenseness of the pronunciation, vowels can be divided into "tense vs. lax" or "long vs. short".
49. In English, in principle, the stress can only fall on the first syllable.
50. The maximal onset principle states that when there is a choice as to where to place a consonant, it is put into the coda rather than the onset.

II. Fill in each of the following blanks with (an) appropriate word(s).
1. Of the three branches of phonetics, the _____ phonetics studies sounds from the speaker's point of view; the _____ phonetics looks at sounds from the hearer's point of view; and the _____ phonetics studies the way sounds travel by looking at sound waves.
2. The _____, mouth, and _____ form the three cavities of the vocal tract.
3. In terms of places of articulation, _____ is a retroflex.
4. When the vocal folds are apart, the air can pass through easily and the sound produced is said to be _____.
5. Consonants are produced by constricting or obstructing the _____, _____ at some place to divert, impede, or completely shut off the flow of air in the oral cavity.
6. Affricates consist of a _____ followed immediately afterwards by a fricative at the same place of articulation.
7. [z, ʃ, ʒ, h] are _____ in terms of manners of articulation.
8. Name four oral stops besides [p] and [t]: _____, _____, _____, _____ and nasals _____, _____, _____.
9. According to the places of articulation, [f] and [v] are _____.
10. In terms of places of articulation, [ʃ] and [ʒ] can be classified into the category of _____.
11. [j] is a _____ in terms of places of articulation.
12. In English and Chinese, vowels with an audible change of quality are called _____.
13. [p⁼, pʰ] are _____ of the same phoneme / p /.
14. [θ, ð] belong to the category of _____ in accordance with their places of articulation.
15. Besides [s], [z], other four sibilants are _____, _____, _____, _____.
16. A syllable that has no _____ is called an open syllable.
17. An example of four consonants occurring after the peak is the word _____.

18. The IPA provides its users with a set of symbols called _____, which can be added to the letter-symbols to make finer distinctions than the letters alone possible.
19. An initial classification will divide the speech sounds into two broad categories: _____ and _____.
20. The three cavities in the articulatory apparatus are pharyngeal cavity, _____, and _____.
21. Name five of the English front vowels: _____, _____, _____, _____, _____.
22. The [p] sound in *peak* is called an _____ [p], and the [p] sound in *speak* is an _____ [p].
23. The main suprasegmental features include _____, _____, and _____.
24. The _____ rule also accounts for the varying pronunciation of the alveolar nasal [n] in some sound combinations.
25. In English, all the front vowels and central vowels are _____ vowels.
26. The features that a phoneme possesses, making it different from other phonemes, are its _____.
27. _____ refers to the degree of force used in producing a syllable.
28. In terms of the height of tongue rising, vowels can be classified as _____, _____ and _____ vowels.

III. Mark the choice that best completes the statement.
1. Phonetics is of a general nature, and it is interested in _____.
   A. all the speech sounds used in all human languages
   B. has speech sounds are produced
   C. how speech sounds differ from each other
   D. how speech sounds can be classified
2. The study to discover how speech sounds in a language form patterns should be included in _____.
   A. phonetics   B. phonology
   C. articulatory phonetics D. acoustic phonetics
3. The sound [l] in _____ is a clear one.
   A. *tell*   B. *quilt*   C. *leaf*   D. *peel*
4. The basic unit in phonology is called _____, and it is a unit that of distinctive value.
   A. phoneme   B. phone   C. allophone   D. sound
5. _____ doesn't form a minimal pair.
   A. *Gap* and *cap*   B. *Pat* and *pad*
   C. *Tip* and *dip*   D. *Map* and *tam*
6. _____ is not in complementary distribution.
   A. *Spot* and *pot*.   B. *Stop* and *top*.
   C. *School* and *cool*.   D. *Light* and *glad*.
7. The following pairs form a minimal pair EXCEPT _____.
   A. *look* and *book*   B. *pin* and *tin*
   C. *kill* and *dill*   D. *beat* and *pee*
8. _____ is not the term used to classify the English consonants in terms of manners of articulation.

Chapter 2
Speech Sounds

    A. Approximant.   B. Lateral.
    C. Plosive.   D. Bilabial.

9. In the following word _____, the articulation of bilabial is not manifested.
    A. *pet*   B. *met*   C. *how*   D. *web*

10. The distinctive feature of the sound [s] is _____.
    A. voiceless alveolar fricative
    B. voiced alveolar fricative
    C. voiceless dental affricative
    D. voiced dental fricative

11. The sounds in _____ are alveolars.
    A. [f] and [v]   B. [t] and [d]
    C. [ʃ] and [ʒ]   D. [k] and [g]

12. The sound with the features bilabial nasal is _____.
    A. [j]   B. [t]   C. [m]   D. [ŋ]

13. Diphthongal glides in English can be heard in following words EXCEPT _____.
    A. *way*   B. *tower*   C. *tide*   D. *how*

14. Words in the pair _____ form a minimal pair.
    A. *beat* and *seen*   B. *pig* and *pad*
    C. *choke* and *joke*   D. *but* and *heart*

15. In the word _____, [l] is palatalized.
    A. *lead*   B. *steal*   C. *lily*   D. *lied*

16. In terms of narrow transcription. [l] is dark in the word _____.
    A. *led*   B. *language*   C. *deal*   D. *clear*

17. Each pair of words manifests complementary distribution EXCEPT _____.
    A. *spot* and *pay*   B. *stop* and *top*
    C. *replay* and *pay*   D. *school* and *cool*

18. For the word *direction*, Americans usually pronounce it as [daɪrɛkʃɜn] whereas most British people say [dɪrɛkʃɜn]. This phenomenon can be interpreted in terms of _____.
    A. phonetic similarity   B. free variation
    C. complementary distribution   D. allophones

19. In all the following words we can find examples of regressive assimilation EXCEPT _____.
    A. *sink*   B. *ninth*   C. *cap*   D. *help*

20. _____ gives the correct description of the sound [u:].
    A. Velar nasal   B. High back tense rounded vowel
    C. Low back lax rounded vowel   D. High front lax unrounded vowel

21. If three consonants should cluster together at the beginning of a word, the first phoneme must be _____.
    A. / p /   B. / t /   C. / l /   D. / s /

22. The vowel in _____ should be nasalized according to the assimilation rules.
    A. *tea*   B. *peep*   C. *flee*   D. *bean*

23. The sound assimilation is not manifested in the spelling of the word _____.
    A. *implausible*   B. *illegal*   C. *irregular*   D. *input*

24. When we produce the back vowels, we hold the _____ part of the tongue higher than the rest of it.

　　　　A. central　　　B. front　　　　C. back　　　　　D. the tip
25. _____ is not the term used to classify the English consonants in terms of manner of articulation.
　　　　A. Stops.　　　B. Liquids.　　　C. Glides.　　　　D. Dental.
26. The one that does not belong to the alveolar is _____.
　　　　A. [t]　　　　B. [m]　　　　　C. [n]　　　　　　D. [r]
27. Sounds like [ʃ], [tʃ], and [j] are realized by the obstruction between the back of the tongue and the hard palate. They belong to the type of _____.
　　　　A. palatal　　　B. glottal　　　C. bilabial　　　　D. velar
28. The distinctive features of the sound [ŋ] are _____.
　　　　A. voiced, nasal,
　　　　B. velarlabial, nasal, voiced
　　　　C. voiced, alveolar, nasal
　　　　D. voiced, labial, palatal
29. The labiodental sounds in English are _____.
　　　　A. [p] and [b]　　　　　　　　B. [f] and [v]
　　　　C. [θ] and [ð]　　　　　　　　D. [k] and [g]
30. According to the rule of _____, the article *an*, instead of *a*, is used before the word *apple*.
　　　　A. nasalization　　　　　　　　B. dentalization
　　　　C. epenthesis　　　　　　　　　D. velarization
31. The sound _____ does not belong to the group of fricative.
　　　　A. [f]　　　　　B. [v]　　　　　C. [k]　　　　　　D. [h]
32. If we follow the English vowel system of Radford, we can describe the vowel [i:] in the way of _____.
　　　　A. high front tense rounded vowel
　　　　B. high back lax unrounded vowel
　　　　C. high front tense unrounded vowel
　　　　D. low back lax rounded vowel
33. _____ does not contain a bilabial sound.
　　　　A. *My*　　　　B. *You*　　　　C. *Buy*　　　　　D. *Pie*
34. _____ ends with an affricate.
　　　　A. *Rack*　　　B. *Such*　　　　C. *Booze*　　　　D. *Tip*
35. The word _____ begins with the sound of a palato-alveolar consonant.
　　　　A. *ship*　　　B. *lip*　　　　C. *zip*　　　　　D. *sip*
36. The articulation of _____ is made with the two pieces of vocal folds pushed towards each other.
　　　　A. uvular　　　B. glottal　　　C. velar　　　　　D. palatal
37. Triphthongal glides in English can be heard in _____.
　　　　A. *tide*　　　B. *toy*　　　　C. *how*　　　　　D. *wire*
38. The word _____ contains a high vowel.
　　　　A. *lot*　　　　B. *mat*　　　　C. *mud*　　　　　D. *boot*
39. All the following words contain front vowels EXCEPT _____.
　　　　A. *book*　　　B. *sleep*　　　C. *slip*　　　　　D. *shed*
40. The sound _____ is usually formed in English by curling the tip of the tongue back behind the alveolar ridge.
　　　　A. [r]　　　　　B. [j]　　　　　C. [h]　　　　　　D. [w]
41. In the word _____, there is no syllabic consonant.

A. *cotton*   B. *bottom*   C. *table*   D. *national*
42. Pitch variation is known as _____ when its patterns are imposed on sentences.
     A. intonation   B. tone   C. pronunciation   D. voice
43. [p] in the word *peak* can be described as _____.
     A. voiced bilabial stop   B. voiceless bilabial stop
     C. voiced bilabial plosive   D. voiceless labiodental stop
44. The description *voiceless alveolar fricative* describes the following consonant _____.
     A. [p]   B. [b]   C. [s]   D. [z]
45. The vowel _____ can be described with features of *mid, central, lax, unrounded*.
     A. [ə]   B. [i:]   C. [ɜ]   D. [ɔ]
46. The idea of _____ is introduced to indicate the difference between [i] and [ɪ], [ɜ] and [ə].
     A. tenseness   B. lip-rounding
     C. height of tongue rising   D. voicing
47. Which branch of phonetics concerns the production of speech sounds?
     A. Acoustic Phonetics.   B. Articulatory Phonetics.
     C. Auditory Phonetics.   D. None of the above.
48. In narrow transcription the word *help* should be presented as _____.
     A. [hɛɫp]   B. [hɛlp]   C. /help/   D. /həɫp/
49. The word below _____ refers to a unit of explicit sound contrast.
     A. morpheme   B. phoneme   C. phonetics   D. phonology
50. Among the following words, _____ does no form a minimal pair with the sound of the word *high*.
     A. *buy*   B. *foe*   C. *lie*   D. *shy*

IV. Answer the following questions as comprehensively as possible, giving examples if necessary.
1. In English, the description of vowels needs to fulfill four basic requirements. What are they? Explain them and offer at least one example.
2. Explain the assimilation rule in phonology with examples.
3. What do you know about RP? Does it change with time?
4. Ananlaze the following with your knowledge about phonological process:
   - cat + s
   assimilate voicing (they already match, so do nothing)
   split sibilants (not applicable here, so do nothing)
   final form: s
   - dog + s
   assimilate voicing: s→z
   split sibilants (not applicable here, so do nothing)
   final form: z
   - bus + s
   assimilate voicing (they already match, so do nothing)
   split sibilants: s→ɪs
   final form: ɪs

参考答案

I.
1. T
2. F. Linguists are concerned with only those sounds that are produced by human speech organs in so far as they have a role to play in linguistic communication.
3. T
4. F. There are segments standing midway and they are called semivowels or semi-consonants. E. g. [j] in ['jeləu] and [w] in [wiː] are semivowels.
5. T
6. F. Stop is usually used to refer to an oral stop, and the term "nasal" is to indicate a nasal stop.
7. F. [tʃ] and [dʒ] are both affricates.
8. T 9. T 10. T 11. T 12. T 13. T
14. F. It should be presented as [bild].
15. F. In terms of manner of articulation, [p] and [b] can be classified into the category of stops.
16. F. [m] is both a bilabial and nasal.
17. F. [i] is also a front vowel.
18. T 19. T
20. F. The mouth, also the termed oral cavity, is one of the three important areas of the human articulatory apparatus.
21. T 22. T
23. F. Cardinal vowels are monophthongs and their quality does not change during their production.
24. F. The distinction between vowels and consonants lies in the obstruction of airstream.
25. T
26. F. The sound [p] is aspirated in the word *peak* and unaspirated in the word *speak*.
27. F. Phonetics is the study of all possible speech sounds while phonology studies the way in which speakers of a language systematically use a selection of these sounds, that is, the sound patterns, to express meaning.
28. F. Sounds in free variation should be assigned to the same phoneme.
29. T 30. T
31. F. The task of a nucleus or peak is often performed by a vowel.
32. F. The least sonorous sounds are stops.
33. T 34. T
35. F. When stops are articulated, complete closure of the articulators are involved so that the airstream cannot escape.
36. T
37. F. Stress, intonation and tone distinguish meaning
38. T.
39. F. The reason is not that simple. In old English, the relation between sound and symbol was much more regular. Some of the sounds, especially the vowels, have undergone changes in the history of English. Furthermore, many English words have been borrowed from other languages throughout history and the irregularity of its

spelling is made worse because of such borrowings.
40. T   41. T   42. T   43. T   44. T
45. F. Acoustic phonetics is the study of the physical propertiesof the sounds produced in speech.
46. T   47. T   48. T
49. F. Received Pronunciation is a pronunciation of British English, originally based on the speech of the upper class of southeastern England and characteristic of the English spoken at the public schools and at Oxford and Cambridge Universities.
50. F. In phonology, the Maximal Onset Principle is a principle determining underlying syllable division. It states that intervocalic consonants are maximally assigned to the onsets of syllables in conformity with universal and language-specific conditions

II.
1. articulatory; auditory; acoustic
2. pharynx; nose
3. [r]
4. voiceless
5. vocal, tract
6. stop
7. fricatives
8. [b][d][k][g];[m][n][ŋ]
9. labiodental
10. dental
11. palatal
12. vowel glides
13. allophones
14. fricatives
15. [ʃ]; [ʒ]; [tʃ]; [dʒ]
16. coda
17. sixths
18. diacritics
19. vowels and consonants
20. oral cavity; nasal cavity
21. [iː]; [i]; [e]; [æ]; [ɑː]
22. aspirated; unaspirated
23. stress, tone, intonation
24. assimilation
25. unrounded
26. distinctive features
27. Stress
28. high; mid; low

III.
1. A   2. B   3. C   4. A   5. D   6. D   7. D   8. D   9. C   10. A
11. B 12. C 13. B 14. C 15. B 16. C 17. C 18. B 19. C 20. B
21. D 22. D 23. D 24. C 25. D 26. B 27. A 28. A 29. B 30. C
31. C 32. C 33. B 34. B 35. A 36. B 37. D 38. D 39. A 40. A
41. D 42. A 43. B 44. C 45. A 46. C 47. B 48. A 49. B 50. B

IV.
1. The four basic requirements are:
 (1) the height of tongue rising (high, mid, low); (2) the position of the highest part of the tongue (front, central, back); (3) the length or tenseness of the vowel (tense vs. lax or long vs. short); (4) lip-rounding (rounded vs. unrounded). Following these requirements, we can describe [iː] as a high front tense unrounded vowel.
2. The assimilation rule assimilates one sound to another by "copying" a feature of a sequential phoneme, thus making the two phonemes similar. Assimilation of neighboring sounds is, for the most part, caused by articulatory or physiological process. When we speak, we tend to increase the case of articulation. For example, while the [iː] sound is non-nasalized in words as *tea*, *peep*, *and flee*, it is nasalized in words like *bean*, *green*, *team* and *scream*. This is because, in all these sounds

combinations the [i:] is followed by a nasal [n] or [m]. To make the pronunciation of the sound combination easier, we actually nasalize the vowel.

3. Received Pronunciation (RP), also called the Queen's (or King's) English and BBC English, is the accent of Standard English in England, with a relationship to regional dialects similar to that of other European languages. Although there is nothing intrinsic about RP that marks it as superior to any other variety, sociolinguistic factors give Received Pronunciation particular prestige in England and Wales. However, since World War II, a greater permissiveness towards allowing regional English varieties has taken hold in education and in the media in England.

Like all accents, RP has changed with time. For example, sound recordings and films from the first half of the 20th century demonstrate that it was usual for speakers of RP to pronounce the /æ/ sound, as in land, with a vowel close to [ɛ], so that land would sound similar to a present-day pronunciation of lend. RP is sometimes known as the Queen's English, but recordings show that even Queen Elizabeth II has changed her pronunciation over the past 50 years, no longer using an [ɛ]-like vowel in words like land. *The* 1993 *Oxford Dictionary* changed three main things in its description of modern RP, although these features can still be heard amongst old speakers of RP. Before World War II, the vowel of cup was a back vowel close to cardinal [ʌ] but has since shifted forward to a central position so that [ɐ] is more accurate; phonetic transcription of this vowel as [ʌ] is common partly for historical reasons.

In the 1960s the transcription /əʊ/ started to be used for the *GOAT* vowel instead of Daniel Jones's /oʊ/, reflecting a change in pronunciation since the beginning of the century. Joseph Wright's work suggests that, during the early 20th century, words such as cure, fewer, pure, etc. were pronounced with a triphthong /iuə/ rather than the more modern /juə/.

The change in RP may even be observed in the home of *BBC English*. The BBC accent of the 1950s was distinctly different from today's: a news report from the 1950s is recognisable as such, and a mock-1950s BBC voice is used for comic effect in programmes wishing to satirize 1950s social attitudes such as the *Harry Enfield Show* and its *Mr. Cholmondley-Warner* sketches. (Source: http://www.answers.com/topic/received-pronunciation)

4. Please refer to 2.2.4 in the textbook. The answer lies in the order in which we applied the rules. In the table provided in this question, the sound [I] derived the surface forms from the underlying form /s/ by first applying the voicing-assimilation rule and then the manner-dissimilation rule. Here is what happens if we simply reverse the order of the two rules:

- *cat* + *s*
  split sibilants (not applicable here, so do nothing)
  assimilate voicing (they already match, so do nothing)
  final form: s
- *dog* + *s*
  split sibilants (not applicable here, so do nothing)
  assimilate voicing: s→z
  final form: z
- *bus* + *s*
  assimilate voicing (they already match, so do nothing)

split sibilants: s→is
assimilate voicing: s→z to match the preceding /I/
(correct) final form: iz

 Once we have more than one rule in our toolbag, we need to be sensitive to the possible interaction among rules. If rule A changes apples to bananas, rule B changes bananas to pears and we start with a bowl containing 2 apples and 2 bananas, show that it matters whether we first apply A then B or first apply B and then A. (Source: http://cspeech.ucd.ie/~fred/teaching/oldcourses/phonetics/rules2.html)

Chapter 3

From Morpheme to Phrase

Concepts & Theories

I. What is Morpheme?
1. Morpheme and Morphology
  MORPHEME is the smallest unit of language in regard to the relationship between sounding and meaning, a unit that cannot be divided into further smaller units without destroying or drastically altering the meaning.
  The systematic study of morpheme is a branch of linguistics called MORPHOLOGY, which investigates the internal structures and rules of morphemes by which words are formed.
2. Types of Morphemes
 (1) Free morpheme and bound morpheme
 (2) Root, affix and stem
   Poly-morphemic words other than compounds may be divided into roots and affixes.
   A ROOT is the base form of a word that cannot be further analyzed without destroying its meaning.
   An AFFIX is the collective term for the type of morpheme that can be used only when added to another morpheme (the root or stem), so affix is naturally bound. Affixes in a language are limited in number, and are generally classified into three subtypes, namely, prefix, suffix and infix, depending on their position around the root or stem of a word.
   A STEM is any morpheme or combination of morphemes to which an inflectional affix can be added.
 (3) Inflectional affix and derivational affix
   This distinction is sometimes known as the distinction between inflectional morphemes and derivational morphemes. Both are concerned with affixes only: roots cannot be divided into inflectional and derivational ones. But these two types of affix have some differences.
   First, inflectional affixes are generally less productive than derivational affixes;
   Second, inflectional affixes do not change the word class of the word they attach to;
   Third, that whether one should add inflectional affixes or not depends very often on other factors within the phrase or sentence at stake.
3. Allomorph and Morphological change
 (1) Allomorph
   Words such as illogical, imbalance, irregular and inactive share a common morpheme in. In other words, *il-*, *im-*, and *ir-* are exceptionally the variation

forms of one morpheme *in-*. These variation forms are called ALLOMORPHs, i.e. allomorphs of the same morpheme owing to the influence of the sounds to which it attaches.
(2) Morphological change
Morphological change takes the form of inflectional changes in affixes.

II. What Is Word?
1. **Word and lexical items**
   WORD is a typical grammatical unit between Morpheme and Word Group (see 3.5). Word is also used as a sounding unit and a writing unit.
2. **Classification of words**
   (1) Variable and invariable words
   ☆ In variable words, one can find ordered and regular series of grammatically different word form; on the other hand, part of the word remains relatively constant. E.g. *follow-follows-following-followed*.
   ☆ Invariable words refer to those words such as *since*, *when*, *seldom*, *through*, *hello*, etc. They have no inflective endings.
   (2) Grammatical words and lexical words
   ☆ Grammatical words, also known as function words, express grammatical meanings. For example, conjunctions, prepositions, articles, and pronouns are grammatical words.
   ☆ Lexical words, also known as content words, have lexical meanings, i.e. those which refer to substance, action and quality, such as nouns, verbs, adjectives, and adverbs, are lexical words.
   (3) Closed-class words and open-class words
   ☆ A word that belongs to the closed-class is one whose membership is fixed or limited. New members are not regularly added. Therefore, pronouns, prepositions, conjunctions, articles, etc. are all closed items.
   ☆ A word that belongs to the open-class is one whose membership is in principle infinite or unlimited. Nouns, verbs, adjectives and many adverbs are all open-class items.
   (4) Word class
   ☆ This division is close to the notion of parts of speech in traditional grammar.
   ☆ Today, word class displays a wider range of more precisely defined categories. Here are some of the categories newly introduced into linguistic analysis.
   - Particles: Particles include at least the infinitive marker *to*, the negative marker *not*, and the subordinate units in phrasal verbs, such as *get by*, *do up*, and *look back*, etc.
   - Auxiliaries: Auxiliaries used to be regarded as verbs. Because of their unique properties, which one could hardly expect of a verb, linguists today tend to define them as a separate word class.
   - Pro-forms: Pro-forms are the forms which can serve as replacements for different elements in a sentence. For example, in the following conversation, *so* replaces *that I can come*.
     A: *I hope you can come*.
     B: *I hope so*.

- Determiners: Determiners refer to words which are used before the noun acting as head of a noun phrase, and determine the kind of reference the noun phrase has. Determiners can be divided into three subclasses: predeterminers, central determiners and postdeterminers.

III. Word Formation (1): From Morpheme to Word

There are two fields that Morphology concerns: (i) the study of INFLECTIONS (also called INFLECTIONAL MORPHOLOGY), as exemplified with bark + -s, and (ii) the study of LEXICAL or DERIVATIONAL MORPHOLOGY (often referred to as WORD-FORMATION).

1. The Inflectional Way of Formation

INFLECTION indicates grammatical relations by adding inflectional affixes, such as number, person, finiteness, aspect and case; the adding of inflectional affixes will not change the grammatical class of the stems (to which they are attached).

2. The Derivational Way of Formation

DERIVATION, in its restricted sense, refers to the process of how new words are formed. It can be further divided into two sub-types: the derivational type (DERIVATION) and the compositional type (COMPOUND). Therefore, "derivation" here is a cover term both for the derivation itself and for the compound.

(1) Derivation

DERIVATION shows a relationship between roots and affixes.

(2) Compound

The term COMPOUND refers to those words that consist of more than one lexical morpheme, or the way to join two separate words to produce a single new word. In compounds, the lexical morphemes can be of different word classes. Compounds can be further divided into two kinds: the endocentric compound and the exocentric compound.

IV. Word Formation (2): Lexical Change

(1) Invention

Since economic activities are the most important and dynamic in human life, many new lexical items come directly from the consumer items, their producers or their brand names.

(2) Blending

Blending is a relatively complex form of compounding, in which two words are blended by joining the initial part of the first word and the final part of the second word, or by joining the initial parts of the two words.

(3) Abbreviation/Clipping

A new word is created by cutting the final part, cutting the initial part or cutting both the final and initial parts of the original words.

(4) Acronym

Acronym is made up from the first letters of the name of an organization, which has a heavily modified headword.

(5) Back-formation

Back-formation refers to an abnormal type of word-formation where a shorter word is derived by deleting an imagined affix from a longer form already in the language.

Chapter 3
From Morpheme to Phrase

(6) Analogical creation

The principle of analogical creation can account for the co-existence of two forms, regular and irregular, in the conjugation of some English verbs.

(7) Borrowing

English in its development has managed to widen her vocabulary by borrowing words from other languages. Greek, Latin, French, Spanish, Arabic and other languages have all played an active role in this process.

V. Word Group and Phrase

Word group is a group of words; it is an expansion of a word. Phrase is a contraction of a clause.

Related Terms

abbreviation

Abbreviation is also called clipping. It refers to a way of creating new words by cutting the final part of, or cutting the initial part of, or cutting both the initial and final parts of the original forms.

acronym

Acronym is made up from the first letters of the name of an organization, which has a heavily modified headword. This process is also widely used in shortening extremely long words of word groups in science, technology and other special fields.

affix

An affix is the collective term for the type of formative that can be used only when added to another morpheme (the root or stem). Affixes are limited in number in a language, and are generally classified into three subtypes, positioned with reference to the root or stem of the word.

allomorph

An allomorph is a concretely realized variant of a morpheme. The classification of morphs as allomorphs or as the tokens of a particular morpheme is based on the similarity of meaning and the complementary distribution: for example, [s], [z], and [ɪz] are considered allomorphs of the plural morpheme.

analogical creation

Analogical creation can account for the coexistence of two forms, regular and irregular, in the conjugation of some English verbs, and it is to be distinguished from overgeneralization, the latter being regarded as a mistake in the use of language.

assimilation

Assimilation refers to the change of a sound as a result of the influence of an adjacent sound, which is more specifically called *contact* or *contiguous* assimilation.

back-formation

It refers to an abnormal type of word-formation where a shorter word is derived by deleting an imagined affix from a longer form already in the language. E.g. *edit* is back formed from *editor*; *peddle* is back formed from *peddler*.

base

Base is any form to which affixes of any kind can be added. This means that any root or stem can be termed a base. But a base differs from a root or a stem.

blending

Blending is a relatively complex form of compounding, in which two words are blended by joining the initial part of the first word and the final part of the second word, or by joining the initial parts of the two words.

borrowings

Borrowings or loans mean the words which have been borrowed from the other languages.

bound morpheme

Morphemes that must appear with at least another morpheme are called bound morphemes. E.g. *-ing* in *fascinating*.

broadening

It is a process to extend or elevate the meaning from its originally specific sense to a relatively general one. For instance, the word *holiday* used to mean *holy day* in religious English. Today it means *a day for rest* regardless of its religious nature. So the meaning is widened.

clipping

Clipping is a way of shortening a longer word into a shorter form.

closed-class word

A word that belongs to the closed-class is one whose membership is fixed or limited. New members are not regularly added. E.g. pronouns, preposition, conjunctions, and articles, etc. are all closed-class items.

compound

It is the result of the process of word formation of composition, a linguistic expression that consists of at least two free morphemes or morpheme constructions. For instance, *bathroom* is made up of (*bath* + *room*).

compounding

Compounding is a way to create a new lexical item through combining two or more roots.

content words

Content words are those that refer to substance, action and quality, and they carry the main content of a language. Content words are also called lexical words.

conversion

Conversion is a process to change a word from one class into another, with little or no phonological change.

derivation

Derivation is the process and result of word formation in which new words are created from already existing words through various processes, e.g. the creation of adjectives from nouns (*professional* ← *profession*), nouns from verbs (*computer* ← *compute*), etc.

derivational affix

Derivational affixes are added to an existing form to create a word. The existing form to which a derivational affix can be added is called a stem. For example, the word *tolerate* is formed by the root *toler-* plus the derivational affix *-ate*.

dissimilation

Dissimilation refers to the influence exercised by one sound segment upon the articulation of another, so that the sounds become less alike, or different.

endocentric compound

A compound which has a center or a head word is termed endocentric compound.

Chapter 3
From Morpheme to Phrase

epenthesis rule

The epenthesis rule is the rule or change in which successive sounds are separated by an intervening segment. E.g. a schwa [ɪ] in *pieces* can be described as an epenthetic vowel inserted between [s] and [z] in underlying [piːs] + [z].

exocentric compound

A compound which has no center or a head word is called exocentric compound.

folk etymology

Folk etymology refers to a change in form of a word or phrase, resulting from an incorrect popular notion of the origin or meaning of the term or from the influence of more familiar terms mistakenly taken to be analogous.

free morpheme

A free morpheme refers to the morpheme which is an independent unit of meaning and can be used freely all by itself. E.g. *help*, *able*.

function words

Words that serve to link the different parts of a language together are called function words. They are also called grammatical words.

grammatical words

Words that express grammatical meanings, such as conjunctions, prepositions, articles and pronouns, are grammatical words.

inflection

Word stems of particular parts of speech are realized in morphologically different word forms that regularly mark different syntactic and semantic functions. Inflection is the manifestation of grammatical relationships through the addition of inflectional affixes, such as number, person, finiteness, aspect, and case, which do not change the grammatical class of the stems to which they are attached.

inflectional affix

Inflectional affixes manifest various grammatical relations or grammatical categories such as number, tense, degree and case. For example, the inflectional affixes that have been retained include:
- (*e*)*s*, indicating plurality of nouns,
- (*e*)*s*, indicating third person singular, present tense,
- (*e*)*d*, indicating past tense for all three persons,
- *ing*, indicating progressive aspect.

initialisms

Initialisms mean combining the initial letters of a composite name to make a new lexical item.

invariable words

Invariable words refer to those words such as *since*, *when*, *seldom*, *through*, *hello*. They do not have inflective endings.

invention

Invention refers to a process of creating new words by letting lexical items come directly from the consumer items, their producers or their brand names into the vocabulary. Words such as *Kodak*, *Coke*, and *Xerox* are examples of this kind.

lexeme

Lexeme is postulated as the abstract unit underlying the smallest unit in the lexical system of a language, which appears in different grammatical contexts.

lexical words

Words that have lexical meanings, that is, they refer to substance, action and quality, such as nouns, verbs, adjectives, and adverbs. They are also known as content words.

loanblending

Loanblending is a process in which part of the form is native and part is borrowed, but the meaning is fully borrowed. For instance, in English, the first parts of the words *coconut* and *Chinatown* came from Spanish and Chinese respectively, but the second parts are of the English origin.

loanshift

Loanshift is a process in which the meaning is borrowed, but the form is native. *Bridge* is an English word, but when it refers to a type of card game, the meaning was borrowed from the Italian word *Ponte*.

loanwords

English in its development has managed to widen her vocabulary by borrowing words from other languages. There are several types of processes with regard to borrowing: loanwords, loanblending and loanshift. The borrowing of loanwords is a process in which both form and meaning are borrowed with only a slight adaptation, in some cases, to the phonological system of the new language that they enter.

loss of sound

The loss of sound can refer to the disappearance of the very sound as a phoneme in the phonological system and it may also occur in utterances at the expense of some unstressed vowels. E.g. *sorh*/sorx/→ *sorrow*/sorɜu/, and *cabinet* changes its pronunciation from /kæbɜnɜt/ to /kæbnɜt/.

metathesis

Metathesis is a process involving an alternation in the sequence of sounds. Metathesis had been originally a performance error, which was overlooked and accepted by the speech community. For instance, the word *bird* was *brid* in Old English.

morph

The phonological and orthographic forms that represent a morpheme are called morphs. For example, the morpheme {sweet} is phonologically represented by [swɪːt] and orthographically by *sweet*. These two forms are morphs of the morpheme {sweet}.

morpheme

Morpheme refers to the smallest meaningful unit of language. Take the word *boyish* as an example. The word obviously consists of two meaningful elements: *boy* and *-ish*. As we all know that the word *boy* means *young*, *male human being* and *-ish* means *having the quality of*. Structurally speaking, the word *boyish* consists of two meaningful components which cannot be analyzed any further. So both *boy* and *-ish* are morphemes.

morphology

Morphology studies the internal structure of words, and the rules by which words are formed.

morphophonology

Morphophonology or morphophonemics is a branch of linguistics referring to the analysis and classification of the phonological factors which affect the appearance of morpheme, and the grammatical factors which affect the appearance of phonemes. At any rate, it studies the interrelationships between phonology and morphology.

Chapter 3
From Morpheme to Phrase

open-class words

An open-class word is one whose membership is in principle infinite or unlimited. With the emergence of new ideas, inventions, etc., new expressions are continually and constantly being added to the lexicon. Nouns, verbs, adjectives and many adverbs are open-class items.

part of speech

Part of speech is the result of the classification of the words of a given language according to form and meaning criteria. Such classifications reach back into antiquity. Because of the different classificatory approaches, the number of parts of speech in the various grammars varies between two and fifteen.

prefixation

Prefixation is a process to form a new word by adding a prefix to the base.

root

A root is the base form of a word that cannot be analyzed without total loss of identity. That is to say, it is that part of the word left when all the affixes are removed. A free root is a word in its own right. Words such as *book*, *walk*, and *root* are examples of this kind. A bound root is often seen as part of a word that can never stand by itself although it bears clear, definite meaning. It must be combined with another root or an affix to form a word. For example, the root *geo* bears the meaning of *the earth*; when it combines with another root *-ology* meaning *a branch of learning*, we get the word *geology*, which means *the study of the earth's structure*.

stem

A stem is any morpheme or combination of morphemes to which an inflectional affix can be added.

suffixation

Suffixation is a process to form a new word by adding a suffix to the base.

variable words

In variable words, one can find ordered and regular series of grammatically different word forms; on the other hand, part of the word remains relatively constant. Thus each ordered series constitutes a paradigm. E.g. *mat*, *mats*.

word formation

Word formation is the investigation and description of processes and rule-governed formation of new complex words on the basis of already existing linguistic resources. Depending on the areas of interest, word formation looks at the structure of the vocabulary from a historical-genetic or synchronic-functional aspect.

Practice

I. Mark the choice that best completes the statement. (20%)

1. In terms of the meaning expressed by words, they can be classified into _____.
   A. grammatical words and lexical words
   B. content words and lexical words
   C. grammatical words and function words
   D. pro-forms and auxiliaries

2. _____ other than compounds may be divided into roots and affixes.
   A. Polymorphemic words   B. Bound morphemes

  C. Free morphemes   D. Monomorphemic words
3. Which two terms can best describe the following pairs of words: *table—tables*, *day break—daybreak*?
  A. Inflection and compound.   B. Compound and derivation.
  C. Inflection and derivation.   D. Derivation and inflection.
4. Which of the following is NOT a process of the lexical change?
  A. INVENTION   B. ACRONYM
  C. LEXICON   D. BLENDING
5. Which of the following is NOT a pre-determiner?
  A. *all*   B. *three times*   C. *half*   D. *that*
6. Nouns, verbs and adjectives can be classified as _____.
  A. lexical words   B. grammatical words
  C. function words   D. form words
7. Morphemes that represent tense, number, gender and case are called _____ morpheme.
  A. inflectional   B. free   C. bound   D. derivational
8. There are _____ morphemes in the word *denationalization*.
  A. three   B. four   C. five   D. six
9. In English *-ise* and *-al* are called _____.
  A. prefixes   B. suffixes   C. infixes   D. stems
10. The three subtypes of affixes are: prefix, suffix and _____.
  A. derivational affix   B. inflectional affix
  C. infix   D. back-formation
11. _____ is a way in which new words may be formed from already existing words by subtracting an affix which is thought to be part of the old word.
  A. Affixation   B. Back-formation   C. Insertion   D. Addition
12. The word *TV* is formed in the way of _____.
  A. acronymy   B. clipping   C. initialism   D. blending
13. The words like *comsat* and *sitcom* are formed by _____.
  A. blending   B. clipping
  C. back-formation   D. acronymy
14. The stem of *internationalists* is _____.
  A. nationalist   B. nation
  C. nationalist   D. internationalist
15. All of them are meaningful EXCEPT for _____.
  A. lexeme   B. phoneme   C. morpheme   D. allomorph

II. Mark the following statements with "T" if they are true or "F" if they are false. (10%)

1. Phonetically, the stress of a compound always falls on the first element, while the second element receives secondary stress.
2. *Fore* as in *foretell* is both a prefix and a bound morpheme.
3. Base refers to the part of the word that remains when all inflectional affixes are removed.
4. In most cases, prefixes change the meaning of the base whereas suffixes change the word-class of the base.

Chapter 3
From Morpheme to Phrase

5. Conversion from noun to verb is the most productive process of a word.
6. Reduplicative compound is formed by repeating the same morpheme of a word.
7. The words whimper, whisper and whistle are formed in the way of onomatopoeia.
8. In most cases, the number of syllables of a word corresponds to the number of morphemes.
9. Back-formation is a productive way of word-formations.
10. Inflection is a particular way of word-formations.
11. Free morphemes may constitute words by themselves.
12. INVENTION is a form of compounding, in which two words are blended by joining the initial part of the first word and the final part of the second word, or by joining the initial parts of the two words.
13. Words are the most stable of all linguistic units in respect of their internal structure.
14. Invariable words do not have inflective endings.
15. A root may also be free or bound, and a root may also be both free and bound.

III. Fill in each of the following blanks with an appropriate word. The first letter of the word is already given. (10%)

1. Different from compounds, d_____ shows a relationship between roots and affixes.
2. S_____ is the smallest component of meaning.
3. L_____ is a process in which part of the form is native and the rest has been borrowed, but the meaning is fully borrowed.
4. All words may be said to contain a root m_____.
5. A small set of conjunctions, prepositions and pronouns belong to c_____ class, while the largest part of nouns, verbs, adjectives and adverbs belongs to o_____ class.
6. B_____ is a reverse process of derivation, and therefore is a process of shortening.
7. C_____ is a process of word formation in which one can, by shifting the word class, change the meaning of a word from a concrete entity or notion to a process or attribution.
8. Words are divided into simple, compound and derived words on the m_____ level.
9. A word formed by derivation is called a d_____, and a word formed by compounding is called a c_____.
10. Bound morphemes are classified into two types: a_____ and b_____.

IV. Explain the following concepts or theories. (20%)

1. Blending
2. Allomorph
3. Closed-class word
4. Morphological rule

V. Answer the following questions briefly. (10%)

1. What do you know about semantic change?
2. What are the phonological changes?

VI. Match each term in Column A with one relevant item in Column B. （10％）

A	B
(1) acronym	a. beseech—besought/beseeched
(2) analogical creation	b. national
(3) derivational morpheme	c. *tea* in English
(4) clipping	d. riffle (ripple + shuffle)
(5) fusion	e. caravan—van
(6) adjective compound	f. editor—edit
(7) back-formation	g. UNESCO
(8) broadening	h. thought-provoking
(9) loanword	i. overwhelmed
(10) Inflectional affix	j. bird—young bird—any kind of bird

VII. Essay questions. （20％）

1. Describe lexical change proper with the latest examples in English, covering at least four aspects.
2. Describe the distinction between inflectional affixes and derivational affixes.

参考答案

I.
1. A 2. A 3. A 4. C 5. D 6. A 7. A 8. C 9. B 10. B
11. B 12. C 13. A 14. D 15. B

II.
1. T 2. T 3. F 4. T 5. T 6. F 7. T 8. F 9. F 10. F
11. T 12. F 13. T 14. T 15. T

III.
1. derivation 2. Sememe 3. Loanblending 4. morpheme
5. close; open 6. Back-formation 7. Conversion 8. morpheme
9. derivative; compound 10. affix; bound root

IV.

1. Blending: It is a process of word-formation in which a new word is formed by combining the meanings and sounds of two words, one of which is not in its full form or both of which are not in their full forms, like *newscast* (news + broadcast), *brunch* (breakfast + lunch).
2. Allomorph: It is any of the variant forms of a morpheme as conditioned by position or adjoining sounds.
3. Close-class word: It is a word whose membership is fixed or limited. Pronouns, prepositions, conjunctions, articles, etc. are all closed-class words.
4. Morphological rule: It is the rule that governs which affix can be added to what type of base to form a new word, e.g. *-ly* can be added to a noun to form an adjective.

Chapter 3
From Morpheme to Phrase

V.
1. There are three kinds of semantic changes, namely, broadening, narrowing, and meaning shift. Class shift and folk etymology also contribute to change in meaning.
   (1) Broadening: Broadening is a process to extend or elevate the meaning from its specific sense to a relatively general one.
   (2) Narrowing: Contrary to broadening, the original meaning of a word can be narrowed or restricted to a specific sense.
   (3) Meaning shift: All semantic changes involve meaning shift. Here meaning shift is understood in its narrow sense, i.e. the change of meaning has nothing to do with generalization or restriction as mentioned above.
   (4) Class shift: By shifting the word class one can change the meaning of a word from a concrete entity or notion to a process or attribution. This process of word formation is also known as zero-derivation, or conversion.
   (5) Folk etymology: Folk etymology refers to a change in form of a word or phrase, resulting from an incorrect popular notion of the origin or meaning of the term or from the influence of more familiar terms mistakenly taken to be analogous.
2. There are four major factors that contribute to the formation of new pronunciation.
   (1) Loss: The loss of sound can first refer to the disappearance of the very sound as a phoneme in the phonological system. The loss of sounds may also occur in utterances at the expense of some unstressed words.
   (2) Addition: Sounds may be lost but they may also be added to the original sound sequence.
   (3) Metathesis: Metathesis is a process involving an alternation in the sequence of sounds. Metathesis had been originally a performance error, which was overlooked and accepted by the speech community.
   (4) Assimilation: Assimilation refers to the change of a sound as a result of the influence of an adjacent sound, which is more specifically called *contact* or *contiguous* assimilation.

VI.
(1) g (2) a (3) b (4) e (5) d (6) h (7) f (8) j (9) c (10) i

VII.
1. Apart from compound and derivation, new words or expressions are created through the following processes.
   (1) Invention: Since economic activities are the most important and dynamic in human life, many new lexical items come directly from the consumer items, their producers or their brand names.
   (2) Blending: Blending is a relatively complex form of compounding, in which two words are blended by joining the initial part of the first word and the final part of the second word, or by joining the initial parts of the two words.
   (3) Abbreviation/clipping: A new word is created by cutting the final part, cutting the initial part or cutting both the final and initial parts of the original words.
   (4) Acronym: Acronym is made up from the first letters of the name of an organization, which has a heavily modified headword.
   (5) Back-formation: Back-formation refers to an abnormal type of word-formation where a shorter word is derived by deleting an imagined affix from a longer form

already in the language.
(6) Analogical creation: The principle of analogical creation can account for the co-existence of two forms, regular and irregular, in the conjugation of some English verbs.
(7) Borrowing: English in its development has managed to widen her vocabulary by borrowing words from other languages. Greek, Latin, French, Spanish, Arabic and other languages have all played an active role in this process.

2. Inflection is the manifestation of grammatical relationships through the addition of inflectional affixes, such as number, person, finiteness, aspect and case, which do not change the grammatical class of the stems to which they are attached. The distinction between inflectional affixes and derivational affixes is sometimes known as a distinction between inflectional morphemes and derivational morphemes. We can tell the difference between them with the following ways:
(1) Inflectional affixes very often add a minute or delicate grammatical meaning to the stem. E.g. *toys*, *walks*, *John's*, etc. Therefore, they serve to produce different forms of a single word. In contrast, derivational affixes often change the lexical meaning. E.g. *cite*, *citation*, etc.
(2) Inflectional affixes do not change the word class of the word they attach to, such as *flower*, *flowers*, whereas derivational affixes might or might not, such as the relation between *small* and *smallness* for the former, and that between *brother* and *brotherhood* for the latter.
(3) Inflectional affixes are often conditioned by nonsemantic linguistic factors outside the word they attach to but within the phrase or sentence. E.g. the choice of *likes* in "The boy likes to navigate on the internet" is determined by the subject *the boy* in the sentence, whereas derivational affixes are more often based on simple meaning distinctions. E.g. The choice of *clever* and *cleverness* depends on whether we want to talk about the property "clever" or we want to talk about "the state of being clever".
(4) In English, inflectional affixes are mostly suffixes, which are always word final. E.g. *drums*, *walks*, etc. But derivational affixes can be prefixes or suffixes. E.g. *depart*, *teacher*, etc.

Further Practice

I. Mark the following statements with "T" if they are true or "F" if they are false. Provide explanations for the false statements.

1. Actually the distinction between closed-class words and open-class words is quite clear-cut.
2. Content words are also known as grammatical words.
3. The word *distempered* has four morphemes.
4. The morphemes *-s* in *dogs* and *-al* in *national* are both bound morphemes.
5. All words contain a root morpheme.
6. All the allomorphs, for instance the plural allomorphs, should be in complementary distribution.
7. The word *task* used to mean *tax imposed*, but today it means *a piece of work*. This represents meaning broadening.
8. One explanation for assimilation process is that in speaking, we tend to exert as little

effort as possible so that we do not want to vary too often places of articulation in uttering a sequence of sounds and this is called *theory of least effort*.
9. Not all monomorphemic words are free morphemes.
10. Like affixes, which can be distinguished into inflectional ones and derivational ones, roots can also be classified into these two groups.
11. The word *homesick* is created by the back-formation of *homesickness*.
12. As sentences consist of words and are often analyzed into words, a word is the smallest unit of language.
13. The word *teaches* consists of only one morpheme.
14. *Berry* in words *strawberry*, *blueberry* is a free morpheme.
15. Roots are independent units of meaning and can be used freely by themselves.
16. A stem can be a bound root, a free morpheme or a derived form itself.
17. Prefixes modify the meaning of a stem, but usually do not change the part of speech of the original word.
18. -'s is an inflectional affix indicating plurality of nouns.
19. If we pronounce the form *running dog* as ´running dog, then metaphorically it refers to a person who follows another person obediently in his wrong doings.
20. All words have morphs but not necessarily allomorphs.
21. The morphological rules can be generalized in spite of some exceptions.
22. The phonological and orthographical realizations of a morpheme are termed morphs.
23. Some linguists maintain that a word group is an extension of word of a particular class.
24. Reduplicative compound is formed by repeating a same word or an almost identical word.
25. We can always tell by the words a compound contains what it means because the meaning of a compound is always the sum of the meanings of its parts.

II. Fill in each of the following blanks with (an) appropriate word(s).

1. _____ is a branch of grammar which studies the internal structure of words and rules by which words are formed.
2. _____ are added to the end of stems.
3. _____ morphemes manifest various grammatical relations or grammatical categories such as number, tense and case.
4. The existing form to which a derivational affix can be added is called a _____.
5. Like derivation, _____ is another popular and important way of forming new words in English. For instance, *blackboard* and *greenhouse* are formed in this way.
6. _____ morphemes cannot be used independently but has to be combined with other morphemes.
7. *Manu* is not an _____ but a root.
8. _____ and _____ are subdivisions of affixes.
9. Rules that govern which affix can be added to what type of stem to form a new word are called _____ rules.
10. In terms of the meaning expressed by words, they can be classified into _____ words and _____ words.
11. The word *disappointment* consists of _____ morphemes.
12. The root of the word *internationalism* is _____.

13. _____ refers to the influence exercised by one sound segment upon the articulation of another, so that the sounds become less alike, or different.
14. The word *bike* is created from the word *bicycle* by undergoing the process of _____.
15. The negative prefix *in-* goes through the process of _____, becoming *im-*, *il-* and *ir-* in words *immobile*, *illegal* and *irrevocable*.
16. Three kinds of semantic changes are _____, _____, and meaning shift.
17. The word *engineer* means "a person trained in a branch of engineering" but with a _____, it can mean "to act as an engineer or to plan; to maneuver".
18. In terms of variability, the word *hello* can be classified into the category of _____ words.
19. _____ is made up from the first letters of the name of an organization and this process is also used in shortening extremely long words of word groups in science, technology and other special fields.
20. _____ is related to language variation in the phonological system of language. It refers to changes in sound leading to changes in form.

III. Mark the choice that best completes the statement.

1. A morpheme that must occur with at least one other morpheme to form a word is called _____.
   A. free morpheme   B. bound morpheme
   C. stem   D. none of the above
2. An affix (in English, usually a suffix) that changes the form of a word without changing its part of speech or basic meaning is called a (an) _____ suffix.
   A. derivational   B. inflectional   C. compounding   D. bound
3. The process of joining together two linguistic forms which can function independently is _____.
   A. compounding   B. conversion   C. blending   D. clipping
4. In the word *carelessness*, *careless* is _____.
   A. a suffix   B. a root   C. a stem   D. a prefix
5. In the sentence *He works hard*, *-s* in the word *works* is _____.
   A. a derivational affix
   B. a free morpheme
   C. an inflectional affix indicating plurality of nouns
   D. an inflectional affix indicating third person singular
6. Each language has grammatical words serving to link different parts of the language together. Grammatical words are also known as _____.
   A. function words   B. content words   C. lexical words   D. link words
7. The word _____ is not a compound.
   A. *sunflower*   B. *friendship*   C. *moonwalk*   D. *miniskirt*
8. Bridge is an English word, but when it refers to a type of card game, the meaning is borrowed from an Italian word. This process of borrowing is termed as _____.
   A. loanblending   B. loanshift   C. loan translation   D. loan-word
9. _____ first suggested treating sentence as "the maximum free form" and word "the minimum free form".

Chapter 3
From Morpheme to Phrase

    A. Bloomfield   B. Quirk
    C. Whorf   D. Saussure

10. In the words maps, dogs, watches, mice and sheep, each of /s/, /z/, /ɪz/, /aɪ/ and /iː/ is a(an) _____ of the plural form.
    A. allomorph   B. allophone
    C. similar phoneme   D. counter phoneme

11. New words and expressions can be created through the following processes EXCEPT _____.
    A. blending   B. convention
    C. analogy   D. back-formation

12. The following words are all created by abbreviation EXCEPT _____.
    A. *prof*   B. *bus*   C. *flu*   D. *edit*

13. All the following words are created by blending EXCEPT _____.
    A. *transistor*   B. *telecast*   C. *modem*   D. *pencil*

14. The following terms all refer to changes in sound leading to changes in form EXCEPT _____.
    A. metathesis   B. assimilation   C. addition   D. narrowing

15. Which of the following statements is NOT true about the inflectional affixes?
    A. They only add a minute or delicate grammatical meaning to the stem.
    B. They do not change the word class of the word they attach to.
    C. They are conditioned by non-semantic linguistic factors outside the word they attach to.
    D. They are only suffixes, which are always word final.

16. Lexeme is _____.
    A. a physically definable unit
    B. a grammatical unit
    C. an indefinable unit
    D. the common factor underlying a set of forms

17. Which of the following processes of lexical change has the Chinese word "十七大" experienced?
    A. Abbreviation.   B. Back-formation.
    C. Blending.   D. Borrowing.

18. All of the following are meaningful EXCEPT _____.
    A. lexeme   B. phoneme   C. morpheme   D. allomorph

IV. Find out the original terms from which the words were back-formed.

1. lase   2. enthuse
3. asset   4. diagnose
5. hairdress   6. drowse
7. donate   8. greed
9. amuse   10. denote
11. helicopt   12. automate
13. spring-clean   14. pettifog
15. sight-read   16. calm
17. self-destruct   18. gangle
19. free-associate   20. chain-react

V. List all the function words you can find in the following paragraph. All the forms of *be* are identified as function words.

In Britain the day after Christmas is called Boxing Day. This is a great day for sports, and many go out to watch football matches, etc. But most people stay at home and have a lazy day.

VI. Classify the following words according to their different kinds of semantic changes.
   a. holiday   b. camp   c. engineer   d. wizard   e. deer
   f. hog   g. task   h. liquid   i. cockroach j. bead
1. Broadening   _____
2. Narrowing   _____
3. Meaning shift   _____
4. Class shift   _____
5. Folk etymology   _____

VII. Break up each of the following words into separate morphemes and classify them into different categories.
   a. disappointed   b. illegal   c. intercontinental   d. refusal,
   e. lukewarm   f. globalization g. uncomfortably   h. receiving
1. Free morpheme   _____
2. Bound morpheme   _____
3. Stem   _____
4. Free root   _____
5. Bound root   _____
6. Inflectional affix _____
7. Derivational affix _____

VIII. Classify the following words in terms of different types of processes with regard to borrowing.
   a. coconut   b. bridge   c. almighty   d. tea   e. loanword
   f. Yankee   g. free verse h. Chinatown i. sputnik
1. loanword   _____
2. loanblend   _____
3. loanshift   _____
4. loan translation   _____

IX. Find out the meaning of the prefix in each of the following words.
1. antecedent _____   2. byproduct   _____
3. enclose   _____   4. foretell   _____
5. overwork   _____   6. postgraduate _____
7. include   _____   8. precede   _____
9. superman   _____   10. transmit   _____

X. Write out the compound words according to the definitions given below. The first part of each compound word has been provided as in A, B, and C.
A. *green*
1. A stretch of land, round a town, where building is not allowed, so that fields, woods etc., remain: _____
2. A shop-keeper who sells vegetables and fruit: _____

Chapter 3
From Morpheme to Phrase

3. A young, inexperienced person, especially man, who is easily cheated: _____

B. *sun*
1. The condition of having sore skin after experiencing the effects of strong sunlight: _____
2. A flash of sunlight, especially through a break in clouds: _____
3. The time when the sun is seen to disappear as night begins: _____

C. *out*
1. A sudden appearance or beginning of something bad: _____
2. A public show of anger: _____
3. Money spent for a purpose: _____

XI. Explain the meaning of the italic words in each of the following sentences.
1. The waiter told us that, if we wished, we could choose something from the cold *table*.
2. John's stories kept the whole *table* amused.
3. There is a *table* of contents at the front of this book.
4. The children were learning their *tables*.
5. The president is at *table* now, but he will see you when he has finished eating.
6. Jimbo immersed his *trunk* in the pail of water and squirted the delighted children.
7. If you travel by train, you can send your *trunk* for a nominal charge.
8. Fifty miles out on deserted highway, your rental car developed a flat tire, I opened the *trunk* and found there was no spare.
9. We stripped off the branches and then sawed the *trunk* into three-foot lengths for firewood.
10. The store had one pair of *trunks* left—green and yellow with blue stripes. I simply couldn't buy them.
11. The *trunk* line of the Illinois Central Railroad runs from Chicago to the New Orleans.
12. Queen Victoria *ruled* for 63 years.
13. *Rule* two straight lines in your notebook.
14. I'm afraid we must *rule* out that possibility.
15. It's against the *rule* to touch the ball in football.

XII. Answer the following questions as comprehensively as possible, giving your own examples.
1. Classify the various types of morphemes used in English.
2. Cite five examples of affixes that attach (relatively) productively to verbs, contribute no or very specific meaning, and do not change category.
3. Is morpheme a grammatical concept or a semantic one?
4. What are the categories newly introduced into linguistic analysis of word class?
5. Explain and comment on the following two sentences:
   a. *He made a little bow—a short sharp thing—to the ladies.*
   b. *He made a little bow—a short sharp thing—for his boat.*

参考答案

I.
1. F. The distinction is not clear-cut, e.g. preposition, though a close-class, is a relatively open one in English.

2. F. Content words are used to refer to lexical words.
3. F. It has three morphemes.
4. T 5. T 6. T 7. T 8. T
9. F. All monomorphemic words are free morphemes.
10. F. Roots cannot be divided into inflectional ones and derivational ones.
11. T
12. F. This is a false notion, because words are further analyzable, i. e., words can be broken into even smaller components, that is, morphemes.
13. F. It consists of two morphemes. (*Teach* is a free morpheme and *-es* is an inflectional suffix).
14. T 15. T
16. F. Some roots are bound morphemes.
17. F. Prefixes modify the meaning of a stem, and usually can change the part of speech of the original word. (E. g. the prefix *en-* in *enlarge*)
18. F. *-'s* is an inflectional affix indicating the possessive case of nouns.
19. F. It should be pronounced as ´running and ´dog.
20. T 21. T 22. T 23. T 24. T
25. F. The meaning of a compound cannot always be inferred from the meaning of its component parts, and sometimes is idiomatic.

II.
1. Morphology   2. Suffixes   3. Inflectional
4. stem   5. compounding   6. Bound
7. affix   8. Prefixes; suffixes 9. morphological
10. grammatical; lexical 11. 3   12. nation
13. Dissimilation   14. abbreviation   15. assimilation
16. broadening; narrowing 17. class shift 18. invariable
19. Acronym   20. phonological change

III.
1. B 2. B 3. A 4. C 5. D 6. A 7. D 8. B 9. A 10. A
11. B 12. D 13. D 14. D 15. D 16. D 17. A 18. B

IV.
1. lase←laser   2. enthuse←enthusiasm
3. asset←assets   4. diagnose←diagnosis
5. hairdress←hairdresser   6. drowse←drowsy
7. donate←donation   8. greed←greedy
9. amuse←amusing   10. denote←denotion
11. helicopt←helicopter   12. automate←automation
13. spring-clean←spring-cleaning 14. pettifog←pettifogge
15. sight-read←sight-reading   16. calm←calmative
17. self-destruct←self-destruction 18. gangle←gangling
19. free-associate←free association 20. chain-react←chain reaction

V.
in, the, after, is, this, is, a, for, and, out, to, but, at, and, a

Chapter 3
From Morpheme to Phrase

VI.
1. broadening: a, g
2. narrowing: b, e, h
3. meaning shift: j
4. class shift: c, f
5. folk etymology: d, i

VII.
a. disappointed: *-dis*, *appoint*, *-ed*
b. illegal: *il-*, *legal*
c. intercontinental: *inter-*, *continent*, *-al*
d. refusal: *refus(e)*, *-al*
e. lukewarm: *luke*, *warm*
f. globalization : *glob(e)*, *-al*, *-iz(e)*, *-ation*
g. uncomfortably: *un-*, *comfort*, *-abl(e)*, *-ly*
h. receiving: *re-*, *-ceiv(e)*, *-ing*
1. free morpheme: *appoint, legal, continent, refus(e), luke, warm, glob(e), comfort, receive*
2. bound morpheme: *-dis, il-, inter-, -al, -iz(e), -ation, un-, -abl(e), -ly, re-, -ed, -ing*
3. stem: *appoint, disappoint, disappointed, legal, illegal, continent, continental, intercontinental, refus(e), glob(e), global, globalize, globalization, comfort, comfortable, uncomfortable, receiv(e)*
4. free root: *appoint, legal, continent, refus(e), luke, warm, glob(e), comfort*
5. bound root: *-ceiv(e)*
6. inflectional affix: *-ed, -ing*
7. derivational affix: *-dis, il-, inter-, -al, -iz(e), -ation, un-, -abl(e), -ly, re-*

VIII.
1. loanwords: i; e; d
2. loanblends: a; h
3. loanshifts: b; f
4. loan translation: c; g

IX.
1. *ante-*: before
2. *by-*: incidental to mean
3. *en-*: to cover or wrap to be
4. *fore-*: before in time
5. *over-*: more(than), excessive
6. *post-*: after in time
7. *in-*: within
8. *pre-*: before
9. *super-*: degree greater than normal
10. *trans-*: across, through

X.
A. 1. greenbelt 2. greengrocery 3. greenhorn
B. 1. sunburn 2. sunbreak 3. sunset
C. 1. outburst 2. outrage 3. outlay

XI.
1. a display of cold food such as salad, etc.
2. everyone sitting at the table
3. list
4. list which young children repeat to learn what number results when a number from 1 to 12
5. at table having a meal
6. a long, flexible snout or nose, esp. of elephant

7. a large box or chest for storing or transporting clothes or other personal effects
8. a covered compartment in an automobile for keeping a spare tire, luggage or other articles
9. the main stem of a tree
10. *plural*: shorts worn by men for swimming or other athletic pursuits
11. of or pertaining to the main body of a channel, or line of a system
12. v. govern; have authority over
13. v. make (a line or lines) on paper with a ruler
14. v. *rule something out*: declare that it cannot be considered, that it is out of the question
15. n. law or custom which guides or controls behavior or action; decision made by an organization, etc. about what must or what must not be done

XII.
1. Morphemes of various types used in English can be classified as follows:
    (1) Morpheme is the smallest unit in terms of relationship between expression and content, a unit which cannot be divided without destroying or drastically altering the meaning, whether it is lexical or grammatical. So, a morpheme is the minimal unit of meaning.
    (2) Free morpheme vs. bound morpheme: A Free Morpheme is one that may constitute a word (free form) by itself, such as, *bed*, *book*, *and tree* etc. Bound Morpheme is one that may appear with at least one other morpheme, such as, *-s* in *dogs*, and *-al* in *national*. All mono-morphemic words are constituted by free morphemes and those polymorphemic words which consist wholly of free morphemes are called compounds.
    (3) Polymorphemic words other than compounds may divide into roots and affixes. A root is the base form of a word, which can not be further analyzed without total loss of identity. That is to say, a root is that part of word left when all the affixes are removed. A stem: is any morpheme or combination of morphemes to which an affix can be added. Affix is the collective term for the type of formative that can be used only when added to another morpheme. Naturally, affixes belong to the type of bound morphemes. (Subtypes include prefix, suffix, infix, and circumflex). Affixes may also be divided into inflectional and derivational types, e.g. *walks* vs. *sleepy*.
    (4) Derivational morphemes can change the syntactic category of the word with which they combine, e.g., *-ish* in *boyish*.
2. Inflectional affixes add a delicate grammatical meaning to the stem, such as *-s* in words *toys*, *walks*, and *John's*. They do not change the category of words such as *-s* indicating plurality in words like *girls* and *flowers*. Inflectional affixes of this kind can be attached to the entire category of regular countable nouns.
3. Morpheme is both a grammatical and a semantic concept. A morpheme may overlap with a phoneme, such as *I*, but usually not, as in *pig*, in which the morpheme is the whole word, i.e. an independent, free morpheme, but the phonemes are /p/, /i/, and /g/.
4. Today, word class displays a wider range of more precisely defined categories. Here are some of the categories newly introduced into linguistic analysis:
    (1) Particles (the infinitive marker *to*, the negative marker *not* and the subordinate units in phrasal verbs, such as *get by*.)

(2) Auxiliaries (*am*, *is*, *are*, *may*, *can*, *has*...)
(3) Pro-form, a word class that can function as a substitute for another item. (Pro-adjective such as in *So is mine*, Pro-verb such as in *better than he did*, Pro-adverb such as in *I hope so too*, and Pro-locative such as in *He is hiding there*)
(4) Determiners are words which are used before the noun (including its premodifiers like adjectives) acting as head of a noun phrase and determine the kind of reference the noun phrase has. For example, *the*, *a*, *some*, and *all* are the common predeterminers. Postdeterminers include cardinal numeral, ordinal numerals, such as *next*, *last*, *a lot of*, etc.

5. Nothing is the same in these two sentences, but we do not perceive the difference until we reach the final word group. *He* in (1) is a person out in society, *He* in (2) is a person building a boat. *Made* in (1) is the performance of an act, and in (2) is the construction of a thing. *Bow* in (1) is a bending of the head or the body in solution; in (2) *bow* is the front or the forward end of a boat. *Little* means small in size—*short* and *sharp*; in (1) *short* and *sharp* refers to a quick and abrupt movement, which implies that *he* is not willing to bow to show respect to the ladies; in (2), *short* and *sharp* refers to the shape of the bow, that is not long, but with a fine cutting edge. The important thing is that we cannot make any of the above distinctions until all the evidence is in, and if we try to jump to conclusions, we will be wrong.

From Word to Text

Concepts & Theories

I. What is Syntax?
Syntax is the study of the rules governing the ways different constituents are combined to form sentences in a language, or the study of the interrelationships between elements in sentence structures.

II. Syntactic Relations
Syntactic relations can be analyzed into three kinds: positional relations, relations of substitutability, and relations of co-occurrence.

1. Positional relation
(1) For language to fulfill its communicative function, it must have a way to mark the grammatical roles of the various phrases that can occur in a clause.

(2) Positional relation or word order, refers to the sequential arrangement of words in a language.

(3) If the words in a sentence fail to occur in a fixed order required by the convention of a language, one tends to produce an utterance either ungrammatical or nonsensical at all.

(4) Positional relations are a manifestation of one aspect of Syntagmatic Relations observed by F. de Saussure. They are also called Horizontal Relations or simply Chain Relations.

(5) Word order is among the three basic ways (word order, genetic and areal classifications) to classify languages in the world: SVO, VSO, SOV, OVS, OSV, and VOS. English belongs to SVO type, though this does not mean that SVO is the only possible word order.

2. Relation of substitutability
(1) The definition of the Relation of Substitutability: The Relation of Substitutability refers to classes or sets of words substitutable for each other grammatically in sentences with the same structure. It also refers to groups of more than one word which may be jointly substitutable grammatically for a single word of a particular set.

(2) Some alternative terms for the Relation of Substitutability: The Relation of Substitutability is also called Associative Relation by Saussure, and Paradigmatic Relation by Hjemslev. To make it more understandable, it is called Vertical Relation or Choice Relation.

Chapter 4
From Word to Text

3. Relation of co-occurrence
   (1) Relation of co-occurrence means that words of different sets of clauses may permit, or require, the occurrence of a word of another set or class to form a sentence or a particular part of a sentence. For instance, a nominal phrase can be preceded by a determiner and adjective(s) and followed by a verbal phrase.
   (2) Relations of co-occurrence partly belong to syntagmatic relations, partly to paradigmatic relations.

III. Grammatical Construction and Its Constituents
1. Grammatical construction
   (1) Grammatical Construction or Construct can be used to mean any syntactic construct which is assigned one or more conventional functions in a language, together with whatever is linguistically conventionalized about its contribution to the meaning or use of the construct contains.
   (2) On the level of syntax, we distinguish for any construction in a language its external and internal properties.
      ☆ The external syntax of a construction refers to the properties of the construction as a whole, that is to say, anything speakers know about the construction that is relevant to the larger syntactic contexts in which it is welcome.
      ☆ The internal syntax of a construction is really a description of the construction's "make-up", with the terms such as "subject, predicate, object, determiner, noun, etc."
2. Constituents and phrase structure
   (1) Constituent is a part of a larger linguistic unit. Several constituents together form a construction: e.g. *the boy* (NP); *ate the apple* (VP); *The boy ate the apple* (S).
   (2) The definition of Immediate Constituent Analysis (IC Analysis): When a tree diagram is used to represent the constituent structure of a grammatical unit (e.g. a phrase or sentence), syntactic categories are used to label the nodes; the most common of these are listed in the following:

Word-level	Phrase-level
N = noun	NP = noun phrase
A = adjective	AP = adjective phrase
V = verb	VP = verb phrase
P = preposition	PP = preposition phrase
Det = determiner	S = sentence or clause
Adv = adverb	
Conj = conjunction	

   (3) Taking the construction *The boy ate the apple* for example again, one can analyze it by means of a TREE DIAGRAM in detail.

☆ Tree diagram

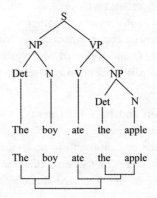

☆ Bracketing

Bracketing is not as common in use, but it is an economic notation in representing the constituent/phrase structure of a grammatical unit.

((The) (girl)) ((ate) ((the) (apple)))

[S[NP[Det The][N girl]][VP[V ate][NP[Det the][N apple]]]]

3. **Endocentric and exocentric constructions**

(1) The definition of endocentric construction: Endocentric construction is one whose distribution is functionally equivalent to that of one or more of its constituents, i. e., a word or a group of words, which serves as a definable centre or head. Usually noun phrases, verb phrases and adjective phrases belong to endocentric types because the constituent items are subordinate to the Head.

(2) The definition of exocentric construction: Exocentric construction refers to a group of syntactically related words where none of the words is functionally equivalent to the group as a whole, that is, there is no definable Centre or Head inside the group, usually including

☆ the basic sentence,

☆ the prepositional phrase,

☆ the predicate (verb + object) construction, and

☆ the connective (*be* + complement) construction.

4. **Coordination and subordination**

Endocentric constructions fall into two main types, depending on the relation between constituents: coordination and subordination.

(1) Coordination: Coordination is a common syntactic pattern in English and other languages formed by grouping together two or more categories of the same type with the help of a conjunction such as *and*, *but* and *or*. These two or more words or phrases or clauses have equivalent syntactic status, each of the separate constituents can stand for the original construction functionally.

(2) Subordination: Subordination refers to the process or result of linking linguistic units so that they have different syntactic status, one being dependent upon the other, and usually a constituent of the other. The subordinate constituents are words which modify the head. Consequently, they can be called modifiers.

IV. Syntactic Function

The syntactic function shows the relationship between a linguistic form and other parts of the linguistic pattern in which it is used.

Names of functions are expressed in terms of subjects, objects, predicators, modifiers, and complements, etc.

1. Subject

(1) Some traditional definitions of subject:
- ☆ In some languages, subject refers to one of the nouns in the nominative case. The typical example can be found in Latin, where subject is always in nominative case.
- ☆ Another traditional definition of the subject is what the sentence is about (i.e., topic).

(2) A workable definition of subject:
- ☆ Word order
  Subject ordinarily precedes the verb in a statement.
- ☆ Pro-forms
  The first and third person pronouns in English appear in a special form when the pronoun is a subject, which is not used when the pronoun occurs in other positions.
- ☆ Agreement with the verb
  In the simple present tense, an -s is added to the verb when a third person subject is singular, but the number and person of the object or any other element in the sentence have no effect at all on the form of the verb.
- ☆ Content questions
  If the subject is replaced by a question word (*who* or *what*), the rest of the sentence remains unchanged.
- ☆ Tag question
  A tag question is used to seek confirmation of a statement. It always contains a pronoun which refers back to the subject, and never to any other elements in the sentence.

2. Predicate

(1) The definition of predicate: Predicate refers to a major constituent of sentence structure in a binary analysis in which all obligatory constituents other than the subject were considered together.

(2) It usually expresses actions, processes, and states that refer to the subject.

(3) The word predicator is suggested for verb or verbs included in a predicate.

3. Object

(1) A traditional definition of object: Object is also a term hard to define. Since, traditionally, subject can be defined as the doer of an action, object may refer to the receiver or goal of an action, and it is further classified into Direct Object and Indirect Object.

(2) In some inflecting languages, object is marked by case labels: the accusative case for direct object, and the dative case for indirect object.

(3) In English, object is recognized by tracing its relation to word order (after the verb and preposition) and by inflections (of pro-nouns).

(4) Modern linguists suggest that object refers to such an item that it can become subject in a passive transformation.

V. Category

The definition of category: The term category refers to the defining properties of the general units such as categories of the noun (number, gender, case and countability) and categories of the verb (tense, aspect, voice).

1. Number

Number is a grammatical category used for the analysis of word classes displaying such contrasts as singular, dual, plural, etc.

(1) In English, number is mainly observed in nouns, and there are only two forms: singular and plural, such as *dog*: *dogs*.

(2) Number is also reflected in the inflections of pronouns and verbs, such as *he laughs*: *they laugh*; *this man*: *these men*.

2. Gender

(1) Gender refers to such contrasts as *masculine*: *feminine*: *neuter*, *animate*: *inanimate*, etc. for the analysis of word classes.

(2) Though there is a statistical correlation between natural gender and grammatical gender, the assignment may seem quite arbitrary in many cases.

(3) English gender contrast can only be observed in pronouns and a small number of nouns, and, they are mainly of the natural gender type.

☆ *he*: *she*: *it*
☆ *prince*: *princess*
☆ *author*: *authoress*

3. Case

(1) The case category is used in the analysis of word classes to identify the syntactic relationship between words in a sentence.

(2) In Latin grammar, cases are based on variations in the morphological forms of the word, and are given the terms *accusative*, *nominative*, *dative*, etc.

(3) There are five cases in ancient Greek and eight in Sanskrit. Finnish has as many as fifteen formally distinct cases in nouns, each with its own syntactic function.

4. Agreement

(1) Agreement (or concord) may be defined as the requirement that the forms of two or more words of specific word classes that stand in specific syntactic relationship with one another, shall also be characterized by the same paradigmatically marked category (or categories).

(2) This syntactic relationship may be anaphoric, as when a pronoun agrees with its antecedent: *Whose is this pen? —Oh, it's the one I lost.*

(3) The syntactic relationship may involve a relation between a head and its dependent, as when a verb agrees with its subject and object: *Each person may have one coin*.

(4) The features of the agreement of number between nouns and verbs are obvious in English. Agreement between gender and number should be shown in noun-adjective relation in French.

VI. Phrase, Clause and Sentence

1. Phrase

There is now a tendency to make a distinction between phrases and word groups.

Chapter 4
From Word to Text

(1) A phrase is a single element of structure containing more than one word, and lacking the subject-predicate structure typical of *clauses*. Traditionally, it is seen as part of a structural hierarchy, falling between a clause and word, e.g., *the three tallest girls* (nominal phrase).

(2) A word group is an extension of a word of a particular class by way of modification with its main features of the class unchanged. Thus we have nominal group, verbal group, adverbial group, conjunction group and preposition group.

2. Clause

(1) The definition of a clause: A clause is group of words with its own subject and predicate included in a larger subject-verb construction, namely, in a sentence.

(2) The classification of clauses: Clauses can also be classified into two kinds, they are, finite and non-finite clauses, the latter referring to what are traditionally called infinitive phrase, participial phrase and gerundial phrase.

3. Sentence

(1) Traditionally, SENTENCE is the minimum part of language that expresses a complete thought.

☆ Sentence: Traditional approach

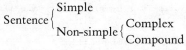

☆ Sentence: Functional approach

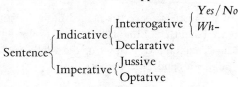

(2) Basic sentence types: Bolinger
Mother fell. (Nominal + intransitive verbal)
Mother is young. (Nominal + copula + complement)
Mother loves Dad. (Nominal + transitive verbal + nominal)
Mother fed Dad breakfast. (Nominal + transitive verbal + nominal + nominal)
There is time. (There + existential + nominal)

(3) Basic sentence types: Quirk
SVC   *Mary is kind.*
             a nurse.
SVA   *Mary is here.*
             in the house.
SV   *The child is laughing.*
SVO   *Somebody caught the ball.*
SVOC   *We have proved him wrong.*
             a fool.
SVOA   *I put the plate on the table.*
SVOO   *She gives me expensive presents.*

VII. Recursiveness

1. What is recursiveness?

(1) Recursiveness mainly means that a phrasal constituent can be embedded within another constituent having the same category, but it has become an umbrella term such important linguistic phenomena as coordination and subordination, conjoining and embedding, hypotactic and paratactic.

(2) Theoretically, there is no limit to the number of embedding of one relative clause into another relative clause, so long as it does not become an obstacle to successful communication. The same holds true for nominal clauses and adverbial clauses.

2. **Means to extend sentences**
1. Conjoining
   (1) The definition of conjoining: Conjoining refers to the process where one clause is coordinated or conjoined with another.
   (2) The conjunctions used in this case are: *and*, *but*, and *or*.
2. Embedding
   (1) The definition of embedding: Embedding refers to the means by which one clause is included in the sentence (main clause) in syntactic subordination.
   (2) The three basic types of subordinate clauses are:
      ☆ Complement clause: *I don't know whether Professor Li needs this book.*
      ☆ Adjunct (or Adverbial) clause: *If you listened to me, you wouldn't make mistakes.*
      ☆ Relative clause: *I saw the man who had visited you last year.*

VIII. Beyond the Sentence

The development of modern linguistic science has helped push the study of syntax beyond the traditional sentence boundary. Linguists are now exploring the syntactic relation between sentences in a paragraph or chapter or the whole text, which leads to the emergence of Text Linguistics and Discourse Analysis.

1. **Sentential connection**
   (1) Hypotactic (subordinate clauses):
      You can phone the doctor if you like. However, I very much doubt whether he is in.
      We live near the sea. So we enjoy a healthy climate.
   (2) Paratactic (coordinate clauses):
      In Guangzhou it is hot and humid during the summer. In Beijing it is hot and dry.
      He dictated the letter. She wrote it.
      The door was open. He walked in.
2. **Cohesion and cohesiveness**
   (1) Cohesion is a concept to do with discourse or text rather than with syntax. It refers to relations of meaning that exist within the text, and defines it as a text.
   (2) Cohesiveness can be realized by employing various cohesive devices:
      ☆ Conjunction
      ☆ Ellipsis
      ☆ Lexical collocation
      ☆ Lexical repetition
      ☆ Reference
      ☆ Substitution, etc.

Chapter 4
From Word to Text

Related Terms

agreement

Agreement may be defined as the requirement that the forms of two or more words of specific word classes that stand in specific syntactic relationship with one another, shall also be characterized by the same paradigmatically marked category or categories.

anaphor

Anaphor is used in a narrow sense to include only reflexives like *myself* and reciprocals like *each other*. The term is related to the notion of binding because *to be bound* means the relation between an anaphor and its accessible subject.

argument of poverty stimulus

Argument of poverty stimulus means that it is impossible for children to acquire some particular language knowledge resulting from the contact of language data in the process of their L1 acquisition.

aspect

Aspect refers to the internal temporal structure of a verb or sentence meaning.

base component

Base component is a term that refers to one of the four components in Chomsky's modified grammar model. The base component and the transformational component together make up the syntactic component. Base component is further divided into categories and lexicon. The categories contain rewriting rules and lexicon contains words with specified features.

binding

The notion binding is borrowed from logic, which refers to the relation between a quantifier and a variable, that is, a variable is bound by a quantifier. *To be bound* refers to the relation between and anaphor and its accessible subject. That is, the former will be coreferential with the latter. And they must be in the same governing category, which is the minimal domain, or the lowest mode in a tree-diagram, containing a dependent element, its governor and an accessible subject.

case

Case is a grammatical category of inflected words which serves to indicate their syntactic function in a sentence and, depending on the function, involves government and agreement. In English, pronouns have three cases of nominative (e.g. *I*, *he*, *she*), accusative (e.g. *me*, *him*, *her*) and genitive (e.g. *my*, *your*, *his*). Nouns have only two cases: general (e.g. *John*, *boy*) and genitive (*John's*, *boy's*). Case systems may vary from language to language and undergo continuous change.

case condition and adjacency condition

As is required by the case condition principle, a noun phrase must have case and case is assigned by V (verb) or P (preposition) to the object position or by AUX (auxiliary) to the subject position. The theory of case condition accounts for the fact that noun phrases appear only in subject and object positions. When a noun phrase moves, it can move only to the position where it can be assigned case, in order to satisfy the condition of case requirement. Under such a condition, when the move-α rule operates to change a sentence, from the active voice to the passive voice, it can move a noun phrase only to the required case receiving position.

category

The term category in some approaches refers to classes and functions in its narrow sense. More specifically, it refers to the defining properties of these general units: the categories of the noun and of the verb.

c-command

C-command, that is, constituent command, goes like this: Node A c-commands node B if and only if the first branching node that dominates A also dominates B (condition: node A does not dominate node B, and vice versa.).

clause

A constituent with its own subject and predicate, if it is included in a larger sentence, is a clause.

cohesion

Cohesion refers to relations of meaning that exist within the text and defines it as a text.

communicative dynamism

Communicative dynamism, CD for short, is a notion first developed by J. Firbas (1964) in research into the relation between structure and function. This notion is based on the fact that linguistic communication is not a static phenomenon, but a dynamic one. CD is meant to measure the amount of information an element carries in a sentence. The degree of CD is the effect contributed by a linguistic element. Take the sentence *He was cross* for example, the lowest degree of CD is carried by *He*, and the highest is carried by *cross*, with the degree carried by *was* ranking between them.

complex sentence

A complex sentence contains two or more clauses, one of which can be incorporated into the other.

concord

Concord, also known as agreement, may be defined as the requirement that the forms of two or more words in syntactic relationship should agree with each other in terms of some categories. In English the determiner and the noun it precedes should concord in number, and the form of a subject should agree with that of the verb in terms of number in the present tense. In other languages, besides number and time, there is also gender concord.

conjoining

Conjoining refers to the process where one clause is coordinated or conjoined with another.

constituent

Constituent is a term used in structural sentence analysis for every linguistic unit, which is part of a larger linguistic unit. Several constituents together form a construction: for example, in the sentence, *Money doesn't grow on trees*, each word is a constituent, as is the prepositional phrase *on trees*. Constituents can be joined together with other constituents to form larger units. If two constituents, A and B, are joined to form a hierarchically higher constituent C, A and B are said to be immediate constituents of C.

construction and constituents

Structural linguists regard the relation between a sentence and its component elements as the relation between a construction and its constituents. Construction is composed of several parts, which can be single words, or groups of words, contiguous or discontiguous, the small units are known as its immediate constituents. The small units themselves can be constructions of specific types. In the sentence *The girl is giggling*, the nominal phrase *the girl* can be further analyzed into *the* (Determiner) + *girl* (Noun). Thus, *the girl* is construction of a nominal phrase, whereas *The* and *girl* are its constituents.

coordination

Coordination is a common syntactic pattern in English and other languages formed by grouping together two or more categories of the same type with the help of a conjunction such as *and*, *but* and *or*.

coordinate sentence

A coordinate sentence is one that contains two clauses joined by a linking word called coordinating conjunction, such as *and*, *but* and *or*.

deep structure

Deep structure may be defined as the abstract representation of the syntactic properties of a construction, i.e. the underlying level of structural relations between its different constituents, such as the relation between the underlying subject and its verb, or a verb and its object.

deictic expression

Deictic expression is a term adopted by C. S. Peirce from formal logic for linguistic expressions that refer to the personal, temporal, or spatial aspect of any given utterance act and whose designation is therefore dependent on the context of the speech situation. Among the many different kinds of deictic expressions are the personal pronouns (*I*, *you*, etc.), adverbial expressions (*here*, *there*, etc.), and the demonstrative pronouns (*this*, *that*, etc.)

embedding

Embedding refers to the means by which one clause is included in the sentence in syntactic subordination.

embedded clause and matrix clause

Embedded clause and matrix clause: a complex sentence contains two or more clauses, one of which is incorporated into the other. That is, the two clauses in the complex sentence hold unequal status, one subordinating the other. The incorporated, or subordinate, clause is normally called an embedded clause, and the clause into which it is embedded is called a matrix clause. For example, in the sentence *Mary told Jane that John liked linguistics*. *Mary told Jane* is a matrix clause, while *John liked linguistics* is an embedded clause.

endocentric construction

Also known as a headed construction, an endocentric construction is one whose distribution is functionally equivalent, or approaching equivalence, to one of its constituents, which serves as the center or head of the whole. Typical endocentric constructions are noun phrases, verb phrases and adjective phrases. They may be further divided into two sub-types: subordinate and coordinate constructions. Those in which there is only one head, with the head being dominant and the other constituents dependent, are subordinate constituents. The coordinate construction has more than one head, in which the two content constituents are of equal syntactic status and no one is dependent on the other.

exocentric construction

Opposite to endocentric construction, it is defined as a construction whose distribution is not functionally equivalent to any of its constituents. There is no noticeable center or head in it.

functional sentence perspective

Functional Sentence Perspective (FSP) is a model of the information structure of sentence, developed in the early 1960s by J. Firbas and others in the tradition of the pre-war Prague School. Parts of a sentence representing given information are said to have the lowest degree of communicative dynamism: these form the theme. Parts representing new information have the highest degree: these form the rheme. Parts which have an intermediate degree are said to form a transition between theme and rheme. The language view reflected from this model about the analysis of sentence is called FSP.

gender

Gender is a lexical-grammatical category, which in most languages of the world divides the nominal lexicon into formally and/or semantically motivated groups, the number of classes varying just as the kind of criteria for the division. However, gender systems in the narrower sense are only those classifications which exhibit a limited number of closed classes as well as agreement.

government

Government, in traditional grammar, refers to lexeme-specific property of verbs, adjectives, prepositions, or nouns that determines the morphological realization (especially case) of dependent elements. It is another type of control over the form of some words by other words in certain syntactic constructions. It differs from concord in that this is a relationship in which a word of a certain class determines that form of others in terms of certain category. In English, for example, the pronoun after a verb or a preposition should be in the object form as in *She gave him a book*.

In the generative approach, the notion is very similar to the traditional idea. The difference is that the latter is defined more rigorously and covers a wider area of relations, not just over the form of words. In government relations, Chomsky suggests there is constituent command, c-command for short. C-command refers to the relation between an element and another of the same level and under the same node in a tree diagram, and any others under the latter element as well.

hierarchical structure

Hierarchical structure refers to the sentence structure that groups words into structural constituents and shows the syntactic categories of each structural constituent, such as NP, VP and PP.

IC Analysis

Immediate Constituent Analysis (IC Analysis) is the analysis of a sentence in terms of its immediate constituents—word groups (or phrases), which are in turn analyzed into the immediate constituents of their own, and the process goes on until the ultimate constituents are reached. In practice, however, for sake of convenience, we usually stop at the level of word.

immediate constituents

Immediate constituents are those immediately, directly below the level of a construction, which may be a sentence or a word group. Theoretically, the construction may also be a word. A word may also be analyzed into its immediate constituents— morphemes, e.g. lovely into {love} and {ly}. The last level of constituents, i.e. the morpheme, is known as the ultimate constituent.

Chapter 4
From Word to Text

innateness hypothesis

Innateness Hypothesis is a hypothesis on the source of human language competence proposed by Chomsky, by which language is product of human brain and human brain is born with Language or Language Acquisition Device which is genetically-based. When a child was born, his/her Language Faculty (LF) is in initial state, with constant exposure to native language, the LF is developed from initial state to steady state.

mood

Mood is grammatical category distinguishing modality, which is a category covering indications either of a kind of speech act or of the degree of certainty with which something is said.

move-α rule

Move-α rule is a general movement rule which accounts for the syntactic behavior of any constituent movement.

number

Number is a grammatical category of nouns which marks quantity. Number can also be applied to other parts of speech through agreement.

NP raising

NP movement does not only occur in passive sentences, but also occurs in raising constructions. There are two types of raising constructions, one containing raising verbs, e.g. *seem*; the other containing raising adjective, e.g. *likely*, *certain*, *possible*. Such constructions are so named because the raising verbs or adjectives can make the NP in the complement clause move the front of the sentence. This movement is called NP raising. For instance, in *It seems that John knows something about it*, the NP *John* can be raised as *John seems to know something about it*.

object

The object may refer to the receiver or goal of an action and it is further classified into direct object and indirect object.

paradigmatic relation

This is a term Saussure used to refer to a relation holding between elements replaceable with each other at a particular place in a structure, or between one element present and the others absent. This relation indicates there are syntactic constrains between words in the sentence. Paradigmatic relation is also known as the vertical or choice relation.

parameters

The language knowledge of UG (Universal Grammar) related to a particular language is known as parameters, which manifests language variations and usually have two parameter values realized by various language differences.

phrase

Phrase is a single element of structure containing more than one word and lacking the subject-predicate structure typical of clauses.

positional relation

Positional relation, or word order, refers to the sequential arrangement of words in a language.

predicate

Predicate refers to a major constituent of sentence structure in a binary analysis in which all obligatory constituents other than the subject were considered together. It usually expresses actions, processes and states that relate to the subject.

principles

The language knowledge of UG related to common rules of human language is called principles, which is, in nature, highly abstracted grammatical knowledge applicable to any human language. A particular language does not necessarily have all such principles, however, no human language can be against such principles.

recursiveness

Though it mainly means that a phrasal constituent can be embedded within another constituent having the same category, recursiveness has become an umbrella term, under which may be brought together several important linguistic phenomena such as coordination and subordination, conjoining and embedding, hypotactic and paratactic.

relation of substitutability

Firstly, relation of substitutability refers to classes or sets of words substitutable for each other grammatically in sentences with the same structure. Secondly, it refers to groups of more than one word which may be jointly substitutable grammatically for a single word of a particular set.

relation of co-occurrence

By the relation of co-occurrence, one means that words of different sets of clauses may permit, or require, the occurrence of a word of another set of class to form a sentence or a particular part of a sentence.

rheme

Rheme is a term used by functional grammarians to refer to what the speaker states about, or in regard to, the starting point of the utterance.

sentence

Sentence is a structurally independent unit that usually comprises a number of words to form a complete statement, question or command.

simple sentence

A simple sentence is one that consists of a single clause which contains a subject and a predicate and stands alone as its own sentence.

subordination

Subordination refers to the process or result of linking linguistic units so that they have different syntactic status, one being dependent upon the other, and usually a constituent of the other.

subordinate construction

Subordinate construction is one of the two subtypes of endocentric construction. That in which there is only one head, with the head being dominant and the other constituents dependent are subordinate construction.

subject

In some languages, subject refers to one of the nouns in the nominative case.

surface structure

Surface structure (S-structure) is the final stage in the syntactic derivation of a construction, which closely corresponds to the structural organization of a construction people actually produce and receive.

syntactic category

A syntactic category usually refers to a lexical category or phrasal category that performs a particular grammatical function.

Chapter 4
From Word to Text

syntactic function
   The syntactic function shows the relationship between a linguistic form and other parts of the linguistic pattern in which it is used.

syntactic movement
   Syntactic movement refers to the movement of any constituent in a sentence out of its original place to a new position. It is indicated by rules traditionally called transformational rules, whose operation may change the syntactic representation of a sentence. It includes NP-movement, *Wh*-movement and other movements.

syntagmatic relation
   Syntagmatic relation is a term used to refer to a relation between one item and others in a sequence, or between elements which are all present, such as the relation between *weather* and the others in the following sentence: *If the weather is nice, we'll go out*. Words in a syntagmatic relation must meet syntactic and semantic conditions. Syntagmatic relation is also known as the horizontal relation, or chain relation.

syntax
   The word syntax, derived originally from Greek, is made up of two morphemes: {syn} and {tax}. The former means *together*, and the latter *to arrange*, hence the literal meaning *a setting out together* or *arrangement*. In linguistics, it refers to the study of the rules governing the way words are combined to form sentences in a language, or simply, the study of the formation of sentences.

Practice

I. Mark the choice that best completes the statement. (20%)

1. Which of the following term does NOT mean the same as the relation of substitutability?
   A. Associative relation.
   B. Paradigmatic relation.
   C. Vertical relation.
   D. Horizontal relation.

2. Clauses can be used as subordinate constituents and the three basic types of subordinate clauses are complement clauses, adjunct clauses and _____.
   A. relative clauses
   B. adverbial clauses
   C. coordinate clauses
   D. subordinate clauses

3. Names of the syntactic functions are expressed in all the following terms EXCEPT _____.
   A. subjects and objects
   B. objects and predicators
   C. modifiers and complements
   D. endocentric and exocentric

4. In English, case is a special form of the noun which frequently corresponds to a combination of preposition and noun and it is realized in all the following channels EXCEPT _____.
   A. inflection
   B. following a preposition
   C. word order
   D. vertical relation

5. In English, theme and rheme are often expressed by _____ and _____.
   A. subject; object
   B. subject; predicate
   C. predicate; object
   D. object; predicate

6. Phrase structure rules have _____ properties.
   A. recursive
   B. grammatical

81

    C. social
    D. functional
7. Which of the following is NOT among the three basic ways to classify languages in the world?
    A. Word order.
    B. Genetic classification.
    C. Areal classification.
    D. Social classification.
8. The head of the phrase *the city Rome* is _____.
    A. *the city*
    B. *Rome*
    C. *city*
    D. *the city Rome*
9. The phrase *on the shelf* belongs to _____ construction.
    A. endocentric
    B. exocentric
    C. subordinate
    D. coordinate
10. The sentence *They were wanted to remain quiet and not to expose themselves* is a _____ sentence.
    A. simple
    B. coordinate
    C. compound
    D. complex

II. Mark the following statements with "T" if they are true or "F" if they are false. (10%)

1. The relations of co-occurrence partly belong to syntagmatic relations, partly to paradigmatic relations.
2. One property coordination reveals is that there is a limit on the number of coordinated categories that can appear prior to the conjunction.
3. According to Standard Theory of Chomsky, deep structures contain all the information necessary for the semantic interpretation of sentences.
4. In English, the object is recognized by tracing its relation to word order and by inflections of pronouns.
5. Classes and functions determine each other, but not in any one-to-one relation.
6. Usually noun phrases, verb phrases and adverbial phrases belong to endocentric types of constriction.
7. In English the subject usually precedes the verb and the direct object usually follows the verb.
8. In the exocentric construction *John kicked the ball*, neither constituent stands for the verb-object sequence.
9. A noun phrase must contain a noun, but other elements are optional.
10. In a coordinate sentence, two (or more) S constituents occur as daughters and co-heads of a higher S.

III. Fill in each of the following blanks with an appropriate word. The first letter of the word is already given. (10%)

1. The subordinate constituents are words which modify the Head and consequently, they can be called m _____.
2. *John believes (that the airplane was invented by an Irishman)*. The part in the bracket is a c _____ clause.
3. In order to account for the case of the subject in passive voice, we have another two terms, p _____ and n _____.
4. There is a tendency to make a distinction between phrase and w _____, which is an extension of word of a particular class by way of modification with its main features

Chapter 4
From Word to Text

of the class unchanged.
5. Recursiveness, together with o _____, is generally regarded as the core of creativity of language.
6. Traditionally, p _____ is seen as part of a structural hierarchy, positioned between clause and word.
7. The case category is used in the analysis of word classes to identify the s _____ relationship between words in a sentence.
8. Clause can be classifies into FINITE and NON-FINITE clauses, the latter including the traditional infinitive phrase, p _____, and gerundial phrase.
9. Gender displays such contrasts as *masculine*: *feminine*: n _____.
10. English gender contrast can only be observed in g _____ and a small number of l _____ and they are mainly of the natural gender type.

IV. **Explain the following concepts or theories.** (20%)
1. Syntax
2. IC analysis
3. Relation of co-occurrence
4. Category
5. Recursiveness

V. **Match each term in Column A with one relevant item in Column B.** (10%)

A	B
(1) syntactic relation	a. number, gender and case
(2) grammatical construction	b. conjoining and embedding
(3) syntactic function	c. syntagmatic relation
(4) category	d. subsitutablity
(5) recusiveness	e. coordination and subordination
(6) positional relation	f. hypotactic and paratactic relations
(7) associative relation	g. conjunction, ellipsis, reference
(8) sentential connection	h. subject, predicate and object
(9) cohesion	i. finite and non-infinite
(10) clause	j. paradigmatic relation

VI. **Answer the following questions briefly.** (10%)
1. What are endocentric construction and exocentric construction?
2. What are the basic functional terms in syntax?

VII. **Essay questions.** (20%)
1. Explain and comment on the following sentence a and b.
   a. *John is easy to please*.
   b. *John is eager to please*.
2. Comment on the statement, "Linguistic structure is hierarchical".

参考答案

I.
1. D 2. A 3. D 4. D 5. B 6. A 7. D 8. D 9. B 10. A

II.
1. T 2. F 3. T 4. T 5. T 6. F 7. T 8. T 9. T 10. T

III.
1. modifiers
2. complement
3. pronouns; nouns
4. word group
5. openness
6. phrase
7. syntactic
8. participial
9. neuter
10. grammatical subject; logical subject

IV.
1. Syntax: Syntax refers to the rules governing the way words are combined to form sentences in a language, or simply, the study of the formation of sentences.
2. IC analysis: Immediate constituent analysis, IC analysis for short, refers to the analysis of a sentence in terms of its immediate constituents-word groups (phrases), which are in turn analyzed into the immediate constituents of their own, and the process goes on until the ultimate sake of convenience.
3. Relation of co-occurrence: By the relation of co-occurrence, one means that words of different sets of clauses may permit, or require, the occurrence of a word of another set of class to form a sentence or a particular part of a sentence. For instance, a nominal phrase can be preceded by a determiner and adjective and followed by a verbal phrase.
4. Category: The term category in some approaches refers to classes and functions in its narrow sense, e.g., noun, verb, subject, predicate, noun phrase, verb phrase, etc. More specifically, it refers to the defining properties of these general units: the categories of the noun, for example, include number, gender, case and countability; and of the verb, for example, tense, aspect, voice, etc.
5. Recursiveness: Though it mainly means that a phrasal constituent can be embedded within another constituent having the same category, recursiveness has become an umbrella term, under which may be brought together several important linguistic phenomena such as coordination and subordination, conjoining and embedding, hypotactic and paratactic. All these are means to extend sentences.

V.
(1) d (2) e (3) h (4) a (5) b (6) c (7) j (8) f (9) g (10) i

VI.
1. An endocentric construction is one whose distribution is functionally equivalent, or approaching equivalence, to one of its constituents, which serves as the center, or head, of the whole. A typical example is *the three small children* with *children* as its head. The exocentric construction, opposite to the first type, is defined negatively as a construction whose distribution is not functionally equivalent to any of its constituents. Prepositional phrases like *on the shelf* are typical examples of this type.
2. The syntactic function shows the relationship between a linguistic form and other parts of the linguistic pattern in which it is used. Names of functions are expressed in terms

Chapter 4
From Word to Text

of subjects, objects, predicate, modifiers, complements, etc. In some languages, subject refers to one of the nouns in the nominative case. Predicate refers to a major constituent of sentence structure in a binary analysis in which all obligatory constituents other than the subject were considered together. It usually expresses actions, processes and states that relate to the subject. Object may refer to the receiver or goal of an action and it is further classified into direct object and indirect object.

VII.
1. The two sentences have similar surface structure. But in spite of this surface similarity the grammar of the two is quite different. "John" has a different logical relationship to "please" in the two sentences. In the first sentence, though it is not apparent from the surface word order, "John" functions as the direct object of the verb "to please"; the sentence means: it is easy for someone to please John. Whereas in the second sentence "John" functions as the subject of the verb "to please"; the sentence means: John is eager that he pleases someone. It cannot be paraphrased as "* It is eager to please John", or as "* Pleasing John is eager". Deep structure specifies these relationships: a. (Someone pleases John) is easy; b. John is eager (John pleases someone).
2. Linguistic structure is hierarchical.
   (1) At the lowest level are bits of distinctive sound meaningless in themselves—the hum of an *m* or the explosion of a *p*— which occur in clumps of one or more that we call syllables. A syllable is the smallest unit that is normally spoken by itself. It is the poet's unit, the unit of rhythm and audibility.
   (2) Above the level of meaningless sounds and syllables are the levels that are segmented both for sound and for meaning. First are words and parts of words that have some recognizable semantic makeup, such as the prefix *trans-* or the suffix-*ism*.
   (3) Above the word level is the level of syntax, which is itself a complex of levels, since the unit that we call a sentence is often made up of a combination of simpler sentences, usually in some abbreviated form; and these in turn contain smaller units termed phrases, such as the prepositional phrase *to the west* and the verb phrase *run fast*.
   (4) Still higher units have to be recognized-question-and-answer, paragraph, discourse—but the larger they get, the harder it is to decide just what the structure is supposed to be. Most linguistic analysis up very recently has stopped with the sentence.
   (5) Stratification—this organization of levels on levels—is the physical manifestation of the "infinite use of finite means", the trait that most distinguishes human communication, the basis of its tremendous resourcefulness. Dozens of distinctive sounds are organized into scores of syllables, which become the carriers of hundreds of more or less meaningful segments of words, and these in turn are built into thousands of words proper. With thousands of words we associate millions of meanings, and on tip of those millions, the numbers of possible sentences and discourses are astronomical.
   (6) Underlying multiple reinvestment is the "structural principle", whereby instead of having unique symbols for every purpose, which would require as many completely different symbols as there are purposes, we use elementary units and recombine them.

Further Practice

I. Mark the following statements with "T" if they are true or "F" if they are false. Provide explanations for the false statements.

1. The syntactic rules of any language are finite in number, but they are capable of yielding an infinite number of sentences.
2. Although, a single word can also be uttered as a sentence, normally a sentence consists of at least a subject, its predicate and an object.
3. The sentences are linearly structured, so they are composed of sequence of words arranged in a simple linear order.
4. a. *John hit upon an idea*.
   b. *An idea hit upon John*.

   In the above sentences, the subject and object constituent by the sentence switch their position. Although sentence b is absurd, it is still grammatical, because *John* and *an idea* are of the same phrasal category.
5. Though they are of a small number, the combinational rules are powerful enough to yield all the possible sentences and rule out the impossible ones.
6. In a sentence like *Mary likes flowers*, both *Mary* and *flowers* are not only Nouns, but also Noun Phrases.
7. The recursive property can basically be discussed in a category-based grammar, but not in a word-based grammar.
8. An XP must contain an X which is called the phrasal head.
9. In the phrase *this very tall girl*, *tall girl* is an obligatory element and the head of the phrase.
10. a. *The man beat the child*.
    b. *The child was beaten by the man*.

    In the above sentences, the movement of *the child* from its original place to a new place is a *WH*-movement.
11. Tense and aspect, the two important categories of the verb, nowadays are viewed as separate notions in grammar.
12. The structuralists regard linguistic units as isolated bits in a structure (or system).
13. IC analysis can help us to see the internal structure of a sentence clearly and it can also distinguish the ambiguity of a sentence.
14. Structural linguists hold that a sentence does not only have a linear structure, but it has a hierarchical structure, made up of layers of word groups.
15. In Saussure's view, the linguist cannot attempt to explain individual signs in a piecemeal fashion. Instead he must try to find the value of a sign from its relation to others, or rather, its position in the system.
16. The theme-rheme order is the usual one in unemotional narration, which is a subjective order.
17. What is new in Halliday is that he has tried to relate the functions of language to its structure.
18. *Sentence* is a basic unit of structure in functional grammar.
19. The interpersonal function of language refers to the idea held by Halliday that language serves to establish and maintain social relations.

Chapter 4
From Word to Text

20. Finite is a function in the clause as a representation, both the representation of outer experience and inner experience.
21. The relations of co-occurrence partly belong to syntagmatic relations, partly to paradigmatic relations.
22. According to Chomsky, grammar is a mechanism that should be able to generate all and only the grammatical sentences of a language.
23. In English, the subject of a sentence is said to be the doer of an action, while the object is the person or thing acted upon by the doer. Therefore, the subject is always an agent and the patient is always the object.
24. In English, the object is recognized by tracing its relation to word order and by inflections of pronouns.
25. Classes and functions determine each other, but not in any one-to-one relation.
26. The syntactic rules of a language are finite in number, and there are a limited number of sentences which can be produced.
27. Structuralism views language as both linearly and hierarchically structured.
28. Phrase structure rules provide explanations on how syntactic categories are formed and sentences generated.
29. UG is a system of linguistic knowledge and a human species-specific gift which exists in the mind of a normal human being.
30. Tense and aspect are two important categories of the verb, and they were separated in traditional grammar.

II. Fill in each of the following blanks with (an) appropriate word(s).

1. As is required by the _____, a noun phrase must have case and case is assigned by verb, or preposition to the _____ position or by auxiliary to the _____ position.
2. Adjacency condition states that a case _____ and a case _____ should stay adjacent to each other.
3. The general movement rule accounting for the syntactic behavior of any constituent movement is called _____.
4. The phrase structure rules, with the insertion of the lexicon, generate sentences at the level of _____.
5. The application of syntactic movement rules transforms a sentence from the level of _____ to that of _____.
6. In English there are two major types of movement, one involving the movement of an NP is called _____ movement and the other a *WH*-word is called _____ movement.
7. a. *The boy ate the apple.*
   b. *The apple was eaten by the boy.*
   In Sentence b, *the boy* and *the apple* are moved from their original positions in Sentence a to new positions, with *the boy* _____ to the right and *the man* _____ to the left.
8. In the sentence *the man was bitten by a dog*, *the man* is both the _____ subject and the _____ object.
9. The decision on where to make the cuts in IC analysis relies on _____: whether a sequence of words can be substituted for a single word and the structure remains the same.

10. IC Analysis is different from the traditional parsing in that IC emphasizes the function of the _____ level-word group, seeing a hierarchical structure of the sentence as well.
11. The subordinate constituents are words which modify the head and consequently, they can be called _____.
12. *John believes (that the airplane was invented by an Irishman).*
    The part in the bracket is a _____ clause.
13. In order to account for the case of the subject in passive voice, we have another two terms, _____ and _____.
14. English gender contrast can only be observed in _____ and a small number of _____ and they are mainly of the natural gender type.
15. There is a tendency to make a distinction between phrase and _____, which is an extension of word of a particular class by way of modification with its main features of the class unchanged.
16. Recursiveness, together with _____, is generally regarded as the core of creativity of language.
17. Normally a sentence consists of at least a subject and a predicate which contains a _____ verb or a verb phrase.
18. The sequential order of words in a sentence suggests that the structure of a sentence is _____.
19. The starting point of an utterance which is known in the given situation and from which the speaker proceeds is named _____.
20. _____ structure can become the sole responsible structure for semantic interpretation by the introduction of the trace theory.

III. Mark the choice that best completes the statement.

1. The sentence *John likes linguistics, but Mary is interested in history* is a _____ sentence.
   A. simple   B. coordinate
   C. complex   D. relational
2. In the sentence *Mary told Jane that John liked linguistics* the introductory word *that* is called _____.
   A. coordinating conjunction   B. conjunction
   C. subordinator   D. embedded word
3. *The student// likes/ the new linguistics professor.* The above segmentation truthfully reveals the _____ nature of sentence structure.
   A. hierarchical   B. linear
   C. horizontal   D. parallel
4. The sentence *The tall man and women left* can be illustrated by tree diagram _____.
   A. (1)   B. (2)
   C. both (1) and (2)   D. neither
   (1)

```
                    S
                  /   \
               NP      VP
              / \       |
            /    \      V
          Det   Adj  NP  |
           |     |   /\  |
          The  tall man and women  left
```

(2)

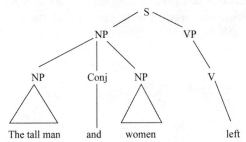

5. According to the following tree diagram, V can only be replaced by _____.
   A. *sat*
   B. *brought*
   C. *pushed*
   D. *none*

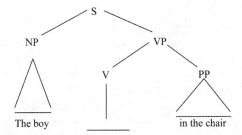

6. a. *John likes linguistics the most.*
   b. *It was linguistics that John liked the most.*
   Which of the following statements about the two sentences (*a* and *b*) given above is NOT true?
   A. In both sentence a and sentence b, *John* is the logical subject.
   B. In structural concept, *John* is the structural subject of a sentence.
   C. *It* in sentence b is the structural subject of the matrix clause.
   D. *John* is the structural subject in both a and b.
7. The conclusion that a set of principles or rules govern language use is based on the observation that _____.
   A. Speakers make acceptability judgment about sentences they have never heard before
   B. Speech is a habit-structure
   C. Imitation accounts for language acquisition
   D. Phonological information must form part of syntactic movement
8. The symbol N indicates a/an _____.
   A. lexical category
   B. phrasal category
   C. intermediate category
   D. lexical insertion rule
9. Of the following combination possibilities, _____ can NOT be generated from the following rule: NP→(Det) (Adj) N (PP) (S).
   A. NP→N
   B. NP→Det Adj S
   C. NP→Det N
   D. NP→Det Adj N PPS
10. An advantage of X-bar syntax over phrase structure syntax is that X-bar syntax _____.

A. avoids a proliferation of redundant intermediate categories
   B. allows us to identify indefinitely long embedded sentences
   C. allows as to postulate categories other than lexical and phrasal
   D. forces us to conclude that the ambiguity of phrases like *the English King* is lexical rather than structural
11. Which set of rules generates the following tree structure?

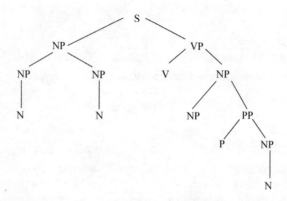

   A. S→NP VP
       NP→N PP
       VP→V NP
       PP→P NP
       NP→N

   B. S→NP VP
       NP→NP NP PP
       VP→V NP PP
       PP→P NP
       NP→N

   C. S→VP VP
       NP→{NP/PP}
       VP→V NP
       PP→P NP
       NP→N

   D. S→NP VP
       NP→NP {NP/PP}
       VP→V NP
       PP→P NP
       NP→N

12. a. *It seems they are quite fit for the job*.
    b. *They seem quite fit for the job*.
    Sentence b is a result of _____ movement.
    A. NP   B. WH
    C. AUX   D. None

13. The head of the phrase *underneath the open window* is _____.
    A. *underneath*   B. *the*
    C. *open*   D. *window*

14. The following statements are in accordance with Halliday's opinion on language EXCEPT _____.
    A. The use of language involves a network of systems of choices
    B. Language is never used as a mere mirror of reflected thought
    C. Language is a system of abstract forms and signs
    D. Language functions as a piece of human behavior

15. Chomsky is more concerned with _____ relations in his approach to syntax.
    A. syntagmatic   B. structural
    C. paradigmatic   D. transformational

16. _____ is a type of control over the form of some words by other words in certain syntactic constructions and in terms of certain category.
    A. Concord   B. Government
    C. Binding   D. C-command
17. Clauses can be used as subordinate constituents and the three basic types of subordinate clauses are complement clauses, adjunct clauses and _____.
    A. relative clauses   B. adverbial clauses
    C. coordinate clauses   D. subordinate clauses
18. Names of the syntactic functions are expressed in all the following terms EXCEPT _____.
    A. subjects and objects   B. objects and predicators
    C. modifiers and complements D. endocentric and exocentric
19. In English, case is a special form of the noun which frequently corresponds to a combination of preposition and noun and it is realized in all the following channels EXCEPT _____.
    A. inflection   B. following a preposition
    C. word order   D. vertical relation
20. Clauses can be classified into finite and non-finite clauses, _____ including the traditional infinitive phrase, participial phrase and gerundial phrase.
    A. the former   B. the latter
    C. both   D. neither
21. It is the _____ on case assignment that states that a case assignor and a case recipient should stay adjacent to each other.
    A. Case Condition   B. Adjacent Condition
    C. Parameter Condition   D. Adjacent Parameter
22. Predication analysis is a way to analyze _____ meaning.
    A. phoneme   B. word
    C. phrase   D. sentence
23. Which of the following italic parts is NOT an idiom?
    A. *How do you do?*
    B. *How did you do?*
    C. He went to it *hammer and tongs*.
    D. They *kept tabs on* the Russian spy.
24. When we say that we can change the second word in the sentence *She is singing in the room* with another word or phrase, we are talking about _____.
    A. government   B. linear relations
    C. syntactic relations   D. paradigmatic relations
25. In the phrase structure rule S→NP VP, the arrow can be read as _____.
    A. has   B. generates
    C. consists of   D. is equal to

IV. Suppose an unfamiliar language has the PS rules as shown in (1). Which two of the sentences given in (2) are generated from these PS rules? Try to provide labeled tree diagrams for them.
    (1) S→V NP NP
        NP→D N A

NP→PN
D→an
N→{cu, gille}
PN→{Tearlach, Calum}
A→{beag, mor}
V→{chunnaic bhail}

(2) a. Calum chunaic an gille.
　　b. Bhuail an gille mor an cu.
　　c. Bhuail an beag cu.
　　d. Chunnaic Tearlach an gille.

V. Answer the following questions as comprehensively as possible, giving examples if necessary.

1. The following two sentences are ambiguous. Show the two readings of each by drawing its respective tree diagrams.
   (1) The tall man and woman left.
   (2) Visiting professor can be interesting.
2. Use an example to show what a tree diagram is (as it is used in Transformational-Generative Grammar).
3. Use an example to show what IC analysis is.
4. What are the three general functions of language according to Halliday?
5. What distinguishes the structural approach to syntax from the traditional one?
6. Some grammar books say there are three basic tenses in English—the present, the past and the future; others say there are only two basic tenses—the present and the past. Explain what tense is and whether it is justifiable to say there is a future tense in English.

参考答案

I.
1. T
2. F. Normally a sentence consists of at least a subject, and its predicate.
3. F. The superficial arrangement of words in a linear sequence does not entail that sentences are simply linearly structured. A close examination of it will reveal its hierarchical nature.
4. T 5. T 6. T 7. T 8. T
9. F. In the phrase *this very tall girl*, *girl* is an obligatory element and the head of the phrase.
10. F. This is an NP-movement.
11. T
12. F. Not isolated bits, but interrelated with each other.
13. T 14. T 15. T
16. F. The theme-rheme order is the usual one in unemotional narration, which is an objective order.
17. T
18. F. The clause is the basic unit of the structure.
19. T
20. F. Actor is a function in the clause as a representation, both the representation of outer experience and inner experience.

Chapter 4
From Word to Text

21. T   22. T
23. F. The subject is not always an agent and the patient is not always the object. As we can see that in the sentence *John was bitten by a dog*, *John* is acted upon.
24. T   25. T
26. F. The syntactic rules of a language are finite in number, yet there is no limit to the number of sentence which can be produced.
27. T   28. T   29. T
30. F. Tense and aspect were not separated in traditional grammar.

II.
1. case condition; object; subject   2. assignor; recipient   3. transformational rule
4. D-structure   5. D-structure; S-structure
6. NP-movement; *WH*-movement
7. postposing; proposing   8. structural; logical   9. substitutability
10. intermediate   11. modifiers   12. complement
13. grammatical subject; logical subject
14. pronouns; nouns   15. word group   16. openness
17. finite   18. linear   19. theme
20. Surface

III.
1. B 2. C 3. A 4. C 5. A 6. D 7. A 8. A 9. B 10. A
11. D 12. A 13. A 14. C 15. A 16. B 17. A 18. D 19. D 20. B
21. B 22. D 23. B 24. D 25. C

IV.
The sentences b and c are generated from the given PS rules:
b. *Bhuail an gille mor an cu.*   c. *Bhuail an beag cu.*

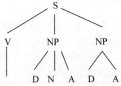
Buail an gille mor an cu.

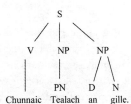
Chunnaic Tealach an gille.

V.
1. (1) Meaning One: The tall man and the tall woman left.

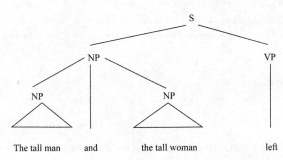

Meaning Two: The tall man and the woman (who is not tall) left.

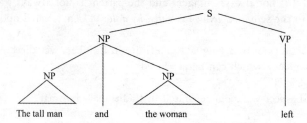

(2) Meaning One: Professor who is visiting can be interesting.

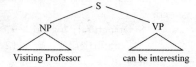

Meaning Two: To visit professor can be interesting.

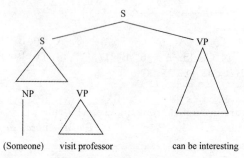

2. A special type of graphic representation used to depict linguistic structures. Borrowed from the concept of a tree, a tree diagram consists of a root and several branching nodes and branches. In such representations of the hierarchical relations and inner structures, nodes represent grammatical categories and the branches represent the relationships of domination. Each pair of nodes has a two-fold relationship, one of dominance and one of precedence. In a tree diagram, S immediately dominates NP and VP, and indirectly all other nodes in the tree, while each node which is to the left of another node precedes the one to the right, provided that none of the nodes dominates the other. Thus VP precedes VP, Det precedes N, and so on. Tree diagrams of natural languages are also subject to certain rules of well-formedness; thus, for example, crossing branches are not allowed. See the example *the professor gives a lecture*.

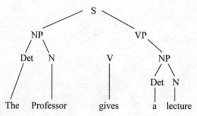

Chapter 4
From Word to Text

3. IC analysis is the short form for Immediate Constituent Analysis. IC analysis can be represented in different ways. Taking the construction *The boy ate the apple* as an example, one can analyze it by means of tree diagrams or bracketing.
   (1) Tree diagrams:

   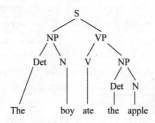

   Or:

   The boy ate the apple

   (2) Bracketing:
   ((The) (boy)) ((ate) ((the) (apple)))

4. Halliday states there are three general functions of language: ideational which is subdivided into experiential and logical, interpersonal and textual. They are related to three grammatical systems: transitivity, mood and theme. In his words, Language serves for the expression of 'content': that is, of the speaker's experience of the real world, including the inner world of his own consciousness. We may call this is the ideational function. Language serves to establish and maintain social relations: for the expression of social roles, which include the communication roles created by language itself—for example, the roles of questioner or respondent, which we take on by asking or answering a question; and also for getting things done, by means of the interaction between one person and another. Through this function, which we may refer to as interpersonal, social groups are delimited, and the individual is identified and reinforced, since by enabling him to interact with others language also serves in the expression and development of his own personality. Finally, language has to provide for making links with itself and with features of the situation in which it is used. We may call this the textual function, since this is what enables the speaker or writer to construct 'text', or connected passages of discourse that is ideationally relevant; and enables the listener or reader to distinguish a text from random set of sentences.

5. Traditionally, the study of syntax is the study of sentence formation, which involves a great deal of the study of the word: the classification of words in terms of parts of speech, the identification of functions of words in terms of subject, predicate, etc. These parts of speech and functions are sometimes called categories (nouns, verbs, number, gender, case, etc). However, the structural approach to syntax is different. This approach regards linguistic units as interrelated with each other in a structure (or system), not as isolated bits (as the traditional approach does). For instance, Saussure's syntagmatic and paradigmatic relations have let people see how much a word in a sentence is related to other words horizontally and vertically in the structure. There are constrains on words in both paradigmatic and syntagmatic relations. Besides, the

traditional approach is prescriptive in nature which the structural one descriptive in nature. The picture about language that the structural linguists have presented is relatively true.
6. Tense is a way languages express the time at which an event described by a sentence occurs. Tense is a linguistic concept, which varies from language to language. Tense indicates the relationship between the form of the verb and the time of the action or state it describes. Thus tense if deictic, i. e. indicating time relative to the time of utterance. Strictly speaking in English, verbs are only recognized in the past or present tense. Past tense is used to describe actions that occurred in the past; present tense is used to describe actions that are currently taking place. The so-called future tense is used to describe an action that will take place in the future, bur not expressed in the same as these two. That is, it is not expressed by morphology, not by the different forms of the verbs, but by various other means, such as *will/shall* + infinitive, *be going to* + infinitive, present progressive aspect, simple present tense and *will/shall* + progressive infinitive. And *will* and *shall* are basically modal verbs like *can* and *may*. Thus it is not justifiable to say that there is a future tense in English.

Chapter 5 Meaning

Concepts & Theories

I. The Definition of Semantics
Semantics is the study of the meaning of linguistic units, words and sentences in particular.

II. G. Leech's View on *Meaning*
G. Leech provides seven categories of meaning.
1. Conceptual meaning. It is denotative in that it is concerned with the relationship between a word and the thing it denotes, or refers to.
2. Associative meaning. It includes the following 5 types.
   (1) Connotative meaning. It is what is communicated by virtue of what language refers to.
   (2) Social meaning. It is what is communicated of the social circumstances of language use.
   (3) Affective meaning. It is what is communicated of the feelings and attitudes of the speaker/writer.
   (4) Reflected meaning. It is what is communicated through association with another sense of the same expression.
   (5) Collocative meaning. It is what is communicated through association with words which tend to occur in the environment of another word.
3. Thematic meaning. It is what is communicated by the way in which the message is organized in terms of order and emphasis.

III. The Referential Theory
1. Referential theory relates the meaning of a word to the thing it refers to, or stands for.
2. Concept is the idea which is conceived through abstraction and through which objects or states of affairs are classified on the basis of particular characteristics and/or relations.
   (1) Ogden and Richards' semantic triangle involves the notion of *Concept*.
   (2) *Sense* is used by Leech as a briefer term for his conceptual meaning.
   (3) The distinction between *sense* and *reference* is comparable to that between *connotation* and *denotation*.

IV. Sense Relations
There are three kinds of sense relations.
1. **Synonymy**

   Synonymy is the technical term for the sameness relation.

   Total synonyms are rare. They may differ (1) in style, (2) in connotation and (3) in dialect.

2. Antonymy

Antonymy is the term for oppositeness relation. There are three kinds of antonymy.
(1) Gradable antonymy
   ☆ The members of a pair differ in terms of degree.
   ☆ Antonyms of this kind are graded against different norms.
   ☆ One member of a pair, usually the term of the higher degree, serves as the cover term.
(2) Complementary antonymy
   ☆ The members of a pair of this type are complementary to each other.
   ☆ The norm in this type is absolute.
   ☆ There is no cover term for the two members of a pair.
(3) Converse antonymy
   The members of a pair do not constitute a positive-negative opposition. They show a reversal relationship between two entities.

3. Hyponymy

Hyponymy refers to the relationship of meaning inclusiveness. The upper term of a certain class name is called superordinate. The lower terms, the members are called hyponyms. The members of the same class are called co-hyponyms.
(1) There are three things for us to notice.
   ☆ Sometimes a superordinate may be a superordinate to itself.
   ☆ A superordinate may be missing sometimes.
   ☆ Hyponyms may also be missing.

V. Componential Analysis

1. Componential analysis is the description of the meaning of lexemes as well as of the inner structure of the lexicon through (structured) sets of semantic features.
2. The meaning of a word is not an unanalysable whole. It may be seen as a complex of different semantic features.
3. Semantic components may help to analyze relationship between words and sentences.
4. There are also difficulties in the analyzing the meaning of a word in terms of semantic components because:
   (1) Many words are polysemous.
   (2) Some semantic components are seen as binary taxonomies.
   (3) There may be words whose semantic components are difficult to ascertain.

VI. Sentence Meaning

This is an area where word meaning and sentence structure come together. There are some theories on sentence meaning.
1. An integrated theory-compositionality
   (1) The principle of compositionality is that the meaning of a sentence depends on the meanings of the constituent words and the way they are combined.
   (2) The basic idea supporting this theory is that a semantic theory consists of two parts: a dictionary and a set of projection rules.
      ☆ The dictionary provides the grammatical classification and semantic information of words.
      ☆ The projection rules are responsible for combining the meanings of words together.

(3) This theory is also an integration of syntax and semantics.
(4) There are problems in this theory:
   ☆ The distinction between semantic marker and distinguisher is not very clear.
   ☆ There are cases in which the collocation of words cannot be accounted for by grammatical markers, semantic markers or selection restrictions.
   ☆ It is hard to explain the meaning of the meta-language of those semantic components.
2. **Logical semantics**
   There are two branches in logical semantics-propositional logic and predicate logic.
   (1) Propositional logic, also known as propositional calculus or sentential calculus, is the study of the truth conditions for propositions: how the truth of a composite proposition is determined by the truth values of its constituent propositions and the connections between them.
      ☆ There are five basic relations: $\sim$ stands for negation; & stands for conjunction which also means *and*; $\vee$ stands for conjunction which also means *or*; $\rightarrow$ means implication; and $\leftrightarrow$ means equivalence.
   (2) Predicate logic or predicate calculus studies the internal structure of simple propositions.
      ☆ An argument is a term which refers to some entity about which a statement is being made. There may be one, two or more than two arguments in one sentence.
      ☆ A predicate is a term which ascribes some property, or relation, to the entity, or entities, referred to.
      ☆ *All* in the analyzed sentence is symbolized by $\forall$ and there is also another existing quantifier as $\exists$.

Related Terms

affective meaning
   Affective meaning refers to what is communicated of the feelings and attitudes of the speaker/writer.
antonym
   Words that are opposite in meaning are antonyms.
antonymy
   Antonymy is the name for oppositeness in sense relation. There are three main subtypes: gradable antonymy, complementary antonymy, and converse antonymy.
argument
   An argument is a term which refers to some entity about which a statement is being made.
associative meaning
   Connotative meaning, social meaning, affective meaning, reflected meaning and collocative meaning are collectively known as associative meaning in the sense that an elementary associationist theory of mental connections is enough to explain their use.
bilingual
   When a person knows or uses two languages, we say that he/she is a bilingual or a bilingual person.

co-hyponym

Hyponyms that share one superordinate are called co-hyponyms.

collocative meaning

Collocative meaning is communicated through association with words which tend to occur in the environment of another word.

complementary antonymy

Complementary antonymy is a kind of antonymy. The members of a pair in this type are complementary to each other. Words that belong to complementary antonymy are *alive*: *dead*, *male*: *female*, etc.

componential analysis

Componential analysis is the description of the meaning of lexemes as well as of the inner structure of the lexicon through (structured) sets of semantic features.

compositionality

The idea that the meaning of a sentence depends on the meanings of the constituent words and the way they are combined is usually known as the principle of compositionality.

concept

Concept is the idea which is conceived through abstraction and through which objects or states of affairs are classified on the basis of particular characteristics and/or relations.

conceptual meaning

Conceptual meaning is logical, cognitive or denotative content.

connotation

Philosophers use connotation to mean the properties of the entity a word denotes. In semantics, connotation is what is communicated by virtue of what language refers to.

converse antonymy

Converse antonymy is a special type of antonymy in that the members of a pair do not constitute a positive-negative opposition. They show the reversal of a relationship between two entities.

denotation

Denotation refers to that part of the meaning of a word or phrase that relates it to phenomena in the real world or in a fictional or possible world.

disjunction

The connective disjunction ? corresponds to the English *or*. Its truth table shows that only when and as long as one of the constituents is true, the composite proposition will be true.

entailment

Entailment is a relationship between two or more sentences. If knowing that one sentence is true gives us certain knowledge of the truth of the second sentence, then the first sentence entails the second.

equivalence

The logical connective equivalence, also called biconditional and symbolized as $\leftrightarrow$, is a conjunction of two implications. That is, p$\equiv$q equals (p→q) & (q→p). It corresponds to the English expression *if and only if ... then*, which is sometimes written as *iff... then*. The condition for the composite proposition to be true is that if and only if both constituent propositions are of the same truth value, whether true or false.

gradable antonymy

Gradable antonymy refers to the gradable oppositeness of meaning, because there are often intermediate forms between two gradable antonyms.

grammatical marker

Grammatical marker is also called syntactic marker, it is used to mark the detailed part of speech of a word.

hyponym

In hyponymy, the more specific term is the hyponym.

hyponymy

Hyponymy refers to the relationship of meaning inclusiveness.

implication

The connective implication→, also known as conditional, corresponds to the English *if ... then*. Its truth table shows that unless the antecedent is true and the consequent is false the composite proposition will be true.

marked (member)

Marked (member) refers to the word that departs from the neutral along some specified parameter.

meaning

Meaning refers to the central semantic notion defined and used differently depending on the theoretical approach. G. Leech recognizes seven types of meaning in his *Semantics*, namely, conceptual meaning, connotative meaning, social meaning, affective meaning, reflected meaning, collocative meaning and thematic meaning.

monolingualism

Monolingualism means commanding of only one language as opposed to bilingualism or multilingualism.

predicate

A predicate in logic semantics is a term which ascribes some property, or relation, to the entity, or entities referred to in a proposition.

predicate logic

Predicate logic, which is also called predicate calculus, studies the internal structure of simple propositions. For example, in predicate logic, the proposition "Socrates is a man." is presented as M(s), in which man (presented by M) is the predicate and Socrates (presented by s) is the argument. The truth value of the proposition varies with the argument.

presupposition

The following relations will give a fundamental definition to the concept of presupposition in logic: S1 presupposes S2 exactly if S1 implies S2 and if not S1 also entails S2.

projection rule

The projection rules are responsible for combining the meanings of words together. In Katz and Fodor's theory of interpretive semantics, a semantic operation which arrives at the interpretation of the whole meaning of a sentence through the step-by-step projection of the meaning of the individual constituents from the lowest level of derivation to the next higher level. Thus, projection rules function over the hierarchic relations of the constituents in the deep structure. According to Katz and Fodor, projection rules simulate the cognitive process in which the speaker and hearer comprehend the whole meaning of the sentence, using their knowledge of the lexicon and of the syntactic relations. The process in which projection rules are applied is known as amalgamation.

proposition

A proposition is what is expressed by a declarative sentence when that sentence is uttered to make a statement.

propositional logic

Propositional logic, also known as propositional calculus, or semantic calculus, is the study of the truth conditions for propositions: how the truth of a composite proposition is determined by the truth value of its constituent propositions and the connections between them.

reference

In the *semantic triangle* proposed by Odgen and Richards, reference is the relationship between words and the things, actions, events, qualities they stand for.

referent

In the *semantic triangle* proposed by Odgen and Richards, *referent* refers to the object in the world of experience.

referential theory

The theory of meaning which relates the meaning of a word to the thing it refers to, or stands for, is known as the referential theory.

reflected meaning

Reflected meaning is what is communicated through association with another sense of the same expression.

selection restriction

Selection restrictions are constraints on the combination process of word meanings into sentence meaning.

semantics

Semantics is a branch of linguistics which examines how meaning is encoded in a language. It is not only concerned with meaning of words as lexical items, but also with levels of language below the word and above it, e.g. meaning of morphemes and sentences.

semantic component

Semantic components are units smaller than the word meaning in componential analysis. For example, the semantic components of the word *boy* is HUMAN, YOUNG and MALE.

semantic distinguisher

Semantic distinguishers have the ability to show the word information that is more idiosyncratic and word-specific, compared to semantic markers in the semantic analysis principle of compositionality.

semantic marker

Semantic markers show the word information that has to do with the more systematic part, or is of a more general nature, compared to semantic distinguishers in the semantic analysis principle of compositionality.

semantic triangle

Semantic triangle is a geometric schema developed by Odgen and Richards to illustrate the dependent relationship between symbol, thought and referent, or in more common terms, sign, meaning and object (of reference).

sense
　　Sense refers to the abstract properties of an entity that a word refers to.
social meaning
　　Social meaning is what is communicated of the social circumstances of language use.
synonymy
　　Synonymy is the technical name for the sameness relation.
superordinate
　　The upper term in the sense relation of hyponymy, the class name, is called superordinate.
taxonomy
　　It refers to the classification of items into classes and sub-classes.
unmarked (member)
　　Unmarked member refers to the linguistic unit which is neutral, natural or expected.

Practice

I. Mark the choice that best completes the statement. (20%)

1. Which of the following is NOT included in G. Leech's seven types of meaning?
   A. Connotative meaning.　　B. Denotative meaning.
   C. Conceptual meaning.　　D. Affective meaning.

2. Of the following pairs of words, _____ belongs to the type of complementary antonyms.
   A. *teacher/student*　　B. *captive/free*
   C. *rich/poor*　　D. *fast/slow*

3. Which of the following is NOT true?
   A. Sense is concerned with the inherent meaning of the linguistic form.
   B. Sense is the collection of all the features of the linguistic form.
   C. Sense is abstract and decontextualized.
   D. Sense is the aspect of meaning dictionary compilers are not interested in.

4. Which of the following is concerned with word meaning?
   A. Compositionality principle.　　B. Truth value judgment.
   C. Logic semantics.　　D. Componential analysis.

5. _____ is a way in which the meaning of a word can be dissected into meaning components, called semantic features.
   A. Predication analysis　　B. Componential analysis
   C. Phonemic analysis　　D. Grammatical analysis

6. *Alive* and *dead* are _____.
   A. gradable antonyms　　B. converse antonyms
   C. complementary antonyms　　D. None of the above

7. _____ deals with the relationship between the linguistic element and the non-linguistic world of experience.
   A. Reference　　B. Concept
   C. Semantics　　D. Sense

8. _____ refers to the phenomenon that words having different meanings have the same form.
   A. Polysemy　　B. Synonymy

C. Homonymy D. Hyponymy
9. Words that are close in meaning are called _____.
   A. homonyms B. polysemies
   C. hyponyms D. synonyms
10. _____ antonyms are also called relational opposites.
    A. Gradable B. Complementary
    C. Converse D. Controversial

II. Mark the following statements with "T" if they are true or "F" if they are false. (10%)

1. Sometimes a superordinate may be a superordinate to itself and a hyponym may be a hyponym of itself.
2. If a proposition p is true, then its negation $\sim p$ is false. And if p is false, then $\sim p$ is true.
3. Linguistic forms having the same sense may have different references in different situations.
4. In the complementary pair *true—false*, there is no cover term.
5. Every word has sense, but not every word has reference.
6. Compositionality is a principle for sentence analysis, in which the meaning of a sentence depends on the meanings of the constituent words and the way they are combined.
7. The meaning of a sentence is the sum total of the meanings of all its components.
8. In English, *color* is the superordinate term for *red*, *green*, *yellow*, etc.
9. The connective *Implication* corresponds to the English *if...then*.
10. We can use meta-meta-language to explain meta-language in the componential analysis.

III. Fill in each of the following blanks with an appropriate word. The first letter of the word is already given. (20%)

1. S_____ can be defined as the study of meaning.
2. Predicate l_____, also called predicate calculus, studies the internal structure of a simple proposition.
3. R_____ means what a linguistic form refers to in the real, physical world; it deals with the relationship between the linguistic element and the non-linguistic world of experience.
4. The word that can be presented by the following semantic components BECOME (x, ($\sim$ALIVE (x))) should be d_____.
5. Two words, or two expressions, which have the same semantic c_____, will be synonymous with each other.
6. A theory which explicitly employs the notion of c_____ is the semantic triangle proposed by Ogden and Richards. In their theory the notion functions as the relation mediator between a word and the thing it refers to.
7. C_____ analysis is based upon the belief that the meaning of a word can be divided into meaning components.
8. There are generally three kinds of sense relations recognized, namely, a_____, s_____ and h_____.
9. An a_____ is a term which refers to some entity about which a statement is being

made in predicate logic analysis.
10. The connective d_____ (∨) corresponds to the English *or*.

IV. Explain the following concepts or theories. (20%)
1. Converse antonymy
2. Hyponymy
3. Componential analysis
4. Reference

V. Answer the following questions. (20%)
1. What is the word in each group that is different form others, pick it out and give the reasons.
   A. *dog, cat, cow, horse, animal*
   B. *trunk, branches, tree, roots, leaves*
   C. *peony, tulip, jasmine, rose, lily, petal*
   D. *pen, pencil, paper, oven, eraser*
2. What are the three kinds of antonymy?

VI. Analyze with your linguistic knowledge. (10%)
For each group of words given below, state what semantic property or properties are shared by the words in group A and B respectively, and what semantic property or properties distinguish the words in A and B.
(1) A. *bachelor, man, son, paperboy, pope, chief*
    B. *bull, rooster, drake, ram*
(2) A. *table, stone, pencil, cup, house, ship, car*
    B. *milk, alcohol, rice, soup*
(3) A. *book, temple, mountain, road, tractor*
    B. *idea, love, charity, sincerity, bravery, fear*

参考答案

I.
1. B 2. B 3. D 4. D 5. B 6. C 7. A 8. C 9. D 10. C

II.
1. T 2. T 3. T 4. F 5. T 6. T 7. F 8. F 9. T 10. F

III.
1. Semantics   2. logic   3. Reference   4. die
5. components   6. concept   7. Componential
8. antonymy; synonymy; hyponymy   9. argument   10. disjunction

IV.
1. Converse antonyms are also called relational opposites. This is a special type of antonymy in that the members of a pair do not constitute a positive-negative opposition. They show the reversal of a relationship between two entities, e.g. *buy-sell, parent-child, above-below*, etc.
2. Hyponymy involves us in the notion of meaning inclusiveness. It is a matter of class membership. That is to say, when x is a kind of y, the lower term x is the hyponym,

and the upper term *y* is the superordinate. Two or more hyponyms of the same one superordinate are called co-hyponyms, e.g. under *flower*, there are *peony*, *jasmine*, *tulip*, *violet*, *rose*, etc., *flower* is the superordinate of *peony*, *jasmine*, etc., *peony* is the hyponym of *flower*, and *peony*, *jasmine*, *tulip*, *violet*, *rose*, etc. are co-hyponyms.
3. Compositional analysis: It defines the meaning of a lexical element in terms of semantic components, or semantic features. For example, the meaning of the word *boy* may be analyzed into three components: HUMAN, YOUNG and MALE. Similarly *girl* may be analyzed into HUMAN, YOUNG and FEMALE.
4. Reference: It is what a linguistic form refers to in the real world; it is a matter of the relationship between the form and the reality.

V.

1. A. *animal* is different from the other words. It is the superordinate of the other words.
   B. *tree* is different from the other words. It is the superordinate of the other words.
   C. *petal* is different from the other words. It is the hypernym of the other words.
   D. *oven* is different from the other words. It is a word other than stationery things.
2. Antonymy is the term for oppositeness relation. There are three subtypes: gradable, complementary and converse antonymy.
   (1) Gradable antonymy
       Gradable antonymy refers to the gradable oppositeness of meaning, because there are often intermediate forms between two gradable antonyms. Gradable antonymy is the commonest type of antonymy. They are mainly adjectives, e.g. *good—bad*, *long—short*, *big—small*, etc.
   (2) Complementary antonymy
       The members of a pair in complementary antonymy are complementary to each other. That is, they divide up the whole of a semantic field completely. Not only the assertion of one means the denial of the other, the denial of one also means the assertion of the other, e.g. *alive—dead*, *hit—miss*, *male—female*, *boy—girl*, etc.
   (3) Converse antonymy
       Converse antonyms are also called relational opposites. This is a special type of antonymy in that the members of a pair do not constitute a positive-negative opposition. They show the reversal of a relationship between two entities, e.g. *buy—sell*, *parent—child*, *above—below*, etc.

VI.

1. (1) The words in A and B are male.
       The words in A are human while in B non-human.
   (2) The words in A and B are inanimate.
       The words in A are instrumental while in B edible.
   (3) The words in A and B are worldly or conceptual.
       The words in A are material while in B spiritual.

Chapter 5
Meaning

❧ Further Practice ☙

I. **Mark the following statements with "T" if they are true or "F" if they are false. Provide explanations for the false statements.**

1. Semantics is the study of the meaning of linguistic units, words, phonemes and sentences in particular.
2. Conceptual meaning is *connotative* in that it is concerned with the relationship between a word and the thing it connotes, or refers to.
3. Philosophers use connotative meaning to refer to what is communicated by virtue or what language refers to.
4. The only way to explain the meaning of *desk* is *a piece of furniture with a flat top and four legs, at which one reads and writes*.
5. The definition of *desk* as *a piece of furniture with a flat top and four legs, at which one reads and writes* may also be called the sense of *desk*.
6. The distinction between sense and reference is not comparable to that between denotation and connotation.
7. We can find total synonyms in English.
8. There is usually an intermediate degree between the pair of two gradable antonyms, and usually the intermediate degree may be lexicalized.
9. The adjectives in complementary antonymy can not be modified by "very".
10. If a pair of words is in relationship of converse antonymy, then the members of this pair do not only constitute a positive-negative opposition, but also show the reversal of a relationship between two entities.
11. One member of the converse antonyms usually presupposes the other.
12. *Young* and *old* are gradable antonyms, so *younger* and *older* are also gradable antonyms.
13. A superordinate usually has several hyponyms, and a hyponym can also have several superordinates.
14. Sometimes a superordinate may be a superordinate to itself.
15. The smallest unit in semantics is word meaning.
16. The meaning of a sentence will be generated by the adding of the individual words in the sentence.
17. According to the grammatical classification and the semantic information, *The colorless green ideas sleep furiously* is a false sentence.
18. &, ∨, ∼ and → are known as two-place connectives.
19. The symbol ↔ corresponds to the English expression *if and only if . . . , then*, which is sometimes written as *iff . . . then*.
20. In logical semantics, the sentence *If the earth is round, animals can't use language* is valid.
21. In logical semantics, the sentence *If the earth is square, animals can't use language* is true.
22. Because $\sim \exists x(S(x) \& \sim C(x))$
    And because $C(x)$
    So, $S(x)$
23. The predicate in logic semantics must be a verb.

24. The word *cat* is given the definition *a small animal with soft fur and sharp teeth and claws, often kept as a pet or in building to catch mice or rats*. This is the sense of the word *cat*.
25. Linguistic forms having the same sense may have different references in different situations.
26. *Dog*, *cat* and *tiger* are co-hyponyms, and their superordinate is animal.
27. Componential analysis is a way proposed by the structural semanticists to analyze word meaning.
28. The meaning of a sentence is the sum total of meanings of all its components, that is, the meaning of a sentence can be worked out by adding up all the meanings of its constituent words.
29. Some sentences may comply perfectly with the grammar rules of the language, but they may not be semantically meaningful.
30. In teaching the meaning of the word, the teachers would often teach the connotative meaning of the word.
31. Philosophers also use connotation to mean the properties of the entity a word denotes.
32. Projection rules are grammatical rules.
33. The dictionary in compositional analysis only deals in the word meaning.
34. Compositionality analysis mainly focuses on the study of social meaning proposed by Leech.
35. Metaphor does not belong to the study domain of componential analysis.
36. In logical semantics, the sentence *If the earth is flat, the earth goes around the sun* is true.
37. The way words are combined into phrases and phrases into sentences determines the meaning of the sentences.
38. Semantic components aim at giving the grammatical rules that combine words together.

II. Fill in each of the following blanks with (an) appropriate word(s).

1. The subject concerning the study of meaning is called _____.
2. In Leech's definition of seven types of meaning, _____ meaning is what is communicated through association with words which tend to occur in the environment of another word.
3. In Leech's definition of meanings, the five meanings—connotative meaning, social meaning, affective meaning, reflected meaning, collocative meaning fall into the category of _____ meaning.
4. There are generally three kinds of sense relations recognized, namely, _____, _____ and _____.
5. There are three main types of antonymy, namely, _____, _____ and _____.
6. The relationship between *good* and *bad* is _____ antonymy.
7. When an antonymy pair shows the reversal of a relationship between two entities, the relationship of this pair is _____ antonymy.
8. On the analogy of distinctive features in phonology, some linguists suggest that there are _____ in semantics.
9. Two words, or two expressions, which have the same semantic components, will be _____ with each other.
10. Words which have all the semantic components of and more semantic components than

Chapter 5
Meaning

another are _____ of the latter.

11. Semantic components like HUMAN, ADULT, MALE are _____, a language used for talking about another language.
12. In the Compositionality principle, the semantic analysis consists of two parts: a dictionary and a set of projection rules. _____ provide(s) the grammatical classification and semantic information of words, while _____ is (are) responsible for combining the meanings of words together.
13. In compositionality analysis, the semantic description of a certain sentence effectively provides a solution to the integration of _____ and _____.
14. In the logical system, propositions will be analyzed into two parts— _____ and _____. The former is a term which refers to some entity about which a statement is being made, and the latter is a term which ascribes some property or relation, to the entity or entities referred to.
15. In the sentence *Tomorrow is Sunday*. _____ is the argument, and _____ is a _____ place predicate.
16. In the field of philosophy we have two terms as connotation and denotation. For example, the _____ of *human* is any person such as John and Mary, and its _____ may be *biped*, *featherless*, *rational*, etc.
17. In Leech's definition of meanings, _____ meaning is only determined by the order of the words in a sentence and the different prominence they each receive.
18. Composite propositions include both _____ and _____ propositions.
19. Language could be formalized. Some philosophers formalized language by _____, some from the generative school formalized language by _____.
20. The suffix of _____ or _____ could be added to some words to make the new words have the semantic features of [+ HUMAN].

III. Mark the choice that best completes the statement.
1. In Leech's definition of meanings, _____ meaning is what is communicated by virtue of what language refers to.
   A. conceptual   B. social   C. connotative   D. collocative
2. _____ refers to the abstract properties of an entity; while _____ refers to the concrete entities having these properties.
   A. Reference, denotation
   B. Connotation, denotation
   C. Sense, connotation
   D. Denotation, connotation
3. We do not have _____ antonymy.
   A. gradable
   B. dialectal
   C. converse
   D. complementary
4. _____ is an unmarked word.
   A. *Bad*   B. *Low*   C. *Old*   D. *Short*
5. To some extent, the difference between gradable and complementary antonyms can be compared to the traditional logical distinction between _____ and _____.
   A. denotation, connotation
   B. contrary, contradictory
   C. partially different, totally different
   D. totally different, partially different
6. _____ is not the study of the truth conditions for propositions.

A. Propositional logic   B. Propositional calculus
   C. Sentential conditions   D. Sentential calculus
7. A (n) _____ is what is expressed by a declarative sentence when that sentence is uttered to make a statement.
   A. sentence   B. utterance   C. proposition   D. statement
8. A very important property of the proposition is that it has a _____. It is either true or false.
   A. reality status   B. truth feature
   C. false value   D. truth value
9. _____ studies the internal structure of simple propositions.
   A. Semantic calculus   B. Propositional logic
   C. Predicate calculus   D. Sentential logic
10. The truth value of a proposition varies with the _____.
    A. predicate   B. argument   C. verb   D. place
11. If p is true and q is false, which of the following has the property of being true?
    A. $\sim p$ B. $p \& q$ C. $p \rightarrow q$ D. $q \rightarrow p$
12. _____ is the collection of all the features of the linguistic form; it is abstract and de-contextualized.
    A. Sense   B. Referent   C. Denotation   D. Symbol
13. In pair _____, X entails Y.
    A. X: *John is a bachelor.* Y: *John is a man.*
    B. X: *I've done my homework.* Y: *I haven't brushed my teeth.*
    C. X: *Some of the students came to my party.*
       Y: *Not all the students came to my party.*
    D. X: *John is married.* Y: *John is a bachelor.*
14. Componential analysis is a way proposed by the _____ semanticists to analyze the word meaning.
    A. structural   B. contextual   C. behavioral   D. conceptual
15. Among the following pairs of words, _____ can be called converse opposites.
    A. *old—young*   B. *alive—dead*
    C. *male—female*   D. *doctor—patient*
16. The pair of words *let* and *rent* in their American usage is one of _____.
    A. gradable antonyms   B. complementary antonyms
    C. dialectal synonyms   D. converse opposites
17. Of the following pairs of words, _____ belongs to the type of complementary antonyms.
    A. *teacher/student*   B. *captive/free*
    C. *rich/poor*   D. *fast/slow*
18. Pair _____ belongs to the category of gradable antonyms.
    A. *over/under*   B. *weak/strong*
    C. *open/shut*   D. *sell/buy*
19. The word which is more general in meaning is called the _____, and the more specific words are called its _____.
    A. homophone, homograph   B. hyponym, co-hyponyms
    C. synonymy, synonyms   D. superordinate, co-hyponyms
20. The following are factors that cause near synonyms EXCEPT _____.

A. conceptual difference B. stylistic difference
C. dialectal difference D. connotative difference
21. Among the following subjects, _____ does not have any relation to semantics.
 A. pragmatics B. psychology
 C. accounting D. statistics
22. The compositionality principle is based on the theory of _____.
 A. sociolinguistics B. structuralism
 C. functional grammar D. generative grammar
23. If we have X and Y which have the semantic features as X [+A] [+B] [+C]; Y [+A] [+B] [+C], then we say that X and Y are _____.
 A. synonyms B. antonyms C. hyponyms D. one word
24. If we have X and Y which have the semantic features as X [+A] [+B] [+C]; Y [+A] [+B] [−C], then we say that X and Y are _____.
 A. synonyms B. antonyms C. hyponyms D. one word
25. Among the following pairs of adjective synonyms, _____ can be used similarly in the aspect of grammar (the place they occur in the sentences).
 A. *powerful/strong* B. *close/near*
 C. *safe/secure* D. *expensive/dear*

IV. Identify the underlined part in each of the following sentences in terms of the type(s) of meanings proposed by Leech. Some may convey more than one type of meaning.

G. Leech once proposed seven types of meaning in his *Semantics* (1981), namely, conceptual meaning, connotative meaning, social meaning, affective meaning, reflected meaning, collocative meaning and thematic meaning. Each of the following underlined parts present at least one particular meaning in addition to conceptual meaning. Identify one particular meaning in each of the sentences below.

1. The sky is gray, the flower is gray, Dora, in her great sorrow, saw a gray cat stealing into the yard.
2. With a long stick, our headmaster went in. All the students were silent.
3. Tomorrow is Sunday, I can go with you.
4. Are you going to Scarborough Fair? Parsley, Sage, Rosemary and Thyme? Remember me to one who lives there; she once was a true love of mine.
5. I ain't nothing to say and I'm going home.
6. —Oh, it's a little bit cold here.
   —Then I will close the window for you.
7. Quietness is requested for the benefit of those who have already retired.
8. Well, dear sir, I really do not like to hear someone barking here.

V. The following pairs are of different sense relations. Put the right sense relation next to each pair. The relations are listed for you below.

synonymy, gradable antonymy, complementary antonymy, converse antonymy, hyponymy, co-hyponyms.

1. good—bad _____
2. fall—autumn _____
3. flower—rose _____
4. desk—chair _____
5. seller—buyer _____

6. give—receive　　　_____
7. dead—alive　　　_____
8. hit—miss　　　_____
9. beautiful—ugly　　　_____
10. bigger—smaller　　　_____

VI. Analyze the following with your linguistic knowledge.

1. What is the relationship between sentence a and sentence b? Give your explanation.
   a. *Mary divorced last month*.
   b. *Mary once married*.
2. The following is the definition of *colorful* in compositionality analysis. Explain the functions and meanings of the brackets below.
   colorful {Adj}
   a. (Color) [abounding in contrast or variety of bright colors] <(Physical Object) or (Social Activity)>
   b. (Evaluative) [having distinctive character, vividness, or picturesqueness] <(Aesthetic Object) or (Social Activity)>
3. Is the following statement true or false? Give your reasons for the choice.
   Usage related aspects of sentential or propositional meaning requires world knowledge and contextual information, which belongs to the domain of pragmatic analysis. So we say semantics is part of pragmatics.
4. Do the following two sentences share the same meaning? Explain with some linguistic knowledge, paying attention to the underlined parts.
   a. <u>Tim was drunk</u>, so he lost his way.
   b. <u>Drunk as was Tim</u>, he lost his way.

VII. Formula.

1. The following are expressions in componential analysis, write down the correspondent expressions and formulas in the blankets.
   (1) _____ = PARENT (x, y) & MALE (x).
   (2) daughter = _____.
   (3) _____ = HUMAN + YOUNG + MALE.
   (4) die = _____.
   (5) take = CAUSE(x,(_____)).
2. Fill in the Truth Table below.

p	q	p & q	p ∨ q	p → q	p ≡ q
T	T	T	( )	T	( )
T	F	( )	T	( )	F
F	T	F	( )	T	( )
F	F	F	F	T	T

3. Put the following sentences into formulas presented by the logic connections, and then explain the formulas in plain English other than the sentences given here.
   (1) All the students are clever.
   (2) Some students are clever.
   (3) Since all students are clever and John is a student, John is clever.
4. Translate the following logical forms into English. (j = John, k = Kathy, m = Maxine, b = book, G = give, S = student, x, y are variables which may be translated as *someone*,

anyone or *everyone* depending on the quantifier.)
(1) $\sim \forall T(x) (L(x, j))$
(2) $\forall T(x) (L(x, \forall S(y)))$
(3) $G(k, m, b)$
(4) $\sim \exists x (T(x) \& L(x, j))$
(5) $\sim \forall x(T(x) \& \sim L(x, \forall S(y)))$

VIII. Decide the relation between each of the following sentence pairs. (E for *a entails b* and P for *a presupposes b*)

1. a. *John killed Mary.*
   b. *Mary is dead.*
2. a. *Tom failed in his math test.*
   b. *Tom took a test.*
3. a. *Tom's dog is bigger than mine.*
   b. *I have a dog.*
4. a. *Allen ate some grapes.*
   b. *Allen ate some fruit.*

IX. What does each *time* used in the following passage mean respectively?

   This passage is taken from *The Green Banana* (Batchelder and Warner 1974) which tells an American author's experience of realizing the importance and greatness of the minor culture in Brazil by realizing the importance of green bananas as glue to fix his leaking engine.

   As a product of American education, I had never paid the slightest attention to the green banana, except to regard it as a fruit whose time^1 had not yet come. Suddenly, on that mountain road, its time^2 had come to meet my need. But as I reflected on it further, I realized that the green banana had been there all along. Its time^3 reached back to the very origins of the banana. The people in that village had known about it for years. It was my own time^4 that had come, all in relation to it. I came to appreciate the special genius of those people, and the special potential of the green banana. I had been wondering for some time^5 about what educators like to call learning moments, and I now knew I had just experienced two of them at once.

X. Answer the following questions as comprehensively as possible, giving your own examples.

1. What is referential theory? Have you found some defects of it?
2. Do you think that there are absolute synonyms in the world? Support your point of view with examples.
3. What is relationship between *young* and *old* in terms of synonymy? Give reasons for your judgment.
4. Do you think that in the relationship of hyponymy, we must have both the superordinate and the hyponym at the same time?
5. How to get the meaning of the sentence *The artist painted a beautiful picture* by integrating the syntactic and semantic rules?
6. What is the compositionality principle? Are there any problems with this theory?
7. Do you agree with the famous quote from *Xunzi* in the following?

   名无固宜,约之以命,约定俗成谓之宜,异于约则谓之不宜;名无固实,约之以命实,约定俗成谓之实名。(*It is not proper or improper to give names to the things in the world. People just acknowledge the names by convention. If the names conform to convention,* they are proper. If not, they are improper. Names do not have the natural referents in the practical world. People just recognize the referents of the names by agreement and public consent. If the things referred to by the names conform to convention, they are proper. If not, they are improper.)

8. How do you understand the sentence *My brother Johnny is a fish* in terms of semantic components analysis? How does the sentence add the property of a fish to *my brother*?
9. How do you understand the following dialogue? Is that an acceptable dialogue?
   — *This drink is better than nothing.*
   — *You are right. Nothing is worse than the drink.*

参考答案

I.

1. F. Semantics is the study of the meaning of linguistic units, words and sentences in particular. Phonemes neither have meanings nor are in the field of semantic study.
2. F. Conceptual meaning is denotative in that it is concerned with the relationship between a word and the thing it denotes, or refers to.
3. F. In the field of philosophy, connotative meaning is used to mean the properties of the entity a word denotes.
4. F. The explanation in the statement above is only one way of showing what a desk is. In other situations, we still have other ways of showing the meaning of a desk.
5. T
6. F. The distinction between sense and reference is comparable to that between connotation and denotation.
7. F. Total synonymy is rare. The so-called synonyms are all context dependent.
8. T 9. T
10. F. If a pair of words is in relationship of converse antonymy, the members of this pair do not constitute a positive-negative opposition. They show the reversal of a relationship between two entities.
11. T
12. F. *Young* and *old* are gradable antonyms but *younger* and *older* are not gradable antonyms, because they involve a relation between two entities.
13. T 14. T
15. F. The smallest units in semantics are semantic features, which make up word meanings.
16. F. Sentence using the same words may mean quite differently if they are arranged in different orders. The meaning of a sentence depends on the meanings of the constituent words and the way they are combined.
17. F. *The green ideas sleep furiously* is a false sentence because the words in it do not confine to the projection rules.
18. F. &, ∨ and → are known as two-place connectives, but ~ is a one-place connective.
19. T 20. T 21. T
22. F. The right inference should be
    Because ~∃x(S(x)&~C(x))
    And because S(x)
    So, C(x)

23. F. The predicate in logic semantics is not necessarily a verb. For example, in sentence Mary is a student. "a student" is the predicate.
24. T 25. T 26. T 27. T
28. F. The meaning of a sentence is not the total sum of meanings of all its components. For example, *The dog bit the man* and *The man bit the dog* consist of exactly the same words, yet are different widely in meaning.
29. T
30. F. In the teaching of the word meaning, teachers would not only teach the connotative meaning but they would often give a concrete referent of the word to better illustrate the meaning of the word.
31. T 32. T
33. F. Besides the word meaning, the dictionary also offers the grammatical information of a certain word.
34. F. Compositionality analysis mainly focuses on the connotative meaning proposed by Leech.
35. T 36. T 37. T
38. F. Semantic components aim at showing the semantic features of the words.

II.
1. semantics   2. collocative   3. associative
4. sameness relation; oppositeness relation; inclusiveness relation
5. gradable antonymy; complementary antonymy; converse antonymy
6. gradable   7. converse   8. semantic features/ semantic components
9. synonyms   10. hyponyms   11. meta-language
12. the dictionary; the projection rules   13. syntax, semantics
14. an argument; a predicate   15. tomorrow; Sunday; one
16. denotation; connotation   17. thematic
18. compound, complex
19. logical semantics, compositionality analysis/principle
20. -ist, -er

III.
1. C 2. B 3. B 4. C 5. B 6. C 7. C 8. D 9. C 10. B
11. C 12. A 13. A 14. A 15. D 16. D 17. B 18. B 19. D 20. A
21. C 22. D 23. A 24. B 25. A

IV.
1. affective meaning   2. thematic meaning   3. conceptual meaning
4. reflected meaning   5. social meaning   6. connotative meaning
7. social meaning   8. connotative and collocative meaning

V.
1. gradable antonymy   2. synonymy   3. hyponymy
4. co-hyponyms   5. converse antonymy   6. converse antonymy
7. complementary antonymy 8. complementary antonymy 9. gradable antonymy
10. converse antonymy

VI.
1. Sentence a entails sentence b. The sense relation between sentence a and sentence b is entailment.

Sentence a and sentence b are in such a relationship that the truth of the second sentence necessarily follows from the truth of the first sentence, while the falsity of the first follows from the falsity of the second.

In terms of semantic components, we can say it is because sentence a contains words which have all the semantic components of a word used in sentence b.

2. In the compositionality analysis, the basic idea is that a semantic theory consists of two parts: a dictionary and a set of projection rules. The dictionary provides the grammatical classification and semantic information of words.

The marker {Adj} right after *colorful* presents the grammatical classification of it. That is, the word *colorful* is an adjective. a and b are two semantic meanings of the same word *colorful*. The information in ( ) has to do with the more systematic part, and is called semantic markers. The information in [ ] is more idiosyncratic, word specific, and is called distinguishers.

The information in < > is the selection restrictions of the word *colorful*. It serves as the projection rules. That is the word *colorful* can only be followed by the kind of information in the < > in each explanation.

By presenting the grammatical marker, semantic markers, distinguishers and selection restrictions, we get a full understanding and the usage of the word *colorful*.

3. Semantics studies the meaning of language. It has a lot of related subjects that study the meaning of language from different perspectives. For example, component analysis studies the word meaning by its semantic features. Compositionality principle studies the sentence meaning by the dictionary meaning and the projection rules. The first two subjects and many other semantic related subjects focus more on the meaning apart from the physical context of language. Yet pragmatics focuses more on the language meaning in its usage in the physical context.

So in a narrow sense, pragmatics and semantics study language meaning from different perspectives. In a broad sense, pragmatics belongs to semantics, because no matter what perspective the pragmatics has, it is a subject concerning the meaning of language.

4. Literally in terms of proposition, the two sentences have the same meaning as *Tim was drunk, and he lost his way*. Yet these two sentences vary in the thematic meaning, as they have different ways of organizing words in the sentences.

The second sentence puts the word *drunk* at the very beginning of the sentence. It stresses the cause for *Tim losing his way*—he was drunk.

VII.

1. (1) father   (2) CHILD(x, y) & ∼MALE(x)   (3) boy
   (4) BECOME(x, (∼ALIVE(x)))   (5) HAVE(x, y)

2.

p	q	p & q	p ∨ q	p → q	p ≡ q
T	T	T	(T)	T	(T)
T	F	(F)	T	(F)	F
F	T	F	(T)	T	(F)
F	F	F	F	T	T

3. (1) ∀x(S(x)→C(x))

For all x, it is the case that, if x is a student, then x is clever.
(2) ∃x(S(x) & C(x))
There are some x's that are both students and clever.
(3) ∀x (S(x)→C(x))
S(j)
So, C(j)
Because for all x, it is the case that if x is a student, then x is clever, and because John is one student, John is also clever.

4. (1) Not all the teachers like John.
(2) All the teachers like all the students.
(3) Kathy gives Maxine a book.
(4) There is not any teacher that likes John.
(5) Some teachers like all the students.

VIII.

1. E 2. P 3. P 4. E

E 和 P 的问题是《语言学教程》中提到的。Saeed 的 *Semantics*（2000）里面有两者的区别：

1. 否定蕴含句，蕴含便不复存在。否定预设句,预设仍然存在。
2. A entails B: we all know that if A then automatically B.
    E.g. The anarchist assassinated the emperor.
        The emperor is dead.
    A presupposes B: B is part of the assumed background against which A is said.
    E.g. The Mayor of Manchester is a woman.
        There is a Mayor of Manchester.
3. Truth value
    Entailment:
    1) if p is true, then q is true.
    2) if q is false, then q is false
    3) if p is false, q is true or false
    4) if q is false, p is true or false.
    Presupposition
    1) if p is true, q is true
    2) if p is false, q is still true
    3) if q is true, then we can not judge weather p is true or false.

IX.

$time^1$ refers to the ripe time of the banana.
$time^2$ refers to the banana's time of being very important because it met my need.
$time^3$ refers to the moment the green banana appeared on the earth.
$time^4$ refers to the moment of my noticing the importance of the green banana.
$time^5$ refers to a period of time.

X.

1. The theory of meaning which relates the meaning of a word to the thing it refers to, or stands for, is known as referential theory. It is generally possible to explain the meaning of a word by pointing to the thing it refers to.

However there are problems with this theory. (1) When we define one term by referring to some particular substance in the world, we are just using the particular substance as an example, an instance, of something more general. That is, there is something abstract (concept) behind the concrete thing we can see with our eyes. (2) There are some words that do not have references. Grammatical words like *but*, *if*, *and* do not refer to anything. And words like *God*, *ghost* and *dragon* refer to imagery things which do not exist in reality. (3) It is not convenient to explain the meaning of a word in terms of the thing it refers to. The thing a word stands for may not always be at hand at the time of speaking. Even when it is nearby, it may take the listener some time to work out its main features.

2. Total synonymy is rare. The so-called synonyms are all context dependent. They all differ from one way to another.

   They may differ in style. In the context *Little Tom __ a toy bear*. *buy* is more appropriate than *purchase*. They may also differ in connotations. That is why people jokingly say *I'm thrifty, you are economical, and he is stingy*. Thirdly, there are dialectal differences. *Autumn* is British while *fall* is American.

3. The relationship between *young* and *old* is gradable antonymy. There are three reasons for the statement above. (1) The words *young* and *old* differ in terms of degree. Between *young* and *old* there are several intermediate degrees. (2) There is no absolute criterion by which we may say someone is young or old. A man of 40 may be young in one person's eye, yet he may be pretty old in another person's eye. (3) In this pair of *young* and *old*, the term for the higher degree old serves as a cover term.

4. In the relation of hyponymy, both the superordinate and the hyponym may be missing sometimes. In English there is no superordinate for the color terms *red*, *green*, *black*, etc. Hyponyms may also be missing. In contrast to Chinese, there is only one word in English for different kinds of uncles：伯伯，叔叔，姑父…

5. We can present the syntactic description by a tree diagram.

   To get the meaning of each word in the sentence we need to refer to the dictionary by examining the grammatical classifications, semantic markers and distinguishers.

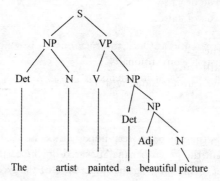

To get the meaning of the whole sentence, we need to combine the meanings of the words according to the projection rules. We use selection restrictions to select the appropriate meanings of the words in one group (e.g. in one NP or one VP). Then we combine the meanings of the words that are comparatively near to each other from the

lower level of the diagram to the higher level. That is, we will first combine the meanings of *beautiful* and *picture*, then those of *the* and *beautiful picture*, then those of *painted* and *the beautiful picture*, and so on. This effectively provides a solution to the integration of syntax and semantics.
6. The compositionality principle is a theory about the obtaining of the sentential meaning. In this theory, the meaning of a sentence depends on the meanings of the constituent words and the way they are combined.

    The basic idea is that a semantic theory consists of two parts: a dictionary and a set of projection rules.

    The dictionary provides the grammatical classification and semantic information of words. The grammatical classification provides detailed information of the parts of speech. The semantic information is further divided into two sub-types: the information which has to do with the more systematic part, or is of a more general nature, is shown by semantic features in round brackets ( ). The information which is more idiosyncratic, word specific is shown by distinguishers in square brackets [ ].

    The projection rules are responsible for combining the meanings of words together. According to the selection restrictions, we select and combine the appropriate meanings of words in one group (e.g. in one NP or VP), from the lowest level to the highest level of a sentence in the tree diagram.

    However, there are problems in this theory. First, the distinction between semantic marker and distinguisher is not very clear. Secondly, there are cases in which the collocation of words can not be accounted for by grammatical markers, semantic markers or selection restrictions. Thirdly, there is trouble in pinning down the meanings in the semantic markers as a meta-language. We can never successfully explain what exactly a meta-language is by itself.
7. This quote is Xun Zi's understanding of the relationship between the word name and the thing it refers to. From this quote, we can find the thought of language arbitrariness and conventionality in *Xun Zi*. I quite agree to his idea.
    (1) Arbitrariness. Xun Zi claims that there is no relationship between a name and its referent. The relationship between the word itself and its referent is only established randomly.
    (2) Conventionality. The correspondence between a word and the substance it refers to is maintained by convention. Once the relationship is coined arbitrarily, it would pass on through history conventionally.
8. The word *fish* has the semantic components of [+ animate] [+ good at swimming]. Johnny is my brother, so he can not be a fish in a real sense. The sentence just adds the semantic component [+ good at swimming] of the word *fish* to Johnny. So from the sentence we could say that Johnny is good at swimming.

    This sentence is a metaphor. By employing metaphor, people can add the semantic components to other words that do not have the added semantic components originally. Of course that process needs the participation of human cognition.
9. In this dialogue, the first speaker wants to say that this drink is passable. At least they have a drink now instead of nothing. On the surface the second speaker seems to agree with the first speaker by saying *You are right*. and by employing an explanatory sentence *nothing is worse than* … .

    Usually in everyday logic *A is better than B* implies *B is worse than A*. But here we have a rare case. *Nothing is worse than* ... means *this is the worst*. So in a deep sense the second speaker doesn't agree with the first speaker at all.

The second part of the dialogue is self-contradictory. In the first sentence, there is agreement which denotes that the drink is OK. Yet the second sentence just expresses the meaning of the drink is the worst.

Although the second part of the dialogue is self-contradictory, we listeners could all accept the sentence as being meaningful. By agreeing on the surface and disagreeing in the depth, the second speaker expresses his feelings humorously and in a stronger way than just saying the disagreement directly.

The understanding of the meaning of the dialogue has gone through the process of *the dialogue is logical* to the *dialogue is illogical* and then back to the state of *the dialogue is logical* in the end.

Chapter 6 Language and Cognition

Concepts & Theories

I. What Is Cognition?
1. **The definition of cognition**
   Cognition is a mental process, information processing/mental process or faculty of knowing, including awareness, perception, reasoning, and judgment.
2. **Three approaches to cognition**
   (1) The formal approach: the study of structural patterns, including the study of morphological, syntactic, and lexical structure.
   (2) The psychological approach: the study of language from the view of relatively general cognitive systems ranging from perception, memory and attention to reasoning.
   (3) The conceptual approach: the study of how language structures (processes & patterns) conceptual content.

II. What Is Psycholinguistics?
1. **The definition of psycholinguistics**
   Psycholinguistics is the study of psychological aspects of language; it usually studies the psychological states and mental activity associated with the use of language.
2. **Six subjects of research within psycholinguistics**
   (1) Language acquisition (L1/L2)
   (2) Language comprehension
   (3) Language production
   (4) Language disorders
   (5) Language and thought
   (6) Neurocognition
3. **Three subjects to be focused on**
   (1) Language acquisition
      Four stages of language acquisition:
      ☆ Holophrastic stage: Shortly after their first birthday, babies begin to understand words, and around that birthday, they start to produce them. Words are usually produced in isolation; this one-word stage can last from two months to a year. Children's first words are similar all over the planet. About half the words are for objects, actions, motions, and routines.
      ☆ Two-word stage: Around 18 months, language changes in two ways. Vocabulary growth increases; the child begins to learn words at a rate of one every two waking hours, and will keep learning that rate or faster through adolescence.
      ☆ Stage of three-word utterances: Children's two- and three-word utterances

look like samples drawn from longer potential sentences expressing a complete and more complicated idea.

☆ Fluent grammatical conversation stage: Normal children can differ by a year or more in their rate of language development, though the stages they pass through are generally the same regardless of how stretched out or compressed and many children speak in complex sentences before they turn two.

— During the grammar explosion, children's sentences are getting not only longer but also more complex, and, they can embed one constituent inside another.

— By the 3, children can use function words more often than they omit them in more than 90% of the sentences that require them.

— Though many of the 3-year-old's sentences are ungrammatical for one reason or another, it is because there are many things that can go wrong in any single sentence. Children rarely scramble word orders and, by the age of three, come to supply most inflections and function words in sentences that require them.

— Children do not seem to favor any particular kind of language. They swiftly acquire free word order, SOV and VSO orders, rich systems of case and agreement, strings of agglutinated suffixes, ergative case marking, and whatever else their language throws at them.

— Children acquiring language acquire gender marking quickly, make few errors. It is safe to say that except for constructions that are rare, predominantly used in written language, or mentally taxing even to an adult, all parts of all languages are acquired before the child turns four.

(2) Language comprehension

The core processes of language comprehension include:

☆ Word recognition

Word lays in the central position in language comprehension because of its extremely important role in transmitting the meaning. Word recognition can be viewed in terms of recognition of spoken words and printed words.

— The perception of spoken words: Speech is distributed in time, a fleeting signal that has few reliable cues to the boundaries between sound segments and words. Features of speech could cause difficulty for listeners. Listeners attempt to map the acoustic signal onto a representation in the mental lexicon almost as the signal starts to arrive. Scholars have put forward some models related to word recognition:

(i) Cohort model: Marslen-Wilson & Welsh (1978) believed that the first few phonemes of a spoken word activate a set or cohort of word candidates that are consistent with the input. These candidates compete with one another for activation. As more acoustic input is analyzed, candidates that are no longer consistent with the input drop out of the set. This process continues until only one word candidate matches the input, the best fitting word may be chosen if no single candidate is a clear winner.

(ii) Interactive model: Interactive model holds that higher processing levels have a direct, *top-down* influence on lower levels. Lexical knowledge can affect the perception of phonemes. There is interactivity in the form of lexical effects

Chapter 6
Language and Cognition

on the perception of sub-lexical units. In certain cases, listeners' knowledge of words can lead to the inhibition of certain phonemes; in other cases, listeners continue to "hear" phonemes that have been removed from the speech signal and replaced by noise.

(iii) Race model: Race model does not agree *top-down* effects, it has two routes that race each other—a pre-lexical route, which computes phonological information from the acoustic signal, and a lexical route, in which the phonological information associated with a word becomes available when the word itself is accessed. When word-level information appears to affect a lower-level process, it is assumed that the lexical route won the race.

—The perception of printed words: Print serves as a map of linguistic structure, readers use the clues to morphological structure that are embedded in orthography in reading the printed words. Phonology and other aspects of linguistic structure are retrieved in reading. In printed word recognition, there are two major questions:

a. The question about how linguistic structure is derived from print: One idea is that two different processes are available for converting orthographic representations to phonological representations. A lexical route is used to look up the phonological forms of known words in the mental lexicon. A non-lexical route accounts for the productivity of reading, that is, it generates pronunciations for novel letter strings as well as for regular words on the basis of smaller units.

b. The question about orthography-to-phonology translation: English, which has been the subject of much of the research on word recognition, has a rather irregular writing system. Readers of English often use letter groups that correspond to the syllable *rime* in spelling-to-sound translation.

☆ Comprehension of sentences

Psycholinguists have addressed the phenomena of sentence comprehension in different ways:

—Serial models: Serial models propose that the sentence comprehension system continually and sequentially follows constraints of a language's grammar with remarkable speed, and describe how the processor quickly constructs one or more representations of a sentence based on a restricted range of information that is guaranteed to be relevant to its interpretation, primarily grammatical information. Any such representation is then quickly interpreted and evaluated, using the full range of information that might be relevant.

—Parallel models: Parallel models emphasize that the comprehension system is sensitive to a vast range of information, including grammatical, lexical, and contextual, as well as knowledge of the speaker/writer and of the world in general. Parallel models describe how the processor uses all relevant information to quickly evaluate the full range of possible interpretations of a sentence.

—It is generally acknowledged that listeners and readers integrate grammatical and situational knowledge in understanding a sentence.

(i) Structural factors in comprehension: Comprehension of written and spoken language can be difficult because it is not always easy to identify the constituents (phrases) of a sentence and the ways in which they relate to one another. Psycholinguists have proposed principles interpreting sentence comprehension with respect to the grammatical constraints.

(ii) Lexical factors in comprehension: The human sentence processor is primarily guided by information about specific words that is stored in the lexicon.

☆ Comprehension of text

—Sentences come in texts and discourses, and the entire text or discourse is relevant to the messages conveyed. Text is the net of propositions that make up the semantic interpretations of individual sentences.

—Readers abstract the main threads of a discourse and infer missing connections, constrained by limitations of short-term memory and guided by how arguments overlap across propositions and by linguistic cues signaled by the text.

—Resonance model holds that information in long-term memory is automatically activated by the presence of material that apparently bears a rough semantic relation to it. Semantic details, including factors such as negation that drastically change the truth of propositions, do not seem to affect the resonance process. It emphasized a more active and intelligent search for meaning as the basis by which a reader discovers the conceptual structure of a discourse. A resonance process serves as a first stage in processing a text, and, reading objectives and details of text structure determine whether a reader goes further and searches for a coherent structure for the text.

(3) Language production

Three questions to be focused on:

—How do people produce single words?

—How do people generate longer utterances?

—How do the representations and processes involved in writing differ from those involved in speaking?

☆ Access to words: Words are planned in several processing steps. Each step generates a specific type of representation, and information is transmitted between representations via the spreading of activation. The three major steps include:

—Conceptualization is deciding what notion to express.

—Word selection corresponds to the chosen concept. The speaker first selects a syntactic word unit which specifies the syntactic class of the word and additional syntactic information. Selecting a syntactic word unit is a competitive process. A unit is selected as soon as its activation level exceeds the summed activation of all competitors. A checking mechanism ascertains that the selected unit indeed maps onto the intended concept.

—Morpho-phonological encoding begins with the retrieval of the morphemes corresponding to the selected words. Sometimes morphologically related items have different effects on the production of target words than do semantically or phonologically related items.

☆ Generation of sentences

Two major steps of sentence generation:

—Conceptual preparation. It is deciding what to say. To make a complicated theoretical argument or to describe a series of events, the speaker needs a global plan.

—Word retrieval. Because sentences are not simply sets of words but have syntactic structure, speakers must apply syntactic knowledge to generate sentences.

Two distinct sets of processes involved in generating syntactic structure.

—Functional planning processes: It is assigning grammatical functions, such as subject, verb, or direct object. These processes rely primarily on information from the message level and the syntactic properties of the retrieved lexicon-grammar units.

—Positional encoding: It uses the retrieved lexicon-grammar units and the functions they have been assigned to generate syntactic structures that capture the dependencies among constituents and their order.

☆ Written language production

—The steps in the production of written language are similar to those in the production of spoken language.

—A major difference is that, once a syntactic lexicon unit and its morphological representation have been accessed, it is the orthographic form instead of phonological form that must be retrieved and produced.

—Phonology plays an important role in this kind of process.

—Writing differs from speaking in that writers have more time available for conceptual preparation and planning. Monitoring and revising typically play a greater role in writing than in speaking.

III. What Is Cognitive Linguistics?

1. The definition of cognitive linguistics

Cognitive linguistics is the scientific study of the relation between the way we communicate and the way we think. It is an approach to language that is based on our experiences of the world and the way we perceive and conceptualize it.

2. Construal and construal operations

Construal refers to the ability to conceive and portray the same situation in different ways

(1) Attention/Salience

We activate the most relevant concepts more than concepts that are irrelevant to what we are thinking about.

(2) Judgment/Comparison

☆ The construal operations of judgment/comparison have to do with judging something by comparing it to something else.

☆ The figure-ground alignment seems to apply to space with the ground as the prepositional object and the preposition expressing the spatial relational configuration. It also applies to our perception of moving objects.

—Since the moving object is typically the most prominent one, because it is moving, it is typically the figure, while the remaining stimuli constitute the ground.

—In order to distinguish static and dynamic figure/ground relations, Langacker (1987) uses the term TRAJECTOR for a moving figure and LANDMARK for

the ground of a moving figure.
  (3) Perspective/Situatedness
    ☆ Perspective generally depends on two things.
      —It depends on where we are situated in relation to the scene we're viewing.
      —It depends on how the scene is arranged in relation to our situatedness.
    ☆ DEIXIS involves linguistic forms that point at something from the speech situation. In cognitive terms, deixis is the use of elements of subject's situatedness to designate something in the scene. There are many other types of deixis:
      —Person deixis: construes the relations between the participants in the speech situation;
      —Social deixis: construes social relations between participants in the discourses;
      —Textual/discursive deixis: construes the relation to previous mention in discourse.
3. Categorization
  (1) The definition of categorization: CATEGORIZATION is the process of classifying our experiences into different categories based on commonalities and differences. Categorization is a major ingredient in the creation of human knowledge, and it allows us to relate present experiences to past ones.
  (2) Three levels in categories:
    ☆ The basic level
      The categories at the BASIC LEVEL are those that are most culturally salient and are required to fulfill our cognitive needs the best. This is the level where we perceive the most differences between *objects* in the world.
    ☆ The superordinate level
      SUPERORDINATE categories are the most general ones. The members of a superordinate category do not have enough features in common to conjure up a common gestalt at this level.
    ☆ The subordinate level
      Often the names for SUBORDINATE LEVEL categories are morphologically complex. They are typically composite forms.
4. Image schemas
  (1) The definition of image schemas: An image-schema is a *skeletal* mental representation of a recurrent pattern of embodied (especially spatial or kinesthetic) experience. They are highly schematic representations of perceptually grounded experience. They emerge from our embodied interactions with the world.
  (2) Different types of image schemas:
    ☆ A center-periphery schema
      — It involves a physical or metaphorical core and edge, and degrees of distance from the core.
    ☆ A containment schema
      — It is an image schema that involves a physical or metaphorical boundary, enclosed area or volume, or excluded area or volume.
      — A containment schema has additional optional properties, such as transitivity of enclosure, objects inside or outside the boundary, protection of an enclosed

object, the restriction of forces inside the enclosure, and the relatively fixed position of an enclosed object.
☆ A cycle schema
— It involves repetitious events and event series. Its structure includes the following: a starting point, a progression through successive events without backtracking, a return to the initial state.
— The schema often has superimposed on it a structure that builds toward a climax and then goes through a decline.
☆ A force schema
— It involves physical or metaphorical causal interaction.
— It includes the following elements: a source and target of the force, a direction and intensity of the force, a path of motion of the source and target, a sequence of causation.
— Some kinds of force schemas are: an attraction schema, a balance schema, a blockage schema, a compulsion schema, a counterforce schema, a diversion schema, an enablement schema, a restraint removal schema.
☆ A link schema
— It consists of two or more entities, connected physically or metaphorically, and the bond between them.
☆ A part-whole schema
— It involves physical or metaphorical wholes along with their parts and a configuration of the parts.
☆ A path schema
— It involves physical or metaphorical movement from place to place, and consists of a starting point, a goal, and a series of intermediate points. This can be exemplified by paths and trajectories.
☆ A scale schema
— It involves an increase or decrease of physical or metaphorical amount, and consists of any of the following: a closed-end or open-ended progression of amount, a position in the progression of amount, one or more norms of amount, a calibration of amount.
☆ A verticality schema
— It involves *up* and *down* relations.

5. Metaphor

Lakoff and Johonson (1980) classify conceptual metaphors into three categories: ontological metaphors, structural metaphors and orientational metaphors.
(1) Ontological metaphors
☆ ONTOLOGICAL METAPHOR means that human experiences with physical objects provide the basis for ways of viewing events, activities, emotions, ideas, etc., as entities and substances. Ontological metaphors can serve various purposes.
☆ By ontological metaphors we give bounded surfaces to less clearly discrete entities (mountains, hedges, street corners) and categorize events, actions and states as substances. Take the experience of rising prices as an example, which can be metaphorically viewed as an entity via the noun inflation.
(2) Structural metaphors

☆ STRUCTURAL METAPHOR plays the most important role because it allows us to go beyond orientation and referring and gives us the possibility to structure one concept according to another. This means that structural metaphors are grounded in our experience.

☆ Structural metaphors imply how one concept is metaphorically structured in terms of another.

(3) Orientational metaphors

☆ ORIENTATIONAL METAPHOR gives a concept a spatial orientation. They are characterized not so much by structuring one concept in terms of another, but by a co-occurrence in our experience.

☆ The orientational metaphors are grounded in an experiential basis, which link together the two parts of the metaphor.

☆ Orientational metaphors are based on human physical and cultural experience. For example, in some cultures the future is in front of us, whereas in others it is in back of us.

6. Metonymy

Radden & Kovecses (1999:30-43) propose two general conceptual configurations: whole ICM and its part(s); parts of an ICM.

7. Blending theory

(1) BLENDING theory is also known as the INTERGRATION theory, proposed by Gilles Fauconnier & Mark Turner (1994, 1995). It is a cognitive operation whereby elements of two or more *mental spaces* are integrated via projection into a new, blended space which has its unique structure.

(2) Blending operates on two input mental spaces to produce a third space, the blend. The blend inherits partial structure from the input spaces and has emergent structure of its own.

(3) There are some conditions needed when two input spaces $I1$ and $I2$ are blended.

☆ Cross-Space Mapping: There is a partial mapping of counterparts between the input spaces $I1$ and $I2$.

☆ Generic Space: It reflects some common, usually more abstract, structure and organization shared by the inputs.

☆ Blend: The inputs $I1$ and $I2$ are partially projected onto a fourth space, the blend.

☆ Emergent Structure: the blend has emergent structure not provided by the inputs. This happens in three interrelated ways:
—Composition
—Completion
—Elaboration

Related Terms

anticipation error

An anticipation error occurs when a word is spoken earlier in the sentence than it should be.

basic level

Basic level is the level where we perceive the most differences between *objects* in the

world.
behaviorist learning theory

Behaviorist learning theory is a theory of psychology which, when applied to first language acquisition, suggests that the learner's verbal behavior is conditioned or reinforced through association between stimulus and response.

bottom-up processing

Bottom-up processing is a process in which lower-level processes are carried out influence from higher-level processes. For example, perception of phonemes being uninfluenced by the words in which they appear.

brain lateralization

Brain lateralization refers to the localization of cognitive and perceptual function in a particular hemisphere of the brain. For example, the right hemisphere processes stimuli more holistically and the left hemisphere more analytically. In most people, the left hemisphere has primary responsibility for language, while the right hemisphere controls visual and spatial skills.

categorization

Categorization is the process of classifying our experiences into different categories based on commonalities and differences. Categorization is a major ingredient in the creation of human knowledge, and it allows us to relate present experiences to past ones. There are three levels in categories: the basic level, the superordinate level, and the subordinate level.

center-periphery schema

Center-periphery schema involves a physical or metaphorical core and edge, and degrees of distance from the core. For example: the structure of an apple, an individual's perceptual sphere, an individual's social sphere, with family and friends at the core and others at the outside.

cognition

Cognition is used in several different loosely related ways. In psychology it is used to refer to the mental processes of an individual, with particular relation to a view that argues that the mind has internal mental states (such as beliefs, desires and intentions) and can be understood in terms of information processing, especially when a lot of abstraction or concretization is involved, or processes such as involving knowledge, expertise or learning for example are at work. Another definition of *cognition* is the mental process or faculty of knowing, including aspects such as awareness, perception, reasoning, and judgment.

cognitive linguistics

Cognitive linguistics is a newly established approach to the study of language that emerged in the 1970s as a reaction against the dominant generative paradigm which pursues an autonomous view of language. Cognitive linguistics is based on human experiences of the world and the way they perceive and conceptualize the world.

cognitive psycholinguistics

Cognitive psycholinguistics is an interdisciplinary direction of research developed at the end of the 1950s in the United States that is concerned with the investigation of mental processes in the acquisition and use of knowledge and language.

cohort theory

Cohort theory hypothesizes that auditory word recognition begins with the formation of a group of words at the perception of the initial sound and proceeds sound by sound with the cohort of words decreasing as more sounds are perceived.

construal operations

Construal operations are conceptualizing processes used in language process by human beings. That is, construal operations are the underlying psychological processes and resources employed in the interpretation of linguistic expressions.

containment schema

Containment schema is an image schema that involves a physical or metaphorical boundary, enclosed area or volume, or excluded area or volume. A containment schema has additional optional properties, such as transitivity of enclosure, objects inside or outside the boundary, protection of an enclosed object, the restriction of forces inside the enclosure, and the relatively fixed position of an enclosed object.

context

As a comprehensive concept in communication theory, context refers to all elements of a communicative situation: the verbal and non-verbal context, the context of the given speech situation and the social context of the relationship between the speaker and hearer, their knowledge, and their attitudes. Catford distinguishes between linguistic context and situational co-text.

critical period

Critical period is an early period of one's life extending to the age of puberty, during which the human brain is most ready to acquire language naturally and effortlessly, a period that coincides with the period of brain lateralization for language function.

cycle schema

Cycle schema involves repetitious events and event series. Its structure includes the following: a starting point, a progression through successive events without backtracking, a return to the initial state. The schema often has superimposed on it a structure that builds toward a climax and then goes through a decline. Examples of cycle schemas are days, weeks, years, sleeping and waking, breathing, circulation, emotional buildup and release.

deixis

Deixis involves linguistic forms that point at something from the speech situation. In cognitive terms, deixis is the use of elements of subject's situatedness to designate something in the scene.

exchange error

Exchange error is a type of error in which two items within a sentence are swapped.

experimental psycholinguistics

As one field of psycholinguistics, experimental psycholinguistics involves the investigation through experiments of the psychological mechanisms for the productions and understanding of speech.

force schema

Force schema involves physical or metaphorical causal interaction. It includes the following elements: a source and target of the force, a direction and intensity of the force, a path of motion of the source and target, a sequence of causation. Here are some kinds of force schemas: an attraction schema, a balance schema, a blockage schema, a compulsion schema, a counterforce schema, a diversion schema, an enablement schema, a restraint removal schema.

frequency effect

Frequency effect describes the additional ease with which a word is accessed due to its

Chapter 6
Language and Cognition

more frequent usage in the language.

garden path sentence

Garden path sentence is a sentence whose beginning suggests that it has a construction which by the end it clearly does not have. The stock example is *The horse raced past the barn fell*: *raced* will be taken at first to be the past sense, but the whole makes sense (cf. *The horse rode past the barn*), only if it is a participle. (cf. *The horse ridden past the barn fell*).

general context effects

General context effects occur when our general knowledge about the world influences language comprehension.

generic metaphor

Generic metaphor occupies a high level on a scale of generality on which conceptual metaphor can be placed. It is composed of generic-level source and target domains. Generic-level metaphors are instantiated, or realized by specific-level ones. Thus, the metaphor EMOTION ARE FORCES is instantiated, or realized, by the specific-level metaphor ANGER IS A HOT IN A CONTAINER.

image schemas

Mark Johnson (1987) defines an image schema as a recurring, dynamic pattern of our perceptual interactions and motor programs that gives coherence and structure to our experience.

image-schema metaphor

Image-schema metaphor is based on image-schemas, such as the path-schema, the force-schema, the contact-schema, etc. In such metaphor, the source domain does not map rich knowledge onto the target domain.

immediacy assumption

The reader is supposed to carry out the processes required to understand each word and its relationship to previous words in the sentence as soon as that word is encountered; this is known as the immediacy assumption.

knowledge-telling strategy

Knowledge-telling strategy means writing down everything they can think of that is relevant to a topic without organizing the information in any way.

knowledge-transforming strategy

Knowledge-transforming strategy involves focusing on potential problems within the planning process.

language production

Language production refers to the processes involved in producing language, predominantly used in connection with the production of spoken language. These processes include planning the utterance with regard to what to say, retrieving the words and integrating them into a sentence, articulating the sentence and monitoring the output. Evidence for such processes comes from hesitation phenomena, pauses, speech errors, anakoluthons, and furthermore self-repair.

link schema

Link schemas consists of two or more entities, connected physically or metaphorically, and the bond between them. Here are some examples of link schemas: a child holding her mother's hand, someone plugging a lamp into the wall, a causal *connection*, kinship *ties*.

macroproposition

Macropropositions are general propositions used to form an overall macrostructure of the story.

macrostructure

Macrostructure is a term from text linguistics (van Dijk) for the global semantic and pragmatic structure of a text. The macrostructure of a text, which includes phonological, graphological, and lexicogrammatical patterning, refers to the largest scale patterns, which are the means where texts can be classified into different text types, such as narrative, exposition, lyric poem, and so on.

mapping

Conceptual metaphors are characterized by a set of conceptual correspondences between elements of the source and target domains. These correspondences are called mappings.

mental lexicon

Mental lexicon is the information about the properties of words, retrievable when understanding language. For example, we may use morphological rules to decompose a complex word like rewritable the first few times we encounter it and after several exposures we may store and access it as a unit or word. It means that frequency of exposure determines our ability to recall stored instances.

mental space

Mental space is a conceptual packet that gets built up on-line in the process of understanding sentences or other nonlinguistic messages. Mental spaces are not the same as conceptual domains. Mental spaces are created in particular situations for the purpose of understanding and thus are smaller and more specific than conceptual domains.

metaphor

Metaphor involves the comparison of two concepts in that one is construed in terms of the other.

minimal attachment theory

Minimal attachment theory is a principle in psychological theories of speech processing, by which, in parsing a sentence, successive words are construed in ways which lead to minimal additions to already established levels of phrase structure.

modularity

Modularity is a principle in psychological theories of speech processing, by which, in parsing a sentence, successive words are construed in ways which lead to minimal additions to already established levels of phrase structure. An explanation, it has been claimed, for the phenomenon of garden path sentences.

morpheme-exchange errors

Morpheme-exchange errors are a type of error that roots or basic forms of two words are switched leaving the grammatical structure unchanged.

ontological metaphors

Ontological metaphors mean that human experiences with physical objects provide the basis for ways of viewing events, activities, emotions, ideas, etc., as entities and substances.

orientational metaphor

Orientational metaphor gives a concept a spatial orientation. Orientational metaphors are characterized not so much by structuring one concept in terms of another, but by a co-occurrence in our experience.

parallel models

Parallel models emphasize that the comprehension system is sensitive to a vast range of information, including grammatical, lexical, and contextual, as well as knowledge of the speaker/writer and of the world in general. Parallel models describe how the processor uses all relevant information to quickly evaluate the full range of possible interpretations of a sentence.

parsing

Parsing is a term that used to refer to description of the syntactic structure of sentences using elementary units such as morphemes, words, phrases and their mutual interrelationships. The goals and methods of parsing are dependent on the grammatical theory in question.

part-whole schema

Part-whole schema involves physical or metaphorical wholes along with their parts and a configuration of the parts. Examples are: the body and its parts, the family and the caste structure of India.

path schema

Path schema involves physical or metaphorical movement from place to place, and consists of a starting point, a goal, and a series of intermediate points. This can be exemplified by paths and trajectories.

perceptual span

Perceptual span is the range of letters from which useful information is extracted.

proposition

Proposition is a term adopted by semantics and speech act theory from philosophy and formal logic. By proposition one usually understands the language-independent common denominator of the meaning of sentences which express the factuality of a given state of affairs.

psycholinguistics

Psycholinguistics is the study of psychological aspects of language; it usually studies the psychological states and mental activity associated with the use of language. It is applied since the 1960s to two main fields: the empirical study of the development of language in children and the investigation through experiments of the psychological mechanisms for the production and understanding of speech.

right-ear advantage

Concerning dichotic listening tasks, in which auditory stimuli are used and the subject has to report what is perceived, the usual pattern of results obtained is one of faster, and more accurate, reports for the stimulus received via the right ear-often described as showing right-ear advantage (REA) for speech over non-speech sounds.

saccades

Saccades are a series of rapid eye movements known during reading process.

scale schema

Scale schema involves an increase or decrease of physical or metaphorical amount, and consists of any of the following: a closed-end or an open-ended progression of amount, a position in the progression of amount, one or more norms of amount, a calibration of amount. Here are some examples of scale schemas: physical amounts, properties in the number system.

schemata

Schemata are packets of stored knowledge.

semantic association network

Semantic association network refers to the frequently used form of knowledge representation that is a graph-like notation system. Originally developed to model association memory, semantic networks have evolved into general knowledge representation schemes. Semantic networks represent by using a hierarchy of concepts organized by a primitive relation such as *is a* or *part of*. Further two-place relations (roles) are defined by using these. The main task is developing semantic networks consisted in establishing the inventory of semantic relations between concepts. Simple semantic network is formally a restricted variant of predicate logic. Current developments in knowledge representation, such as KL-ONE, are based on semantic networks.

serial models

Serial models propose that the sentence comprehension system continually and sequentially follows the constraints of a language's grammar with remarkable speed. Serial models describe how the processor quickly constructs one or more representations of a sentence based on a restricted range of information that is guaranteed to be relevant to its interpretation, primarily grammatical information.

source domain

Source domain is the means that we use in order to describe the experience.

specific context effects

Specific context effects involve information obtained from earlier parts of a discourse.

specific-level metaphor

Specific-level metaphor occupies a low level on a scale of generality on which conceptual metaphor can be replaced. It is composed of specific-level source and target domains. Specific-level metaphors are instantiations, or special cases, of generic-level ones. Thus, the metaphor ANGER IS HOT FLUID IN A CONTAINER is an instantiation, or special case, of the generic-level metaphor EMOTIONS ARE FORCES.

spoonerism

Spoonerism or slip of the tongue refers to the phenomenon that the initial letter or letters of two words are transposed.

strategic knowledge

Strategic knowledge is knowledge of the methods used in constructing a writing plan in order to make it coherent and well-organized.

structural metaphor

Structural metaphor plays the most important role because it allows us to go beyond orientation and referring and gives us the possibility to structure one concept according to another. This means that structural metaphors are grounded in our experience. Structural metaphors imply how one concept is metaphorically structured in terms of another.

superordinate

Superordinate categories are the most general ones. The members of a superordinate category do not have enough features in common to conjure up a common gestalt at this level.

subordinate level

At subordinate level we perceive the differences between the members of the basic level categories. Often the names for subordinate level categories are morphologically complex. They are typically composite forms.

target domain

Target domain is the experience being described by the metaphor.

Chapter 6
Language and Cognition

verticality schema

Verticality schema involves "up" and "down" relations. Here are some examples of verticality schemas: standing upright, climbing stairs, viewing a flagpole, watching water rise in a tub. According to Johnson, some image schemas also represent spatial orientations and relations: UP-DOWN, FRONT-BACK, PART-WHOLE, CENTER-PERIPHERY, and so on.

Practice

I. Mark the choice that best completes the statement. (20%)

1. The formal approach of the study of language and cognition does NOT include the study of _____ structure.
   A. morphological   B. syntactic   C. lexical   D. semantic
2. _____ lays in the central position in language comprehension because of its extremely important role in transmitting the meaning.
   A. Morpheme   B. Word   C. Phrase   D. Sentence
3. Psycholinguists have proposed that the human sentence processor is primarily guided by information about specific words that is stored in the _____.
   A. lexicon   B. syntax   C. semantics   D. sound system
4. Readers abstract the main threads of a discourse and infer missing connections, constrained by limitations of short-term memory and guided by how _____ overlap across propositions and by linguistic cues signaled by the text.
   A. themes   B. arguments   C. subjects   D. objects
5. Which of the following is NOT one of the aspects of process of language production?
   A. Conceptualization and linearization.   B. Self-monitoring.
   C. Gesturing during speech.   D. Self-instructing.
6. _____ is the process of classifying our experiences into different categories based on commonalities and differences.
   A. Judgment   B. Comparison
   C. Categorization   D. Salience
7. _____ metaphor means that human experiences with physical objects provide the basis for ways of viewing events, activities, emotions, ideas, etc., as entities and substances.
   A. Structural   B. Orientational
   C. Ontological   D. Semiotic
8. A _____ schema is an image schema that involves a physical or metaphorical boundary, enclosed area or volume, or excluded area or volume.
   A. containment   B. center-periphery
   C. cycle   D. force
9. A _____ schema involves a physical or metaphorical core and edge, and degrees of distance from the core.
   A. containment   B. center-periphery
   C. cycle   D. force
10. A _____ schema consists of two or more entities, connected physically or metaphorically, and the bond between them.
    A. link   B. part-whole   C. path   D. scale

II. **Mark the following statements with "T" if they are true or "F" if they are false.** (15%)

1. The psychological approach basically addresses the structural patterns exhibited by the overt aspect of linguistic forms, largely abstracted away from or regarded as autonomous from any associated meaning.
2. The conceptual approach includes the study of morphological, syntactic, and lexical structure.
3. The conceptual approach is concerned with the patterns in which and the processes by which conceptual content is organized in language.
4. An important focus of psycholinguistics is the largely unconscious application of grammatical rules that enable people to produce and comprehend intelligible sentences.
5. In the 1960s and early 1970s numerous psychologists and linguists used the transformational-generative model proposed by Rene Dirven to discover how children come to know the grammatical processes that underlie the speech they hear and to investigate the processing and comprehension of language: spoken or written.
6. In 1989, the first conference on cognitive linguistics was organized in Duisburg, Germany, by Chomsky.
7. Charles Darwin, the founder of Evolution Theory, was one of the first keeping the dairy of his son's speech development.
8. The main linguistic accomplishments during the first year of life are control of the speech musculature and sensitivity to the phonetic distinctions used in the parents' language.
9. Shortly before their first birthday, babies begin to understand words, and around that birthday, they start to produce them.
10. Around 12 months, language changes in two ways. Vocabulary growth increases; the child begins to learn words at a rate of one every two waking hours, and will keep learning that rate or faster through adolescence.
11. Before they put words together, babies cannot comprehend a sentence.
12. Normal children can differ by a year or more in their rate of language development, though the stages they pass through are generally the same regardless of how stretched out or compressed and many children speak in complex sentences before they turn two.
13. In cognition, we can direct our attention towards parts of the perceived scenery. In perception, it has to do with the activation of conceptual structures. That is, we activate the most relevant concepts more than concepts that are irrelevant to what we're thinking about.
14. Construal operations are conceptualizing processes used in language process by human beings. That is, construal operations are the underlying psychological processes and resources employed in the interpretation of linguistic expressions.
15. In order to distinguish between static and dynamic figure/ground relations, Langacker (1987) uses the term LANDMARK for a moving figure and TRAJECTOR for the ground of a moving figure.

Chapter 6
Language and Cognition

III. Fill in each of the following blanks with an appropriate word. The first letter of the word is already given. (15%)
1. C_____ linguistics has addressed the structuring within language of such basic conceptual categories as those of space and time, scenes and event, entities and processes, motion and location, and force and causation.
2. Shortly before their f_____ birthday, babies begin to understand words, and around that birthday, they start to produce them.
3. P_____ models emphasize that the comprehension system is sensitive to a vast range of information, including grammatical, lexical, and contextual, as well as knowledge of the speaker/writer and of the world in general.
4. In generating sentences, the first step is again c_____ preparation-deciding what to say.
5. The most popular principle interpreting sentence comprehension with respect to the grammatical constraints is Minimal a_____ which defines structurally simpler, and it claims that structural simplicity guides all initial analyses in sentence comprehension.
6. Evidence for the distinction between functional and positional processes comes from the finding that some speech errors can best be explained as errors of functional e_____.
7. C_____ operations are conceptualizing processes used in language process by human beings.
8. In cognitive terms, d_____ is the use of elements of subject's situatedness to designate something in the scene.
9. Linguistically, names for s_____ categories are often mass nouns when basic level terms are count nouns.
10. Often the names for s_____ level categories are morphologically complex. They are typically composite forms.
11. Mark Johnson defines an image s_____ as a recurring, dynamic pattern of our perceptual interactions and motor programs that gives coherence and structure to our experience.
12. The t_____ domain is the experience being described by the metaphor and the source domain is the means that we use in order to describe the experience.
13. O_____ metaphors are based on human physical and cultural experience. For example, in some cultures the future is in front of us, whereas in others it is in back of us.
14. M_____ in the cognitive literature is modeled as idealized cognitive models (ICMs) by Lakoff, conceptual mappings by Radden & Kovecses, domain highlighting by Croft.
15. Fauconnier and Turner propose and discuss B_____ theory, a cognitive operation whereby elements of two or more mental spaces are integrated via projection into a new, blended space which has its unique structure.

IV. Explain the following concepts or theories. (20%)
1. Force schema
2. Cognitive linguistics
3. Scale schema
4. Link schema

V. Match the examples about whole ICMs and its parts in Column B with their corresponding definitions in Column A. (10%)

A	B
(1) Thing-and-part ICM	a. *How old are you?* for "what is your age"?
(2) Scale ICM	b. Bill smoked *marijuana*
(3) Constitution ICM	c. *England* for "Great Britain"
(4) Event ICM	d. *jerk* for "stupidity"
(5) Category-and-Member ICM	e. *crude* for "crude oil"
(6) Category-and-Property ICM	f. *wood* for "forest"
(7) Reduction ICM	g. *to author* a new book
(8) Action ICM	h. *slow road* for "slow traffic resulting from the poor state of the road"
(9) Perception ICM	i. *the pill* for "birth control pill"
(10) Causation ICM	j. *sight* for "thing seen"

VI. Essay questions. (20%)
    1. Illustrate the three approaches to the study of language and cognition.
    2. Define the term *metonymy* in the cognitive literature.

参考答案

I.
1. D   2. B   3. A   4. B   5. D   6. C   7. C   8. A   9. B   10. A

II.
1. F   2. F   3. T   4. T   5. F   6. F   7. T   8. T   9. T   10. F
11. F   12. T   13. F   14. T   15. F

III.
1. Cognitive   2. first   3. Parallel
4. conceptual   5. attachment   6. encoding
7. Construal   8. deixis   9. superordinate
10. subordinate   11. schema   12. target
13. Orientational   14. Metonymy   15. Blending

IV.
1. Force schema involves physical or metaphorical causal interaction. It includes the following elements: a source and target of the force, a direction and intensity of the force, a path of motion of the source and target, a sequence of causation. Here are some kinds of force schemas: an attraction schema, a balance schema, a blockage schema, a compulsion schema, a counterforce schema, a diversion schema, an enablement schema, a restraint removal schema.
2. Cognitive linguistics is a newly established approach to the study of language that emerged in the 1970s as a reaction against the dominant generative paradigm which

pursues an autonomous view of language. Cognitive linguistics is based on human experiences of the world and the way they perceive and conceptualize the world.
3. Scale schema involves an increase or decrease of physical or metaphorical amount, and consists of any of the following: a closed-end or open-ended progression of amount, a position in the progression of amount, one or more norms of amount, a calibration of amount. Here are some examples of scale schemas: physical amounts, properties in the number system.
4. Link schema consists of two or more entities, connected physically or metaphorically, and the bond between them. Here are some examples of link schemas: a child holding her mother's hand, someone plugging a lamp into the wall, a causal *connection*, kinship *ties*.

V.
(1) c (2) a (3) f (4) b (5) i (6) d (7) e (8) g (9) j (10) h

VI.
1. There exist three approaches to the study of language and cognition: the formal approach, the psychological approach and the conceptual approach.
   (1) The formal approach basically addresses the structural patterns exhibited by the overt aspect of linguistic forms, largely abstracted away from or regarded as autonomous from any associated meaning. This approach includes the study of morphological, syntactic, and lexical structure.
   (2) The psychological approach looks at language from the perspective of relatively general cognitive systems ranging from perception, memory, attention to reasoning. It also investigates language both for its formal properties and for its conceptual properties. Thus, the latter kind of investigation has included analyses of semantic memory, the association of concepts, the structure of categories, inference generation, and contextual knowledge. However, these studies have largely remained within certain circumscribed areas.
   (3) The conceptual approach is concerned with the patterns in which and the processes by which conceptual content is organized in language. Since the term STRUCTURE will be used to refer both to patterns and to process, the conceptual approach can more simply be said to address how language structures conceptual content.
2. Metonymy, in the cognitive literature, is modeled as idealized cognitive models (ICMs) by Lakoff (1987), conceptual mappings by Radden & Kovecses (1999), domain highlighting by Croft (2002), combinations of mappings and highlighting by Ruiz de Mendoza (2000), scenarios by Panther & Thornburg (1999) and more generally as reference-point activation by Langacker (1999) and Barcelona (2000). On the basis of the ontological realms, we may distinguish three categories: the world of "concept", the world of "form", and the world of "things" and "events". These realms roughly correspond to the three entities that comprise the well-known semiotic triangle as proposed by Ogden and Richards (1936): thought, symbol and referent. The interrelations between entities of the same or from different ontological realms lead to various ICMs and possibilities for metonymy.

Further Practice

I. Match each term in Column A with one relevant item in Column B.

1. Match the theories in Column A with the related terms in Column B.

A	B
(1) As soon as people hear speech, they start narrowing down the possible words that they may be hearing. A word is identified as soon as there is only one possibility left.	a. Immediacy Assumption
(2) It describes the additional ease with which a word is accessed due to its repeated occurrence in the discourse or context.	b. Semantic Association Network
(3) People initially construct the simplest syntactic structure when interpreting the structure of sentences.	c. Frequency effects
(4) The reader is supposed to carry out the processes required to understand each word and its relationship to previous words in the sentence as soon as that word is encountered.	d. Spoonerism
(5) Context mechanism which represents the relationships between various semantically related words.	e. Assimilation Theory
(6) Initial letter or letters of two words are transposed.	f. Psycholinguistics
(7) A theory which emphasizes on the importance of background knowledge in "normal" situations where we might memorize linguistic material.	g. Cohort theory
(8) Investigating the psychological reality of linguistic structures.	h. Morpheme-Exchange Error
(9) Roots or basic forms of two words are switched leaving the grammatical structure unchanged.	i. General Context Effects
(10) General knowledge about the world influences language comprehension.	j. Minimal Attachment Theory

2. Match the examples about parts of an ICM in Column A with their corresponding definitions in Column B.

A	B
(1) *Nixon* bombed Hanoi	a. Action ICM.
(2) *to blanket* the bed; *to dust* the room	b. Perception ICM.
(3) *I am parked there* for *My car*	c. Causation ICM.

Chapter 6
Language and Cognition

continued

A	B
(4) *Waterloo* for *battle fought at Waterloo*	d. Production ICM.
(5) *There goes my knee* for *There goes the pain in my knee*	e. Control ICM.
(6) *healthy complexion* for *the good state of health bringing about the effect of healthy complexion*	f. Possession ICM.
(7) *Do you still love me? — Yes, I do.*	g. Containment ICM.
(8) a self-contradictory utterance	h. Location ICMs.
(9) *I've got a Ford* for *car*	i. Sign and Reference ICMs.
(10) *The bottle is sour* for *milk*	j. Modification ICM.

II. Mark the following statements with "T" if they are true or "F" if they are false. Provide explanations for the false statements.

1. Psychology of Language includes non-verbal communication such as gestures and facial expressions.
2. Linguists tend to favor descriptions of spontaneous speech as their main source of evidence, whereas psychologists mostly prefer experimental studies.
3. The three major strands of psycholinguistic research are comprehension, production, and acquisition.
4. One of the most important factors that affects word recognition is how frequently the word is used in a given discourse or context.
5. Word recognition plays a significant part in deciding which meaning is the most appropriate.
6. It is typically the case that the perceptual span encompasses about three or four letters to the left of fixation and some fifteen letters to the right of fixation.
7. Gereral context effects occur all the time, because a crucial aspect of language comprehension involves making use of any relevant general knowledge that we possess.
8. In general terms, subsequent ability to remember the propositions depends on the length of time they spend in the working buffer.
9. Macropropositions are general propositions used to form an overall macrostructure of the story.
10. According to Garrett's model, there are altogether five different levels of representation involved in speaking a sentence and their sequence is message-level representation, functional-level representation, phonetic-level representation, positional-level representation, and articulatory-level representation.
11. One of the most detailed theories of the writing process was proposed by Garrett.
12. Speakers decide on the grammatical structure of a proposed utterance in the positional-level representation.
13. The psychological approach basically addresses the structural patterns exhibited by the overt aspect of linguistic forms, largely abstracted away from or regarded as autonomous from any associated meaning.
14. The conceptual approach includes the study of morphological, syntactic, and lexical structure.
15. The conceptual approach is concerned with the patterns in which and the processes by

which conceptual content is organized in language.
16. An important focus of psycholinguistics is the largely unconscious application of grammatical rules that enable people to produce and comprehend intelligible sentences.
17. In the 1960s and early 1970s numerous psychologists and linguists used the transformational-generative model proposed by Rene Dirven to discover how children come to know the grammatical processes that underlie the speech they hear and to investigate the processing and comprehension of language; spoken or written.
18. In 1989, the first conference on cognitive linguistics was organized in Duisburg, Germany, by Chomsky.
19. Charles Darwin, the founder of Evolution Theory, was one of the first keeping the dairy of his son's speech development.
20. The main linguistic accomplishments during the first year of life are control of the speech musculature and sensitivity to the phonetic distinctions used in the parents' language.
21. Shortly before their first birthday, babies begin to understand words, and around that birthday, they start to produce them.
22. Around 12 months, language changes in two ways. Vocabulary growth increases; the child begins to learn words at a rate of one every two waking hours, and will keep learning that rate or faster through adolescence.
23. Before they put words together, babies cannot comprehend a sentence.
24. Normal children can differ by a year or more in their rate of language development, though the stages they pass through are generally the same regardless of how stretched out or compressed and many children speak in complex sentences before they turn two.
25. In cognition, we can direct our attention towards parts of the perceived scenery. In perception, it has to do with the activation of conceptual structures. That is, we activate the most relevant concepts more than concepts that are irrelevant to what we're "thinking about".
26. Construal operations are conceptualizing processes used in language process by human beings. That is, construal operations are the underlying psychological processes and resources employed in the interpretation of linguistic expressions.
27. In order to distinguish between static and dynamic figure/ground relations, Langacker (1987) uses the term LANDMARK for a moving figure and TRAJECTOR for the ground of a moving figure.
28. Visual and spatial skills are under the control of the left hemisphere in most people.
29. In general, the two-word stage begins roughly in the second half of the child's second year.
30. In modern linguistics, speech is regarded as more basic than writing.

III. Fill in each of the following blanks with (an) appropriate word(s).

1. Conceptual metonymy is a _____ process in which one conceptual entity, the vehicle, provides mental access to another conceptual entity, the target, within the same conceptual domain.
2. _____ were presented as structured patterns of knowledge related to recurring situations, which are reflected linguistically in the lexical relations between verbs and in the syntax of clauses.

Chapter 6
Language and Cognition

3. The notion of _____ segregation was first introduced into psychology by the Danish psychologist Rubin and later integrated into the more comprehensive framework of perceptual organization by the gestalt psychologists.
4. The mapping of conceptual metaphor involves two domains, one is the _____ and the other is the target domain.
5. According to cognitive linguistics, the _____ level category is the parasitic category of the basic level category.
6. Prototypes are not the fixed reference points for cognitive categories but are liable to keep shifting as the _____ changes.
7. _____ relations like -OVER- and -UNDER-, -UP- and -DOWN-, -IN- and -OUT- are regarded as image schemas.
8. According to cognitive linguistics, conceptual metaphor and conceptual _____ are cognitive models.
9. In cognitive linguistics, the use of _____ and _____ has been generalized and the former one stands for the figure, whereas the later one refers to the other entity in the relation.
10. Personification is a type of _____ metaphor that involves understanding nonhuman entities, or things, in terms of human beings.

IV. Answer the following questions as comprehensively as possible, giving examples if necessary.
1. According to Garett's theory, how many levels of representation are involved in speaking a sentence, and what are they?
2. According to Hayes and Flower, what does writing process consist of?

V. Analyze with your linguistic knowledge.
1. *HAPPY IS UP; SAD IS DOWN*
2. *ARGUMENT IS WAR*

VI. Analyze the following with your linguistic knowledge.
a. *doggie go out* (Approximate meaning: *The dog went out*)
b. *gara, rara, beb, beb, beb* (No apparent meanings)
c. [kuk$_I$] (Approximate meaning: *I want cookies*)
d. [gag$_I$ nad$_I$] (Approximate meaning: *The dog has been naughty*)
1. Put the letters for the child's utterances above in chronological order.
2. Name the stage and provide an explanation for each stage.

VII. Answer the following questions.
1. List the stages of children's language acquisition, and provide examples if possible.
2. What is your understanding of *cognitive model* in cognitive linguistics?
3. What do you know about *Image Schemas* proposed by Mark Johnson?
4. What is *figure/ground* segregation introduced by the Danish psychologist Rubin?
5. Explain the so-called *blending theory* proposed by Fauconnier & Turner.

参考答案

I.
1. (1) g (2) c (3) j (4) a (5) b (6) d (7) e (8) f (9) h (10) i

2. (1) e (2) a (3) f (4) h (5) b (6) c (7) j (8) i (9) d (10) g

II.
1. F. Psychology of Communication includes non-verbal communication such as gestures and facial expressions.
2. T
3. F. The three major strands of psycholinguistic research are comprehension, production, and communication.
4. T
5. F. Semantic context effect plays a significant part in deciding which meaning is the most appropriate.
6. T 7. T 8. T 9. T
10. F. According to Garrett's model, there are altogether five different levels of representation involved in speaking a sentence and their sequence is message-level, functional-level, positional-level, phonetic-level and articulatory-level.
11. F. One of the most detailed theories of the writing process was proposed by Hayes and Flower.
12. F. Speakers decide on the grammatical structure of a proposed utterance in the functional-level representation.
13. F. The formal approach basically addresses the structural patterns exhibited by the overt aspect of linguistic forms, largely abstracted away from or regarded as autonomous from any associated meaning.
14. F. The formal approach includes the study of morphological, syntactic, and lexical structure.
15. T 16. T
17. F. Transformational-generative model was proposed by Chomsky.
18. F. In 1989, the first conference on cognitive linguistics was organized in Duisburg, Germany, by Rene Dirven.
19. T 20. T 21. T
22. F. Around 18 months, language changes in two ways. Vocabulary growth increases; the child begins to learn words at a rate of one every two waking hours, and will keep learning that rate or faster through adolescence.
23. F. Before they put words together, babies can comprehend a sentence using its syntax.
24. T
25. F. In perception, we can direct our attention towards parts of the perceived scenery. In cognition, it has to do with the activation of conceptual structures. That is, we activate the most relevant concepts more than concepts that are irrelevant to what we're thinking about.
26. T
27. F. In order to distinguish between static and dynamic figure/ground relations, Langacker (1987) uses the term TRAJECTOR for a moving figure and LANDMARK for the ground of a moving figure.
28. F. In most people, the left hemisphere has primary responsibility for language, while the right hemisphere controls visual and spatial skills.
29. T 30. T

III.
1. cognitive
2. Frames
3. figure/ground segregation
4. source domain
5. superordinate
6. context
7. Locative
8. metonymy
9. trajector; landmark
10. ontological

IV.
1. According to his model, there are five different levels of representation involved in speaking a sentence, and they occur in the following sequence:
   (1) The message-level representation: this is an abstract, pre-linguistic representation of the idea or ideas that the speaker wants to communicate.
   (2) The functional-level representation: this is an outline of the proposed utterance having grammatical structure; in other words, the slots for nouns, adjectives, and so on are allocated, but there are no actual words to fill the slots.
   (3) The positional-level representation: this differs from the functional level representation in that it incorporates the words of the sentence that is to be produced.
   (4) The phonetic-level representation: this indicates some of the necessary information about the ways in which words in which intended sentence is pronounced.
   (5) The articulatory-level representation: this is the final representation and contains a set of instructions for articulating the words in the sentence in the correct order.
2. According to Hayes and Flower, writing essentially consists of three inter-related processes:
   (1) The planning process, which involves producing ideas and arranging them into a writing plan appropriate to the writer's goals.
   (2) The sentence generation process, which translates the writing plan into actual sentences that can be written down.
   (3) The revision process, which involves an evaluation of what has been written so far; this evaluation can encompass individual words at one extreme or the overall structure of the writing at the other extreme.

V.
1. Orientational metaphor gives a concept a spatial orientation. They are characterized not so much by structuring one concept in terms of another, but by a co-occurrence in our experience. The orientational metaphors are grounded in an experiential basis, which link together the two parts of the metaphor. The link verb *is*, part of the metaphor, should be seen as the link of two different co-occurring experiences. For example, MORE IS UP. This metaphor is grounded in the co-occurrence of two different kinds of experiences: adding more of a substance and perceiving the level of the substance rise. Orientational metaphors are based on human physical and cultural experience. For example, in some cultures the future is in front of us, whereas in others it is in back of us. Now let us study some orientational metaphors and give a brief hint about how each metaphorical concept might have arisen from human physical and cultural experience (Lakoff & Johnson, 1980):

   HAPPY IS UP; SAD IS DOWN
   a. I'm feeling *up*.
   b. That *boosted* my spirits.

    c. My spirits *rose*.

    d. You're in *high* spirits.

    e. Thinking about her always gives me a *lift*.

    f. I'm feeling *down*.

    g. I'm *depressed*.

    h. He's really *low* these days.

    i. I *fell* into a depression.

    j. My spirits *sank*.

    From these sentences above, it is obvious that drooping posture typically goes along with sadness and depression, erect posture with a positive state.

2. STRUCTURAL METAPHOR plays the most important role because it allows us to go beyond orientation and referring and gives us the possibility to structure one concept according to another. This means that structural metaphors are grounded in our experience. Structural metaphors imply how one concept is metaphorically structured in terms of another. For example, ARGUMENT IS WAR leads to an English expression like "He attacked every weak point in my argument."

    a. Your claims are *indefensible*.

    b. He *attacked every weak point* in my argument.

    c. His criticisms were *right on target*.

    d. I *demolished* his argument.

    e. I've never *won* an argument with him.

    f. You disagree? Okay, *shoot*!

    g. If you use the *strategy*, he'll *wipe you out*.

    h. He *shot down* all of my arguments.

    It is obvious that we don't just talk about argument in terms of war. We can actually win or lose arguments. We see the person we are arguing with as an opponent. We attack his positions and we defend our own. We gain and lose ground. We plan and use strategies. If we find a position indefensible, we can abandon it and take a new line of attack. Many of the things we do in arguing are partially structured by the concept of war.

VI.

1. b; c; d; a

2. (1) b: The pre-language/babbling stage: Children have not yet begun to learn speech sounds. They simply *coo* or *babble*.

    (2) c: The one-word/holophrastic stage: Children use one word (e.g. [kukɪ]) to express the meaning of a sentence (e.g. *I want cookies*)

    (3) d: The two-word stage: Children's utterances contain two words (e.g. [gagɪ nadɪ]) with syntactic and semantic relations between them.

    (4) a: The telegraphic speech stage: Children's utterances contain more words (e.g. *doggie go out*), yet only content words expressing the main message.

VII.

1. There are four stages of children's language acquisition:

    (1) Holophrastic stage: Language acquisition begins very early in the human lifespan, and begins, with the acquisition of a language's sound patterns. The main linguistic accomplishments during the first year of life are control of the speech

Chapter 6
Language and Cognition

musculature and sensitivity to the phonetic distinctions used in the parents' language. Shortly before their first birthday, babies begin to understand words, and around that birthday, they start to produce them. Words are usually produced in isolation; this one-word stage can last from two months to a year. Children's first words are similar all over the planet. About half the words are for objects: food (*juice*, *cookie*), body parts (*eye*, *nose*), clothing (*diaper*, *sock*), vehicles (*car*, *boat*), toys (*doll*, *block*), household items (*bottle*, *light*), animals (*dog*, *kitty*), and people (*dada*, *baby*). Children differ in how much they name objects or engage in social interaction using memorized routines, though all children do both.

(2) Two-word stage: Around 18 months, language changes in two ways. Vocabulary growth increases; the child begins to learn words at a rate of one every two waking hours, and will keep learning that rate or faster through adolescence. Children's two-word combinations are highly similar across cultures. Even before they put words together, babies can comprehend a sentence using its syntax.

(3) Stage of three-word utterances: Children's two- and three-word utterances look like samples drawn from longer potential sentences expressing a complete and more complicated idea.

(4) Fluent grammatical conversation stage: Between the late two-word and mid-three-word stage, children's language blooms into fluent grammatical conversation rapidly, sentence length increases steadily. Because grammar is a combinatorial system, the number of syntactic types increases exponentially, doubling every month, reaching the thousands before the third birthday. Normal children can differ by a year or more in their rate of language development, though the stages they pass through are generally the same regardless of how stretched out or compressed and many children speak in complex sentences before they turn two. Though many of the 3-year-old's sentences are ungrammatical for one reason or another, it is because there are many things that can go wrong in any single sentence. It is safe to say that except for constructions that are rare, predominantly used in written language, or mentally taxing even to an adult (like *The horse that the elephant tickled kissed the pig*), all parts of all languages are acquired before the child turns four!

2. Cognitive model is a whole bundle of contexts or context net related to a certain category and experienced by us and stored in our memory. Here the context refers to the corresponding cognitive categories or mental concept called up by words and a cognitive representation of the interaction between the concepts. Cognitive models are open-ended and descriptions of cognitive models are never exhaustive, but always highly selective. Cognitive models are not isolated cognitive entities, but interrelated. Since it is the context networks experienced by individuals and stored in their mind, cognitive models are subjective and vary between different individuals. For the convenience of description, cognitive models depend on cognitive individuals' living and cultural environment, since the forming of cognitive models is based on experience and experience occurs in culture. Cognitive models are almost the same with cognitive domain, frame, idealized cognitive model.

3. Mark Johnson proposes IMAGE SCHEMAS. He defines an image schema as a recurring, dynamic pattern of our perceptual interactions and motor programs that

gives coherence and structure to our experience. Image schematic structures have two characteristics: they are pre-conceptual schematic structures emerging from our bodily experience and they are constantly operating in our perceptual interaction, bodily movement through space, and physical manipulation of objects. Image schemas exist at a level of abstraction, operate at a level of mental organization between propositional structures and concrete images, and serve repeatedly as identifying patterns in an indefinitely large number of experiences, perceptions, and image formation for objects or events that are similarly structured in the relevant ways.

(1) A center-periphery schema: It involves a physical or metaphorical core and edge, and degrees of distance from the core. For example: the structure of an apple, an individual's perceptual sphere, an individual's social sphere, with family and friends at the core and others at the outside.

(2) A containment schema: It is an image schema that involves a physical or metaphorical boundary, enclosed area or volume, or excluded area or volume. A containment schema has additional optional properties, such as transitivity of enclosure, objects inside or outside the boundary, protection of an enclosed object, the restriction of forces inside the enclosure, and the relatively fixed position of an enclosed object.

(3) A cycle schema: It involves repetitious events and event series. Its structure includes the following: a starting point, a progression through successive events without backtracking, a return to the initial state. The schema often has superimposed on it a structure that builds toward a climax and then goes through a decline. Examples of cycle schemas are *days*, *weeks*, *years*, *sleeping* and *waking*, *breathing*, *circulation*, *emotional buildup* and *release*.

(4) A force schema: It involves physical or metaphorical causal interaction. It includes the following elements: a source and target of the force, a direction and intensity of the force, a path of motion of the source and target, a sequence of causation. Here are some kinds of force schemas: an attraction schema, a balance schema, a blockage schema, a compulsion schema, a counterforce schema, a diversion schema, an enablement schema, a restraint removal schema.

(5) A link schema: It consists of two or more entities, connected physically or metaphorically, and the bond between them. Here are some examples of link schemas: *a child holding her mother's hand*, *someone plugging a lamp into the wall*, *a causal connection*, *kinship ties*.

(6) A part-whole schema: It involves physical or metaphorical wholes along with their parts and a configuration of the parts. Examples are: *the body and its parts*, *the family* and *the caste structure of India*.

(7) A path schema: It involves physical or metaphorical movement from place to place, and consists of a starting point, a goal, and a series of intermediate points. This can be exemplified by *paths* and *trajectories*.

(8) A scale schema: It involves an increase or decrease of physical or metaphorical amount, and consists of any of the following: a closed-end or open-ended progression of amount, a position in the progression of amount, one or more norms of amount, a calibration of amount. Here are some examples of scale schemas: *physical amounts*, *properties in the number system*.

(9) A verticality schema: It involves "up" and "down" relations. Here are some

examples of verticality schemas: *standing upright*, *climbing stairs*, *viewing a flagpole*, *watching water rise in a tub*. According to Johnson, some image schemas also represent spatial orientations and relations: UP-DOWN, FRONT-BACK, PART-WHOLE, CENTER-PERIPHERY, and so on.

4. Figure/ground segregation was first introduced into psychology by the Danish psychologist Rubin a century ago and later integrated into the more comprehensive framework of perceptual organization by the gestalt psychologists. Figure has special properties such as form or shape, structure, coherence, and lying in front of the ground. The properties of ground are that it is formless and its contour seems belong to figure, it has no structure, it is uniform, and it lies behind figure. All in all, the figure is perceived as being more prominent than the ground, and psychological research has shown that it is more likely to be identified and remembered, and to be associated with meaning, feeling and aesthetic values. Figure/ground segregation should follow prominence principle, since figure has perceptive prominence. Usually entities which are small, moving and having gestalt features are assigned the status of figure.

5. Fauconnier & Turner propose and discuss BLENDING or INTEGRATION theory, a cognitive operation whereby elements of two or more "mental spaces" are integrated via projection into a new, blended space which has its unique structure. They present examples of blending, analyze the blending process, provide a taxonomy of blends, and argue for the ubiquity and importance of blending as a cognitive resource.

   (1) Blending operates on two input mental spaces to produce a third space, the blend. The blend inherits partial structure from the input spaces and has emergent structure of its own.

   (2) The blending theory suggests a new way of thinking about what constitutes a novel inference. Because the mapping operation involves integrated frames rather than isolated predicates, the choice of one particular framing over another necessarily results in a different set of attendant inferences.

   (3) Besides the acquisition of unknown facts, a novel inference might involve a new construal of a well-understood phenomenon, a change in prominence of a particular element, or simply the availability of connected frames.

Chapter 7 Language, Culture and Society

Concepts & Theories

I. Language and Culture
1. The relationship between language and culture

Generally, the relation between Language to Culture is that of part to whole, for Language is part of Culture.

The knowledge and beliefs that constitute a people's culture are habitually encoded and transmitted in L.

Anthropological study of linguistics: study of language in a sociocultural context.

(1) Bronislaw Malinowski (1884-1942):

The meaning of a word greatly depends upon its occurrence in a given context.

Language functions as a link in human activity, a mode of action.

(2) J. R. Firth (1890-1960): theory of the context of situation

The relevant features of the participants, persons, personalities.

The relevant objects.

The effects of the verbal action.

who speaks what to whom and when and to what end

(3) Dell Hymes (1927-): Ethnography of communication

Speech situation.

Situation, event, and act.

SPEAKING: situation, participants, ends, act sequence, key, instrumentalities, norms, and genres

(4) Sapir-Whorf Hypothesis

Edward Sapir (1884-1939) and Benjamin Lee Whorf (1897-1941)

Our language helps mould our way of thinking and, consequently, different languages may probably express speakers' unique ways of understanding the world.

Linguistic determinism: L may determine our thinking patterns.

Linguistic relativity: different languages offer people different ways of expressing the world around.

2. More about Sapir-Whorf hypothesis

Two versions of the Sapir-Whorf Hypothesis have been developed, a strong version and a weak version. The strong version of the theory refers to the claim the original hypothesis suggests, emphasizing the decisive role of language as the shaper of our thinking patterns. The weak version of this hypothesis, however, is a modified type of its original theory, suggesting that there is a correlation between language, culture and thought, but the cross-cultural differences thus produced in our ways of thinking are relative, rather than categorical.

Chapter 7
Language, Culture and Society

3. To which extent do we need culture in our linguistic study?

A study of linguistic issues in a cultural setting can greatly promote our understanding of Motivation and directionality in language change.

A sociolinguistic study of combining form *-gate* and its derivations:

Findings:
(1) This suffix enjoys a rich productivity in American English.
(2) Words derived from this source inevitably take on a culturally pejorative implication.

Tentative conclusions:
(1) *Watergate* will stay in English for quite a long time.
(2) Its structural status becomes stable.
(3) The pejorative semantic implicature will stay.

4. **Culture in language teaching classroom**

Principally, there are at least three objectives for us to teach culture in our language class:
(1) To get the students familiar with cultural differences;
(2) To help the students transcend their own culture and see things as the members of the target culture will;
(3) To emphasize the inseparability of understanding language and understanding culture through various classroom practices

II. Language and society

1. How does language relate to society?

The relationship between language and society has long been recognized and examined. Evidence for this claim, discrete as it might be, can be conveniently gathered from the works by those great philosophers and grammarians either in the Graeco-Roman tradition or in the Indian history.

During the whole 20th century, a great deal of efforts has been taken to treat the inquiry of linguistics as a MONISTIC or AUTONOMOUS PURSUIT of an independent science. Strongly influenced by this dominant view of linguistic science, a separation of the structural study of language from its social context of usage was claimed, justified, and reinforced. The resurrection of a DUALISTIC VIEW of linguistic inquiry, however, came into being in the 1960s, along with the development of sociolinguistics as an opposition to the dominant theory of Chomskyan linguistics.

2. **A situationally and socially variationist perspective**

There has been a maxim in sociolinguistics which claims that *You are what you say* (Lakoff 1991). Following this claim, we may expand the scope of our observation by introducing some social factors that are believed to influence our language behavior in a social context. Among these factors, some major ones include (1) class, (2) gender, (3) age, (4) ethnic identity, (5) education background, (6) occupation, and (7) religious belief.

(1) Class: William Labov conducted a rather meticulous survey at several departments in the City of New York. The objective for having this sociolinguistic investigation was to examine the relationship between speakers' social status and their phonological VARIATIONS. And it turned out that class and style were two major factors influencing the speakers' choice of one phonological variant over another. Based on these findings, Labor explicitly delineated the patterns of

stratification by class and style and, more importantly, successfully introduced class as an indispensable sociolinguistic variable. Ever since its publication in the middle of the 1960s, this research paradigm has become the mainstream in sociolinguistics.

(2) Gender: WOMEN REGISTER in the language takes on the following features:
☆ Women use more "fancy" color terms such as mauve and beige.
☆ Women use less powerful curse words.
☆ Women use more intensifiers such as terrible and awful.
☆ Women use more tag questions.
☆ Women use more statement questions.
☆ Women's linguistic behavior is more indirect and, hence, more polite than men's.

3. What should we know more about sociolinguistics?

SOCIOLINGUISITIC STUDY OF SOCIETY: things that we are interested in include bilingualism or multilingualism, language attitudes, language choice, language maintenance and shift, language planning and standardization, vernacular language education, to name some important ones.

SOCIOLINGUISTIC STUDY OF LANGUAGE: if we want to know more about some linguistic variations in language use by turning to potential sociocultural factors for a description and explanation, we are doing a sociolinguistic study of language. Consequently, we are more interested in examining micro linguistic phenomena such as structural variants, address forms, gender differences, discourse analysis, Pidgin and Creole languages, and other more language related issues.

4. What implications can we get from sociolinguistics?

(1) First, we'll have a look at sociolinguistics in language classrooms.
☆ Sociolinguistics has contributed to a change of emphasis in the content of language teaching.
☆ It has also contributed to innovations in materials and activities for the classroom.
☆ It has contributed to a fresh look at the nature of language development and use.
☆ It has contributed to a more fruitful research in this field.

(2) Second, let us have a look at sociolinguistics in law courts. The inquiry of the relationship between language and law has opened another avenue for the application of sociolinguistic findings to some more practical issues in society.

(3) Lastly, we turn to sociolinguistics in clinic settings. The analysis of dialogues between doctors and patients in a hospital context has also attracted the interest of some researchers in sociolinguistics.

III. Successful communication occurs:
(1) When the hearer can see, feel, and understand issues from the speaker's point of view.
(2) When the hearer and speaker know each other's intention.
(3) When two parties adopt a dynamic dialogue pattern.

IV. Summary

We have introduced some important theories and practices in a sociocultural inquiry of linguistic issues. As we have indicated, a more systematic pursuit of this kind did not start until the 1960s, with the occurrence of sociolinguistics as a new force in the study of language. After almost 40 years' development, this innovative movement has gained much momentum and vitality by incorporating the insights from other relevant sciences and has gradually secured its position as a legitimate pursuit in linguistics (cf. Chomsky 1995). On the other hand, as has been shown above, the study of the relationship between language, culture, and society is a rather intriguing task.

Related Terms

applied sociolinguistics

This is a term that covers several linguistic subdisciplines as well as certain interdisciplinary areas that use linguistic methods: language pedagogy, psycholinguistics, language acquisition, second language acquisition, translation, contrastive analysis, language planning, lexicography, computational linguistics, ethnolinguistics, sociolinguistics, and others. Applied linguistics differs from theoretical linguistics in that the latter is concerned with the formal structure of language as an autonomous system of signs. The term *applied linguistics* is in some cases misleading, since in many of the subdisciplines language is studied from both a theoretical and practical (i.e. applied) perspective. Moreover, some areas should be considered *applications* of linguistics. Applied linguistics has become a field of growing linguistic interest, as evidenced by the many journals devoted to these allied studies which have been launched since the 1960s.

bilingualism

Bilingualism refers to a linguistic situation in which two standard languages are used either by an individual or by a group of speakers such as the inhabitants of a particular region of nation.

communicative competence

Coined by D. Hymes in his ethnography of communication, this term is a critical expansion of N. Chomsky's concept of competence. Communicative competence is the fundamental concept of a pragma-lingusitc model of linguistic communication: it refers to the repertoire of know-how that individuals must develop if they are to be able to communicate with one another appropriately in the changing situations and conditions. In this model, speaking is understood as the action of transmitting symbols (i.e. interaction). Communicative competence is the descriptive goal of various social-psychological disciplines.

context of situation

Context of situation is used by Firth to cover all the relevant circumstances in which a specific act of speech takes place. It can be summarized as the relevant features, the verbal action, and the non-verbal action of the participants, the relevant objects and the effects of the verbal action. The term was originally that of the anthropologist B. Malinowski. E.g. when a specific person says on a specific occasion *Well played*!, it might be part of the context of situation that the speaker is sitting, with others, watching a cricket match, that a batsman has driven for four through covers, that the speaker is from a certain background, and so on. In the analysis of a language, features recurring in individual utterances (considered again as specific acts of speech) will be related to specific types of situation and to specific features in them.

directionality

A term refers to the issue regarding the direction of derivation among parts of a generative grammar. Specifically as part of a controversy between *Generative Semantics* and *Interpretive Semantics* in the early 1970s: i.e. should syntactic representations of sentences be derived from their semantic representations, or vice versa?

ethnography of communication

Ethnography of communication is a term introduced by D. H. Hymes in the early 1960s for the study of the uses and patterns of speaking in a society, as distinct from an account of the language system. Thus in some communities ritual utterances are a central feature of ceremonial; in others they are not. In some, close friends will tend to greet each other with formal insults; in some, verbosity in speech is appreciated; in some, requests will tend to be made directly rather than indirectly; and so on. The domain of the ethnography of speaking covered features such as these which were seen as falling between the usual scope of linguistics, and that of ethnography in general.

linguistic universality

Linguistic universality is a property that all languages have, or a statement that holds for all languages.

multilingualism

Multilingualism refers to a linguistic situation in which more than two languages are used either by an individual or by a group of speakers such as the inhabitant of a particular region of nation.

sociolinguistics

The term refers to any study of language in relation to society. Commonly, for the late 1960s, of studies of variation in language by Labov and his followers. In that sense, sociolinguistics might be defined as the study of correlations between linguistic variables (e.g. the precise phonetic quality of a vowel, or the presence or absence of a certain element in a construction) and non-linguistic variables such as the social class of speakers, their age, sex, etc. Increasingly, from the end of the 1970s, of a range of loosely connected investigations, including conversation analysis as conducted especially by sociologists, the study of relations in general between language and ideology or language and power, linguistic aspects of social psychology, etc.

speech community

Speech community refers to any group of people whose language or use of language can be taken as a coherent object of study. Speakers of English can be treated as such a community; also, e.g. speakers with a distinct variety that one might call "Birmingham English", spoken or usually spoken by part of the population of Birmingham. So might any other population that meets some test of coherence, whether large or small, bilingual or monolingual, in a single place or scattered.

Practice

I. Mark the choice that best completes the statement. (20%)

1. _____ is concerned with the social significance of language variation and language use in different speech communities.

    A. Psycholinguistics   B. Sociolinguistics

Chapter 7
Language, Culture and Society

    C. Applied linguistics   D. General linguistics

2. Which of the following is NOT seen as the representatives of an anthropological orientation from North America?
   A. Franz Boasts.   B. Edward Sapir.
   C. John Firth.   D. Benjamin Lee.

3. _____ developed his own theory of Context of Situation.
   A. Franz Boasts   B. Edward Sapir
   C. John Firth   D. Benjamin Lee

4. _____ is the first three stages in the Evolutionary Stages of Basic Color Words proposed by Berlin and Kay.
   A. *White/black → green/yellow → red*
   B. *Red → green/yellow → white/black*
   C. *White/black → red → green/yellow*
   D. *Green/yellow → white/black → red*

5. _____ do(es) NOT belong to the sociolinguistic study of language.
   A. Address forms   B. Bilingualism
   C. Gender differences   D. Pidgin

6. _____ in a person's speech or writing usually ranges on a continuum from casual or colloquial to formal or polite according to the type of communicative situation.
   A. Regional variation   B. Changes in emotions
   C. Variation in connotations   D. Stylistic variation

7. A _____ is a variety of language that serves as a medium of communication among groups of people for diverse linguistic backgrounds.
   A. lingua franca   B. register
   C. Creole   D. national language

8. Although _____ are simplified languages with reduced grammatical features, they are rule-governed, like any human language.
   A. vernacular languages   B. creoles
   C. pidgins   D. sociolects

9. In normal situations, _____ speakers tend to use more prestigious forms than their _____ counterparts with the same social background.
   A. female; male   B. male; female
   C. old; young   D. young; old

10. A linguistic _____ refers to a word or expression that is prohibited by the *polite* society from general use.
    A. slang   B. euphemism   C. jargon   D. taboo

II. Mark the following statements with "T" if they are true or "F" if they are false. (10%)

1. At the start of the 19th century, an anthropological orientation in the study of language was developed both in England and North America.
2. The Firthian tradition was further developed by the founder of systemic-functional linguistics, Halliday.
3. The investigation of basic color vocabulary conducted by Brent Berlin and Paul Kay revealed the same findings as the Sapir and Whorf hypothesis.
4. There are ONLY two basic color words in the language Dani.
5. Kaplan claims that the structural organization of a text tends to be culturally specific.

6. There has been a maxim from Lakoff in sociolinguistics which claims that *You are what you say*.
7. William Labov's objective for having the sociolinguistic investigation was to examine the relationships between speakers' gender and their phonological variations.
8. Carl Rogers states that real communication takes place when we listen with understanding.
9. Linguistic universality is a property that all languages have, or a statement that holds for all languages.
10. The bound root *-gate* enjoys a rich productivity in American English, such as in the words *Billygate*, *Debategate* and *Ricegate*.

III. Fill in each of the following blanks with an appropriate word. Notice the first letter of the word is already given. (20%)

1. The social group isolated for any given study is called the speech c_____.
2. As early as in the 1920s, a school of a_____ study of linguistics came into being in England.
3. What Firth emphasized in the theory of Context of Situation is quite similar to a more updating sociological a_____ in language use.
4. The experience and his study of Hopi, an American Indian language, helped Whorf develop his unique understanding of linguistic r_____, which is widely known as the SAPIR-WHORF HYPOTHESES.
5. The resurrection of a d_____ view of linguistic inquiry, however, came into being in the 1960s, along with the development of sociolinguistics as an opposition to the dominant theory of Chomskyan linguistics.
6. Lakoff's hypotheses suggest that here exists a women r_____ in the language.
7. We can either classify sociolinguistic studies by means of hierarchical division, or alternatively, by means of an o_____ categorization.
8. Hyme's theory of Communicative C_____ was introduced into language teaching in the middle of the 1970s.
9. Successful communication occurs when the two parties adopt a d_____ dialogue pattern.
10. A pidgin typically lacks in i_____ morphemes.

IV. Explain the following concepts or theories. (20%)
1. Speech community
2. Communicative competence
3. Context of situation
4. Linguistic universality

V. Answer the following questions. (30%)
1. What might be the suggestive principles for cross-cultural communication?
2. What is Sapir-Whorf Hypothesis?
3. Summarize the important contributions of sociolinguistics.

参考答案

I.
1. B 2. C 3. C 4. C 5. B 6. D 7. A 8. C 9. A 10. D

Chapter 7
Language, Culture and Society

II.
1. F 2. T 3. F 4. T 5. T 6. T 7. F 8. T 9. T 10. F

III.
1. community   2. anthropological   3. axiom   4. relativity   5. dualistic
6. register   7. orientational   8. Competence   9. dynamic   10. inflectional

IV.
1. Speech community refers to any group of people whose language or use of language can be taken as a coherent object of study. Speakers of English can be treated as such a community; also, e.g. speakers of a distinct variety that one might call "Birmingham English", spoken or usually spoken by part of the population of Birmingham. So might any other population that meets some test of coherence, whether large or small, bilingual or monolingual, in a single place or scattered.
2. communicative competence: Coined by D. Hymes in his ethnography of communication, this term is a critical expansion of N. Chomsky's concept of competence. Communicative competence is the fundamental concept of a pragma-linguistic model of linguistic communication; it refers to the repertoire of know-how that individuals must develop if they are to be able to communicate with one another appropriately in the changing situations and conditions. In this model, speaking is understood as the action of transmitting symbols (i.e. interaction). Communicative competence is the descriptive goal of various social-psychological disciplines.
3. context of situation: Used by Firth to cover all the relevant circumstances in which a specific act of speech takes place. It can be summarized as the relevant features, the verbal action, and the non-verbal action of the participants, the relevant objects and the effects of the verbal action. The term was originally that of the anthropologist B. Malinowski. E.g. when a specific person says on a specific occasion *Well played*!, it might be part of the context of situation that the speaker is sitting, with others, watching a cricket match, that a batsman has driven for four through covers, that the speaker is from a certain background, and so on. In the analysis of a language, features recurring in individual utterances (considered again as specific acts of speech) will be related to specific types of situation and to specific features in them.
4. linguistic universality: Linguistic universality is a property that all languages have, or a statement that holds for all languages.

V.
1. Some suggestive principles are provided below as basic guidelines to cross-cultural communication:
    First of all, successful communication occurs when the hearer can see, feel and understand issues from the speaker's point of view.
    Second, successful communication occurs when the speaker and hearer know each other's intention.
    Third, successful communication occurs when the tow parties adopt a dynamic dialogue pattern.
2. What is Sapir-Whorf Hypothesis?
    Whorf attended some linguistic courses given by Sapir at Yale University and found particular resonance between his own ideas and those of Sapir. This experience and his study

of Hopi, an American Indian language, helped him develop his unique understanding of linguistic relativity, which is widely known as the Sapir-Whorf Hypotheses. What this hypothesis suggests is like this: our language helps mould our way of thinking and, consequently, different languages may probably express our unique ways of understanding the world. Following this argument, two important points could be captured in this theory. On the one hand, language may determine our thinking patterns; on the other, similarity between languages is relative. The greater their structural differentiation is, the more diverse their conceptualization of the world will be. For this reason, this hypothesis has alternatively been referred to as linguistic determinism and linguistic relativity.

3. Summarize the important contributions of sociolinguistics.
   (1) Sociolinguistics has contributed to a change of emphasis in the content of language teaching;
   (2) It has also contributed to innovations in materials and activities for the classroom;
   (3) It has helped to form a fresh look at the nature of language development and use;
   (4) It has contributed to a more fruitful research in this field.

Further Practice

I. Fill in each of the following blanks with (an) appropriate word(s).

1. At the start of the 20th century: an anthropological _____ in the study of language was developed both in England and in North America. What characterized this new tradition was its study of language in a _____ context.

2. _____ community refers to any group of people whose language or use of language can be taken as a coherent object of study. Speakers of English can be treated as such a community.

3. Malinowski claimed that *In its primitive uses, language functions as a link in concerted human _____... It is a mode of action and not an instrument of reflection.*

4. Like Sapir, though far less directly, Firth seemed to suggest the creativity and _____ of linguistic idiosyncrasy in language use.

5. And the _____ tradition in this respect was further developed by the founder of systemic-functional linguistics, M. A. K. Halliday, whose contributions to sociolinguistics could be better seen from his understanding of language from a socially _____ or international perspective, his functional interpretation of _____ as a resource for meaning potential, and his linguistic model in the study of literature.

6. Whorf attended some linguistic coursed given by Sapir at Yale University and found particular _____ between his own ideas and those of Sapir. This experience and his study of Hopi, an American Indian language, helped him develop his unique understanding of linguistic _____, which is widely known as the SAPIR-WHORF HYPOTHESES. This hypothesis has alternatively been referred to as linguistic _____ and linguistic relativity-a view which was first expounded by the German ethnologist, Wilhelm von Humboldt.

7. Eugene Nida claims that there are five types of sub-culture we should be fully aware of: _____ culture; linguistic culture; _____ culture; _____ culture and social culture.

8. The strong version of Sapir-Whorf hypothesis refers to the claim the original hypothesis suggests, emphasizing the decisive role of language as the _____ of our thinking

Chapter 7
Language, Culture and Society

patterns. The weak version of this hypothesis, however, is a modified type of its original theory, suggesting that there is a _____ between language, culture, and thought, but the cross-cultural differences thus produced in our ways of thinking are relative, rather than categorical.

9. A study of linguistic issues in a cultural setting can greatly promote our understanding of motivation and _____ in language change.
10. The resurrection of a _____ view of linguistic inquiry, however, came into being in the 1960s, along with the development of sociolinguistics as an opposition to the dominant theory of Chomskyan linguistics.
11. In the middle of 1960s, William Labov, a famous sociolinguist, conducted a rather meticulous survey at several departments in the City of New York. The objective for having this sociolinguistic investigation was to examine the relationship between speakers' social status and their phonological _____. And it turned out that class and _____ were two major factors influencing the speakers' choice of one phonological variant over another.
12. Lakoff's hypotheses suggest that here exists a women _____ in the language.
13. _____, as an interdisciplinary study of language use, attempts to show the relationship between language and society.
14. If we want to know more about a given society or community by examining the linguistic behavior of its members, we are doing a sociolinguistic study of _____. That is we are doing sociolinguistics at a macro level of investigation. On the other hand, if we want to know more about some linguistic variations in language use by turning to potential sociocultural factors for a description and explanation, we are doing a sociolinguistic study of _____. Consequently, we are more interested in examining micro linguistic phenomena.
15. The social group isolated for any given study is called the speech _____.
16. Speech _____ refers to any distinguishable form of speech used by a speaker or group of speakers.
17. From the sociolinguistic perspective, a speech variety is no more than a _____ variety of a language.
18. Language standardization is also called language _____.
19. Social variation gives rise to _____ which are subdivisible into smaller speech categories that reflect their socioeconomic, educational, occupational background, etc.
20. _____ variation in a person's speech or writing usually ranges on a continuum from casual or colloquial to formal or polite according to the type of communicative situation.
21. A regional dialect may gain status and become standardized as the national or _____ language of a country.
22. The standard language is a _____, socially prestigious dialect of language.
23. Language varieties other than the standard are called nonstandard, or _____ languages.
24. In sociolinguistics, we have two things to think about: _____ things and their use in a sociocultural context.

II. Mark the following statements with "T" if they are true or "F" if they are false. Provide explanations for the false statements. (10%)

1. Language as a means of social communication is a homogeneous system with a

homogeneous group of speakers.
2. The goal of sociolinguistics is to explore the nature of language variation and language use among a variety of speech communities and in different social situations.
3. From the sociolinguistic perspective, the term *speech variety* can not be used to refer to standard language, vernacular language, dialect or pidgin.
4. The most distinguishable linguistic feature of a regional dialect is its grammar and uses of vocabulary.
5. A person's social backgrounds do not exert a shaping influence on his choice of linguistic features.
6. Every speaker of a language is, in a stricter sense, a speaker of a distinct idiolect.
7. A lingua franca can only be used within a particular country for communication among groups of people with different linguistic backgrounds.
8. A pidgin usually reflects the influence of the higher, or dominant, language in its lexicon and that of the lower language in their phonology and occasionally syntax.
9. Bilingualism and diglossia mean the same thing.
10. The use of euphemisms has the effect of removing derogatory overtones and the disassociative effect as such is usually long-lasting.

III. Answer the following questions as comprehensively as possible, giving examples if necessary.
1. What does Firth's concept of *context of situation* include?
2. Explain the following comic show lines concerning Pidgin in the field of the Sociolinguistic Study of Language. What are the reasons for developing such a variety in language?

   These lines are taken from a famous comic strip in *Papua New Guinea*:

   Sapos yu kaikai planti pinat, bai yu kamap strong olsem phantom. Fantom, yu pren tru bilong mi. Inap yu ken helpim mi nau? Fantom, em i go we?

   Translation:

   If you eat plenty of peanuts, you will come up strong like the phantom. Phantom, you are a true friend of mine. Are you able to help me now? Where did he go?
3. How do you interpret the sentence *Sex is what you are born with; gender is what you're given*? The following checklist of alternatives to sexist language was produced by a publisher giving advice to authors.

To be avoided	To be preferred
man-made	artificial, synthetic, manufactured
Man's achievements	human achievements, our achievements
If a man drove 50 miles at 60 mph …	If a person drove 50 miles at 60 mph …
the best man for the job	the best person (or candidate) for the job
manpower	workforce, staff, labour, human resources

(1) Do you agree with the premise that the *words to be avoided* are in fact sexist?
(2) Do you agree that the *words to be preferred* are better?
(3) Explain your decisions and suggest better alternatives where possible.

Chapter 7
Language, Culture and Society

参考答案

I.

1. orientation; sociocultural
2. Speech
3. activity
4. diversity
5. Firthian, semiotic, grammar
6. resonance; relativity; determinism
7. ecological; religious; material
8. shaper; correlation
9. directionality
10. dualistic
11. variations; style
12. register
13. Sociolinguistics
14. society; language
15. community
16. variety
17. dialectal
18. planning
19. sociolects
20. Stylistic
21. official
22. superposed
23. vernacular
24. structural

II
1. F 2. T 3. F 4. F 5. F 6. T 7. F 8. T 9. F 10. F

III.
1. Firth, a leading figure in a linguistic tradition later known as the London School, tried to set up a model for illustrating the close relationship between language use and its co-occurrent factors. In the end, he developed his own theory of context of situation, which can be summarized as follows:

   The relevant features of the participants: persons, personalities.
   The verbal action of the participants
   The non-verbal action of the participants
   The relevant objects.
   The effects of the verbal action.

2. A simplified language derived from two or more languages is called a pidgin. It is a contact language developed and used by people who do not share a common language in a given geographical area. It is used in a limited way and the structure is very simplistic. Since they serve a single simplistic purpose, they usually die out. However, if the pidgin is used long enough, it begins to evolve into a more rich language with a more complex structure and richer vocabulary. Once the pidgin has evolved and has acquired native speakers (the children learn the pidgin as their first language), it is then called a Creole. An example of this is the Creole above from Papua New Guinea, Tok Pisin, which has become a National language.

   Reasons for the development of Pidgins
   In the nineteenth century, when slaves from Africa were brought over to North America to work on the plantations, they were separated from the people of their community and mixed with people of various other communities, therefore they were unable to communicate with each other. The strategy behind this was so they couldn't come up with a plot to escape back to their land. Therefore, in order to finally communicate with their peers on the plantations, and with their bosses, they needed to form a language in which they could communicate. Pidgins also arose because of colonization. Prominent languages such as French, Spanish, Portuguese, English, and

Dutch were the languages of the colonizers. They traveled, and set up ports in coastal towns where shipping and trading routes were accessible.

There is always a dominant language which contributes most of the vocabulary of the pidgin, this is called the superstrate language. The superstrate language from the Papua New Guinea Creole example above is English. The other minority languages that contribute to the pidgin are called the substrate languages. (Source: http://logos.uoregon.edu/explore/socioling/pidgin.html)

3. Please refer to the part about *linguistic sexism* on Page 172-173 in the textbook. This list of sexist terms shows not only what may be avoided but also how they may be avoided. In the company of people who are made uncomfortable by sexist terms, there is a polite and linguistically acceptable alternative in most cases. The often quoted *person aperture cover* for *man hole* is both a hoax and a parody of the intention of the language. If the gender of the person being discussed is unknown or could be female or male, there are several alternatives. One is to use *She or he should show his/her tickets*, or even *S/he should show ...* (only common on forms and questionnaires). Another is to use the plural *Customers should show their tickets* or to use the second person pronoun instead— *Please show your ticket*. Use of the passive is an alternative though it may lead to less clarity— *Tickets should be shown*. It's worth pointing out that many attempts have been made to devise new and neutral pronouns, though none has become common. S/he is possibly the nearest to popularity.

(Source: http://www.putlearningfirst.com/language/23sexism/sexist.html)

Chapter 8 Language in Use

Concepts & Theories

I. Speech act theory
1. **Performatives and constatives**
   (1) Performative: In speech act theory an utterance which performs an act, such as *Watch out* (= a warning).
   (2) Constative: An utterance which asserts something that is either true or force. E.g. Chicago is in the United States.
   (3) Felicity conditions of performatives:
      ☆ There must be a relevant conventional procedure, and the relevant participants and circumstances must be appropriate.
      ☆ The procedure must be executed correctly and completely.
      ☆ Very often, the relevant people must have the requisite thoughts, feelings and intentions, and must follow it up with actions as specified.
2. **A theory of the illocutionary act**
   (1) Locutionary act: A distinction is made by Austin in the theory of speech acts between three different types of acts involved in or caused by the utterance of a sentence. A locutionary act is the saying of something which is meaningful and can be understood.
   (2) Illocutionary act: An illocutionary act is using a sentence to perform a function.
   (3) Perlocutionary act: A perlocutionary act is the results or effects that are produced by means of saying something.

II. The theory of conversational implicature
1. **The cooperative principle**
   (1) The cooperative principle (CP)
      Cooperative principle refers to the *co-operation* between speakers in using the maxims during the conversation. There are four conversational maxims:
      ☆ The maxim of quantity:
         a. Make your contribution as informative as required.
         b. Don't make your contribution more informative than is required.
      ☆ The maxim of quality: Try to make your contribution one that is true.
         a. Don't say what you believe to be false.
         b. Don't say that for which you lack adequate evidence.
      ☆ The maxim of relation: Say things that are relevant.
      ☆ The maxim of manner: Be perspicuous.
         a. Avoid obscurity of expression.
         b. Avoid ambiguity.
         c. Be brief.

d. Be orderly.

(2) Conversational implicature: The use of conversational maxims to imply meaning during conversation is called conversational implicature.

2. **Violation of the maxims**

   Give the cases of violation of the maxims.

3. **Characteristics of implicature**

   (1) Calculability

   Hearers work out implicature based on literal meaning, CP and its maxims, context.

   (2) Cancellability/defeasibility

   If the linguistic or situational contexts changes, the implicature will also change.

   (3) Non-detachability

   Implicature is attached to the semantic content of what is said, not to the linguistic form; implicatures do not vanish if the words of an utterance are changed for synonyms.

   (4) Non-conventionality

   Implicature is different from its conventional meaning of words. It is context-dependent. It varies with context.

III. Post-Gricean developments

1. Relevance theory

   This theory was formally proposed by Dan Sperber and Deirdre Wilson in their book *Relevance: Communication and Cognition* in 1986. They argue that all Gricean maxims, including the CP itself, should be reduced to a single principle of relevance, which is defined as: Every act of ostensive communication communicates the presumption of its own optimal relevance.

2. The Q- and R-principles

   These principles were developed by L. Horn in 1984. The Q-principle is intended to invoke the first maxim of Grice's Quantity, and the R-principle the relation maxim, but the new principles are more extensive than the Gricean maxims.

   The definition of the Q-principle (hearer-based) is:
   (1) Make your contribution sufficient (cf. quantity);
   (2) Say as much as you can (given R).

   The definition of the R-principle (speaker-based) is:
   (1) Make your contribution necessary (cf. Relation, Quantity 2, Manner);
   (2) Say no more than you must (given Q).

3. The Q-, I- and M-principles

   This tripartite model was suggested by S. Levinson mainly in his 1987 paper *Pragmatics and the Grammar of Anaphor: A Partial Pragmatic Reduction of Binding and Control Phenomena*.

Related Terms

calculability

Implicatures can be worked out on the basis of some previous information. That is their calculability.

Chapter 8
Language in Use

cancellability

Cancellability is also known as defeasibility. The presence of a conversational implicature relies on a number of factors: the conventional meaning of words used, the Cooperative Principle, the linguistic and situational contexts, etc. So if any of them changes, the implicature will also change, or even be cancelled.

constatives

In the early stage of J. L. Austin's philosophy of language, including the first part of his 1958 lectures on speech act theory, this term denoted utterances that describe or depict facts or states of affairs and so may be either true or false. In this sense, *constative* corresponds to the philosophical term *statement*.

context

As a comprehensive concept in communication theory, *context* refers to all elements of a communicative situation: the verbal and nonverbal context, the context of the given speech situation and the social context of the relationship between the speaker and the hearer, their knowledge, and their attitudes.

conversational implicature

Proposed by Grice, it is a type of implied meaning, which is deduced on the basis of the conventional meaning of words together with the context, under the guidance of the CP and its maxims.

cooperative principle

Grice believes there must be some mechanisms governing the production and comprehension of people's utterances. He suggests that there is a set of assumptions guiding the conduct of conversation, in other words, we seem to follow some principle like the following: Make our conversation contribution such as is required, at the stage at which it occurs, by the accepted purpose or direction of the talk exchange in which you are engaged", and this principle is known as the cooperative principle. To specify the CP further, Grice introduces four maxims of it.

division of pragmatic labor

The use of a marked (relatively complex and/or prolix) expression when a corresponding unmarked (simpler, less *effortful*) alternate expression is available tends to be interpreted as conveying a marked message (one which the unmarked alternative would not or could not have conveyed).

entailment

Entailment is a logical relationship between two sentences in which the truth of the second necessarily follows from the truth of the first, while the falsity of the first follows from the falsity of the second.

felicity conditions

Conditions for performatives to meet to be appropriate or felicitous are called felicity conditions.

horn scale

This notion was originally proposed by L. Horn, referring to a set of quantitative elements, arranged in the order of informativeness as $<all, most, many, some, few>$, $<always, often, sometimes>$.

illocutionary act

It is the act of expressing the speaker's intention, as well as the act performed in saying something.

locutionary act

It is the act of uttering words, phrases, clauses. It is the act of conveying literal meaning by means of syntax, lexicon and phonology.

non-conventionality

It means that conversational implicature is by definition different from the conventional meaning of words.

non-detachability

It is meant that a conversational implicature is attached to the semantic context of what is said, not to the linguistic form. Therefore it is possible to use a synonym and keep the implicature intact.

ostensive communication

From the speaker's side, communication should be seen as an act of making clear one's intention to express something. This act is called ostensive act. In other words, a complete characterization of communication is that it is ostensive-inferential.

performatives

This concept is proposed by Austin. He claims that some sentences do not describe things, and they cannot be said to be true or false. The uttering of these sentences is, or is a part of, the doing of an action. So they are called performatives.

perlocutionary act

It is the act performed by or resulting from saying something; it is the consequence of, or the change brought about by the utterance; it is the act performed by saying something such as *You have left the door wide open*.

pragmatics

Pragmatics studies how meaning is conveyed in the process of communication. The essential difference between pragmatics and traditional semantics is that pragmatics considers meaning in context and traditional semantics studies meaning in isolation from the context of use.

presumption of optimal relevance

It means that every utterance comes with a presumption of the best balance of effort against effect. On the one hand, the effects achievable will never be less than is needed to make it worth processing. On the other hand, the effort required will never be more than is needed to achieve these effects. In comparison to the effects achieved, the effort needed is always the smallest.

Q-principle & R-principle

They are proposed by Horn who attempts to reduce all the Grice's maxims to two principles. They are as follows: Q-principle (hearer-based): make your contribution sufficient, say as much as you can (given R); R-principle (speaker-based): make your contribution necessary; say no more than you must (given Q).

relevance theory

This theory was formally proposed by Dan Sperber and Deirdre Wilson. They regard that all Gricean maxims, including the CP itself, should be reduced to a single principle of relevance: Every act of ostensive communication communicates the presumption of its own optimal relevance.

speech act theory

Speech act is an utterance conceived as an act by which the speaker does something. By saying *I name this ship the Queen Elizabeth* a speaker will, in the appropriate

Chapter 8
Language in Use

circumstances, perform the act of naming it. Speech act theory was first proposed by John L. Austin in his book *How to Do Things with Words* (1962). The theory was developed by J. R. Searle at the end of the 1960s, on the basis of work by Austin. It included, among other things, a division of such acts into representatives, directives, commissives, expressives, and declarations.

Practice

I. Mark the choice that best completes the statement. (20%)

1. What essentially distinguishes semantics and pragmatics is whether in the study of meaning _____ is considered.
   A. reference B. speech act C. practical usage D. context
2. A sentence is a _____ concept, and the meaning of a sentence is often studied in isolation.
   A. pragmatic B. grammatical C. mental D. conceptual
3. If we think of a sentence as what people actually utter in the course of communication, it becomes a (n) _____.
   A. constative B. directive C. utterance D. expressive
4. Which of the following is true?
   A. Utterances usually do not take the form of sentences.
   B. Some utterances cannot be restored to complete sentences.
   C. No utterances can take the form of sentences.
   D. All utterances can be restored to complete sentences.
5. Speech act theory did NOT come into being until _____.
   A. in the late 50's of the 20th century B. in the early 1950's
   C. in the late 1960's D. in the early 21st century
6. _____ is the act performed by or resulting from saying something; it is the consequence of, or the change brought about by the utterance.
   A. A locutionary act B. An illocutionary act
   C. A perlocutionary act D. A performative act
7. According to Searle, the illocutionary point of the representative is _____.
   A. to get the hearer to do something
   B. to commit the speaker to something's being the case
   C. to commit the speaker to some future course of action
   D. to express the feelings or attitude towards an existing state of affairs
8. All the acts that belong to the same category share the same purpose, but they differ _____.
   A. in their illocutionary acts B. in their intentions expressed
   C. in their strength or force D. in their effect brought about
9. _____ is advanced by Paul Grice.
   A. Cooperative Principle
   B. Politeness Principle
   C. The General Principle of Universal Grammar
   D. Adjacency Principle
10. In the following dialogue, B does not give enough information that is required, and he has flouted the maxim of _____.

A: *Do you know where Mr. Smith lives?*
B: *Somewhere in the southern suburbs of the city.*

  A. quality B. quantity C. relation D. manner

II. Mark the following statements with "T" if they are true or "F" if they are false. (10%)

1. Implicatures can be worked out on the basis of some previous information. That is their calculability.
2. It would be impossible to give an adequate description of meaning if the context of language use was left unconsidered.
3. What essentially distinguishes semantics and pragmatics is whether in the study of meaning the context of use is considered.
4. The major difference between a sentence and an utterance is that a sentence is not uttered while an utterance is.
5. The meaning of a sentence is abstract, but context-dependent.
6. The meaning of an utterance is decontexualized, therefore stable.
7. Utterances always take the form of complete sentences
8. Speech act theory was originated with the British philosopher John Searle.
9. Speech act theory started in the late 50's of the 20th century.
10. Austin made the distinction between a constative and a performative.

III. Fill in each of the following blanks with an appropriate word. The first letter of the word is already given. (20%)

1. P_____ is the study of how speakers of a language use sentences to effect successful communication.
2. The notion of c_____ is essential to the pragmatic study of language.
3. C_____ were statements that either state or describe and were thus verifiable.
4. A l_____ act is the act of uttering words, phrases, clauses. It is the act of conveying literal meaning by means of syntax, lexicon and phonology.
5. The i_____ act performed by the speaker is that by making such an utterance he has expressed, his intention of speaking, i.e. asking someone to close the door.
6. In his early study, Austin made a distinction of utterances between p_____ and c_____.
7. In the utterance *I name the ship the Queen Elizabeth* the word name is a p_____ verb.
8. In daily conversation people do not usually say things directly but tend to imply them and the implied meaning is termed by Grice as i_____.
9. a. *I saw a boy.*   b. *I saw a child.*
   The logical relationship between the above two sentences can be called e_____.
10. In Zipf's principle of least effort, he recognized two competing forces: the force of u_____, or speaker's economy, and the force of d_____, or hearer's economy.

IV. Explain the following concepts or theories. (20%)

1. Conversational implicature
2. Performatives
3. Locutionary act
4. Q-principle (Horn)

Chapter 8
Language in Use

V. Analyze the following situations. （10%）
1. Explain the following remarks with examples and make some comments.
   Both semantics and pragmatics are concerned with meaning, but the difference between them can be traced to two different uses of the verb mean: a. What does X mean? b. What did you mean by X?
2. Do you think Speaker B is cooperative in the following conversation? Support your argument with Cooperative Principle.
   Speaker A: *When is the bus coming?*
   Speaker B: *There has been an accident further up the road.*

VI. Essay questions. （20%）
   What do you know about Paul Grice's Cooperative Principle? Explain with examples.

参考答案

I.
1. D 2. B 3. C 4. B 5. A 6. C 7. B 8. C 9. A 10. B

II.
1. T 2. T 3. T 4. F 5. F 6. F 7. F 8. F 9. T 10. T

III.
1. Pragmatics   2. context   3. Constatives
4. locutionary   5. illocutionary   6. performatives; constatives
7. performative   8. implicature   9. entailment
10. unification; diversification

IV.
1. Conversational implicature: In our daily life, speakers and listeners involved in conversations are generally cooperating with each other. In other words, when people are talking with each other, they must try to converse smoothly and successfully. In accepting speakers' presuppositions, listeners have to assume that a speaker is not trying to mislead them. This sense of cooperation is simply one in which people having a conversation are not normally assumed to be trying to confuse, trick, or withhold relevant information from one another. However, in real communication, the intention of the speaker is often not the literal meaning of what he or she says. The real intention implied in the words is called conversational implicature.
2. Performative: In speech act theory an utterance which performs an act, such as *Watch out* (= a warning).
3. Locutionary act: A locutionary act is the saying of something which is meaningful and can be understood.
4. Horn's Q-principle: (1) Make your contribution sufficient (cf. quantity); (2) Say as much as you can (given R).

V.
1. Pragmatics is the study of the use of language in communication, particularly the relationships between sentences and the contexts and situations in which they are used. Pragmatics includes the study of
   (1) How the interpretation and use of utterances depends on knowledge of the real

world;

(2) How speakers use and understand speech acts;

(3) How the structure of sentences is influenced by the relationship between the speaker and the hearer.

Pragmatics is sometimes contrasted with semantics, which deals with meaning without reference to the users and communicative functions of sentences.

2. Yes, B is cooperative. On the face of it, B's statement is not an answer to A's question. B doesn't say *when*. However, A will immediately interpret the statement as meaning *I don't know* or *I am not sure*. Just assume that B is being *relevant* and *informative*. Given that B's answer contains relevant information, A can work out that *an accident further up the road* conventionally involves *traffic jam*, and *traffic jam* preludes *bus coming*. Thus, B's answer is not simply a statement of *when the bus comes*; it contains an implicature concerning *when the bus comes*.

VI.

1. His idea is that in making conversation, the participants must first of all be willing to cooperate; otherwise, it would not be possible for them to carry on the talk. This general principle is called the Cooperative Principle, abbreviated as CP. It goes as follows: make your conversational contribution such as required at the stage at which it occurs by the accepted purpose or direction of the talk exchange in which you are engaged.

   To be more specific, there are four maxims under this general principle:

   The maxim of quantity

   Make your contribution as informative as required (for the current purpose of the exchange).

   Do not make your contribution more informative than is required.

   The maxim of quality

   Do not say what you believe to be false.

   Do not say that for which you lack adequate evidence.

   The maxim of relation

   Be relevant.

   The maxim of manner

   Avoid obscurity of expression.

   Avoid ambiguity.

   Be brief (avoid unnecessary prolixity).

   Be orderly.

Further Practice

I. Mark the following statements with "T" if they are true or "F" if they are false. Provide explanations for the false statements.

1. What essentially distinguishes semantics and pragmatics is whether in the study of meaning the context of use is considered.

2. If we take a sentence for what people actually utter in the course of communication, it becomes an utterance.

3. All the utterances take the form of sentences.

4. Austin proposed the distinction between performatives and constatives, but soon he

Chapter 8
Language in Use

noticed that the difference between them is not absolute and gave up that distinction.
5. The second major theory in pragmatics is the theory of conversational implicature. It is proposed by a philosopher Grice.
6. Implicatures are calculable, because hearers are able to work out them according to some previous information. This characteristic is called calculability.
7. The Speaker's Meaning usually refers to the use of sentence with a meaning other than the conceptual meaning.
8. Constatives refer to sentences uttered by the speaker in company with the actual doing of something.
9. Perlocutionary Act refers to the making of a statement, offer, promise, etc. in uttering a sentence, by virtue if the conventional force associated with it.
10. *Anyway, women are women* is an example of violating Quality maxim.
11. If a synonymous word is used to replace a word in the utterance, the implicature is possible to be kept intact.
12. CP is, in a sense, comparable to illocutionary force in speech act theory in that they are both concerned with the contextual side of meaning.
13. Relevance theory is claimed to be able to reduce Gricean maxims, including CP itself, to a single principle.
14. According to Levinson, the Q-, I-, and M-principles are Grice's two maxims of Quantity and a maxim of Manner reinterpreted neo-classically.
15. Additional clauses cannot cancel implicatures.

II. Fill in each of the following blanks with (an) appropriate word(s).
1. The fact that speakers try to convey conversation implicatures and hearers are able to understand them suggests that implicatures are _____.
2. _____ is also known as defeasibility.
3. By _____ is meant that a conversational implicature is attached to the semantic content of what is said.
4. Dan Sperber and Deirdre Wilson argue that all Gricean maxims should be reduced to a single principle of _____.
5. Dan Sperber and Deirdre Wilson agree with Grice that communication is not simply a matter of encoding and decoding. It also involves _____.
6. The _____ -based Q-principle is a sufficiency condition in the sense that information provided is most the speaker is able to.
7. In Stephen Levinson's view, _____ is a measure of timely helpfulness with respect to interaction goals.
8. Levinson renames the second maxim of Quantity the Principle of _____.
9. In Levinson's view, only the _____ minimization has to do wit the I-principle.
10. Levinson also calls his principle "_____".
11. If we think of a sentence as what people actually utter in the course of communication, it becomes an _____.
12. The meaning of a sentence is _____, and decontexualized.
13. _____ were sentences that did not state a fact or describe a state, and were not verifiable.
14. A(n) _____ act is the act of expressing the speaker's intention; it is the act performed in saying something.

15. A(n) _____ is to commit the speaker himself to some future course of action.
16. A(n) _____ is to express feelings or attitude towards an existing state.
17. There are four maxims under the cooperative principle: the maxim of _____, the maxim of quality, the maxim of relation and the maxim of manner.

III. Mark the choice that best completes the statement.
1. The first major theory in the study of language in use was proposed by a philosopher _____.
   A. William   B. Chomsky   C. Austin   D. Grice
2. The hearer's shutting the window is the _____ act of the utterance *It is cold in here*.
   A. illocutionary   B. perlocutionary
   C. locutionary   D. none of the above
3. All the following people make revision on Grice's CP and its maxims except _____.
   A. Wilson   B. Levinson   C. Horn   D. Austin
4. The presence of a conversational implicature relies on a number of factors: the conventional meaning of words used, the CP, the linguistic and situational contexts, etc... So if any of them changes, the implicature will also change or even be cancelled. This fact shows the _____ of implicature.
   A. calculability   B. cancellability
   C. non-detachability   D. non-conventionality
5. Here are three utterances: a. *John's a genius*. b. *John's a big brain*. c. *John's an idiot*. When utterance a and b imply c, they show the _____ of conversational implicature.
   A. calculability   B. cancellability
   C. non-detachability   D. non-conventionality
6. Tautologies like *Boys are boys*, and *War is war*, are extreme examples in which _____ is violated.
   A. the first Quality maxim   B. the second Quality maxim
   C. the first Quantity maxim   D. the second Quantity maxim
7. Cancellability is also known as _____.
   A. calculability   B. non-detachability
   C. defeasibility   D. non-conventionality
8. The hearer-based Q-principle is first proposed by _____.
   A. Dan Sperber   B. Deirdre Wilson
   C. Laurence Horn   D. Stephen Levinson
9. In Levinson's view, the maxims of Quantity have to do with the quantity of _____.
   A. information   B. relevance
   C. connotation   D. denotation
10. In Levinson's view, only the semantic minimization has to do with the _____.
    A. the Q-principle   B. the I-principle
    C. the M-principle   D. the R-principle

IV. Answer the following questions as comprehensively as possible, giving examples if necessary.
1. Provide a situation in which Speaker B's utterance in the following conversation is relevant.
   A: *I do think our boss is at his wit's end, don't you?*
   B: *Huh, did you visit your parents this Christmas?*
2. Analyze the following sentences in terms of the distinction between performatives and

Chapter 8
Language in Use

constatives and try to provide other examples in your analysis.
- A. *I do* (sc. take this woman to be my lawful wedded wife) — as uttered in the course of the marriage ceremony.
- B. *I name this ship the Queen Elizabeth*.
- C. *I bequeath my watch to my brother* — as occurring in a will.
- D. *I pour some liquid into the tube*.

3. What do you know about Relevance Theory proposed by Dan Sperber and Deirdre Wilson?
4. Do you agree that the sentence *The president was assassinated* entails that *The president is dead*? Illustrate the difference between *implicature* and *entailment* with examples.

参考答案

I.
1. T 2. T
3. F. Most utterances take the form of sentences, yet some utterances are not, and some cannot even be restored to complete sentences.
4. T 5. T 6. T 7. T 8. T
9. F. That is not perlocutionary, but illocutionary act.
10. F. It violates the maxim of Quantity.
11. T 12. T 13. T 14. T
15. F. Additional clause can cancel the implicature. For instance, *There are 11 girls playing in the soccor field and there is an old man, who is their coach*.

II.
1. calculable
2. Cancellability
3. Non-Detachability
4. relevance
5. inference
6. hearer
7. relevance
8. Informativeness
9. semantic
10. heuristics
11. utterance
12. abstract
13. Performatives
14. illocutionary
15. commissive
16. expressive
17. quantity

III.
1. C 2. B 3. D 4. B 5. C 6. C 7. C 8. C 9. A 10. B

IV.
1. B's utterance violates the maxim of Relation by changing the topic initiated by Speaker A. This violation implies that Speaker B did not want to discuss A's remarks about their boss, and perhaps, A has committed a social gaffe.
2. In order to define performatives, Austin refers to those sentences which conform to the old prejudice in that they are used to describe or constate something, and which thus are true or false; and he calls such sentences *constatives*. In contrast to them, Austin defines *performatives* as follows:
   (1) Performative utterances are not true or false, that is, not truth-evaluable; instead when something is wrong with them then they are *happy* or *unhappy*.
   (2) The uttering of a performative is, or is part of, the doing of a certain kind of action (Austin later deals with them under the name illocutionary acts), the performance of which, again, would not normally be described as just *saying* or

describing something.

    For example, when Peter says *I promise to do the dishes* in an appropriate context then he thereby does not just say something, and in particular he does not just describe what he is doing; rather, in making the utterance he performs the promise; since promising is an illocutionary act, the utterance is thus a performative utterance. If Peter utters the sentence without the intention to keep the promise, or if eventually he does not keep it, then although something is not in order with the utterance, the problem is not that the sentence is false; it is rather *unhappy*, or *infelicitous*, as Austin also says in his discussion of so-called felicity conditions. In the absence of any such flaw, on the other hand, the utterance is to be assessed as *happy* or *felicitous*, rather than as *true*.

(3) As Austin later notices himself, Sentences A, B and C belong (more or less strikingly) to what Austin calls, explicit performatives; there are also *implicit*, *primitive*, or *inexplicit* performatives. When, for instance, one uses the word *Go!* in order to command someone to leave the room then this utterance is part of the performance of a command; and the sentence, according to Austin, is neither true nor false; hence the sentence is a performative; — still, it is not an explicit performative, for it does not make explicit that the act the speaker is performing is a command.

(4) Sentence D is a constative, and it can also be used to do things.

3. Sperber and Wilson's theory begins with some watershed assumptions that are typical of pragmatic theories. Namely, it agrees that all utterances are encountered in some context, frequently make use of sentences, and that all utterances convey a number of implicatures. In addition, they posit the notion of *manifestness*, which is when something is grasped either consciously or unconsciously by a person.

    They further note that it will be manifest to people who are engaged in inferential communication that each other have the notion of relevance in their minds. This will cause each person engaged in the interaction to arrive at the *presumption of relevance*, which is the notion that (1) *implicit messages are relevant enough to be worth bothering to process*, and (2) *the speaker will be as economical as they possibly can be in communicating it*.

    The core of the theory is the *principle of relevance*, one of the four Gricean maxims, which states that any utterance addressed to someone automatically conveys the presumption of its own optimal relevance. In this way, the vast majority of acts of communication will implicitly make manifest the intent to communicate. However, the actual process of deciphering other implicit interpretations is largely left to the communicators themselves by using mental shorthands, or heuristics.

    For Sperber and Wilson, relevance is conceived as relative or subjective, as it depends upon the state of knowledge of a hearer when they encounter an utterance. However, they are quick to note that their theory does not attempt to exhaustively define the concept of *relevance* in everyday use, but tries to show an interesting and important part of human speech. (Source: http://en.wikipedia.org/wiki/Relevance_theory)

4. Implicature is a technical term in the linguistic branch of pragmatics coined by Paul Grice. It refers to what is *suggested* in an utterance, even though not expressed nor *strictly implied* (that is, entailed) by the utterance. The statement *The president was assassinated* not only suggests that *The president is dead* is true, but requires that it be

true. The first sentence could not be true if the second were not true; if the president were not dead, then whatever it is that happened to him would not have counted as a (successful) assassination.

Similarly, unlike implicatures, entailments cannot be cancelled; there is no qualification that one could add to *The president was assassinated* which would cause it to cease entailing *The president is dead* while also preserving the meaning of the first sentence.

In pragmatics, entailment is the relationship between two sentences where the truth of one requires the truth of the other.

For example, the sentence a. *The president was assassinated* entails b. *The president is dead*. Notice also that if b. is false, then a. must necessarily be false. To show entailment, we must show that a. true forces b. to be true and b. false forces a. to be false.

Entailment differs from implicature (in their definitions for pragmatics), where the truth of one a. suggests the truth of the other b., but does not require it. For example, the sentence a. *Mary had a baby* and b. *got married* implicates that a. *she had a baby* before b. *the wedding*, but this is cancellable by adding —*not necessarily in that order*. Entailments are not cancellable.

Entailment also differs from presupposition in that in presupposition, the truth of what one is presupposing is taken for granted. A simple test to differentiate presupposition from entailment is negation. For example, both *The king of France is ill* and *The king of France is not ill* presuppose that there is a king of France. However *The president was not assassinated* no longer entails *The president is dead*. Presupposition remains under negation, but entailment does not. (Source: http://en.wikipedia.org/wiki)

Chapter 9 Language and Literature

Concepts & Theories

I. Stylistics
1. **The definition of stylistics**
   Stylistics is a branch of linguistics which studies the features of situationally distinctive uses (varieties) of language, and tries to establish principles capable of accounting for the particular choices made by individual and social groups in their use of language.
2. **The developmental stages of stylistics**
   (1) The 1960s was a decade of formalism.
   (2) The 1970s is a decade of functionalism.
   (3) The 1980s is a decade of discourse stylistics.
   (4) The 1990s is a decade in which socio-historical and socio-cultural stylistic studies are a main preoccupation.

II. Some General Features of the Literary Language
1. **Foregrounding and the grammatical form**
   In literary texts, the grammatical system of the language is often exploited, experimented with, or made to deviate from other, more everyday, forms of language, and as a result creates interesting new patterns in form and in meaning.
2. **Different figurative usages of language**
   (1) The literal meaning of a word or expression is its basic or original meaning. It is usually the first meaning of a word in the dictionary.
   (2) A figurative word or phrase is used in a different way from its usual meaning, to give you a particular idea or picture in the mind.
   (3) Trope is another word for the figurative use of language. It further divided into simile, metaphor, metonymy, synecdoche and so on.
   (4) A simile is a way of comparing one thing with another, of explaining what one thing is like by showing how it is similar to another thing.
   (5) A metaphor makes an implied comparison between two unlike elements.
   (6) Metonymy refers to the act of referring to something by the name of something else that is closely connected with it.
   (7) Synecdoche refers to using the name of part of an object to talk about the whole thing, or vice versa.
3. **The analysis of literary language**
   In one word, we look at the deviation or marked phenomena on different levels of language:
   (1) the level of lexis
   (2) the level of word order and syntax

(3) the level of textual patterns and discourses

III. The Language in Poetry

1. **Sound patterning**
   (1) Rhyme is the use of words in a poem or song that have the same sound, especially at the ends of lines.
   (2) In end rhyme the last word of a line has the same final sound as that of the last word of another line, sometimes immediately above or below, sometimes one or more lines away. It is presented as cVC.

2. **Different forms of sound patterning**
   (1) Alliteration has the initial consonants from different words identical. It is presented as Cvc.
   (2) Assonance describes different syllables with a common vowel. It can be presented as cVc.
   (3) Consonance has different syllables ending with the same consonants. It can be presented as cvC.
   (4) Reverse rhyme describes syllables sharing the vowel and initial consonant. It can be presented as CVc.
   (5) Pararhyme describes syllables having the same initial and final consonants but different vowels. It can be presented as CvC.
   (6) Repetition has two complete match of CVC.

3. **Stress and metrical patterning**
   (1) In poems we have stressed and unstressed syllables.
   (2) Metre refers to the arrangement of strong and weak stresses in lines of poetry that produces the rhythm.
   (3) Units of metre are called feet. We have different types of feet, namely, iamb, trochee, anapest, dactyl, spondee, pyrrhic and so on.
      ☆ An iambic foot contains two syllables, an unstressed syllable followed by a stressed one.
      ☆ A trochaic foot contains two syllables, a stressed syllable followed by a stressed one.
      ☆ An anapestic foot consists of three syllables. Two unstressed syllables are followed by a stressed one.
      ☆ A dactylic foot consists of three syllables. A stressed syllable is followed by two unstressed syllables.
      ☆ A spondaic foot consists of two stressed syllables.
      ☆ A pyrrhic foot consists of two unstressed syllables.
   (4) Lines that contain different numbers of feet.
      ☆ Dimetre refers to lines that contain two feet.
      ☆ Trimetre refers to lines that contain three feet.
      ☆ Tetrametre refers to lines that contain four feet.
      ☆ Pentametre refers to lines that contain five feet.
      ☆ Hexametre refers to lines that contain six feet.
      ☆ Heptametre refers to lines that contain seven feet.
      ☆ Octametre refers to lines that contain eight feet.

4. **Conventional forms of metre and sound**

(1) Couplets are two lines of verse, usually connected by a rhyme.
(2) Quatrains are four lines of verse, usually connected by a rhyme. They are quite common in English poetry.
(3) Blank verse consists of lines in iambic pentametre which do not rhyme.
(4) Sonnet refers to a poem that has 14 lines, each containing 10 syllables, and a fixed pattern of rhyme.
(5) Free verse refers to poetry that does not have a fixed structure and does not rhyme.
(6) Limericks refers to a humorous short poem, with two long lines that rhyme with each other, followed by two short lines that rhyme with each other and ending with a long line that rhymes with the first two.

5. **The poetic functions of sound and metre**
   (1) Different sound and metre in poems could be used for aesthetic pleasure.
   (2) Different sound and metre in poems could be used to conform to a convention/style/poetic form.
   (3) Different sound and metre in poems could be used to express or innovate with a form.
   (4) Different sound and metre in poems could be used to demonstrate technical skill, and for intellectual pleasure.
   (5) Different sound and metre in poems could be used for emphasis or contrast.
   (6) Different sound and metre in poems could be used for onomatopoeia function.

6. **How to analyze poetry?**
   When we analyze poetry we should focus on the following aspects:
   (1) Information about the poem.
   (2) The way the poem is structured.
      ☆ Layout—are the lines grouped into stanzas of equal or unequal lengths?
      ☆ Number of lines.
      ☆ Length of lines.
      ☆ Regular metre.
      ☆ End rhymes.
      ☆ Other forms of sound patterning.

IV. The Language in Fiction

1. **Functional prose and point of view**
   (1) There are three levels of discourse in fiction—the level between the novelist and the reader, the level between the narrator and the narratee, and the level between character A and character B.
   (2) I-narrator refers to the narrator of the story who is also a character in the story. I-narrator is also called a first-person narrator.
   (3) Third-person narrator refers to the narrator of the story who is not a character in the story.
   (4) Schema refers to the generalized knowledge about the sequence of events in particular sociocultural contexts, for example, going to a restaurant, purchasing a ticket, borrowing a book.
   (5) Schema-oriented language refers to the language told from the viewpoint of a certain character in the story.
   (6) Deixis refers to the characteristic function of linguistic expressions that relate to the

Chapter 9
Language and Literature

personal, and temporal aspect of utterances depending upon the given utterance situation.

2. **Speech and thought presentation**
   (1) Speech presentation. We have five kinds of speech presentation.
      ☆ DS Direct Speech: *"That is unfair!"*
      ☆ IS Indirect Speech: *He said that was unfair!*
      ☆ FIS Free Indirect Speech: *He hoped she would come.*
      ☆ NRSA Narrator's Representation of Speech Acts: *He expressed thanks.*
      ☆ NRS Narrator's Representation of Speech: *They talked.*
   (2) Thought presentation. We have five kinds of thought presentation.
      ☆ DT Direct Thought: *"He will be late." John thought.*
      ☆ IT Indirect Thought: *John thought he would be late.*
      ☆ FIT Free Indirect Thought: *He would be late.*
      ☆ NRTA Narrator's Representation of Thought Acts: *John considered her offer.*
      ☆ NRT Narrator's Representation of Thought: *John thought for a long time.*
   (3) Stream of consciousness writing refers to the free association of ideas and impressions in the mind in writing.

3. **Prose style**
   (1) Authorial style refers to a way of writing which recognizably belongs to a particular writer.
   (2) Text style deals in how linguistic choices help to construct textual meaning.

4. **How to analyze the language of fiction**
   When analyzing fiction we should pay attention to:
   (1) patterns of lexis
   (2) patterns of textual organization
   (3) foregrounded features, including figures of speech
   (4) whether any patterns of style variation can be discerned
   (5) discoursal patterning of various kinds, like turn-taking or patterns of inferencing
   (6) patterns of viewpoint manipulation, including speech and thought presentation

V. The Language in Drama

Stylists are concerned with the text on the pate, rather than the performance on the stage.

1. **How should we analyze drama**
   We can analyze drama as poetry, fiction or conversation.

2. **Analyzing dramatic language**
   We can examine the conversation in a drama from different angles.
   (1) Turn quantity and length can help us get the importance of the characters in the play.
   (2) Exchange sequence can help us understand the characters' feelings and intensions or the writer's style.
   (3) Production errors can be used to convey some feelings of the characters.
   (4) The cooperative principles could help readers understand the conversation and the play.
   (5) We could discover the relative status and changes in status of characters by observing the language in the play.
   (6) Register is the term used in linguistics to describe the relationship between a particular style of language and its context of use.

(7) We can discover the characters of the persons in the drama by observing the quantity of their speech.

3. How to analyze dramatic texts?
When we analyze dramatic texts, we should
(1) Paraphrase the text.
(2) Write a commentary on the text.
(3) Select a theoretical approach.

VI. The Cognitive Approach to Literature
1. The cognitive approach focuses on the cognitive structure and process of the linguistic choices in literature.
2. Figure and ground is one tool in cognitive analysis. A figure is like a foreground feature. It is also known as attention or attractors in cognitive linguistics. The opposite of figure is ground which is often neglected.
3. Image schemata can be loosely described as being the recurring patterns of our everyday perceptual interactions and bodily experiences. People use the image-schematic patterns in order to make meaning of the world when new situations arise.
4. Cognitive metaphor works by mapping specific characteristics of a source domain onto a target domain. There are three main types:
   (1) Structural cognitive metaphor;
   (2) Ontological cognitive metaphor;
   (3) Oriental cognitive metaphor.

Related Terms

alliteration

Alliteration means syllables which have identical initial consonants. The initial sound /f/ in *Fair is foul and foul is fair* is a good example of it.

anapest

An anapestic foot consists of three syllables; two unstressed syllables are followed by stressed one.

assonance

Assonance describes syllables with a common vowel (cVc).

authorial style

When people talk of style, they usually mean authorial style. This refers to the *world view* kind of authorial style. In other words a way of writing which recognizably belongs to a particular writer, say Jane Austen or Ernest Hemingway. This way of writing distinguishes one author's writing from that of others, and is felt to be recognizable across a range of texts written by the same writer, even though those writings are bound to vary as a consequence of being about different topics, describing different things, having different purposes and so on. It is this ability to perceive authorial style in the writings of a particular author that enables us to write pastiches and parodies.

blank verse

Blank verse consists of lines in iambic pentameters which do not rhyme.

cognitive metaphor

Cognitive metaphor works by mapping specific characteristics of a source domain onto a target domain. There are three main types, namely structural cognitive metaphor,

ontological cognitive metaphor and orientational cognitive metaphor.
consonance
　　Syllables ending with the same consonants (cvC) are described as having consonance.
couplets
　　Couplets are two lines of verse, usually connected by a rhyme.
dactylic foot
　　A dactylic foot is similar to an anapest, except reversed—a stressed syllable is followed by two unstressed ones.
deixis
　　Deixis refers to the characteristic function of linguistic expressions that relate to the personal, and temporal aspect of utterances depending upon the given utterance situation.
end rhyme
　　End rhyme means that the last word of a line (of a poem) has the same final sounds as the last word of another line, sometimes immediately above or below, sometimes one or more lines away.
feet
　　Units of meter are called feet.
figure and ground
　　In the Figure and Ground relationship, the prominence of the *figure* is important. It is like a foregrounded feature. A figure can be character, location, or thing and is often new or in motion and s thus prominent. The foregrounded literary elements, i.e. the figures, are also know as attention or attractors in cognitive linguistics, while their opposite, i.e. the ground, is known as neglect.
foregrounding
　　Foregrounding is artistically motivated deviation which exists in all levels of language—vocabulary, sound, syntax, meaning, graphology, etc.
free verse
　　Free verse refers to poetry that does not have a fixed structure and does not rhyme.
iambic foot
　　An iambic foot contains two syllables, an unstressed syllable followed by a stressed one. An example of it is: *and pa*lm *to pa*lm *is ho*ly *pa*lmer's *ki*ss (The stressed syllables are written in bold letters)
iambic pentameter
　　A ten-syllable line which has stress on alternate syllables and starts with an unstressed syllable is known as iambic pentameter.
image schemata
　　Image schemata can be loosely described as being the recurring patterns of our everyday perceptual interactions and bodily experiences. For example, whenever we stand up from a chair or sit down on it, or go into or out of a room we experience the image-schematic distinction between *up and down* and *in and out* respectively.
I-narrators
　　The person who tells the story may also be a character in the fictional world of the story, relating the story after the event. In this case the critics call the narrator a First-Person Narrator or I-Narrator because when the narrator refers to himself or herself in the story the first person pronoun *I* is used. First person narrators are often said to be *limited* because they don't know all the facts or *unreliable* because they trick the reader by withholding information or telling

untruths. This often happens in murder and mystery stories.

limericks

Limericks refers to a humorous short poem, with two long lines that rhyme with each other, followed by two short lines that rhyme with each other and ending with a long line that rhymes with the first two.

literal meaning

The first meaning for a word that a dictionary definition gives is usually its literal meaning.

literary stylistics

There is a very close relationship between language and literature. The part of linguistics that studies the language of literature is termed literary stylistics. It focuses on the study of linguistic features related to literary style.

litotes

A figure of speech consisting of an understatement in which an affirmative is expressed by negating its opposite, as in *This is no small problem*.

metaphor

There is a formal difference however, in that the words like or as do not appear. A metaphor, like a simile, also makes a comparison between two unlike elements; but unlike a simile, this comparison is implied rather than stated.

metonymy

Metonymy is a figurative use of language which means the act of referring to something by the name of something else that is closely connected with it.

meter

When stress is organized to form regular rhythms, the term used for it is meter.

pararhyme

When two syllables have the same initial and final consonants but different vowels (CvC), they pararhyme.

pyrrhic

Pyrrhic is a term used to refer to a pyrrhic foot which consists of two unstressed syllables.

quatrains

Stanzas of four lines, known as Quatrains, are very common in English poetry. Oliver Goldsmith's *When lovely Woman Stoops to Folly* written in 1766 is in quatrains.

register

Register is the term used in linguistics to describe the relationship between a particular style of language and its context of use. As language users, we can recognize a wide range of styles even though we might not be able to actively produce them. An example of linguistic register is legal discourse-we recognize a legal document when we see one, but lawyers are generally the only people who are trained to produce those legal documents using appropriate linguistic choices.

reverse rhyme

Reverse rhyme describes syllables sharing the vowel and initial consonant, (CVc), rather than the vowel and final consonant as is the case in rhyme.

rhyme

Rhyme is the use of words in a poem or song that have the same sound, especially at the ends of lines.

Chapter 9
Language and Literature

schema

schema refers to the generalized knowledge about the sequence of events in particular sociocultural contexts, for example, going to a restaurant, purchasing a ticket, borrowing a book.

schema-oriented language

Viewpoint (as in fictional language) is also schema-oriented. It is worth noting that different participants in the same situation will have different Schemas, related to their different viewpoints.

simile

A simile is a way of comparing one thing with another, of explaining what one thing is like by showing how it is similar to another thing, and it explicitly signals itself in a text, with the words *as* or *like*. The phrase *as cold as ice* is a common simile; the concept of coldness is explained in terms of an actual concrete object. The word *as* signals that the trope is a simile.

sonnet

Sonnet refers to a poem that has 14 lines, each containing 10 syllables, and a fixed pattern of rhyme.

spondee

A term used to refer a spondaic foot. A spondaic foot consists of two stressed syllables; lines of poetry rarely consist only of spondees.

stream of consciousness writing

The term *stream of consciousness* was originally coined by the philosopher William James in his *Principle of Psychology* (1890) to describe the free association of idea and impressions in the mind. It was later applied to the writing of William Faulkner, James Joyce, Virginia Woolf and others experimenting early in the 20th century with the novelistic portrayal of the free flow of thought. Perhaps the most famous piece of stream of consciousness writing is that associated with Leopold Bloom in Joyce's Ulysses.

stressed syllable

In English words of two syllables, one is usually uttered slightly louder, higher, held for slightly longer, or otherwise uttered slightly more forcefully than the other syllable in the same word, when the word is said in normal circumstances. This syllable is called the stressed syllable.

synecdoche

Synecdoche is usually classed as a type of metonymy. Synecdoche refers to using the name of part of an object to talk about the whole thing, and vice versa.

text style

Text style looks closely at how linguistic choices help to construct textual meaning. Just as authors cm be said to have style, so can text. Critics can talk of the style of Middlemarch, or even parts of it, as well as the style of George Eliot. When the style of texts or extract from texts is examined, we are even more centrally concerned with meaning that with the world view version of authorial style discussed above, and so when we examine text style we will need to examine linguistic choices which are intrinsically connected with meaning and effect on the reader. All of the areas we have looked at so far in this book could be relevant to the meaning of a particular text and its style; as can areas like lexical and grammatical patterning, even the positioning of something as apparently insignificant as a comma.

third-person narrators

If the narrator is not a character in the fictional world, he or she is usually called a Third-Person Narrator, because reference to all the characters in the fictional world of the story will involve the use of the third-person pronouns, *he*, *she*, *it* or *they*. This second main type of narrator is arguably the dominant narrator type.

trochee

A term used to call a trochaic foot. A trochaic foot contains two syllables with the stressed syllable comes first, followed by an unstressed syllable. *Willows whiten*, *aspens quiver* is an example of it.

trope

A word refers to language used in a figurative way for a rhetorical purpose. Tropes take different forms such as simile, metaphor, metonymy, synecdoche etc.

Practice

I. Mark the choice that best completes the statement. (20%)

1. We might say that _____ was a decade of formalism in stylistics.
   A. the 1960s   B. the 1970s   C. the 1980s   D. the 1990s
2. *They were short of hands at harvest time* can be classified as a type of _____.
   A. simile   B. metaphor   C. metonymy   D. antonomasia
3. Most people are familiar with the idea of _____ in poetry, and indeed for some, this is what defines poetry.
   A. meter   B. lines   C. rhyme   D. rhythm
4. The sound patterning _____ is consonance.
   A. Cvc   B. cVc   C. cvC   D. CVc
5. The sound patterning CvC is _____.
   A. Repetition   B. Pararhyme   C. Reverse rhyme D. Assonance
6. An ANAPESTIC foot consists of three syllables: _____.
   A. Two stressed syllables followed by an unstressed one
   B. Two unstressed syllables followed by a stressed one
   C. A stressed syllable followed by two unstressed ones
   D. An unstressed syllable followed by two stressed ones
7. Robert Browning's poem *Andrea del Sarto* is _____.
   A. couplets   B. quatrains   C. free verse   D. blank verse
8. The term STREAM OF CONSCIOUSNESS was originally coined by _____ in his *Principle of Psychology* to describe the free association of ideas and impressions in the mind.
   A. William James   B. Henry James
   C. William Faulkner   D. James Joyce
9. _____ is the term used in linguistics to describe the relationship between a particular style of language and its context of use.
   A. Turn quantity   B. Exchange sequence
   C. Status   D. Register
10. When stress is organized to form regular rhythms, the term used for it is _____.
    A. meter   B. beat   C. rhyme   D. rhythm

Chapter 9
Language and Literature

II. Mark the following statements with "T" if they are true or "F" if they are false. (10%)

1. The 1960s was decade of formalism, the 1970s a decade of discourse stylistics, and the 1980s a decade of functionalism.
2. Trope refers to language used in a figurative way for a rhetorical purpose.
3. We say that the sentence *the world is like a stage* is simile.
4. The term *stream of consciousness* is to describe the free association of ideas and impressions in the mind, and was originally coined by William Faulkner.
5. Text style looks closely at how linguistic choices help to construct textual meaning.
6. Direct thought is quite often used to represent imaginary conversations, which characters have with themselves or others.
7. Blank verse consists of lines in iambic pentameter that has rhyme.
8. The layout of a poem is particularly significant in the interpretation of visual poetry.
9. Because metaphors are not explicitly signaled, metaphor and simile cannot be identified.
10. In the poem, lines with more than six feet are hexameter.

III. Fill in each of the following blanks with an appropriate word. The first letter of the word is given. (20%)

1. A line that contains five iambs is in iambic pentametre. Similarly, lines that contain two feet (of any kind) are described as d_____.
2. An i_____ foot contains two syllables, an unstressed syllable followed by a stressed one.
3. R_____ rhyme describes syllables sharing the vowel and initial consonant, CVc, rather than the vowel and the final consonant as is the case in rhyme.
4. When stress is organized to form regular rhythms, the term used for it is m_____.
5. C_____ are two lines of verse, usually connected by a rhyme.
6. S_____ refers to using the name of part of an object to talk about the whole thing, and vice versa.
7. In the word *pilgrim*, _____ is a stressed syllable while _____ is an unstressed syllable.
8. The part of linguistics that studies the language of literature is termed as l_____ stylistics. It focuses on the study of linguistic features related to literary style.
9. Stanzas of four lines are called q_____.
10. An a_____ foot consists of three syllables; two unstressed syllables are followed by a stressed one.

IV. Explain the following concepts or theories. (20%)

1. Stream of consciousness writing
2. Simile
3. Iambic pentameter
4. Register

V. Match each term in Column A with one relevant item in Column B. (10%)

A	B
(1) Alliteration	a. will-all
(2) Assonance	b. with-will
(3) Consonance	c. live-love
(4) Reverse rhyme	d. me-my
(5) Pararhyme	e. come-love
(6) Iamb	f. Willows whiten aspens quiver
(7) Trochee	g. One for the master, and one for the dame
(8) Dactyl	h. and palm to palm is holy palmer's kiss
(9) Spondee	i. Without cause be he pleased, without cause be he cross
(10) Anapest	j. and a black-/Back gull bent like an iron bar slowly

VI. Essay questions. (20%)
1. What did Walter Nash propose on how to analyze dramatic texts?
2. Name five different forms of sound patterning and explain them.

参考答案

I.
1. A 2. C 3. C 4. C 5. B 6. B 7. D 8. A 9. D 10. A

II.
1. F 2. T 3. T 4. F 5. T 6. T 7. F 8. T 9. F 10. F

III.
1. dimetre   2. iambic   3. Reverse   4. meter   5. Couplets
6. Synecdoche   7. pil; grim   8. literary   9. quatrains   10. anapestic

IV.
1. The term *stream of consciousness* was originally coined by the philosopher William James in his principle of psychology (1890) to describe the fee association of idea and impressions in the mind. It was later applied to the writing of William Faulkner, James Joyce, Virginia Woolf and others experimenting early in the 20th century with the novelistic portrayal of the free flow of thought.

2. A simile is a way of comparing one thing with another, of explaining what one thing is like by showing how it is similar to another thing, and it explicitly signals itself in a text, with the words as or like. The phrase as cold as ice is a common simile; the concept of coldness is explained in terms of an actual concrete object. The word *as* signals that the trope is a simile.

3. An iambic pentameter is a ten-syllable line which has stress on alternate syllables and starts with an unstressed syllable. It is a very specific and popular form in English poetry.

4. Register is the term used in linguistics to describe the relationship between a particular

style of language and its context of use. As language users, we can recognize a wide range of styles even though we might not be able to actively produce them. An example of linguistic register is legal discourse-we recognize a legal document when we see one, but lawyers are generally the only people who are trained to produce those using appropriate linguistic choices.

V.
(1) d (2) e (3) a (4) b (5) c (6) h (7) f (8) g (9) j (10) i

VI.
1. Walter Nash (1989) suggests that dramatic texts can be analyzed in a series of stages, starting with the most basic and least controversial, and working up to the most sophisticated and debatable. If you are required to analyze a dramatic text, you may find it useful to refer to these guidelines. The stages he outlines are as follows:
   —**paraphrase the text**—**i. e. put it into your own words**
      This can be quite a crude approach, but it ensures that your basic understanding of the text is sound. It is a chance to check any unfamiliar words or grammatical constructions. It also allows you to check how each of the characters contributes to the plot of the play. Although your paraphrase should be as close to the content of the original as possible, there may be still some room for ambiguities or different interpretations. As far as possible you should note these, perhaps by indicating the various possible interpretations in different paraphrases.
   —**write a commentary on the text**
      This is where you interpret what significance of the extract you are analyzing is in the context of the play as a whole; how does it contribute to the development of the plot and the evolution of the characters? This is also a chance to check any literary allusions and ambiguities which give the text more than one possible reading.
   —**select a theoretical approach, perhaps from those discussed above**
      This will be a narrower process, where you consider the text from a specific point of view, applying one theoretical model of the way language and communication work. This needs to be very thorough and detailed, and it is more likely to be debatable whether the approach you have selected is appropriate. Applying a theoretical model to the text may leave you feeling that you have learnt very little that is new, or that you have learnt a great deal—it is far more *chancey* than either the paraphrase or the commentary in terms of what you get out of it.

2. (1) Alliteration
      The initial consonants are identical in alliteration (Cvc). As you can see, pleasures and prove, thought both start with /p/, have different consonant clusters: /pl / and /pr/. Therefore they are not completely alliterative.
   (2) Assonance
      Assonance describes syllables with a common vowel (cVc).
   (3) Consonance
      Syllables ending with the same consonants (cvC) are described as having consonance.
   (4) Reverse rhyme
      Reverse rhyme describes syllables sharing the vowel and initial consonant, CVc, rather than the vowel and the final consonant as is the case in rhyme.

(5) Pararhyme

When two syllables have the same initial and final consonants but different vowels (CvC), they pararhyme.

Further Practice

I. Fill in each of the following blanks with (an) appropriate word(s).

1. The part of linguistics that studies the language of literature is termed _____, and it focus on the study of linguistic features related to _____.
2. _____ describes language use, which departs in some way from everyday use of language.
3. A simile is a way of _____ one thing with another, of explaining what one thing is like by showing how it is _____ to another thing, and it explicitly signals itself in a text, with the words as or like.
4. A metaphor, like a simile also makes a comparison between two _____, but unlike a simile, this comparison is _____ rather than stated.
5. _____ refers to using the name of part of an object to talk about the whole thing, and vice versa.
6. End rhyme is where the _____ of a line has the _____ final sounds as the last word of another line.
7. Where two syllables have the same initial and final consonants, but different vowels, they _____.
8. A spondaic foot consists of two _____; a pyrrhic foot consists of two unstressed syllables.
9. If the narrator is not a character in the fictional world, he or she is usually called a _____.
10. The branch of stylistics _____ has its research focus on image schemata, figure and ground, etc.
11. Another word for the figurative use of language is _____, which refers to language used in a figurative way for the rhetorical purpose.
12. Actually, some use of figurative language such as metaphor and synecdoche can be classified as _____ deviation.
13. _____ consists of lines in iambic pentametre which do not rhyme, while _____ do not have a fixed structure and do not rhyme.
14. Poems have more _____ deviation than novels and dramas.
15. Sometimes the sentence meaning and the utterance meaning of the same sentence should be quite different. So we have to adopt _____ analysis in stylistics.

II. Mark the following statements with "T" if they are true or "F" if they are false. Provide explanations for the false statements.

1. Sometimes novelists use definite reference for the first mentioning of certain details in the novel by positioning readers as people who are familiar to those details.
2. As we move from NRS to DS the speech contribution of the character becomes more and more muted.
3. The FIS usually occurs in a form which appears at first sight to be IS but also has DS features.
4. Direct thought tends to be used for presenting conscious deliberative thought, and it

occurs in quotation marks.
5. As direct thought takes the same linguistic form as the soliloquy does in drama, it is usually ambiguous as to whether the character involved is thinking aloud or talking to the audience.
6. The free indirect thought gives the effect that readers can get a distanced *bird's-eye view* of the characters.
7. Usually the language used in stream of consciousness writing is characterized by a highly elliptical sentence structure but is very cohesive.
8. The language in the writing of stream of consciousness always breaks the Gricean maxims of Quantity and Manner. So it can not be successfully communicative.
9. Stylistic analysis of dramatic texts has tended to follow either of the two approaches: drama as poetry and drama as conversation.
10. One important quality that makes drama a genre is its emphasis on verbal interaction, and the way relationships between people are constructed and negotiated through what they say.
11. The analysis of the exchange sequence in drama will reveal the social status, and changes in status, of characters.
12. If a character is shy or hesitated, he or she will make production errors.
13. Register refers to the relationship between a particular style of language and the users.
14. The analysis of turn quantity and length may help us to tell central characters from minor characters.
15. Drama differs fundamentally from fiction in that it usually lacks a narrative voice.
16. Most characters in a novel have their individual schemata.
17. First-person narrators are often said to be *limited* because they don't know all the facts or *unreliable* because they trick the reader by withholding information or telling untruths, so we should abandon first-person narrator in the novel.
18. We could not get the background information in a play because there is not a narrator that can tell us that.

III. Mark the choice that best completes the statement.
1. Among the following concerns, _____ does NOT belong to the domain of stylistic studies.
   A. what is implied by a certain turn taking way in a certain context
   B. the rhetorical tools used in a certain passage
   C. how a text is constructed
   D. the relationship between a dialect speaker and the society that the speaker is in
2. Among the following linguists, _____ deals in formalism in stylistics.
   A. Halliday   B. Jakobson   C. Leech   D. Bakhtin
3. Among the following, _____ is NOT a deviation at the vocabulary level.
   A. *And I Tieresias have foresuffered all*.
   B. *... the widow-making unchilding unfathering deeps*.
   C. *And storms bulge his fame*.
   D. *Our hearts' charity's hearth's fire, our thoughts' chivalry's throng's Lord*.
4. The sentence *Talent Mr. Micawber has, capital Mr. Micawber has not* can be classified as _____ deviation.
   A. vocabulary   B. syntactic   C. phonological   D. semantic

5. *The White House* as in *The White House is going to visit China next month* is the figurative speech of _____.
   A. simile   B. metaphor   C. synecdoche   D. metonymy
6. *live-with-will* and *come-love* can be described as _____.
   A. alliteration   B. consonance   C. assonance   D. pararhyme
7. Among the following terms, _____ does not describe a certain kind of foot.
   A. anapest   B. repetition   C. iamb   D. spondee
8. A trochaic heptameter poem is said to have _____ feet in each line and _____ syllables in each foot.
   A. 6, 2   B. 7, 2   C. 6, 3   D. 7, 3
9. The famous play *Romeo and Juliet* has the format of _____.
   A. iambic pentametre   B. iambic hexametre
   C. dactylic pentametre   D. dactylic hexametre
10. _____ refers to a poem that has 14 lines, each containing 10 syllables, and a fixed pattern of rhyme.
    A. free verse   B. blank verse   C. sonnet   D. limericks
11. The first-person narrator would NOT appear in _____.
    A. novels   B. poems   C. dramas   D. NRS
12. The sentence *John gave his father a cap which he took it to his house.* is very fuzzy because it has fuzzy _____.
    A. verbs   B. names   C. deixises   D. grammar
13. In the stream of consciousness writing, the stream of consciousness is _____.
    A. DT   B. IT   C. FIT   D. NRT
14. Stylists focus on _____ when they analyze drama.
    A. the performance   B. the text of drama
    C. the playing skills   D. the style
15. _____ studies the cognitive structure and process of the linguistic choices in literature.
    A. Cognitive metaphor   B. Cognitive pragmatics
    C. Cognitive linguistics   D. Cognitive stylistics

IV. Classify the deviations in each of the following into different categories.

   Vocabulary deviation: _____
   Syntactic deviation: _____
   Semantic deviation: _____
   Phonological deviation: _____
   Graphological deviation: _____

1. The major again pressed to his blue eyes the tips of the fingers that were disposed on the edge of the wheeled chair with **careful carelessness**, after the Cleopatra model and Mr. Dombey bowed.
2. "May God starve **ye** yet," yelled an old Irish woman who now threw open a nearby window and stuck out her head. "Yes, and you," she added, catching the eye of one of the policeman. "You bloody **murthering thafe**! Crack my son over the head, will you, you hard-hearted, **murthering divil**? Ah, **ye**—"
3. **Alone** she cuts and binds the grain,
   And sings a melancholy strain;

Chapter 9
Language and Literature

O listen! for the vale profound
Is overflowing with the sound.
4. Do not go **gentle** into that good night.
5. My only **love** sprung from my only **hate**. Too early seen unknown and known too late! Prodigious birth of love that it is to me, that I must **love a loathed enemy**. *-Romeo and Juliet*
6. **Me up at does**
   out of the floor
   quietly Stare
   a poisoned mouse
   still who alive
   is asking what
   have i done that
   You wouldn't have
7. Return to her? ... No, rather I abjure all **roofs** and choose ...
8. We left the town refreshed and **rehatted**.
9. O what a noble mind is here **o'erthrown**!
   The **courtier's, soldier's, scholar's eye, tongue, sword.**
10. Till **a'** the seas gang dry, my dear,
    And the rocks melt **wi'** the sun
    I will love thee still, my dear,
    While the sands **o'** life shall run.
11. "Don't be such a harsh parent, father!"
    "Don't **father** me!" -H.G. Wells
12.   A Christmas Tree
                         Star
                     If you are
              A love compassionate,
         You will walk with us this year,
    We face a glacial distance, who are here
                     Huddled
                  At your feet
13. Valuing himself not a little upon his elegance, being indeed a proper man of his person, this **talkative** now applied himself to his dress.

V. Identify the figures of speech in each of the following sentences, using the given letters to indicate the type of the figures of speech. (*A* for simile, *B* for metaphor, *C* for antonomasia, *D* for synecdoche, *E* for metonymy, *F* for litotes and *G* for Repetition)
1. Mr. Martin bought the pack of Camels on Monday night in the most crowded cigar store on Broadway.
2. The pen is mightier than the sword.
3. Childhood is like a swiftly passing dream.
4. Woe to them who call evil good and good evil.
5. This is no small problem.
6. All the world's a stage.
7. They are short of hands at harvest time.

8. Justice took no note of Joe; and he paid the same tribute to Justice.
9. She's an angel and he's a lion in battle.
10. So are you to my thoughts as food to life.
11. I know it helped put me at ease when I felt like the new kid at school at my first economic summit in Ottawa in 1981.
12. He is something of a political chameleon.
13. The school should provide students a fleeting chance to move on to college, productive jobs, decent incomes and a foothold in the culture.
14. The MYM15 billion proposed stock swap with Novell gives Lotus the technical muscle to provide a lot of those connections.
15. You can get a good cup at Susan's café.
16. We are human and human beings are far from perfect. To be human implies that we will make mistakes. But it is more than that we feel human. We now feel entitled.
17. Both sides are looking for a virgin birth, a deal with no obvious father.
18. If we try to implement these ideas (that English should be replaced by Hindi and the 15 recognized state languages), India will become a Tower of Babel.
19. There is a mixture of the tiger and the ape in the character of a Frenchman.
20. Her behavior when her husband is away causes the neighbors to raise their eyebrows.

VI. Answer the following questions as comprehensively as possible, giving examples if necessary.

1. Why do poets use sound and metrical patterning?
2. How should we analyze poetry?
3. How should we analyze the language of fiction?
4. The following are two quotes of First Appearance Soliloquy from two characters (Liu Mengmei (柳梦梅/生,主角) and the messenger(报子,龙套)) in *The Peony Pavilion*.

【真珠帘】〔生上〕河东旧族、柳氏名门最。论星宿,连张带鬼。几叶到寒儒,受雨打风吹。谩说书中能富贵,颜如玉,和黄金那里？贫薄把人灰,且养就这浩然之气。〔鹧鸪天〕"刮尽鲸鳌背上霜,寒儒偏喜住炎方。凭依造化三分福,绍接诗书一脉香。能凿壁,会悬梁,偷天妙手绣文章。必须砍得蟾宫桂,始信人间玉斧长。"

小生姓柳,名梦梅,表字春卿。原系唐朝柳州司马柳宗元之后,留家岭南。父亲朝散之职, 母亲县君之封。〔叹介〕所恨俺自小孤单,生事微渺。喜的是今日成人长大,二十过头,志 慧聪明,三场得手。只恨未遭 时势,不免饥寒。赖有始祖柳州公,带下郭橐驼,柳州衙 舍,栽接花果。橐驼遗下一个驼孙,也跟随俺广州种树,相依过活。虽然如此,不是男儿 结果之场。每日情思昏昏,忽然半月之前,做下一梦。梦到一园,梅花树下,立着个美人, 不长不短,如送如迎。说道:"柳生,柳生,遇俺方有姻缘之分,发迹之期。"因此改名梦 梅,春卿为字。正是:"梦短梦长俱是梦,年来年去是何年！"

【九回肠】〔解三酲〕虽则俺改名换字,俏魂儿未卜先知？定佳期盼煞蟾宫桂,柳梦梅不卖 查梨。还则怕嫦娥妒色花颓气,等的俺梅子酸心柳皱眉,浑如醉。〔三学士〕无萤凿遍了邻 家壁,甚东墙不许人窥！有一日春光暗度黄金柳,雪意冲开了白玉梅。〔急三枪〕那时节走 马在章台内,丝儿翠,笼定个百花魁。虽然这般说,有个朋友韩子才,是韩昌黎之后,寄 居赵佗王台。他虽是香火秀才,却有些谈吐,不免随喜一会。

门前梅柳烂春晖,梦见君王觉后疑。
心似百花开未得,托身须上万年枝。

-*Liu Mengmei's first appearance soliloquy*

Chapter 9
Language and Literature

（净扮报子上）诏从日月威光远，兵洗江淮杀气高。

-*Messenger A's first appearance soliloquy*

(1) Find the similarities between the two quotes in terms of content and text pattern.

(2) Find the rhythm pattern of the underlined part.

(3) Tell the differences between the two soliloquies in the aspect of textual patterns and content.

(4) What can you infer from the comparison of the two quotes from an important figure（柳梦梅）and an unimportant figure（报子）in terms of content and textual patterns?

5. The following quote is from Du Liniang in *The Peony Pavilion*.

［前腔］（贴持酒台，随旦上）娇莺欲语，眼见春如许。寸草心，怎报的春光一二！

This part can be said to be marked because it is the first appearance soliloquy from the very important figure in the play—Du Liniang（杜丽娘）. Usually the first appearance soliloquy of an important figure in an ancient drama should include the introduction of the figure's self entity, his/her background, the figure's past and future actions or even the plot of the play, and it is usually long. Yet it is short compared with the prominence of the female character. Could you give some possible reasons to explain why the playwright arranged her soliloquy this way?

6. Can you list some functions of language? What function do you think can distinguish literature from other forms of language? Give detailed illustration.

7. How should we say that a play actor is communicatively successful?

8. The following is taken from Shaw's *Major Barbara*. Read the dialogue and tell who the dominant person is and who is not with the language/turn arrangement features in the text.

(Context: Lady Britonart, a woman of about fifty, is writing at her writing desk in a rather grand room. Her son, Stephen, a young man, comes in.)

Stephen: What's the matter?

Lady B: Presently, Stephen.

(Stephen walks submissively to the settee and sits down. He takes up a Liberal weekly called *The Speaker*.)

Lady B: Don't begin to read, Stephen. I shall require all your attention.

Stephen: It was only when I was waiting—

Lady B: Don't make excuses, Stephen. (He puts down *The Speaker*.) Now! (She finishes her writing; rises and comes to the settee.) I have not kept you waiting very long, I think.

Stephen: Not at all, mother.

Lady B: Bring me my cushion. (He takes the cushion from the chair at the desk and arranges it for her as she sits down on the settee.) Sit down. (He sits down and fingers his tie nervously.) Don't fiddle with your tie, Stephen: there is noting the matter with it.

Stephen: I beg your pardon. (He fiddles with his watch chain instead.)

Lady B: Now are you attending to me, Stephen?

Stephen: Of course, mother.

Lady B: No: it's not of course. I want something much more than your everyday matter-of-course attention. I am going to speak to you very seriously, Stephen. I wish you would let that watch chain alone.

Stephen: (Hastily relinquishing the chain.) Have I done anything to annoy you, mother? If so, it was quite unintensional.

Lady B: (astonished) Nonsense! (With some remorse.) My poor boy, did you think I was angry with you?

Stephen: What is it then, mother? You are making me very uneasy.

Lady B: (squaring herself at him rather aggressively) Stephen: may I ask how soon you intend to realize that you are a grown-up man, and that I am only a woman?

Stephen: (amazed) Only a —

Lady B: Don't repeat my words, please: it is a most aggravating habit. You must learn to face life seriously, Stephen. I really cannot bear the whole burden of our family affairs any longer. You must advise me: you must assume the responsibility.

Stephen: I!

Lady B: Yes, you, of course. You were 24 last June. You've been at Harrow and Cambridge. You've been to India and Japan. You must know a lot of things, now; unless you have wasted your time most scandalously. Well, advise me.

9. The following is a poem by Tennyson-*The Eagle*. Analyze the poem according to the requirements and answer the questions that follow.

    The Eagle
HE clasps the crag with crooked hands;
Close to the sun in lonely lands,
Ringed with the azure world, he stands.
The wrinkled sea beneath him crawls;
He watches from his mountain walls,
And like a thunderbolt he falls.

(1) What is the stress and metrical pattern of this poem?

(2) Is there any rhyme pattern in this poem?

(3) In line one of this poem, there is a recurrence of plosives, e.g. /t/, /k/ and /g/. What effects do they produce?

(4) Is there any figurative use of language in this poem?

参考答案

I.

1. literary stylistics; literary style   2. deviation/ foregrounding
3. comparing, similar   4. different elements; implied   5. Synecdoche
6. last word; same   7. pararhyme   8. stressed syllables
9. third-person narrator   10. cognitive stylistics   11. trope
12. semantic   13. blank verse; free verse   14. grammatical
15. pragmatic

II.

1. T
2. F. As we move from DS to NRS the speech contribution of the character becomes more and more muted.
3. T   4. T   5. T
6. F. The free indirect thought gives the effect that readers can get close to the thinking

Chapter 9
Language and Literature

character.
7. F. Usually the language used in stream of consciousness writing is characterized by a highly elliptical sentence structure and the language is not very cohesive.
8. F. The language in the writing of stream of consciousness always breaks the Gricean maxims of Quantity and Manner, but it can be successfully communicative, because the unreasonable writing behavior is related to a relevant authorial purpose. In other words, it serves to achieve the author's writing goal.
9. F. We can also analyze drama as fiction.
10. T   11. T   12. T
13. F. Register refers to the relationship between a particular style of language and the context of use.
14. T   15. T   16. T
17. F. We shouldn't abandon the writing style of first-person narrators, because by employing first-person narrator, the writer would usually pull the distance between the writer and the readers near.
18. F. In the play, the chorus, the soliloquy of the actors and the narrators could all serve the function of giving new information to the audience.

III.
1. D   2. B   3. D   4. B   5. D   6. C   7. B   8. B   9. A   10. C
11. D   12. C   13. A   14. B   15. D

IV.
vocabulary deviation: 8, 11, 13
syntactic deviation: 6, 3, 4, 9, 13
semantic deviation: 1, 5, 7
phonological deviation: 9, 2, 10
graphological deviation: 6, 12

V.
1. C   2. E   3. A   4. G   5. F   6. B   7. D   8. G   9. B   10. A
11. A   12. A   13. B   14. E   15. E   16. G   17. C   18. C   19. D   20. E

VI.
1. Some of the reasons given by Thornborrow and Wareing (1998) can give us an idea of the range of effects sound and meter can have. Reasons for poets using sound and metrical patterning include:
   (1) For aesthetic pleasure—sound and metrical patterning are fundamentally pleasing, in the way that music is; most people enjoy rhythms and repeated sounds. Children in particular seem to like verse for this reason.
   (2) To conform to a convention/style/poetical form—as with clothes and buildings, poetry has fashions, and different forms of sound patterning have been popular at different times. The time at which they were writing has a greet influence on why poets selected the forms they did.
   (3) To express or innovate with a form—poets innovate to create new poetic forms, and also to challenge assumptions about the forms of language which are considered appropriate to poetry.
   (4) To demonstrate technical skill, and for intellectual pleasure—there is a kind of

satisfaction to be derived form the cleverness of some poems and magic of form and meaning being perfectly combined. Poets show their skill with words in the same way as athletes demonstrate their ability to run fast or leap hurdles.

(5) For emphasis or contrast—some metrical pattern, such as the *slow spondees*, or sudden changes in a previously regular pattern, draw your attention to that place in the poem.

(6) Onomatopoeia—When the rhythm of a line or its sound imitates the sound of what is being described, this is known as Onomatopoeia.

2. The following checklist provided by Thornborrow and Wareing (1998) may help to cover the areas of discussion when analyzing poetry.

(1) Information about the poem

If this information is available to you, somewhere in your analysis give the title of the poem, the name of the poet, the period in which the poem was written, the genre to which the poem belongs, e.g. lyric, dramatic, epic sonnet, or satire, etc. You might also mention the topic, e.g. whether it is a love poem, a war poem or a nature poem.

(2) The way the poem is structured

These are structural features that you should check for; there may well be others we have omitted. Don't worry if you don't find any examples of reverse rhyme, or a regular metrical pattern in your poem. What matters is that you looked, so if they had been there, you wouldn't have missed them.

You don't need to write about all the headings below. Working through them is the process of getting to know the poem. After that you can select which are the interesting features you want to discuss.

— Layout—are the lines grouped into stanzas of equal/unequal lengths?
— Number of lines.
— Length of lines-count the syllables; are lines of regular syllable length?
— Regular meter-which syllables carry stress? Are there an equal number of unstressed syllables between the stressed ones? How many feet (stressed syllables) are there in a line? Comment on the type of foot and the number of feet per line- or say that there is no regular metrical pattern. Finding no regular meter is not to say that there is no exploitation of meter however. A poem can be written in free verse and can occasionally use particular metrical patterns for emphasis, or onomatopoeic effect.
— End rhymes—plot the end rhyme, if there is any. You could check with a reference source such as the essay by Jon Stalwartly at the end of the Norton Anthology, to see if the meter and end rhyme conform to a particular style of poem (e.g. ballad or a sonnet).

3. The language features we should examine to elucidate the style of a text or a corpus of and author's writing may include the following aspects:

— patterns of lexis (vocabulary);
— patterns of grammatical organization;
— patterns of textual organization (how the units of textual organization, from sentences to paragraphs and beyond, are arranged);
— foregrounded features, including figures of speech;
— whether any patterns of style variation can be discerned;

Chapter 9
Language and Literature

— discoursal patterning of various kinds, like turn-taking or patterns of inferencing;

— patterns of viewpoint manipulation, including speech and thought presentation.

4. (1) Both soliloquies introduce something related to the plot or background of the play. The first quote introduces Liu's background, his identity, the background of the play and his future action or the future plot. The second introduces the background of the play.

   Both soliloquies have some set patterns. The first has tune, plain words and poem. The second has a couplet.

   (2) The first sentence in the first soliloquy has the end rhyme as *ababab*.

   (3) From the aspect of quality and quantity, the first soliloquy is greater than the second one. The first quote has so many forms like tune, plain words and poems. But the second one has very simple format-couplet. The first quote has much more words than the second quote. The content relating to the background of the speaker is a lot more than the second one.

   (4) From the comparison above we can get the conclusion that the first appearance soliloquy that has more words or more content related to the speaker would most probably belong to the important character in the play, and vice versus. As is known to all that Liu is the hero in the play, and the messenger is just a minor role in the play, we could infer that First Appearance Soliloquies would most probably differ according to the prominence of its speaker.

5. It is true that Du Liniang is a central role in the play *The Peony Pavilion*, but her First Appearance Soliloquy is comparatively short. There may be several reasons for the marked phenomenon.

   (1) Maybe before the appearance of Du, there are other people who have introduced her; or in the following part, she is going to be introduced again by others.

   (2) If there is no other person to introduce Du. The writer may want to create a familiar scene in the reader's mind by not introducing her. The writer may want us to feel that we have already known this girl or we have seen this girl somewhere-just like Liu's feeling toward Du. In this sense, the writer is involving the readers in this play, thus creating a successful effect of the play among the readers.

   On the other hand, by only presenting some words relating to the feeling toward the scenery, the playwright may want to indicate Du's character of being sensitive and her beauty like spring. It is also another kind of introduction-not very direct, but has greater effect than the direct introduction.

6. Language has so many functions, and different linguists classify them in different ways. Roughly speaking, there are seven functions of language, namely, informative function, interpersonal function, performative function, recreational function, phatic function, emotive function and metalingual function.

   Literature is carried out by language, so it also has the seven functions. The function that distinguishes literature from other forms of language should be the recreational function.

   By different deviations and different forms from the everyday language we use, the literature forms create some phonological, textual or syntactic structures which present the beauty of language. Different word choices, grammatical choices and textual structural choices make the text beautiful. By indulging in the beauty of language, both the writer and the reader would benefit from the recreational function of language.

7. An actor on the stage should not only communicate with the other actors. He/she has to communicate with the audience too. So on the one hand, he/she should try to communicate effective with other characters on the stage, in the play. That is to say the actor should try to involve himself/herself in the play to be communicatively successful. On the other hand, he/she should have the audience in mind. The actor should remember to convey the meanings in the play or everything related to the play to the audience clearly and fully. That is to say the actor should speak out everything clearly, he/she should try to make the performance on the stage understandable by the audience. The actor should also convey the writer's meaning clearly.

   So if we say that an actor in the play is communicatively successful, we not only say that he/she could act like the figure in the play, he/she should also communicate the writer's intension successful to the audience.

8. Stephen and Lady B are equal from the aspect of the numbers of the turns taken. Yet from the aspect of the content in each turn and the types of speech act we can find that they are quite unequal—with Lady B being the dominant role and Stephen the dominated role in the conversation.

   (1) From the aspect of content in each turn. There are all together 38 sentences in the passage and of these Lady B speaks 27 while her son, Stephen, produces only 11. In terms of number of words, Lady B produces 205 out of a total of 254, about four times as many as those spoken by Stephen.

   Besides, Lady B not only controls what is talked about, but also how her son should listen to her.

   Furthermore, she twice interrupts Stephen abruptly.

   (2) From the aspect of speech act types. Many of Lady B's utterances are commands of statements which have the illocutionary force of commanding.

   Stephen's utterances consist mostly of genuine questions, sincere apologies and humble explanations.

   The above analysis shows that Lady B is a domineering and aggressive person. In contrast, Stephen is shown to be submissive and nervous.

9. This poem by Tennyson portrays a scene: On a clear day, a man looks up at a mountain peak and sees an eagle. The eagle looks down at the sea and then plunges down toward prey.

   (1) This poem is in iambic tetrameter. Every verse consists of eight syllables with an alternating stress pattern of weak, strong, weak, strong. The eight syllables can be divided into four feet. The first syllable of each foot is weak and the second is strong.

   (2) The poem has regular rhyme. The first three verses all rhyme as well as the final three. Thus, the rhyme scheme is a,a,a,b,b,b.

   We also have alliteration such as in *lonely lands* and in *clasps-crag-crooked*.

   (3) The recurrence of plosives, e.g. /t/, /k/ and /g/. present the harsh condition on the mountain and the firmness of the eagle. The harsh consonants suggest the lack of comfort on this mountain top and the powerfulness of the eagle.

   (4) We have simile, metaphor and personification in the poem.

Chapter 9
Language and Literature

Tennyson compares the eagle with a man, which is personification. The word *stands*, the pronoun *he*, the word *hands* are not words that are usually associated with the eagle, instead they are usually used to refer to human beings.

The sentence *And like a thunderbolt he falls.* is a simile.

The sentence *He watches from his mountain walls*, is a metaphor.

These figurative uses of language has visualized the eagle and presented its features before the readers.

Tennyson's poem *The Eagle*, though short, has regular rhyme and other poetic devices such as iambic tetrameter, alliteration, personification and simile. The first three verses are rather different from the final three. The first three stanzas focus on the *eagle* but the final three focus on the eagle's world and nature. The literary devices of the poem and the powerful imagery combine to make it a classic in the world of English poetry.

Chapter 10 Language and Computer

Concepts & Theories

I. Definition of Computer Literacy and Computer Linguistics
1. Computer literacy refers to people who have sufficient knowledge and skill in the use of computers and computer software.
2. Computer linguistics is a branch of applied linguistics, dealing with computer processing of human language.

II. Computer-assisted language learning (CALL)
1. CALL deals with computer assisted language teaching and learning in particular.
2. There are four phases in the course of CALL development.
3. There are relevant technology in use of teaching areas.
   (1) Teachers are able to design programs to fit their own lessons.
   (2) LAN could be used to establish class activities or connect the teachers and students, or even be used to get connected to the Internet.
   (3) Advanced storing technology makes it possible for a huge amount of information to be stored.
   (4) It is possible for students to hear the digitized sound via computer.
   (5) USB is very convenient and has a strong ability to store information.

III. Machine Translation
1. MT (Machine Translation) refers to the use of machine (usually computers) to translate texts from one natural language to another.
2. Research methods
   (1) The linguistic approach
   (2) The transfer approach
   (3) The interlingual approach
   (4) The knowledge-based approach, including:
       ☆ Linguistic knowledge independent of context (semantics).
       ☆ Linguistic knowledge that relates to context, sometimes called pragmatic knowledge (pragmatics).
       ☆ Common sense/real world knowledge (non-linguistic knowledge).
3. MT quality
   (1) Machines are capable of making mistakes that human translators would not make in the translation.
   (2) Machines are not as intelligent as human beings dealing with the meaning and words arrangement in the translation.
4. MT and the Internet
   Individual PC and the software on it would be replaced by the network computers.

Translation tools would just be some additional part of certain software of the Internet service.
5. MT and human translation
   (1) MT is cost-effective and labor-saving. It can produce rough translation.
   (2) Human translation is more concrete and intellectual.
   (3) There is a trend of combining MT and human translation.

IV. Corpus Linguistics
1. **The definition of corpus linguistics**
   Corpus linguistics deals with the principles and practice of using corpora in language study.
2. **Criticisms and the revival of corpus linguistics**
   Criticisms came from Chomsky and other linguists. But corpus linguistics developed very fast in spite of the criticisms.
3. **Concordance**
   Concordance refers to a list of all the words which are used in a particular text or in the works of a particular author, together with a list of the contexts in which each word occurs (usually not including highly frequent grammatical words such as articles and prepositions).
4. **Text encoding and annotation**
   Annotation could make the implicit information of certain linguistic unit explicit.
   Leech describes 7 maxims which should apply in the annotation of text corpora.
   (1) It should be possible to remove the annotation from an annotated corpus in order to revert to the raw corpus.
   (2) It should be possible to extract the annotation by itself from the text.
   (3) The annotation scheme should be based on guidelines which are available to the end user.
   (4) It should be made clear how and by whom the annotation was carried out.
   (5) The end user should be made aware that the corpus annotation is not infallible, but simply a potentially useful tool.
   (6) Annotation schemes should be based as far as possible on widely agreed and theory-neutral principles.
   (7) No annotation scheme has the prior right to be considered as a standard.
   However, it is not very easy to observe some of Leech's seven maxims.
5. **The roles of corpus data**
   Corpus data is essential in the following fields.
   (1) Speech research
   (2) Lexical studies
   (3) Semantics
   (4) Sociolinguistics
   (5) Psycholinguistics

V. Computer Mediated Communication
1. Computer mediated communication (CMC) is distinguished by its focus on language and language use in computer networked environments, and by its use of methods of discourse analysis to address that focus.
2. There are different kinds of CMCs as mail and news, PowerPoint, blog, chatroom and

so on.
3. Emoticons or smileys
   (1) An emoticon is a sequence of ordinary characters you can find on your computer keyboard. Emoticons are used in e-mail, chat, SMS and other forms of communication using computers.
   (2) Smiley refers to the emoticon which is a smiling face that people use to say *don't take what I just wrote too seriously*.

Related Terms

audiolingualism

Audiolingualism is the method of foreign-language instruction based on structuralist principles and drawing on stimulus-response theory. Its proponents believed that language learning is primarily a matter of developing proper mechanical habits, through positive reinforcement of correct utterances; that target language forms should be presented in spoken form before introducing their written representation; that analogy is a more effective mode of language learning than analysis, and that linguistic forms should be presented in a context rather than as isolated items.

CAI

CAI is an abbreviation for computer assisted instruction. By CAI, we mean the use of computer in a teaching program.

CAL

CAL, computer-assisted learning, refers to the use of a computer in both teaching and learning in order to help the learner achieved educational objectives.

CALL

CALL, computer-assisted language learning, refers to the use of a computer in the teaching or learning of a second or foreign language.

computational linguistics

Computational linguistics can be seen as a branch of applied linguistics, dealing with computer processing of human language.

It includes the analysis of language data by programmed instruction, electronic production of artificial speech and the automatic recognition of human speech, research on automatic translation between natural languages and the text processing and communication between people and computers.

computer corpus

A computer corpus is a large body of machine-readable texts.

computer literacy

Computer literacy refers to the skill possessed by those people who have sufficient knowledge and skill in the use of computers and computer software.

Computer Mediated Communication

Computer Mediated Communication (CMC) is distinguished by its focus on language and language use in computer networked environments and by its use of methods of discourse analysis to address that focus.

computer system

The machine itself together with a keyboard, printer, screen, disk drives, programs etc., is known as a computer system.

Chapter 10
Language and Computer

concordance
　　Concordance refers to a list of all the words which are used in a particular text or in the works of a particular author, together with a list of the contexts in which each word occurs (usually not including highly frequent grammatical words such as articles and prepositions). Concordances have been used in the study of word frequencies, grammar, discourse and stylistics.

content analysis
　　Content analysis is concerned with describing the content of documents in a form suitable for computer processing.

corpus
　　Corpus, plural form corpora, refers to a collection of linguistic data, either compiled as written texts or as a transcription of recorded speech.

corpus linguistics
　　Corpus linguistics deals with the principles and practice of using corpora in language study.

emoticons
　　An emoticon is a sequence of ordinary characters you can find on your computer keyboard. Emoticons are used in e-mail, chat, SMS and other forms of communication using computers.

Esperanto
　　Esperanto is an artificial language, thought to be the most successful interlingua of international understanding. Esperanto consists of a very simple phonetic-phonological, morphological, and syntactic structure.

evaluation
　　Evaluation is concerned with the measurement of the effectiveness of retrieval.

information retrieval
　　An information retrieval system does not inform the user on the subject of his inquiry. It merely informs on the existence and whereabouts of documents relating to its request.

information structure
　　Information structure is concerned with exploiting relationships, between documents to improve the efficiency and effectiveness of retrieval strategies.

interlingua
　　Interlingua is either a completely freely invented language or a language derived from natural languages through simplification which is used for international communication.

LAN
　　LAN, local area networks, are computers linked together by cables in a classroom, lab or building.

MT
　　MT, short for machine translation, refers to the use of machine (usually computers) to translate texts from one language to another.

smiley
　　The most popular emoticon is the smiling face that people use to say *don't take what I just wrote too seriously*.

speech synthesis
　　Speech synthesis refers to the electronic production of artificial speech.

Practice

I. Mark the choice that best completes the statement. (20%)

1. Computational linguistics can be seen as a branch of _____ linguistics.
   A. applied   B. corpus   C. statistical   D. historical
2. The following statements are about CAI EXCEPT _____.
   A. *the use of computer in a teaching program*
   B. *seeing problems on the part of teachers*
   C. *also called computer-managed instruction*
   D. *aiming at both teaching and learning*
3. In recent _____ courseware students are able to interact with the computer and perform higher-level tasks while exploring a subject or problem.
   A. CAI   B. CAL
   C. computer managed   D. computer directed instruction
4. Which of the following activities belongs to CALL?
   A. Learning English by Power-Point.   B. Designing a flash program.
   C. Learning computer language C++.   D. Seeing an English video.
5. Compact disk technology has many uses in foreign language education, including the following EXCEPT _____.
   A. information retrieval   B. interactive audio materials
   C. communicating through LAN   D. interactive multimedia programs
6. _____ is chief concern in computational linguistics; it refers to the use of machine to translate text from one language to another.
   A. CAL   B. CALL   C. MT   D. PLATO
7. In the _____, the MT research was very modest without the participation of the linguistic experts.
   A. early 1950s   B. late 1960s   C. 1970s   D. 1980s
8. In the early 1990s, research on MT was invigorated by the coming of _____ based methods, notably the introduction of statistical methods and of example-based translation.
   A. corpus   B. machine   C. computer   D. program
9. In _____ approach of MT, it is generally believed that translation relies heavily on information and abilities that are not specifically linguistic.
   A. the transfer   B. the interlingual
   C. knowledge-based   D. informational
10. _____ is distinguished by its focus on language and language use in computer networked environments and by its use of methods of discourse analysis to address that focus.
    A. CMC   B. MT   C. CAI   D. CALL

II. Mark the following statements with "T" if they are true or "F" if they are false. Provide explanations for the false statements. (10%)

1. The old linguistic rule-based approaches can still function a lot in the machine translation of the kind of colloquial messages found on the Internet.
2. By a computer, we can calculate the number of occurrences of a word so that information on the frequency of the word may be gathered.
3. The computer has the ability to search for a particular word, sequence of words, or

Chapter 10
Language and Computer

perhaps a part of speech in text. That is referred to as concordance.
4. The analysis of the boundaries of a fuzzy expression by computer is the contribution of corpus linguistics to syntax.
5. One of the roles for corpora in Psycholinguistics lies in the analysis of language pathologies, where an accurate picture of abnormal data must be constructed before it is possible to hypothesize and test what may be wrong with the human language processing system.
6. A computer system refers to the hardware of the computer.
7. We can employ certain translation programs to do the machine translation.
8. Database can be used to assist the linguistic research by providing the analyzing programs.
9. The information stored on one CDROM is less than that on the diskette.
10. By certain technology, we can connect the LAN to the Internet.

III. Fill in each of the following blanks with an appropriate word. The first letter of the word is already given. (20%)

1. P_____ is an application which enables one to create slide shows on the computer screen.
2. If corpora are said to be u_____, it appears in its existing raw state of plain text, whereas a _____ corpora have been enhanced with various types of linguistic information.
3. In order to keep the blog going, the manager should keep p_____ on it.
4. When a group of students communicate with each other online simultaneously, it is said that they are contacting each other in a virtual c_____.
5. In knowledge-based approach of translation, a translator should have the s_____ knowledge, p_____ knowledge and n_____ knowledge.
6. If in the MT, we are to translate English into Chinese, Chinese is called the t_____ language, while English is called the s_____ language.
7. For the MT by the interlingual approach, we have to first of all translate the s_____ language into the i_____, and then into the t_____ language.
8. If we should analyze the grammar features of a certain language the most efficient and quickest way is to analyze the c_____ of the language.
9. By corpus linguists one can carry out the study of the language pathologies, the occurrences of speech errors in natural conversations, etc. These studies belong to the field of p_____ study.
10. When we employ computer as the assisting tool in our linguistic research, after we input certain information or commands through the input devices, the part that carries out the tasks and does the calculation is the p_____.

IV. Give the full forms of the following abbreviated terms. (10%)

1. PLATO
2. ICALL
3. LAN
4. CMC
5. CD-ROM
6. CDI
7. MT
8. FAHQT

9. IR
10. DR

V. Explain the following concepts or theories.（20%）
1. Emoticon
2. CMC
3. Audiolingualism
4. Corpus

VI. Essay questions.（20%）
1. What is Chomsky's idea towards the *corpus*?
2. What are the seven maxims proposed by Leech which should be applied to the annotation of text corpora?

参考答案

I.
1. A 2. D 3. B 4. A 5. C 6. C 7. A 8. A 9. C 10. A

II.
1. F 2. T 3. F 4. F 5. T 6. F 7. T 8. F 9. F 10. T

III.
1. PowerPoint   2. unannoted; annotated   3. posting
4. chatroom   5. semantic; pragmatic; non-linguistic
6. target; source 7. source; interlingua; target   8. corpus
9. psycholinguistic 10. processor

IV.
1. programmed logic for automated teaching operation
2. intelligent computer-assisted language learning
3. local area networks
4. Computer Mediated Communication
5. compact disk-read only memory
6. computer disk-interactive
7. machine translation
8. fully automatic high quality translation
9. information retrieval
10. data retrieval

V.
1. An emoticon is a sequence of ordinary characters you can find on your computer keyboard. Emoticons are used in e-mail, chat, SMS and other forms of communication using computers.
2. Computer Mediated Communication (CMC) is distinguished by its focus on language and language use in computer networked environments and by its use of methods of discourse analysis to address that focus.
3. Audiolingualism is the method of foreign-language instruction based on structuralist principles and drawing on stimulus-response theory. Its proponents believed that

language learning is primarily a matter of developing proper mechanical habits, through positive reinforcement of correct utterances; that target language forms should be presented in spoken form before introducing their written representation; that analogy is a more effective mode of language learning than analysis, and that linguistic forms should be presented in a context rather than as isolated items.
4. Corpus, plural corpora. A collection of linguistic data, either compiled as written texts or as a transcription of recorded speech.

VI.
1. In Chomsky's point of view, corpus can never be a useful tool for the linguist.

    First, in Chomsky's idea, the linguists must seek to model language competence rather than performance.

    Secondly, he holds the idea that the only way to account for a grammar of a language is by sentences. It is the syntactic rules of a language that Chomsky considers finite.

    Thirdly, Chomsky believes that corpus methodology is not the best method of studying language even if language is a finite structure. There are some exceptions that can not be explained by the corpus.
2. (1) It should be possible to remove the annotation from an annotated corpus in order to revert to the raw corpus.
   (2) It should be possible to extract the annotation by themselves from the text.
   (3) The annotation scheme should be based on guidelines which are available to the end user.
   (4) It should be made clear how and by whom the annotation is carried out.
   (5) The end user should be made aware that the corpus annotation is not infallible, but simply a potentially useful tool.
   (6) Annotation schemes should be based as far as possible on widely agreed and theory-neutral principles.
   (7) No annotation scheme has the a prior right to be considered as a standard.

Further Practice

I. Mark the following statements with "T" if they are true or "F" if they are false. Provide explanations for the false statements.
1. There is no need of human participation during the process of MT.
2. The distinction between CAL and CAI is that the former aims at seeing educational problems on the part of the learner, whereas the latter emphasizes the use of a computer in both teaching and learning in order to help the learner achieve educational objectives.
3. The electronic production of artificial speech and the automatic recognition of human speech belong to the study of computational linguistics.
4. In the market of CALL, the programs are all basic drill-and-practice software programs.
5. If we want to interact with others via computer, we must use LAN.
6. While digitized sound is far superior to tape recorded sound, the space needed to store digitized sound is relatively large.
7. Artificial intelligence, dependence grammar, transformation-generative grammar, Montague semantics are all relevant theories to MT.
8. According to the majority transfer view of MT, all the analysis work is done in the

context of the source language alone.
9. Translation is, by its nature, an exercise in comparative linguistics.
10. Interlingua is a kind of language that can be understood by most of the Europeans.
11. The interlingual approach in MT research is more advanced than the transfer approach.
12. Nowadays MT is developing so fast, we could have a large scale of successful machine translation without any human perfection.
13. It is a trend now to use abbreviations for some full words in our writing. For example, we could use 4 for *for*, u for *you*.
14. We have a set standard of emoticons on the Internet.
15. The most popular emoticons are the smiling faces.
16. Statistics can also be employed in the calculating of data features in corpus.
17. Chomsky is among the few linguists who support corpus linguistics.
18. Corpus linguistics can be said to have great help in the research of many other linguistic branches.
19. Online dictionary is also a kind of MT.
20. In knowledge-based approach, we should have the context knowledge and semantic knowledge.
21. All theories related to natural language processing could be used in MT.
22. Corpus linguistics and MT are two independent fields that both employ the computer as a tool.
23. The larger space a storage device has, the slower the accessing of certain information would be.
24. We could use computers to analyze the stylistic features of certain texts.
25. CAI and CAT refers to the same entity from different angles.
26. PowerPoint can not run the slides itself. It needs human involvement to run.
27. A corpus could be annotated or unannotated.
28. Corpus linguistics depends solely on quantitative analysis.

II. Fill in each of the following blanks with (an) appropriate word(s).
1. _____ emphasizes the use of a computer in both teaching and learning in order to help the learner achieve educational objectives.
2. When CAI is called _____, it refers to the use of computers to monitor student progress to direct students into appropriate lessons, material, etc.
3. _____ refers to the use of a computer in the teaching or learning of a second or foreign language.
4. In _____, teachers can observe students' activities and progress and make comments to individual student from a teacher station similar to that found in an audio lab.
5. Since the 1970s development of MT has continued in three main strands: (1) _____ tools for translators, (2) operational MT systems involving _____ in various ways and (3) _____ research toward the improvement of MT methods.
6. It is widely accepted that MT works best in _____ and _____ environment.
7. The practical approaches of MT research can be further divided into three strands, namely, _____, _____, _____.
8. In transfer approach of MT the bulk of the analysis work in MT relies on _____

Chapter 10
Language and Computer

about the specific pair languages.
9. The benefits of using an _____ is that only one part is required for each language and therefore further languages can be added easily.
10. If we want to browse messages and receive e-mails via computer, we should use _____.
11. The enlargement of _____ of the computer makes it possible for us to use and carry large size of information on the computer.
12. _____ which refers to the electronic production of artificial speech should be carried out with the involvement of computers.
13. When doing the on-time translation, it is better for the translator to have the assistance from the _____.
14. The translation way of changing every source language into one set form of language and then putting the set form of language into the target language is called the _____ approach.
15. Usually we could ascribe to an electronic forum or society by our _____.
16. _____ is an online journal comprised of links and postings in reverse chronological order, meaning the most recent posting appears at the top of the page.
17. A _____ is a set of instructions to a computer, it can tell the computer how to analyze a corpus.
18. _____ linguistics utilizes a large can principled collection of natural texts as the basis for analysis.

III. Mark the choice that best completes the statement.

1. A computer system is made up of the following EXCEPT _____.
   A. computer   B. disk   C. program   D. printer
2. CAI program may include the following EXCEPT _____.
   A. a computer rectifying program
   B. a monitoring system
   C. a directing system
   D. a group discussion system via computer
3. _____ could save time and labor in translation of some highly repetitive texts or texts that do not require highly involvement of human intelligence.
   A. CAI   B. Electronic dictionaries
   C. MT   D. Many translators
4. Which of the following terms is NOT a translation tool?
   A. Dictionary and terminological databanks.
   B. Multilingual word processing.
   C. Terminology resources.
   D. Input and output transference.
5. In _____ approach of the MT research, there is a component which has the correspondence lexicon which is a comprehensive list of the source-language patterns and phrases mapped to a target language.
   A. the linguistic   B. the interlingual approach
   C. the transfer   D. the knowledge-based approach
6. It can be predicted that in the future, _____ would be replaced by _____.
   A. MT tools equipped on individual computers, on-line MT software and dictionaries

B. on-line MT software and dictionaries, MT tools equipped on individual computers
   C. network computers, individual PCs
   D. soft disks, u-disks
7. Language corpus usually focuses on _____ rather than _____.
   A. structure, meaning   B. performance, competence
   C. competence, performance   D. meaning, structure
8. To mark the different features of linguistic units in the corpus, we use _____.
   A. dictionaries   B. glossary   C. annotation   D. terminology
9. _____ can be used as a tool in comparing different usages of the same word in a corpus.
   A. Encoding   B. Comparison
   C. Glossary transfer   D. Concordance
10. By means of _____, one can send the same mail to a number of correspondents or send large files and graphs by way of _____.
    A. duplicating, adding   B. adding, duplicating
    C. e-mail, attachment   D. duplicating, attachment
11. The utility of the corpus is increased when it has been _____.
    A. concorded   B. sorted   C. annoted   D. disannoted
12. The _____ information has been made _____ through the process of concrete annotation.
    A. implicit, explicit   B. explicit, implicit
    C. clear, not clear   D. unmarked, marked
13. An information retrieval system informs the user on _____.
    A. the subject of his inquiry
    B. the content of his inquiry
    C. the existence and whereabouts of documents relating to his request
    D. the answers to his question
14. The _____ is concerned with executing the search strategy in response to a query.
    A. input   B. processor   C. IR system   D. output
15. _____ can help us work out the value of the fuzzy expression *soon* in *I will get there soon*.
    A. Corpus and statistics   B. Data computing
    C. MT   D. CMC
16. Among all the following types of translations, _____ fits for the machine translation most.
    A. spoken language translation
    B. diplomatic conversation
    C. large amounts of news documents
    D. exact technique translation
17. Statistics can be used in _____ as an assisting tool.
    A. corpus construction   B. corpus analysis
    C. CALL   D. CAI
18. By authoring programs, teachers could _____.
    A. have access to LAN
    B. teach in a chatroom
    C. communicate with students via e-mails

Chapter 10
Language and Computer

  D. design their own teaching software
19. The application of WORD2003 is a kind of _____ software.
  A. word compiling   B. word processing
  C. word presenting   D. word inputting
20. PowerPoint is a kind of _____ software.
  A. illuminating   B. teaching   C. presenting   D. system
21. Doing exercises on the computer requires _____.
  A. computer-students interaction
  B. students communication
  C. teacher-students interaction
  D. finishing all exercises at once
22. We could add the following in the PowerPoint EXCEPT _____.
  A. a text   B. a database   C. flash   D. weblink

IV. Give the full forms of the following abbreviated terms.
1. CAI
2. CALL
3. CAL
4. CD

V. Choose the correct items that are required.
1. Put the correct number that leads the statement in Column B next to the appropriate terms in Column A.
 Column A:
 (1) Phase I of CALL development   (   )
 (2) Phase II of CALL development   (   )
 (3) Phase III of CALL development   (   )
 (4) Phase IV of CALL development   (   )
 Column B:
 a. Word processing has adapted to language teaching by enabling students to compose and try out their writings in a non-permanent form.
 b. Teaching programs cannot be generated in CALL.
 c. The computer was used as a trigger for interaction between the students
 d. The computer was no longer an individual resource for each student. It came to be seen as the focal point for group work.
 e. During this period, computers were large main frame machines kept in research institutions.
 f. Teaching programs first became electric, pragmatic and student-oriented, rather than assuming massive models of language or theories of teaching.
 g. The mode was normally self-instruction with one student per computer, sometimes gathered together into a computer laboratory parallel to a language laboratory.
2. In the history of MT, there are roughly three stages, put the correct numbers in Column B of the features of each stage after the right stages in Column A.
 Column A:
 (1) The independent work by MT researchers (in the early 1950s) (   )
 (2) Towards good quality output (around 1960)   (   )
 (3) The development of translation tools. (since 1970s)   (   )

Column B:
a. Word processing appeared.
b. The use of human assistance was regarded as an interim arrangement.
c. Researchers began to look for sophisticated translation tools, that is, translation workstations.
d. Researchers suggested the major involvement of human translators both for the pre-editing of input texts and for the post-editing of the output.
e. The period was marked by the assumption that the goal of MT must be the development of fully automatic system producing high quality translations.
f. The MT researchers had to turn to crude dictionary based approaches, that is, predominantly word-for-word translation, and to the application of statistical methods.
3. The following examples are different types of translations. Put the numbers of those that are fit for the MT system in the bracket.
(   )

a. The production of draft versions for authors writing in a foreign language, who need assistance in producing an original text.
b. To produce *rough* translations of scientific and technical documents that may be read by only one person who wants merely to find out the general content.
c. Translation of important business correspondence.
d. The real-time on-line translation of television subtitles.
e. The translation of Shakespeare's Sonnets into Chinese for a literature course book.

VI. Answer the following questions.
1. What is computational linguistics? Give examples of what computational linguistics studies.
2. What is CALL? Illustrate with examples of the types of CALL.
3. What is the impact of the Internet on MT?
4. Which MT approach does the following translation employ, give the reasons.
   (T for target language, S for source language)
   S→ abstract presentation of S→abstract presentation of T→T
5. Is the following statement true or false? State your reasons.
   The Internet has all the functions that a LAN can perform, so it is not necessary for us to build LAN, we could just connect our computers to the Internet to conduct the necessary teaching activities.
6. What advantages have the advances in computer technology given to the corpus based lexicographic research over the earlier work?

参考答案

I.
1. F. Sometimes human participation is required in the process of machine translation.
2. F. CAI aims at seeing educational problems on the part of the teacher. CAL emphasizes the use of a computer in both learning and teaching in order to help the learner achieve educational objectives.
3. T

4. F. Nowadays, a vast array of drill-and-practice programs are still available. However, an increasing number of innovative and interactive programs are being developed.
5. F. LAN is just one means for us to interact with others via computer, we can also employ Internet.
6. T   7. T
8. F. According to the majority transfer view of MT, a certain amount of analysis of the source text is done in the context of the source language and a certain amount of work on the translated text is done in the context of the target language.
9. T
10. F. Interlingua is either a completely freely invented language or a language derived from natural languages through simplification which is used for international communication.
11. F. Both approaches are from different angles in the MT. They have their own advantages and limits. We shouldn't say that one is greater than another.
12. F. Usually we should have human participation to make qualified translation after the machine translation.
13. F. In some informal situation we could use the short forms, yet in some formal occasion we should be cautious to use them.
14. F. We have a set standard of emoticons on our computer keyboard.
15. T   16. T
17. F. Chomsky strongly opposed corpus linguistics as it examines performance rather than competence.
18. T   19. T   20. T   21. T
22. F. Corpus linguistics could assist MT in some aspect.
23. F. The speed of accessing of certain information would depend on quality of both hardware and software.
24. T   25. T
26. F. PowerPoint can run the slides itself.
27. T
28. F. Corpus linguistics depends on both quantitative and qualitative analytical techniques.

II.
1. CAL/computer assisted learning.
2. computer-managed instruction
3. CALL/computer-assisted language learning.   4. LAN
5. computer-based, human assistance, *pure* theoretical
6. domain-specific, controlled
7. the transfer approach, the interlingual approach, knowledge-based approach.
8. comparative information   9. interlingua   10. the Internet
11. storage   12. Speech synthesis   13. MT
14. interlingual   15. e-mail (address)/ messenger mailbox
16. Blog/Webblog   17. program   18. Corpus

III.
1. B   2. D   3. C   4. D   5. C   6. A   7. B   8. C   9. D   10. C   11. C   12. A
13. C   14. B   15. D   16. C   17. B   18. B   19. B   20. C   21. A   22. B

IV.
1. computer-assisted instruction
2. computer-assisted language learning
3. computer-assisted learning
4. compact disk

V.
1. (1) g; b; e;   (2) f   (3) c; d   (4) a   2. (1) d; f   (2) b; e   (3) a; c
3. a. b. d

VI.
1. Computational linguistics can be seen as a branch of applied linguistics, dealing with computer processing of human language. It includes the analysis of language data so as to establish the order in which learners acquire various grammatical rules or the frequency of occurrence of some particular item. It also includes electronic production of artificial speech and the automatic recognition of human speech and includes research on automatic translation between natural languages. It also includes text processing and communication between people and computers.
2. CALL, computer-assisted language learning, refers to the use of a computer in the teaching or learning of a second or foreign language. It may take the forms of:
    (1) activities which parallel learning through other media but which use the facilities of the computer. e.g. using the computer to present a reading text.
    (2) activities which are extensions or adaptations of print-based or classroom based activities. e.g. computer programs that teach writing skills by helping the student develop a topic and thesis statement and by checking a composition for vocabulary, grammar and topic development.
    (3) activities which are unique to CALL. e.g. practicing oral English through Internet.
3. The Internet is having further profound impacts that will surely change the future prospects for MT.
    One of the predictions is that the stand-alone PC with its array of software for word-processing, databases, games, etc. will be replaced by network computers which would download systems and programs from the Internet as and when required. In this case, the one-off purchase of individually packaged MT software, dictionaries, etc. would be replaced by remote stores of MT programs, dictionaries, grammars, translation archives, etc. which would presumably be paid for according to usage.
    Another profound impact of the Internet concerns with the nature of the software itself. What Internet services are seeking is information in whatever language it may have been written or stored—translation is just one means to that end. Users will need an integration of information retrieval, extraction and summarization systems with translation. So it is probable that in future years there will be fewer "pure" MT systems but many more computer-based tools and applications where automatic translation is just one component.
4. This translation way belongs to the transfer approach in MT. The process of changing source language into the abstract presentation of source language and the process of changing the abstract presentation of source language to the abstract presentation of target language is actually the transferring process.
5. The above statement is not totally right.
    The Internet has connecting points by which people connect either their computers

or LANs to it. If we connect all the computers in a LAN to the Internet via individual connecting points, that would be faster for each computer in this LAN, but on the other hand it would also be time consuming, money consuming and energy consuming.

It is a waste of the Internet resource. If each point on the Internet only has one computer, it is waste of the Internet resource. If we have a LAN on each point, we will certainly make full use of this connecting point to the Internet.

Some performance would be better carried out in a LAN than on the Internet. For example, if we want to conduct a virtual classroom discussion, it would be more convenient and faster if we use the LAN directly.

6. First, computers have made possible the collection and storage of very large corpora from a variety of sources. Complete texts or large chunks of texts can bee stored on a computer so that analyses are not limited to sentence length excerpts.

In addition, computers facilitate analyses that are more complete and reliable. Unlike human readers, who are likely to miss certain occurrences of a word, computers can find all the instances of a word in a corpus and generate an exhaustive list of them. On occurrences are lost.

Furthermore, computers can analyze the patterns of word associations on a far more complex scale than is possible by hand. For example, when a word occurs thousands or tens of thousands of times in a corpus, it is unfeasible to ask a person to count and sort all the other words that occur within four words on each side of that word. With a computer, tasks like this can be completed within a couple of minutes.

Chapter 11 Language and Foreign Language Teaching

Concepts & Theories

I. The Relation Between Linguistics and Language Teaching
(1) Language teaching is part of applied linguistics and applied linguistics is part (or a branch) of linguistics.
(2) Some knowledge of linguistics will not only help language teachers to better understand the nature of language, but also help them better understand how to teach language.
(3) Language teachers do need a theory (maybe theories) of language in order to teach language effectively. They need to know at least how the language they teach works.
(4) Language teachers must present the real language and the entire language, not merely its phonology or lexicon or syntax. To discover the real language and to obtain some understanding of it, language teachers may well turn to linguistics. Language teachers should draw on linguists' achievements rather than teach linguistics in every language classroom.
(5) Language teachers should also be aware that there is no unified school of linguistics; rather, there are a variety of linguistic theories. Teachers should be aware that there are conflicts among the various schools of linguistics, with successive schools disavowing their predecessors.
(6) Theoretical views of language explicitly or implicitly inform the approaches and methods adopted in language teaching.
(7) Linguistics, as the science of language, should be of fundamental importance for teachers of language.

II. Linguistics and Language Learning
1. Understanding the role of linguistics in the studies of language acquisition and learning
    (1) Many language learning theories are proposed based on certain linguistic theories. In fact, knowledge in linguistics lies at the root of understanding what language learners can learn, how they actually learn and what they learn ultimately.
    (2) By saying "knowledge in linguistics can serve language learning", we do not mean how language learners can facilitate or enhance their learning process by studying linguistics.
    (3) Although certain language learners certainly benefit from a knowledge of linguistics, it is not sensible to recommend the majority of language learners to study linguistics while they are still struggling with the task of learning the language itself.
2. Grammar and language learning
    (1) As a compromise between the "purely form-focused approaches" and "purely

Chapter 11
Language and Foreign Language Teaching

meaning-focused" approaches, a recent movement called FOCUS ON FORM seems to take a more balanced view on the role of grammar in language learning.

(2) The key point in FOCUS ON FORM is that although language learning should generally be meaning-focused and communication-oriented, it is still necessary and beneficial to focus on form occasionally. Focus on form often consists of an occasional shift of attention to linguistic code features—by the teacher and/or one or more students—triggered by perceived problems with comprehension or production.

(3) One question raised on the practice of focus on form: What elements of language are most amenable to focus on form? Two variables concerning the amenability of language elements to focus on form are:

☆ The relevance of Universal Grammar (UG)
  - According to the advocates of focus on form, if an L2 structure is part of UG, the amenability is high; otherwise, the amenability is low. In focus on form, different measures will be taken depending on whether the amenability of a form (structure) is high or low.
  - The study of UG has attracted considerable attention from many second language acquisition researchers because knowledge of linguistic universals may help shape L2 acquisition in a number of ways. For example, it can provide explanations for developmental sequences and language transfer. The study of UG is now needed in language learning research in the most practical sense.

☆ Complexity of language structures
  - The variable of complexity is not any easier to tackle. It can be assumed that less complex structures have higher amenability, but complexity is hard to define.
  - Formally simple structures can be functionally complex and formally complex items are not necessarily functionally complex.

(4) At the present time it is generally agreed grammar has its due value in language learning.

3. Input and language learning

(1) Language learning can take place when the learner has enough access to input in the target language. This input may come in written or spoken form. In the case of spoken input, it may occur in the context of interaction or in the context of non-reciprocal discourse.

(2) Views diverge greatly as to what kind of input should be provided for language learners.

☆ Authentic input
  - Those who have more faith in meaning-focused language instruction tend to insist on providing authentic input.
  - Ideally, materials at all levels should provide frequent exposure to authentic input which is rich and varied.

☆ Comprehensible input (Krashen)
  - Krashen brought forward the concept of "i + 1" principle, i.e. the language that learners are exposed to should be just far enough beyond their current competence so that they can understand most of it but still be challenged to make progress.

☆ Premodified input
  – Material that is finely tuned in advance to the learner's current level.
☆ Interactively modified input
  – Material that is modified when the teacher and the learners interact.

(3) Although the value of input in language learning is self-evident, research on input has been hampered by many problems, one of which is the lack of linguistic analysis of different types of input.

4. Interlanguage in language learning

(1) Correct production requires learners to construct language for their messages. When learners construct language for expression, they are not merely reproducing what they have learned. Rather they are processing and constructing things.

(2) The conception of language output as a way to promote language acquisition is to some extent in line with CONSTRUCTIVISM.
☆ A constructivist view of language argues that language (or any knowledge) is socially constructed.
☆ Learners learn language by cooperating, negotiating and performing all kinds of tasks. In other words, they construct language in certain social and cultural contexts.

(3) The type of language constructed by second or foreign language learners who are still in the process of learning a language is often referred to as INTERLANGUAGE.
☆ Interlanguage is often understood as a language system between the target language and the learner's native language.
☆ It is imperfect compared with the target language, but it is not mere translation from the learner's native language either.
☆ Interlanguage is a dynamic language system, which is constantly moving from the departure level to the native-like level.
☆ Studies on interlanguage can be done in two ways:
  – Investigating the psychological, biological or neurological mechanisms involved in the production of interlanguage;
  – Investigating the linguistic features of interlanguage.

III. Linguistics and Language Teaching

1. The relationships between linguistics and language teaching

Virtually all aspects of language teaching can have implications from linguistics.

(1) At the macro level, linguistic theories influence our general orientation in approaches to language teaching.

(2) At the micro level, linguistic knowledge helps teachers to better explain the specific language items they teach.

2. The discourse-based view of language teaching

(1) The essential point of the discourse-based view of language takes into account the fact that linguistic patterns exist across stretches of text.

(2) The discourse-based view of language focuses on complete spoken and written texts and on the social and cultural contexts in which such language operates.

(3) The discourse-based view of language teaching aims at developing discourse competence, which is similar to the well-known concept of COMMUNICATIVE COMPETENCE.
☆ What is communicative competence?

Chapter 11
Language and Foreign Language Teaching

- Communicative competence refers to what a learner knows about how a language is used in particular situations for effective and appropriate communication.
- Communicative competence includes knowledge of the grammar and vocabulary, knowledge of rules of speaking, knowledge of how to use and respond to different types of speech acts and social conventions, and knowledge of how to use language appropriately.

(4) According to discourse theorists, it is believed that language learning will successfully take place when language learners know how and when to use the language in various settings and when they have successfully cognized various forms of competence such as grammatical competence (lexis, morphology, syntax and phonology) and pragmatic competence (e.g., speech acts).

(5) In the case of foreign/second language learning, language learners are encouraged to deal with accomplishing actions, which are thought to help them acquire the target language.

(6) Communicative Language Teaching (CLT) and Task-based Language Teaching (TBLT) are the best known examples of such a theory. In the CLT or TBLT classroom, students are expected to learn by performing tasks.
  ☆ Two broad types of tasks: real-world tasks and pedagogical tasks.
    - A real-world task is very close to something we do in daily life or work.
    - Pedagogical tasks are those activities that students do in the classroom but that may not take place in real life. (Information Gap)

(7) Drawbacks of the discourse-based view of language teaching:
  ☆ It overemphasizes the role of external factors in the process of language acquisition and gives little importance to internal learning processes.
  ☆ It is similar to the behavioristic view of language acquisition in those environmental factors and input are at the very center in attempting to explicate the acquisition process.
  ☆ It overstresses the role of knowledge of competence and functions in acquiring a language, and hence fails to notice universal principles that guide language acquisition.

3. The Universal Grammar and language teaching

(1) Language teaching theories based on Chomsky's Universal Grammar
  ☆ A native speaker possesses a kind of linguistic competence.
  ☆ A child is born with knowledge of some linguistic universals.
  ☆ While acquiring his mother tongue, a child compares his innate language system with that of his native language and modifies his grammar.
  ☆ Language learning is not a matter of habit formation, but an activity of building and testing hypothesis.
  ☆ As for the construct of a sentence, TG grammar describes it as composed of a deep structure, a surface structure and some transformational rules.
  ☆ Input is poor and deficient in two ways:
    - Input is *degenerate* because it is damaged by performance features such as slips, hesitations or false starts. Accordingly, the input is not an adequate base for language learning.
    - Input is devoid of grammar corrections. It does not normally contain *negative*

   evidence, the knowledge from which the learner could exercise what is *not* possible in a given language.
   (2) Implications of UG for language learning and teaching. (Advantages & Drawbacks)
      ☆ Advantages of UG for language learning and teaching:
         – UG has generated valuable predictions about the course of interlanguage and the influence of the first language.
         – UG has provided invaluable information regarding L2 teaching as to how L2 teachers (or educational linguists) should present vocabulary items and how they should view grammar.
      ☆ Drawbacks of UG for language learning and teaching:
         – UG's primary aim is to account for how language works, not acquisition.
         – UG is only concerned with the core grammar of language (syntax).
         – The communication function is discarded in UG.
         – Chomsky is concerned only with *competence*; there can be little likelihood of SLA researchers carrying out empirical research.

IV. Linguistics and Syllabus Design
1. What is syllabus design?
   (1) Syllabus design is a bridge between language teaching theory and language teaching practice.
   (2) Syllabus design translates theoretical understanding of language teaching and sets up an operable framework for language teaching.
   (3) The most important part of syllabus design is selecting and sequencing language items.
   (4) The selecting and sequencing of language items should be based on a sound understanding of the language system itself.

2. A clarification of terms: syllabus and curriculum
   (1) The terms curriculum and syllabus are sometimes used interchangeably, sometimes differentiated, and sometimes misused and misunderstood.
   (2) Two senses of *curriculum*:
      ☆ Curriculum refers to the substance of a program of studies of an educational institution or system, such as the school curriculum, the university curriculum;
      ☆ Curriculum can also refer to the course of study or content in a particular subject, such as the mathematics curriculum or the history curriculum, similar to the *syllabus* for a given subject or course of studies.
   (3) A syllabus is a specification of what takes place in the classroom, which usually contains the aims and contents of teaching and sometimes contains suggestions of methodology.
   (4) A curriculum provides:
      ☆ General statements about the rationale about language, language learning and language teaching;
      ☆ Detailed specification of aims, objectives and targets learning purpose; and
      ☆ Implementation of a program.

3. Theoretical views behind syllabus design
   (1) Selection involves two sub-processes:
      ☆ The restriction of the language to a particular dialect and register;

Chapter 11
Language and Foreign Language Teaching

☆ The selection from within the register of the items that are to be taught.
(2) Linguists' contribution:
☆ They provide both the description of a L2 and understanding of how the components make up the whole of the language system.
☆ Reference back to linguistic categories will ensure that all aspects of language that need to be taught are included.

4. Types of syllabus
(1) Structural syllabus
☆ Structural syllabus is influenced by structuralist linguistics. The structural syllabus is a grammar-oriented syllabus based on a selection of language items and structures.
☆ The vocabulary and grammatical rules included in the teaching materials are carefully ordered according to factors such as frequency, complexity and usefulness.
☆ The major drawback of such a syllabus is that it concentrates only on the grammatical forms and the meaning of individual words, whereas the meaning of the whole sentence is thought to be self-evident, whatever its context may be. As a result, students trained by a structural syllabus often prove to be communicatively incompetent.
(2) Situational syllabus
☆ The situational syllabus does not have a strong linguistic basis, yet it can be assumed that the situationalists accept the view that language is used for communication.
☆ The aim of this syllabus is specifying the situations in which the target language is used. The selection and organization of language items are based on situations.
☆ Because it relies on structuralist grammar, it is essentially grammatical. The situations described in a textbook cannot be truly *authentic*.
☆ The arrangement of the situations is not systematic.
(3) Communicative syllabus
☆ The communicative syllabus aims at the learner's communicative competence.
☆ Based on a notional-functional syllabus, it teaches the language needed to express and understand different kinds of functions, and emphasizes the process of communication.

5. Components of syllabus
(1) Aims/goals: General statements about what must be accomplished by the end of the course.
(2) Objectives/targets/requirements: Specific statements about what content or skills that students must master in order to attain the goals.
(3) Non-language outcomes: Affect cultivation, such as confidence, motivation, interest, etc.
(4) Learning strategies, thinking skills, interpersonal skills, etc.
☆ Cultural understanding
☆ Learning contents
☆ Knowledge: vocabulary list, grammar items
☆ Skills: listening, speaking, reading and writing

☆ Functions and notions
☆ Topics
☆ Culture
(5) Implementation
☆ Approaches/methodologies
☆ Teaching principles
☆ Teaching suggestions
☆ Recommendation of textbooks/materials
(6) Assessment/Evaluation: Who, what, how and for what purposes
☆ Who should carry out assessment/evaluation?
☆ What should be evaluated?
☆ How is evaluation best done?
☆ For what purposes should evaluation be done?

6. Current trends in syllabus design
(1) The co-existence of the old and the new
(2) The emphasis on the learning process
(3) The inclusion of non-linguistic objectives in syllabus
(4) The emergence of the multi-syllabus

V. Contrastive Analysis and Error Analysis

1. Contrastive Analysis (CA)
   (1) What is language transfer?
   ☆ It is a well-established notion that the native language plays important roles in the course of second language acquisition, though we do not know enough about what roles it actually plays.
   ☆ The study of the roles that the native language plays in known as the research of LANGUAGE TRANSFER, by which is meant the psychological process whereby prior learning is carried over into a new learning situation, or the influence resulting from the similarities and differences between the target language and any other language that has been previously acquired.
   (2) What is contrastive analysis?
   ☆ It is a way of comparing languages (e.g. L1 and L2) in order to determine potential errors for the ultimate purpose of isolating what needs to be learned and what does not need to be learned in a second language learning situation.
   ☆ Its goal is to predict what areas will be easy to learn and what areas will be difficult to learn.
   ☆ CA is associated in its early days with behaviorism and structuralism.
   (3) Main assumptions underlying CA:
   ☆ Language is a habit and language learning involves establishment of a new set of habits.
   ☆ Previously learned L1 interferes with the learning of L2; the major source of error in the production and/or reception of a second language is the native language; the greater the differences between L1 and L2, the more frequent the errors will occur.
   ☆ Errors in L2 can be accounted for by considering the differences between L1 and L2.

Chapter 11
Language and Foreign Language Teaching

☆ Transfer occurs from L1 to L2. An important part of L2 learning is learning the differences. Similarities can be safely ignored as no new learning is involved.

☆ There is a need for careful analyses of similarities and differences between L1 and L2.

☆ Teachers should focus on areas of negative transfer.

(4) Problems of CA:

☆ Differences between L1 and L2 can be defined linguistically, but difficulties involve psychological considerations. Linguistically difficult items may not be psychologically difficult.

☆ There is substantive evidence that CA cannot predict all errors. On the other hand, some predicted errors (based on CA) do not occur.

☆ CA fails to predict actual difficulties and some difficulties predicted do not always materialize.

(5) Nowadays in the literature, the term *contrastive analysis* is gradually been replaced by *the study of cross-linguistics influences*.

2. Error Analysis (EA)

(1) The Error Analysis movement

☆ The fact that not all errors are explicable by CA resulted in a disillusionment with contrastive analysis.

☆ Gradually CA was replaced by the ERROR ANALYSIS movement.

☆ A major claim of error analysis movement is that many errors made by L2 learners were caused by factors other than L1 interference.

☆ Errors are not just to be seen as something to be eradicated, but rather can be important in and of themselves.

(2) The distinctions between errors and mistakes made in the literature on error analysis:

☆ Error
  — Errors usually arise from the learner's lack of knowledge;
  — It represents a lack of competence.

☆ Mistake
  — Mistakes often occur when learners fail to perform their competence.

(3) The classification of errors in terms of the source of errors:

☆ Interlingual errors (or transfer errors): Interlingual errors occur when the learner misuses an item because it shares features with an item in the native language.

☆ Intralingual errors (developmental errors): Intralingual errors are errors within the target language itself, such as OVERGENERALIZATION, which arises when the learner applies a rule in a situation where the rule does apply.

(4) The classification of errors in terms of the nature of errors:

☆ Omissions: The absence of an item that must appear in a well-formed utterance, e.g., *She sleeping*.

☆ Additions: The presence of an item that must not appear in well-formed utterances, e.g., *He is works in a factory nearby*.

☆ Double markings: The use of a tense marker twice in one sentence, e.g., *We didn't went there*.

☆ Misformations: The use of the wrong form of the morpheme or structure,

e.g., *The dog eated the chicken*.
☆ Misorderings: The incorrect placement of a morpheme (group) in an utterance, e.g., *What John is doing?*
(5) The procedure of error analysis:
☆ Recognition: Dealing with a sentence produced by the language learner, we should first ask whether the sentence is grammatically correct.
☆ Description: If the erroneous sentence is intelligible, we compare it with the correct sentence produced by a native speaker and list the errors and mistakes.
☆ Explanation: When an error is recognized and described, we attempt to answer the question *Why did the learner commit this error?*
(6) Problems of error analysis:
☆ It is inadequate to rely on errors to study how L2 is learned.
☆ It is difficult to determine what an error is.
☆ Error analysis over-stresses production data and fails to account for error avoidance.

VI. Corpus Linguistics and Language Teaching
1. Four common types of corpora
   (1) General corpora
       ☆ A general reference corpus is not a collection of material from different specialist areas technical, dialectal, juvenile, etc..
       ☆ It is a collection of material which is broadly homogeneous, but which s gathered from a variety of sources so that the individuality of a source is obscured, unless the researcher isolates a particular text.
   (2) Specialized corpora
       ☆ This kind of corpora is useful for language for specific purposes.
       ☆ If we need find out what language is used in a certain profession, then we select texts from that profession.
   (3) Sample corpora
       ☆ This is a kind of genre-based corpus.
       ☆ It is a collection of a large number of short extracts randomly selected from all kinds of genres.
   (4) Monitor corpora
       ☆ This kind of corpus is gigantic, ever moving store of text.
       ☆ It has the capacity to hold a state of the language for research purposes.
2. What uses can we make of corpora?
   The most important use that we can make of corpora is that we can find very useful information about how language is actually used. Corpora usually provide the following types of information.
   (1) Frequency information
       ☆ Selecting what to teach.
       ☆ Selecting what to focus on.
       ☆ Deciding what senses to focus on.
   (2) Context and co-text information
       ☆ Contexts are the situational environments in which language is used.
       ☆ Co-texts are the linguistic environments.

☆ Sometimes it is very difficult to tell the differences of two words or phrases which have similar meaning. However, if we look at the context and co-text in which they are used, the difference becomes clear.

(3) Grammar information

What the corpora show is far more complicated than what grammar books tell about grammar.

(4) Collocation and phraseology information

It is usually difficult for second and foreign language learners to learn which words are frequently used together, e.g. *make effort* or *take effort*

(5) Pragmatics information

Information from corpora can tell us how language is actually used in communication.

VII. Summary

1. Linguistic theories have influenced language teaching decisions at various stages (such as defining the goals of learning, designing syllabus, organizing the teaching content, determining the methods and approach, setting assessment criteria, etc.).
2. All these stages are connected with each other, and behind any chain of decisions is a certain view of language and language learning.
3. So far little success has been made in the implementation of an ideal model though the trends in linguistic theories have pushed applied linguists and language teachers to move towards the communicative end since the early 1970s.
4. Two major points on the applications and implications that linguistic theories have in the field of language teaching.

    ☆ Language teaching is a very practical business. Instead of being carried away by miscellaneous linguistic notions, a language teacher must always be aware of the learners' needs.

    ☆ Linguistics is not the only theoretical field which has impact on language teaching practice. Other studies such as pedagogy and psychology also exert strong influences. Linguistics has to be placed appropriately in relation to other theoretical fields.

Related Terms

achievement test

An achievement test assesses how much a learner has mastered the contents of a particular course. Clearly, the items in such a test should be based on what has been taught. The midterm and final examinations held in schools and universities are often typical tests of this kind.

affective filter

Affective filter is the term Stephen Krashen has used to refer to the complex of negative emotional and motivational factors that may interfere with the reception and processing of comprehensible input. Such factors include: anxiety, self-consciousness, boredom, annoyance, alienation, and so forth.

applied linguistics

Applied linguistics is, in a broader sense, the study of linguistics and other theories in relation to any language-related problems. Here applied linguistics looks to psychology, neurophysiology, information theory, sociology, anthropology, philosophy, cognitive science, etc. as well as linguistics. The problems it attempts to solve include speech pathology, machine translation, and national language planning policy, various facets of communication research, and many others.

In a narrower sense, applied linguistics serves to bridge the gap between the theories of linguistics and the practice of foreign language teaching. It interprets the results of linguistic theories and makes them user-friendly to the language teacher and learner.

aptitude test

An aptitude test attempts to measure the learner's aptitude or natural abilities to learn languages. This type of test usually consists of several different tests which measure respectively the ability to identify and remember sound patterns in a new language, the ability to identify the grammatical functions of different parts of sentences, the ability to work out meanings without explanation in a new language, and the ability to remember words, rules and so on in a new language. In order to assess these abilities, artificial languages are often employed.

backwash effect

Backwash effect describes the effect of testing on teaching. Backwash can be harmful or beneficial. Positive backwash happens when student study and learn those things which teachers intend them to study and learn. On the other hand, negative backwash means the converse. For example, if teachers measure writing skill only through multiple-choice items, then there will be pressure to practice such items, rather than writing itself. In this case, the backwash would be negative.

behaviorist learning theory

Behaviorist learning theory is a theory of psychology which, when applied to first language acquisition, suggests that the learner's verbal behavior is conditioned or reinforced through association between stimulus and response.

communicative competence

The concept *communicative competence* was proposed by D. H. Hymes in 1971. It has four components: *possibility*—the ability to produce grammatical sentences; *feasibility*—the ability to produce sentences which can be decoded by the human brain; *appropriateness*—the ability to use correct form of language in a specific socio-cultural context; *performance*—the fact that the utterance is completed.

communicative syllabus

A communicative syllabus aims at the learner's communicative competence. Based on a notional-functional syllabus, it teaches the language needed to express and understand different kinds of functions, and emphasizes the process of communication.

communicative tests

Based on the psycholinguistic-sociolinguistic approach, communicative tests are intended to check the testee's communicative competence. They set out to show whether how well the candidates can perform a set of specified activities.

constructivism

A constructivist view of language argues that language (or any knowledge) is socially constructed. Learners learn language by cooperating, negotiating and performing all kinds of tasks. In other words, they construct language in certain social and cultural contexts.

construct validity

In testing a form of validity which is based on the degree to which the items in a test

Chapter 11
Language and Foreign Language Teaching

reflect the essential aspects of the theory on which the test is based, namely, the construct. For example, the greater the relationship which can be demonstrated between a test of communicative competence in a language and the theory of communicative competence, the greater the construct validity of the test.

content validity

In testing a form of validity which is based on the degree to which a test adequately and sufficiently measures the particular skills or behavior it sets out to measure.

contrastive analysis

Contrastive analysis is a linguistic subdiscipline concerned with the synchronic, comparative study of two or more languages or language varieties. Generally, both differences and similarities in the languages are studied, although the emphasis is usually placed on differences thought to lead to interference. Here the role of theoretical linguistics consists primarily in developing suitable grammar models that make it possible to compare languages systematically, especially in view of interference. Contrastive analysis emphasized the study of phonology and morphology. It did not address communicative contexts, i.e. contrasting socio-pragmatic conditions that influence linguistic production.

criterion-referenced test

Criterion-referenced test is a test that measures a student's performance according to a particular standard or criterion that has been agreed upon. The student must reach this level of performance to pass the test, and a student's score is therefore interpreted with reference to the criterion score, rather than to the scores of other students.

curriculum

The concept *syllabus* is often used interchangeably with *curriculum*, but curriculum is also used in a broader sense, referring to all the learning goals, objectives, contents, processes, resources and means of evaluation planned for students both in and out of the school.

diagnostic test

A diagnostic test is designed to discover mainly what the testee does not know about the language. For example, a diagnostic English pronunciation test may be used to show which sounds a student is and is not able to pronounce. A test of such kind can help the teacher to find out what is wrong with the previous learning and what should be included in the future work.

empirical validity

A measure of the validity of a test, arrived at by comparing the test with one or more criterion measures, such as comparing between this one and other valid tests obtained at the same time or later.

error

To be very precise, an error is the grammatically incorrect form. However, it also refers generally to the learner's misuse or misunderstanding of the target language, may it be grammatical or pragmatic.

error analysis

In second language acquisition, error analysis studies the types and causes of linguistic errors. This sometimes includes the evaluation and correction of errors. Errors may by classified according to (i) modality; (ii) levels of linguistic description; (iii) form; (iv) type; and (v) cause. In the evaluation of errors, the level of error, the degree of communication breakdown, and the tendency towards fossilization play an equally important role.

face validity

In testing the degree to which a test appears to measure the knowledge or ability it claims to measure, based on the subjective judgment of an observer.

fossilization

Fossilization is a process that sometimes occurs in second language learning in which incorrect linguistic features (such as the accent or a grammatical pattern) become a permanent part of the way a person speaks or writes in the target language.

input hypothesis

According to Krashen's idea, learners acquire language as a result of comprehending input addressed to them. The language that learners are exposed to should be just far enough beyond their current competence that they can understand most of it but be still challenged to make progress. Input should neither be so far beyond their reach that they are overwhelmed, nor so close to their current stage that they are not challenged at all. This is the concept of $i + 1$.

instrumental motivation

Instrumental motivation is a term used to refer to the learner's desire to learn a second language because it is useful for some functional, instrumental goals, such as getting a job, passing an examination, or reading for information.

interlanguage

Interlanguage is a language system between the target language and the learner's native language, the relatively systematic transition from initial knowledge of a language to native proficiency during the process of language acquisition. Often manifested as an unstable set of productive characteristics, interlanguage includes the rules of both the native language and the target language as well as a set of rules that belongs to neither, but rather manifests universal principles inherent in the language learner's competence.

language aptitude test

Language aptitude test is a test which measures a person's aptitude for second language learning and which can be used to identify those learners who are most likely to succeed.

lapse

Lapses refer to slips of the tongue or pen made by either foreign language learners or native speakers.

mistake

Mistakes refer to language forms grammatically correct but improper in a communicational context.

needs analysis

Needs analysis or needs assessment (in language teaching and language program design) refers to the process of determining the needs for which a learner or group of learners requires a language and arranging the needs according to priorities. Needs assessment is a part of curriculum development and is normally required before a syllabus can be developed for language teaching.

negative transfer

In learning a second language learners will subconsciously use their mother tongue knowledge. This is known as language transfer. When the structures of the two languages are different, negative transfer or interference occurs and results in errors.

Chapter 11
Language and Foreign Language Teaching

notional-functional syllabus
   In language teaching a syllabus in which the language content is arranged according to the meanings a learner needs to express through language and the functions the learner will use the language for.

overgeneralization
   Overgeneralization is a type of error made when a learner knows some rules of the language but applies them in the wrong place.

parallel test reliability
   Parallel test reliability is an estimate of the reliability of a test, usually employing a correlation between two or more forms of a test which are equivalent in content and difficulty.

placement test
   Placement test is a test which is designed to place students at an appropriate level in a program or course.

procedural syllabus
   Procedural syllabus is also called task-based syllabus. It is a syllabus organized around the tasks, rather than in terms of grammar or vocabulary. For example, using the telephone to obtain information, drawing maps based on oral instructions, giving instructions to others, etc.

process syllabus
   In teaching, process syllabus is a syllabus that specifies the learning experience and processes students will encounter during a course, rather than the learning outcome.

proficiency test
   The purpose of proficient test is to discover what the testee already knows about the target language. A proficiency test is not concerned with any particular course but the learner's general level of language mastery. An example of proficiency test is the American TOEFL, which is used to measure the English language proficiency of foreign students who wish to study in the USA. The former EPT and the current PETS tests offered by the Ministry of Education also belong to this category.

reliability
   Reliability can be defined as consistency. If a test produces the same or very similar results when given to the same candidate twice in succession or marked by different people, it is regarded as having high degree of reliability.

situational syllabus
   Situational syllabus is a syllabus which selects, organizes and presents language items based on situations, e.g. at the bank, at the supermarket, at home, etc.

strategic competence
   Strategic competence refers to a speaker's ability to exploit verbal or non-verbal communication strategies when communication problems arise, compensating for deficiencies in other areas of competence.

structural syllabus
   Influenced by structuralist linguistics, the structural syllabus is a grammar oriented syllabus based on a selection of language items and structures. The vocabulary and grammatical rules such as the teaching materials are carefully ordered according to factors such as frequency, complexity and usefulness.

structural tests
   Based on the psychometric-structuralist approach, the structural tests focus on the

linguistic competence of the testees. What is to be tested is mainly the knowledge of the language structure represented by any of the four skills.

syllabus

A syllabus is the planning of a course of instruction. It is a description of the course content, teaching procedures and learning experiences.

traditional grammar

A type of grammar first developed in Europe in the eighteenth century, based on Aristotelian logic and ancient Greek and Latin grammars, as an aid to learning these languages and interpreting classical texts. Its general characteristics are: (i) classification of data into formal categories, e.g. sentence type, part of speech; (ii) classification based on logical, semantic, syntactic, and extralinguistic criteria, with little attention paid to functional aspects of communication; (iii) primarily a prescriptive attitude i.e. concerned with judgments such as *correct*, *incorrect*, *affected*, *awkward*; (iv) usually written rather than spoken language as the subject; (v) grammatical explanations often confusing synchronic and diachronic aspects-a point especially criticized from a structuralist perspective; (vi) rules that are not explicit or exhaustive; they appeal to the reader's intuition.

transfer

Transfer is a term borrowed from psychology. Originally it means the intensifying or retardative influence of earlier behavioral patterns in learning new behavioral patterns. In linguistics, transfer means the transfer of linguistic features of the mother tongue onto the foreign language. A distinction is made between positive transfer (based on similarities between the two languages) and negative transfer.

validity

Validity is the degree to which a test measures what it is meant to measure. If a test wants to measure the level of pronunciation and intonation of the candidates, but gives them a written test task to do, for example, the validity of the test will be very low.

Practice

I. Mark the choice that best completes the statement. (20%)

1. Two variables concerning the amenability of language elements to focus on form are the relevance of _____ and complexity of language structures.
   A. UG   B. SLA   C. ESP   D. interlanguage

2. Knowledge of linguistic universals may help to shape L2 acquisition in a number of ways. For example, it can provide explanations for developmental sequences and language _____.
   A. analysis   B. transfer
   C. word-learning   D. grammar-learning

3. _____ is material that is finely tuned in advance to learner's current level.
   A. Authentic input   B. Comprehensible input
   C. Premodified input   D. Interactively modified input

4. A curriculum does NOT provide _____.
   A. general statements about the rationale about language
   B. detailed specification of aims, objectives and targets learning purpose
   C. implementation of a program

Chapter 11
Language and Foreign Language Teaching

D. a specification of what takes place in the classroom

5. _____ syllabuses are more concerned with the classroom processes which stimulate learning than with the knowledge or skills that students are supposed to master.
   A. Structural   B. Functional
   C. Communicative   D. Task-based

6. _____: This kind of corpus is gigantic, ever moving store of text.
   A. General corpora   B. Specialized corpora
   C. Sample corpora   D. Monitor corpora

7. The _____ syllabus is grammar oriented syllabus based on a selection of language items and structures.
   A. Structural   B. Functional
   C. Communicative   D. Task-based

8. _____ refers to the extent to which the test adequately covers the syllabus area to be tested.
   A. Face validity   B. Empirical validity
   C. Construct validity   D. Content validity

9. In the _____ or TBLT classroom, students are expected to learn by performing tasks.
   A. CLT   B. UG   C. CLL   D. CAI

10. _____ can be regarded as one of the intralingual errors (developmental errors).
    A. *Although ... but ...*   B. *Because ... so ...*
    C. *Good, good study...*   D. *He goed there to...*

II. Mark the following statements with "T" if they are true or "F" if they are false. (10%)

1. Overgeneralization is a common error made by an early foreign language learner.
2. Focus on form often consists of an occasional shift of attention to linguistic code features-by the teacher and/or one or more students-triggered by perceived problems with comprehension or production.
3. According to the advocates of focus on form, if an L2 structure is part of UG, the amenability is low; otherwise, the amenability is high.
4. Language learning can take place when the learner has enough access to input in the target language.
5. In the case of written input, it may occur in the context of interaction or in the context of non-reciprocal discourse.
6. Learners learn language by cooperating, negotiating and performing all kinds of tasks. In other words, they construct language in certain social and cultural contexts.
7. In the case of foreign/second language learning, language learners are encouraged to deal with accomplishing actions, which are thought to help them acquire the target language.
8. The child is born with knowledge of some linguistic universals.
9. UG's primary aim is to account for acquisition, not how language works.
10. EA is a way of comparing L1 and L2 to determine potential errors for the purpose of isolating what needs to be learned and what not.

III. Fill in each of the following blanks with an appropriate word. The first letter of the word is already given. (10%)

1. As a compromise between the *purely form-focused approaches* and the *purely meaning-*

focused approaches, a recent movement called focus on f_____ seems to take a more balanced view on the role of grammar in language learning.
2. Two variables concerning the a_____ of language elements to focus on form are the relevance of Universal Grammar (UG) and the complexity of language structures.
3. Language learning can take place when the learner has enough access to i_____ in the target language.
4. The type of language constructed by second or foreign language learners who are still in the process of learning a language is often referred to as i_____.
5. P_____ tasks are those activities that students do in the classroom but that may not take place in real life.
6. Language c_____ make it possible for materials developers to select authentic, natural and typical language.
7. Communicative c_____ refers to what a learner knows about how a language is used in particular situations for effective and appropriate communication.
8. A s_____ is a specification of what takes place in the classroom, which usually contains the aims and contents.
9. In the main assumptions underlying CA, teachers should focus on areas of n_____ transfer.
10. The intralingual error, o_____ arises when the learner applies a rule in a situation where the rule does not apply.

IV. Explain the following concepts or theories. (20%)
1. Communicative competence
2. Input Hypothesis
3. Focus on Form
4. Interlanguage
5. Constructivism
6. Contrastive Analysis

V. Essay questions. (20%)
1. How many common types of corpora are there in terms of function?
2. What uses can we make of corpora?

参考答案

I.
1. A 2. B 3. C 4. D 5. D 6. D 7. A 8. D 9. A 10. D

II.
1. F 2. T 3. F 4. T 5. F 6. T 7. T 8. T 9. F 10. F

III.
1. form   2. amenability   3. input
4. interlanguage   5. Pedagogical   6. corpora
7. competence   8. syllabus   9. negative
10. overgeneralization

IV.
1. Communicative competence: The concept was proposed by D. H. Hymes in 1971. It

has four components: *possibility* (i. e. the ability to produce grammatical sentences); *feasibility* (i. e. the ability to produce sentences which can be decoded by the human brain); *appropriateness* (i. e. the ability to use correct form of language in a specific socio-cultural context); and performance (i. e. the fact that the utterance is completed).
2. Input Hypothesis: According to Krashen's idea, learners acquire language as a result of comprehending input addressed to them. The language that learners are exposed to should be just far enough beyond their current competence that they can understand most of it but still be challenged to make progress. Input should neither be so far beyond their reach that they are overwhelmed, nor so close to their current stage that they are not challenged at all. This is the concept of $i + 1$.
3. As a compromise between the *purely form-focused approaches* and *purely meaning-focused approaches*, a recent movement called FOCUS ON FORM seems to take a more balanced view on the role of grammar in language learning. Although language learning should generally be meaning-focused and communication-oriented, it is still necessary and beneficial to focus on form occasionally. Focus on form often consists of an occasional shift of attention to linguistic code features-by the teacher and/or one or more students-triggered by perceived problems with comprehension or production.
4. The type of language constructed by second or foreign language learners who are still in the process of learning a language is often referred to as interlanguage. It is often understood as a language system between the target language and the learner's native language. Interlanguage is a dynamic language system, which is constantly moving from the departure level to the native-like level.
5. A constructivist view of language argues that language (or any knowledge) is socially constructed. Learners learn language by cooperating, negotiating and performing all kinds of tasks. In other words, they construct language in certain social and cultural contexts.
6. A way of comparing L1 and L2 to determine potential errors for the purpose of isolating what needs to be learned and what not. Its goal is to predict what areas will be easy to learn and what will be difficult. It associated in its early days with behaviorism and structuralism.

V.
1. In terms of function, there are four common types of corpora:
    (1) General corpora. A general reference corpus is not a collection of material from different specialist areas technical, dialectal, juvenile, etc. it is a collection of material which is broadly homogeneous, but which is gathered from a variety of sources so that the individuality of a source is obscured, unless the researcher isolates a particular text useful for language research as a whole.
    (2) Specialized corpora. This kind of corpus is useful for language for specific purposes. If we need find out what language is used in a certain profession, then we select texts from that profession.
    (3) Sample corpora. This is a kind of genre-based corpus. It is a collection of a large number of short extracts randomly selected from all kinds of genres.
    (4) Monitor corpora. This kind of corpus is gigantic, ever moving store of text. It has the capacity to hold a state of the language for research purposes.

2. The most important use that we can make of corpora is that we can find very useful information about how language is actually used. Corpora usually provide the following types of information:
   (1) Frequency information. Corpora can tell us how frequently certain language items or structures are used. This kind of information is useful when we try to select what to each, select what to focus on, and decide what senses to focus on in the language classroom.
   (2) Context and co-text information. Contexts are the situational environments in which language is used. Co-texts are the linguistic environments. Sometimes it is very difficult to tell the differences of two words or phrase which have similar meaning. However, if we look at the context and co-text in which they are used, the difference becomes clear.
   (3) Grammatical information. We usually refer to grammar books for grammatical information. However, what the corpora show is far more complicated than what grammar books tell about grammar. For example, information from corpora has shown that conditionals in English are far more than 3 (first, second and third conditionals).
   (4) Collocation and phraseology information. It is usually difficult for second and foreign language learners to learn which words are frequently used together. A search in corpus will do the job.
   (5) Pragmatics information. Information from corpora can tell us how language is actually used in communication.

Further Practice

I. Mark the following statements with "T" if they are true or "F" if they are false. Provide explanations for the false statements.

1. All normal human beings acquire their native language at a given time of life and in an appropriate linguistic environment that provides sufficient language exposure.
2. Language acquisition is a genetically determined capacity that all humans are endowed with.
3. Our language faculty permits us to acquire any human language to which we are exposed, including deaf children acquiring a sign language.
4. Children acquire a language simply as internalizing individual expressions of language.
5. Human brain can store all the words and expressions of a language.
6. Since language acquisition is primarily the acquisition of the grammatical system of language, every specific rule allowed by the grammatical system of a language must be acquired.
7. Integrative motivation occurs when the learner's goal is functional.
8. In SAL, learners have come to the task of acquiring a language with their L1 knowledge.
9. Input can only be spoken.
10. The optimum age for SAL always accords with the maxim of *the younger the better*.
11. Applied linguistics helps teachers to make decision on what to teach and what approach to take.
12. Transformational-generative linguistics sets out to describe the current spoken language

people use in communication.
13. Regardless of their ethnic and cultural background, children of all colors and societies follow roughly the same route/order of language development, though they may differ in the rate of learning.
14. For functional linguists, learning language is learning to mean. In order to be able to mean, one has to master a set of language rules which have direct relation to sentence forms.
15. Achievement test assesses how much a learner has mastered the contents of a particular course.
16. The success of a syllabus relies much on the teacher's knowledge about the learners and their present mastery of the language.
17. The design of the syllabus includes the arrangement of content, preparation of materials, selection of teaching methods and techniques.
18. Situational syllabus specifies the situations in which the target language is used, so it is communicative in nature.
19. The concept of function refers to the meaning one wants to express.
20. The full communicative syllabus stresses what we should teach is communication through language rather than language for communication.
21. While errors always go with language learners, mistakes may always occur to native speakers.
22. TOEFL is considered as an example of achievement test.
23. According to Lado, two basic requirements that a test must fulfill are validity and reliability.
24. Communicative tests are based on psychological and sociolinguistic methods.
25. The reliability coefficient of a test should be between 0.5 and 0.9.
26. Writing is hard to design and score, for it is too subjective.
27. It is possible that a test is reliable, yet not valid.
28. The popular teaching material *English 900* is a representative of audio-lingual method.
29. Empirical validity is obtained by comparing the test with one or more criterion measures.
30. In language learning, language which a learner hears or receives and from which he or she can learn is called input.

II. Fill in each of the following blanks with (an) appropriate word(s).

1. That different languages have a similar level of complexity and detail, and reflect general abstract properties of the common linguistic system is called _____ Grammar.
2. Language acquisition is primarily the acquisition of the _____ system of language.
3. Behaviorist suggested that a child's verbal behavior was conditioned through association between a _____ and the following response.
4. The language which a learner hears or receives and which he or she learns is the _____.
5. Simple, modified speech used by parents, baby-sitter, etc., when they talk to young children who are acquiring their native language is called _____ speech.
6. _____ refers to a single word that appears in children's early speech and functions as a complex idea or sentence.

7. In SLA, _____ refers to the use of one's first language rule which leads to an error or inappropriate form in the target language.
8. In SLA, the approximate language system that a second language learner constructs which represents his or her _____ competence in the target language is called interlanguage.
9. In order to learn a second language, the learner often desires to communicate with native speakers of the target language and that desire shows the _____ motivation of the learner.
10. A _____ syllabus teaches the language needed to express and understand different kinds of functions, and emphasizes the process of communication.
11. Communicative language teaching complemented by explicit grammar instruction is called a communicative-_____ approach.
12. The old way of including grammar in second language teaching is called the _____ grammar instruction.
13. The post-structuralist's view on learning language is that the learner tests his own _____ against what the native speaker says.
14. The explanation of errors implies that we try to make hypothesis about the _____ processes which have caused the learner to commit the error.
15. Today it is accepted that _____ cannot account for all the difficulties and errors that learners have in the learning process.
16. The _____ approach to language testing is claimed to be scientific, because it uses statistical analysis to examine the test results as well as the test itself.
17. A _____ test is not concerned with any particular course but the learner's general level of language mastery.
18. If a certain test results correspond with those of the U.S. TOEFL test, we can say that this test has _____ validity.
19. If a test does not produce the same or very similar results when given to the same candidates twice in succession, we can say this test doest not have _____.
20. _____ is the degree to which a test measures what it is meant to measure.
21. *Error* refers generally to the learner's misuses or misunderstanding of the target language. Error may be _____ or _____.
22. Many people who take the _____ approach to language teaching doubt validity and reliability as standard test requirements.
23. Positive _____ happens when students study and learn those things which teachers intend them to study and learn.
24. *Affective Filter* is the term Stephen Krashen has used to refer to the complex of negative _____ and _____ factors that may interfere with the reception and processing of comprehensible input.
25. In 1957, Robert Lado published his *Linguistic Across Cultures* in which he presented a large quantity of data and stated the importance of _____ analysis.

III. Mark the choice that best completes the statement.
1. The statements concerning the one-word stage of which _____ is NOT true.
    A. This stage comes after babbling stage.
    B. At this stage children learn that sounds are related to meanings.
    C. The kinds of words that occur at this stage include simple nouns, verbs and many

Chapter 11
Language and Foreign Language Teaching

   function words such as prepositions, articles etc.
   D. Children use the same word for things with a similar appearance, at this stage.
2. _____ is an error caused by negative transfer.
   A. *Goed*   B. *Comed*   C. *Foots*   D. *He come tomorrow*
3. Communicative competence includes the following ones EXCEPT _____.
   A. knowledge of the grammar and vocabulary of the language
   B. knowledge of rules of writing
   C. knowing how to use and respond to different types of speech acts
   D. knowing how to use language appropriately
4. According to the acculturation view, the acquisition of a second language involves, and is dependent on, the acquisition of the _____ of the target language community.
   A. culture   B. customs
   C. conventions   D. tradition
5. Integrative motivation occurs when _____.
   A. the learner's goal is functional
   B. the learner wants to secure a desirable job
   C. the learner desires to pass GRE
   D. the learner's goal is social
6. _____ offers precise information concerning how grammar can be learned.
   A. Formalist models of grammar
   B. Generative models of grammar
   C. Functional models of grammar
   D. None of the above
7. Spoken input may come when the learner does the following EXCEPT _____.
   A. tries to talk to a native speaker
   B. watches TV
   C. reads a drama
   D. listens to a radio
8. Interactively modified input is _____.
   A. language challenging enough for learners to make progress
   B. language that is finely tuned in advance to the learners current level
   C. material that is modified when the teacher and learners communicate
   D. material that is modified to become optimal input
9. Learners are likely to make _____.
   A. mistakes   B. errors
   C. lapses   D. all of the above
10. *Errors are the indication that the learner fails to change his old linguistic habits into new habits of the second language* is the attitude held by _____.
    A. structuralists
    B. functional grammarians
    C. transformational-generative grammarians
    D. formalists
11. Which of the following best states the behaviorist view of child language acquisition?
    A. Humans are equipped with neural prerequisites of language and language use.
    B. Language acquisition is the species-specific property of human beings.
    C. Children are born with an innate ability to acquire language.

D. Language acquisition is a process of habit formation.
12. According to Krashen, _____ refers to the gradual and subconscious development of ability in the first language by using it naturally in daily communication situations.
    A. learning   B. acquisition
    C. competence   D. performance
13. The _____ is a syllabus in which the language content is arranged in terms of speech acts together with the language items needed for them.
    A. structural syllabus   B. situational syllabus
    C. notional syllabus   D. functional syllabus
14. _____ refers to the extent to which the test adequately covers the syllabus area to be tested.
    A. Face validity   B. Empirical validity
    C. Construct validity   D. Content validity
15. The major factors in syllabus design are the following ones EXCEPT _____.
    A. describing the course content
    B. selecting participants
    C. process
    D. evaluation

IV. Answer the following questions as comprehensively as possible, giving examples if necessary.
1. Explain with an example the difference between acquisition and learning.
2. According to Corder, in what way are errors significant?
3. Expound on the Natural Approach to language instruction.
4. List the ten components of a communicative syllabus.
5. State the requirements for a good test.
6. Name the four major types of test.
7. State the difference between syllabus and curriculum.
8. List the major drawback of a structural syllabus.
9. What are the problems of a notional-functional syllabus?
10. State the procedure of error analysis.
11. Some people say *A large percentage of the errors are directly related to the learner's mother tongue*. Do you agree with this opinion? Please explain with examples.
12. A teacher drilled his/her students in the structure called indirect questions:
    a. *Can you tell me where my key is?*
    b. *Do you know when our teacher will come?*
    c. *Did you say she had failed the exam?*

    As a direct result of the drills, all the students were able to produce the structure correctly in class. After class, a student came up to the teacher and asked, *Could you tell me where is professor Wang?*, which shows that only minutes after the class the student used the structure incorrectly in spontaneous speech. What do you think is the reasons for this misuse? Could we say that the lesson was a waste of time? Why or why not?

Chapter 11
Language and Foreign Language Teaching

参考答案

I.
1. T 2. T 3. T
4. F. It is misleading. In fact what is acquired is not a bunch of utterances but a set of rules, conditions, and elements that allow one to speak and understand speech.
5. F. In principle, no human brain can store all the words and expressions of a language.
6. F. What is actually acquired by young children are some general rules and defy individual irregular cases.
7. F. Integrative motivation occurs when the learner's goal is social.
8. T
9. F. In put may take the form of exposure in nature settings or formal instruction; it may be spoken or written.
10. F. It doesn't accord with the maxim of the younger the better. It has been demonstrated that adolescents are quicker and more effective L2 learners than young children.
11. T
12. F. Structuralism sets out to describe the current spoken language people use in communication.
13. T
14. F. One has to master a set of language functions, not rules, which have direct...
15. T 16. T
17. F. Syllabus design also has to include means of course evaluation.
18. F. Since the situational syllabus relies on whatever linguistic description available, and at its time this meant structural grammar, such a syllabus is essentially grammatical.
19. F. The concept of function means what one can do with the language.
20. T 21. T
22. F. TOEFL is an example of proficiency test.
23. T 24. T
25. F. The reliability coefficient of a test should be between 0.7 and 0.9.
26. F. Writing is easy to design, yet hard to score, for it is too subjective.
27. T 28. T 29. T 30. T

II.
1. universal
2. grammatical
3. stimulus
4. input
5. caretaker
6. Holophrase
7. interference
8. transitional
9. integrative
10. communicative
11. grammatical
12. discrete-point
13. hypothesis
14. psychological
15. transfer
16. psychometric-structuralist
17. proficiency
18. empirical
19. reliability
20. validity
21. grammatical; pragmatic
22. communicative
23. backwash
24. emotional; motivational
25. contrastive

III.
1. C 2. D 3. B 4. A 5. D 6. D 7. C 8. C 9. D 10. A
11. D 12. B 13. B 14. D 15. A

IV.
1. Acquisition refers to the gradual and subconscious development of ability in the first language by using it naturally in daily communicative situations. Learning, however, is defined as a conscious process of accumulating knowledge of a second language usually obtained in school settings. Is more commonly learned but to some degree may also be acquired, depending on the environmental setting and the input received by the L2 learner. A rule can be learned before it is internalized (i.e., acquired), but having learned a rule does not necessarily preclude having to acquire it later. For example, an English language learner may have learned a rule like the third person singular *-s*, but is unable to articulate the correct form in casual and spontaneous conversation because the rule has not yet been acquired. This shows that conscious knowledge of rules does not ensure an immediate guidance for actual performance.

2. As stated by Corder (1967), errors are significant in three different ways:
   (1) They tell the teacher, if he undertakes a systematic analysis, how far towards the goal the learner has progressed and consequently what remains for him to learn.
   (2) They provide the researcher with evidence of how language is learned or acquired, what strategies or procedures the learner is employing in his discovery of the language.
   (3) They are indispensable to the learner himself, because we can regard the making of errors as a device the learner uses in order to learn. It is a way the learner has of testing his hypothesis about the nature of the language he is learning. The making of errors then is a strategy employed both by children acquiring their mother tongue and adults learning a second language.

3. Natural Approach is the approach to language instruction developed by T. Terrell, and based on Krashen's second language acquisition theory. Krashen offers five interrelated hypotheses regarding language acquisition:
   (1) *Acquisition/learning hypothesis*, where two types of linguistic knowledge can be distinguished: *acquired* and *learned*. Acquired knowledge is used unconsciously and automatically in language comprehension and production learned knowledge is used in careful speech or *edited* writing.
   (2) *Monitor hypothesis*: every language learner has a built-in *monitor* which is used to *edit* one's speech or writing.
   (3) *Input hypothesis*: acquisition occurs only when the language learner comprehends natural language. Input, if it is to be acquired, must be comprehensible.
   (4) *Natural order hypothesis*: morphology and syntax are acquired according to a *natural*, predictable order.
   (5) *Affective filter hypothesis*: language acquisition occurs only in non-threatening environments. When a language learner is placed in a stressful or otherwise unfavorable learning environment, an *affective filter* is raised, which prevents the learner from acquiring language.

   Drawing on these five hypotheses, Terrell developed six guiding principles for the natural approach:

Chapter 11
Language and Foreign Language Teaching

  (a) comprehension is an essential precondition to production;
  (b) speech emerges in stages;
  (c) the emergence of speech is characterized by grammatical errors;
  (d) speech is promoted when language learners work in pairs or in groups;
  (e) language is only acquired in a low anxiety environment;
  (f) the goal of language learning is proficiency in communication skills. Krashen's later studies increasingly acknowledge the importance of explicit grammar explanation and emphasize reading as a strategy for vocabulary acquisition. The natural approach has become a well-established approach in foreign-language instruction.

4. Janice Yalden (1983) lists ten components of a communicative syllabus:
  (1) as detailed a consideration as possible of the purposes for which the learners wish to acquire the target language;
  (2) some idea of the setting in which they will want to use the target language (physical aspects need to be considered, as well as social setting);
  (3) the socially defined role the learners will assume in the target language, as well the roles of their interlocutors;
  (4) the communicative events in which the learners will participate: everyday situations, vocational or professional situations, academic situations, and so on;
  (5) the language functions involved in these events, or what the learner will need to be able to do with or through the language;
  (6) the notions involved, or that the learner will need to be able to talk about;
  (7) the skills involved in the *knitting together* of discourse: discourse and rhetorical skills;
  (8) the variety or varieties of the target language that will be needed, and the levels in the spoken and written language which the learners will need to reach;
  (9) the grammatical content that will be needed;
  (10) the lexical content that will be needed.

5. Taking a psychometric-structuralist view, Lado (1061) proposes two basic requirements that a test must fulfill: validity and reliability.
  (1) Validity: Validity is the degree to which a test measures what it is meant to measure. If candidates are familiar with the topic, for example, the validity of the test will be reduced. Listed below are several kinds of validity: a. Content validity. Content validity refers to the extent to which the test adequately covers the syllabus area to be tested. This form of validity is especially important in an achievement test, which should reflect both the content and the balance of the teaching. Content validity can be affected by the length, selection of topics, and some other factors of the test. b. Construct validity. If the test proves the theoretical construction which it is based, it can be said to have construct validity. For example, a teacher believing in linguistic competence designs a test of such competence in a language. If this test demonstrates great relationship with the theory of linguistic competence, the test then has a high degree of construct validity. c. Empirical validity. If the results of a test correlate with some external criteria, the test can be said to possess empirical validity. Empirical validity can be *concurrent*, when test results match the results of other valid tests or independent measures or *predictive*, when test results correspond with another criterion such as

success in a particular job at a later time. For instance, China's EPT test claims itself scientific and authoritative because its results correspond with those of U.S. TOEFL test. d. Face validity. Unlike the other three forms of validity, Face validity is based on the subjective judgment of an observer. If the test appears to be measuring what it intends to measure, the test is considered to have face validity.

(2) Reliability: Reliability can be defined as consistency. If a test produces the same or very similar results when given to the same candidate twice in succession or marked by different people, it is regarded as having high degree of reliability. Reliability can be affected by two kinds of error. The extrinsic sources of error consist of the variability of the testers and testees, and the variability of the test situation. The intrinsic sources of error are within the test itself. These occur when there is a lack of stability or equivalence. a. stability reliability. A measuring device is stable if it gives the same reading when used twice on the same object, assuming there is no change in the object between the two measurements stability reliability is also called test-retest reliability, because it is estimated by testing and retesting the same candidates, and then correlating their scores. b. Equivalence reliability. A measuring device is equivalent to another if they produce the same results when used on the same objects. To estimate equivalence reliability, the tester can either construct two parallel tests with the same items of the same degree of difficulty, or compare two tests of similar nature.

(3) Validity and reliability under criticism: Many people who take the communicative approach to language teaching cast doubts on validity and reliability as standard test requirements. One of their reasons is that there does not exist an absolute validity. If its theoretical foundation is linguistic competence, test with high content construct or concurrent validity may still fail to show how well the learner can use the language in communicative contexts. Therefore, validity only exists in correspondence with specified criteria. If the criteria themselves are not appropriate, then the validity of the test is not of much value.

6. Classified by different aims, there are at least four major types of test:

(1) Aptitude test: Aptitude test attempts to measure the learner's aptitude or natural abilities to learn languages. This type of test usually consists of several different tests which measure respectively the ability to identify and remember sound patterns in a new language, the ability to identify the grammatical functions of different parts of sentences, the ability to work out meanings without explanation in a new language, and the ability to remember words, rules and so on in a new language. In order to assess these abilities, artificial languages are often employed.

(2) Proficiency test: The purpose of proficient test is to discover what the testee already knows about the target language. A proficiency test is not concerned with any particular course but the learner's general level of language mastery. An example of proficiency test is the American TOEFL, which is used to measure the English language proficiency of foreign students who wish to study in the USA. The former EPT and the current PETS tests offered by the Ministry of Education also belong to this category.

(3) Achievement test: An achievement test assesses how much a learner has mastered the contents of a particular course. Clearly, the items in such a test should be based on what has been taught. The midterm and final examinations held in schools and

universities are often typical tests of this kind.
   (4) Diagnostic test: A diagnostic test is designed to discover mainly what the testee does not know about the language. For example, a diagnostic English pronunciation test may be used to show which sounds a student is and is not able to pronounce. A test of such kind can help the teacher to find out what is wrong with the previous learning and what should be included in the future work.
7. Syllabus is the planning of a course of instruction. It is a description of the course content, teaching procedures and learning experiences. The concept *syllabus* is often used interchangeably with *curriculum*, but curriculum is also used in a broader sense, referring to all the learning goals, objectives, contents, processes, resources and means of evaluation planned for students both in and out of school.
8. A structural syllabus is a grammar oriented syllabus based on a selection of language items and structures. The major drawback of a structural syllabus is that it concentrates only on the grammatical forms and the meaning of individual words, whereas the meaning of the whole sentence is thought to be self-evident, whatever its context may be. Students are not taught how to use these sentences appropriately in real situations. As a result, students trained by a structural syllabus often prove to be communicatively incompetent.
9. First of all it is impossible to make an exhaustive list of notions and language forms, and it is difficult to order them scientifically. Secondly, there is no one-to-one relationship between notions/functions and language forms. A sentence like *It is cold today* can serve as greeting, suggestion, refusal, and probably some other functions. Thirdly, the notional-functional syllabus language as isolated units, only they are notional rather than structural isolates. Such a syllabus cannot achieve the communicative competence which it aims at.
10. The procedure of error analysis consists of the following steps:
    (1) Recognition: Dealing with a sentence produced by the language learner we should first ask whether the sentence is grammatically correct. If the answer is negative, then errors exist. If the answer is positive, then we further check whether the sentence is appropriate in the communicative context-a negative answer indicates a mistake.
    (2) Description: If the erroneous sentence is intelligible, we compare it with the correct sentence produced by a native speaker and list the errors and mistakes. If the meaning of the sentence is not clear, we may refer to the learner's native language to find out what he means and carry out a contrastive analysis. Taking into consideration the use of language in social contexts, we can describe mistakes as well as errors.
    (3) Explanation: When an error is recognized and described, we attempt to answer the question *why did the learner commit this error*? In other words, we make hypothesis about the psychological processes which have caused the learner to commit the error. This will lead us to provide answers to a fundamental question *how do people learn language*?
11. Yes, a large percentage of the errors are directly related to the learner's mother tongue. In pronunciation, for example, the Chinese learners of English tend to produce a full syllable instead of a consonantal sound, because in Chinese, syllables very often end in vowels. Thus a *good old friend* [ə ˈguːd ˈəuld ˈfrend] is pronounced as

[ə ˈɡuːdəˈəuldə ˈfrend]. At the level of lexicon, some words are constantly mixed up, e.g. borrow and lend, except and besides. In syntax, Chinese learners often commit errors in tense and person-number agreement. Also, they tend to use a comma between two complete sentences because this is perfectly acceptable in Chinese.

12. The misuse shows a separation of the abstract grammatical rules from the everyday use of language. The core of the teaching method above could be said as the habit formation through repetition.

    (1) This method seems to concerns only the formation and performance of habits but not problem-solving. As a result, the students may only know the form, but not know when and where this form is used, which is essential to the actual use of language. This type of teaching reveals the defect of the traditional grammar teaching, that is, it concentrates only on the grammatical forms and the meaning of individual words, whereas the meaning of the whole sentence is thought to be self-evident. Therefore, in conscious training, students may be able to use a grammatical structure correctly, while in the spontaneous and subconscious speech, they may fail to still take the structure into consideration. In other words, they may not know how to use that specific form or expression in a daily communication.

    (2) The fact that this teaching method is not perfect does not mean that there is no need to teach grammar. Therefore, it would be inappropriate to label such a lesson as a waste of time. It is true that the students should be taught how to produce appropriate utterances given a communicative situation; yet, they have to know the correct form first, which is greatly related to grammar. It is generally agreed that grammar has its due value in language learning.

    (3) What's more, there can be some improvements to this lesson. It would be appreciated to add the communicative oriented tasks in it, which will make the students understand more clearly the situations the pattern is supposed to be used in, and also help the students apply them to the spontaneous communication.

Chapter 12 Theories and Schools of Modern Linguistics

Concepts & Theories

I. Modern Linguistics and Saussure

Modern linguistics began from Swiss linguist Fernimand de Saussure (1857—1913), who is often described as *father of modern linguistics* and *a master of a disciple which he made modern*.

Saussure was the first to notice the complexities of language. He believed that language is a system of signs.

Saussure's ideas on the nature of sign, on the relational nature of linguistic units, on the distinction of langue and parole and of synchronic and diachronic linguistics, etc. pushed linguistics into a brand new stage.

In short, all linguistics in the 20th century are Saussurean linguistics.

II. The Prague School

1. **Basic knowledge about the Prague School**
   (1) The Prague School can be traced back to its first meeting under the leadership of V. Mathesius (1882—1946) in 1926.
   (2) This school practiced a special style of synchronic linguistics, and its most important contribution to linguistics is that it sees language in terms of function.
   (3) Of the many ideas developed in the Prague School, three points are of special importance:
   ☆ The synchronic study of language is fully justified.
   ☆ There was an emphasis on the systemic character of language.
   ☆ Language was looked on as functional.

2. **The Prague School's major contribution: phonology and phonological oppositions**
   (1) The Prague School is best known and remembered for its contribution to phonology and the distinction between phonetics and phonology.
   (2) Phonetics belonged to parole whereas phonology belonged to langue.
   (3) N. Trubetzkoy (1890—1938) proposed three criteria in classifying distinctive features:
   ☆ Their relation to the whole contrastive system.
   ☆ Relations between the opposing elements.
   ☆ Their power of discrimination.

   These oppositions can be summarized as follows:
   ☆ bilateral opposition
   ☆ multilateral opposition
   ☆ proportional opposition
   ☆ isolated oppositions
   ☆ private opposition

☆ gradual opposition
☆ equipollent opposition
☆ neutralizable opposition
☆ constant opposition.

3. **Functional sentence perspective (FSP)**
   (1) Functional Sentence Perspective is a theory of linguistic analysis which refers to an analysis of utterance (or texts) in terms of the information they contain.
   (2) The principle is that the role of each utterance part is evaluated for its semantic contribution to the whole.
   (3) The movement from the initial nation (Theme) to the goal of discourse (Rheme) reveals the movement of the mind itself.
   (4) The notion of Functional Sentence Perspective is used to deal with the effect of the distributing of known (or given) information and new information in discourse.
   (5) The notion Communicative Dynamism (CD) is developed to measure the amount information an element carries in a sentence.
   (6) FSP is the distribution of various degrees of CD. In other words, the initial elements of a sequence carry the lowest degree of CD, and with each step forward, the degree of CD becomes incremental till the element that carries the highest.

III. The London School

The London School generally refers to the kind of linguistic scholarship in England. The man who turned linguistics proper into a recognized distinct academic subject in Britain was J. R. Firth (1890—1960). Firth was influenced by the anthropologist B. Malinowski (1884—1942). In turn he influenced his student, the well-known linguist M. A. K. Halliday. Malinowski, Firth and Halliday all stressed the importance of context of situation and the system aspect of language. Thus, London School is also known as systemic linguistics and functional linguistics.

1. **Malinowski's theories**
   (1) The most important part of his theorizing concerned the functioning of language.
   (2) Malinowski believed that utterances and situation are bound up inextricably with each other and the context of situation is dispensable for the understanding of words.
   (3) Malinowski distinguished three types of context of situation:
   ☆ Situations in which speech interrelates with bodily activity.
   ☆ Narrative situations.
   ☆ Situations in which speech is used to fill a speech vacuum-phatic communion.
   (4) His concepts of *linguistic environment* and *meaning as functions in the context of situation* provided useful background for further development of linguistics carried out by Firth.

2. **Firth's theories**
   (1) Firth regarded language as a social process, as a means of social life, rather than simply as a set agreed-upon semiotics and signals.
   (2) He held that in order to live, human beings have to learn, and learning language is a means of participating in social activities. Language is a means of doing things and of making others do things. It is a means of acting and living.

(3) Firth did not see language as something wholly inborn or utterly acquired.
(4) He held that meaning is use, thus defining meaning as the relationship between an element at any level and its context on that level.
(5) He defined the context of situation as including the entire cultural setting of speech and the personal history of the participants rather than as simply the context of human activity going on at the moment.
(6) Firth put forward the idea that in analysing typical context of situational one has to take into consideration both situational context and linguistic context of a text:
  ☆ The internal relations of the text
    The syntagmatic relations between the elements in the structure
    The paradigmatic relations between units in the system and find their values
  ☆ The internal relations of the context of situation
    The relations between text and non-linguistic elements, and their general effects
    The analytical relations between *bits* and *pieces* of the text and the specific elements within the situation.

3. Halliday and systemic-functional grammar

Systemic-Functional Grammar has two components: Systemic-Functional and Functional Grammar.
(1) Systemic Grammar, which aims to explain the internal relations in language as a system network, or meaning potential;
  ☆ In Systemic Grammar, the notion of system is made of a central explanatory principle, the whole of language being conceived as *a system of systems*.
  ☆ The system is a list of choices that are available in the grammar of a language.
  ☆ The system network in Systemic Grammar chiefly describes three components of function, or three metafunctions (the ideational function, the interpersonal function, and the textual function).
  ☆ Each of the metafunctions is a complex system consisting of other systems, and choices are simultaneously made from the three functions. This is the close relationship between Systemic Grammar and Functional Grammar.
(2) Functional Grammar, which aims to reveal that language is a means of social action.
  ☆ According to Halliday, the adult's language has to serve many functions. The grammar system has a functional output and a structural output.
  ☆ The ideational function is to convey new information, to communicate a content that is unknown to the hearer.
  ☆ The interpersonal function embodies all uses of language to express social and personal relations. This function is realized by mood and modality.
  ☆ The textual function refers to the fact that language has mechanisms to make any stretch or written discourse into a coherent and unified text and make a living passage different from a random list of sentences.
  ☆ Systemic-Functional Grammar, unlike traditional grammar which takes the sentence as the target unit, takes clause as the basic unit. It aims to provide a taxonomy for sentences, a means of descriptively classifying particular sentences.

IV. American Structuralism

American Structuralism is a branch of synchronic linguistics that emerged independently in the United States at the beginning of the 20th century.

It developed in a very different style from that of Europe, under the leadership of the anthropologist Franz Boas (1858—1942).

1. Early period: Boas and Sapir

(1) In the *Introduction to Handbook of American Indian Languages* (1911), F. Boas discussed the framework of descriptive linguistics. He held that such descriptions consist of three parts: the sound of languages, the semantic categories of linguistic expression, and the process of grammatical combination in semantic expression.

(2) Edward Sapir (1884—1939) was an eminent anthropological linguist.

(3) Sapir's work is best summed up in his *Language: An Introduction to the Study of Speech* (1921), the only book he wrote.

(4) His *Language* deals with a wide range of problems, such as the elements of speech, the sounds of language, form in language, grammatical process, grammatical concepts, types of linguistic structure, and historical change.

(5) In discussing the relations between speech and meaning, Sapir holds that the association of speech and meaning is a relation that may be, but need not be, present.

(6) In discussing the relation between language and thought, Sapir holds that although they are intimately related, they are not to be considered the same.

(7) Sapir also noticed the universal features of language. He believes that without language, there is no culture.

2. Bloomfield's theory

(1) The principal representative of American descriptive linguistics is L. Bloomfield (1887—1949).

(2) Bloomfield's *Language* (1933) was once held as the model of scientific methodology and greatest work of linguistics on both side of the Atlantic.

(3) For Bloomfield, linguistics is a branch of psychology, and specifically of the positivist brand of psychology known as behaviourism.

(4) Behaviourism is a principle of scientific method, based on the belief that human beings cannot know anything they have not experienced.

(5) Behaviourism in linguistics holds that man's use of language is a process of stimulus-response.

(6) Bloomfield's stimulus-response theory:

☆ The first principle: When one individual is stimulated, his speech can make another individual react accordingly.

☆ The second principle: The division of labour and all human activities based on the division of labour are dependent on language.

(7) The distance between the speaker and hearer, two separate nervous systems, is bridged up by sound waves.

3. Post-Bloomfieldian linguistics

(1) American linguists such as Z Harris (1909—), C. Hockett (1916—2000), G. Trager, H. L. Smith, A. Hill, and R. Hall further developed structuralism, characterized by a strict empiricism.

Chapter 12
Theories and Schools of Modern Linguistics

(2) Z. Harris's *Methods in Structural Linguistics* (1951) is generally taken as marking the maturity of American descriptive linguistics.

(3) Charles Francis Hockett's *A Course in Modern Linguistics* (1958) is a well-known textbook in the American descriptive tradition.

(4) The most significant figure in continuing the structuralist tradition may be Kenneth Pike (1912—2000), who and his followers have a special name for their technique of linguistic analysis-tagmemics.
  - ☆ The ultimate aim of tagmemics is to provide a theory which integrates lexical, grammatical and phonological information.
  - ☆ All languages have three interrelated hierarchies: phonological, grammatical, and referential.
  - ☆ On each level of the three hierarchies, there are four linguistic units having the four following features: Slot, Class, Role, and Cohesion.
  - ☆ These basic units are called grammatical units, or tagmemes.

V. Transformational-Generative Grammar

(1) Transformational-Generative Grammar appeared in America in the late 1950s. The founder was A. N. Chomsky (1928—).

(2) TG Grammar has seen five stages of development:
  - ☆ The Classical Theory
  - ☆ The Standard Theory
  - ☆ The Extended Standard Theory
  - ☆ The Revised Extended Standard Theory
  - ☆ The Minimalist Program

1. The innateness hypothesis

(1) Chomsky believes that language is somewhat innate, and that children are born with what he calls a language acquisition device, which is a unique kind of knowledge that fits them for language learning. This is the Innateness Hypothesis.

(2) The Innateness Hypothesis states that there are aspects of linguistic organization that are basic to the human brain and that make it possible for children to acquire linguistic competence in all its complexity with little instruction from family or friends.

(3) Chomsky argues that language acquisition device (LAD) probably consists of three elements: a hypothesis-maker, linguistic universal, and an evaluation procedure.

2. What is generative grammar?

(1) A generative grammar is *a system of rules that in some explicit and well-defined way assigns structural descriptions to sentences*.

(2) Chomsky believes that every speaker of a language has mastered and internalized a generative grammar that expresses his knowledge of his language.

(3) Chomsky puts forward three different levels to evaluate grammars on:
  - ☆ Observational adequacy level
  - ☆ Descriptive adequacy level
  - ☆ Explanatory adequacy level

(4) Chomsky insists on the hypothesis deduction method and his research is called evaluation process.

3. **three features of the classical theory**
   (1) Emphasis on generative ability of language
   (2) Introduction of transformational rules
   (3) Grammatical description regardless of meaning
4. **The standard theory**
   (1) The Standard Theory is marked by Aspects of the Theory of Syntax (1965).
   (2) In this book, Chomsky made a remarkable change by including a semantic component in his grammatical model.
   (3) He says a generative grammar should consist of three components: syntactic, phonological and semantic.
5. **The extended standard theory**
   (1) In the Extended Standard Theory, Chomsky revised his Standard Theory twice.
   (2) The first revision is called the Extended Standard Theory (EST). The second revision is called the Revised Extended Standard Theory (REST).
   (3) In his first revision of the Standard Theory, Chomsky moved part of semantic interpretation to the surface structure.
   (4) Semantic interpretation does play certain roles in the surface structure, but Chomsky still believed that semantics is determined by the deep structure.
   (5) Chomsky's second revision involves the whole theoretical framework. The most remarkable change is that Chomsky now completely puts semantic interpretation in the surface structure. And, accordingly, from semantic interpretive rules is derived logical form representation. Hence, semantics was left out of the domain of syntax.
6. **Later theories**
   (1) In the 1980s, Chomsky's TG Grammar entered the fourth period of development with the theory of Government and Binding (GB).
   (2) It consists of X-bar Theory, θ Theory, Bounding Theory, Government Theory, Case Theory, Control Theory, and Binding Theory.
   (3) In 1992, Chomsky wrote an essay *A Minimalist Program for Linguistic Theory*, collected in his The Minimalist Program (1995), marking a new stage of his generative grammar.
   (4) The Minimalist Program is characterized by several remarkable changes:
      ☆ Some of the discrete analytical models in the GB are discarded and the two levels of analysis, the deep structure and the surface structure, are left out.
      ☆ The important concept of *government* in the previous theory is rejected and the facts interpreted by the theory of government are replaced by several revised concepts.
   (5) In the late 1990s, Chomsky further developed the minimalist theory in his *Minimalist Inquiries: The Framework* (1998).
   (6) Chomsky holds that the initial states of human languages are the same whereas the states of acquiring different languages are not.
   (7) A universal grammar is a theory for studying the initial states, and particular grammars are theories for studying the states of acquisition.
   (8) While the faculty of language consists of a cognitive system that stores information such as sound, meaning, and structure, the performance system retrieves and uses the information.
   (9) The development of TG Grammar can be regarded as a process of constantly minimalizing theories and controlling the generative powers, and the Minimalist

Chapter 12
Theories and Schools of Modern Linguistics

Program and the Minimalist Inquiries are just some logical steps in this process.

7. Main features of TG grammar

Chomsky's TG Grammar differs from the structural grammar in a number of ways:
(1) rationalism
(2) innateness
(3) deductive methodology
(4) emphasis on interpretation
(5) formalization
(6) emphasis on linguistic competence
(7) strong generative powers
(8) emphasis on linguistic universals

VI. Revisionists or Rebels?

1. Case Grammar
   (1) Case Grammar is an approach that stresses the relationships of elements in a sentence. It is a type of generative grammar developed by C. J. Fillmore in the late 1960s.
   (2) In this grammar, the verb is regarded as the most important part of the sentence, and has a number of relationships with various noun phrases. These relationships are called Cases.
   (3) The obvious attractions of Case Grammar include the clear semantic relevance of notions such as agency, causation, location, advantage to someone, etc.
   (4) In spite of the defects of the theory and methods of analysis, Case Grammar has been an important undertaking in drawing the attention of an initially skeptical tradition of linguistic study to the importance of relating semantic cases or thematic roles to syntactic descriptions.

2. Generative Semantics
   (1) Generative Semantics was developed in the late 1960s and early 1970s, as a reaction to Chomsky's syntactic-based TG Grammar.
   (2) The leading figures of this approach are J. R. Roses, G. Lakoff, J. D. McCawley, and P. Postal.
   (3) Generative Semantics considers that all sentences are generated from a semantic structure.
   (4) This semantic structure is often expressed in the form of a proposition that is similar to logical proposition in philosophy.
   (5) Generative Semantics holds that there is no principal distinction between syntactic processes and semantic processes.
   (6) Generative Semantics has collapsed before the end of the 1970s.
   (7) While Generative Semantics is no longer regarded as a viable model of grammar, there are innumerable ways in which it has left its mark on its successors.

Related Terms

American structuralism

American structuralism is a general term for variously developed branches of structuralism pioneered above all by E. Sapir (1884—1939) and L. Bloomfield (1887—1949). Although the various schools cannot be clearly distinguished from one another, a distinction is made between two general phases: the so-called 'Bloomfield Era,' and distributionalism, with Z. Harris as chief representative. Common to all braches are certain scientific prerequisites which decisively influenced the specific methodological orientation of American structuralism.

behaviorism

Behaviorism is a direction of psychological research founded by J. B. Watson(1878—1959) and modeled after natural science that takes aim at the methods of self-observation (introspection) as well as the description of the consciousness(such as feelings, thoughts, impulsive behavior). Behaviorism investigates objectively observable behaviors as a reaction to changes in environmental circumstances. The stimulus-response model (developed through experiments on animals) as well as the fundamental categories of *conditioned reflexes* and conditioning provides the point of departure for behaviorist research. According to these theories, behavior is analyzed as a reaction to particular environmentally conditioned external or internal stimuli and is thereby predictable based on the exact characterization of the corresponding instance of stimulus. Behaviorism has become particularly significant in educational psychology. Its principle of the learning process as a conditioning process, which was further developed in educational psychology, was also applied to the process of language acquisition. The conception of behaviorism is most clearly expressed in Bloomfield's antimentalist concept of language, especially in his taxonomic method of description which is itself geared towards those methods used in the natural sciences.

colligation

Colligations are morphologically and syntactically motivated conditions for the ability of linguistic elements to be combined. These conditions, as expressed in government or valence, can lead to differences in meaning: *The car stopped* vs. *The car stopped honking*.

communicative dynamism

Communicative dynamism is based on the fact that linguistic communication is not a static phenomenon, but a dynamic one. CD (short for Communication Dynamism) is meant to measure the amount of information an element carries in a sentence.

delicacy

Delicacy is Halliday's term for greater or lesser detail in grammatical description. E.g. a distinction between masculine, feminine, and neuter pronouns (*he*, *she*, *it*) is made in English only in the third-person singular. It is therefore more delicate than those between singular and plural, or between third person and first or second.

functional sentence perspective

Prague School term introduces by Matthesius (1929) for denoting the analysis of a sentence in respect to its communicative function. The basis of the sentence is known information, called the theme (topic, given), while that which is said about the known information is considered to be the rheme (comment, new). This semantic classification, which has both semantic and contextual aspects, is reflected in word order, use of pronouns, articles, and intonation.

interpersonal function

Interpersonal function is one of the three metafunctions of language according to M. A. K Halliday's systemic functional grammar. Halliday. It embodies all uses of language to express social and personal relations.

Chapter 12
Theories and Schools of Modern Linguistics

ideational function
Ideational function is one of the three metafunctions of language according to M. A. K. Halliday's systemic functional grammar. It is to convey new information, to communicate a content that is unknown to the hearer.

mood
Mood is a grammatical category of verbs which expresses the subjective attitude of the speaker towards the state of affairs described by the utterance.

modality
Modality is a semantic category which expresses the attitude of the speaker towards what is expressed in the sentence. In its wider sense, modality refers not only to the morphologically formed moods of indicative, subjunctive, and imperative, but also to the different sentence types (statement, question, command).

phatic communication
Phatic communication was defined by the anthropologist B. Malinowski in the 1920s as *a type of speech in which ties of union are created by a mere exchange of words*.

phonematic units
A phonematic unit is one associated with a single position in a linear structure, as opposed to a prosody, whose domain is (at least potentially) larger.

prosodic phonology
Prosodic phonology is an account of phonology developed by Firth and his followers, and distinguished from others by two main features. One is the polysystemic principle. The other is the role of prosodies in accounting for interdependencies between successive places in a structure. It did not develop further after Firth's death in 1960 and later theories of non-linear phonology were at first conceived independently.

residue
Residue refers to the rest of the clause. It has three functional elements: the *Predicator*, *Complement*, and *Adjunct*.

scale of delicacy
Scale of delicacy refers to a scale to arrange systems according to the fineness of the distinction.

systemic-functional grammar
Halliday's Systemic-Functional Grammar is a sociologically oriented functional linguistic approach and one of the most influential linguistic theories in the twentieth century. It has two components: systemic grammar and functional grammar. Systemic grammar aims to explain the internal relations in language as a system network, or meaning potential. And this network consists of subsystems from which language users make choices. Functional grammar aims to reveal that language is a means of social interaction, based on the position that language system and the forms that make it up are inescapably determined by the uses or functions which they serve.

tagmemes
Tagmeme is a term used in Tagmemics, a model of linguistic analysis developed by Pike, R. E, a post-Bloomfieldian linguist. Tagmemes refer to the basic grammatical units on each level of the interrelated hierarchies, namely, phonological, grammatical and referential existing in all languages.

tagmemics
Tagmemics is a model of linguistic analysis developed by Pike, R. E. Longacre and

other linguists who continued the structuralist tradition in the 1950s. For Pike, a language has its own hierarchical systems independent of meaning. All languages have three interrelated hierarchies: phonological, grammatical, and referential. On each level of the three hierarchies, there are four linguistic units having the four following features: Slot, Class, Role and Cohesion.

The ultimate aim of tagmemics is to provide a theory which integrates lexical, grammatical, and phonological information. This theory is based on the assumption that there are various relations in language, and these relations can be analyzed into different units.

textual function

Textual function is one of the three metafunctions of language according to M. A. K Halliday's systemic functional grammar. It refers to the fact that language has mechanisms to make any stretch of spoken or written discourse into a coherent and unified text and make a living passage different from a random list of sentences.

transitivity

Transitivity is the grammar of the clause in its ideational aspect. It consists of six different processes: Material Process, Behavioral Process, Mental Process, Verbal Process, Relational Process, and Existential Process.

Practice

I. Mark the choice that best completes the statement. (20%)

1. The person who is often described as *father of modern linguistics* is _____.
   A. Firth   B. Saussure   C. Halliday   D. Chomsky
2. The most important contribution of the Prague School to linguistics is that it sees language in terms of _____.
   A. function   B. meaning   C. signs   D. system
3. The principal representative of American descriptive linguistics is _____.
   A. Boas   B. Sapir   C. Bloomfield   D. Harris
4. Generally speaking, the _____ specifies whether a certain tagmeme is in the position of the Nucleus or of the Margin in the structure.
   A. Slot   B. Class   C. Role   D. Cohesion
5. _____ Grammar is the most widespread and the best understood method of discussing Indo-European languages.
   A. Traditional   B. Structural   C. Functional   D. Generative
6. _____ Grammar started from the American linguist Sydney M. Lamb in the late 1950s and the early 1960s.
   A. Stratificational   B. Case
   C. Relational   D. Montague
7. In Halliday's view, the _____ function is the function that the child uses to know about his surroundings.
   A. personal   B. heuristic   C. imaginative   D. informative
8. The rheme in the sentence *On it stood Jane* is _____.
   A. *On it*   B. *stood*   C. *On it stood* D. *Jane*
9. Chomsky follows _____ in philosophy and mentalism in psychology.
   A. empiricism   B. behaviorism   C. relationalism D. mentalism

Chapter 12
Theories and Schools of Modern Linguistics

10. TG grammar has seen _____ stages of development.
    A. three   B. four   C. five   D. six

II. Mark the following statements with "T" if they are true or "F" if they are false. (10%)
1. Following Saussure's distinction between langue and parole, Trubetzkoy argued that phonetics belonged to langue whereas phonology belonged to parole.
2. The subject-predicate distinction is the same as the theme and rheme contrast.
3. London School is also known as systemic linguistics and functional linguistics.
4. According to Firth, a system is a set of mutually exclusive options that come into play at some point in a linguistic structure.
5. American Structuralism is a branch of diachronic linguistics that emerged independently in the United States at the beginning of the twentieth century.
6. The Standard Theory focuses discussion on language universals and universal grammar.
7. American descriptive linguistics is empiricist and focuses on diversities of languages.
8. Chomsky's concept of linguistic performance is similar to Saussure's concept of parole, while his use of linguistic competence is somewhat different from Saussure's langue.
9. Firth attempted to integrate linguistic studies with sociological studies.
10. If two sentences have exactly the same ideational and interpersonal functions, they would be the same in terms of textual coherence.

III. Fill in each of the following blanks with an appropriate word. The first letter of the word is already given. (10%)
1. The Prague School practiced a special style of s_____ Linguistics.
2. The Prague School is best known and remembered for its contribution to phonology and the distinction between p_____ and phonology.
3. The man who turned linguistics proper into a recognized distinct academic subject in Britain was J._____.
4. Halliday's Systemic Grammar contains a functional component, and the theory behind his Functional Grammar is s_____.
5. Systemic-Functional Grammar is a s_____ oriented functional linguistic approach.
6. Structuralism is based on the assumption that grammatical categories should be defined not in terms of meaning but in terms of d_____.
7. In the history of American linguistics, the period between 1933 and 1950 is also known as B_____ Age.
8. D_____ in language theories is characteristic of America.
9. The starting point of Chomsky's TG grammar is his i_____ hypothesis.
10. Chomsky argues that LAD probably consists of three elements, that is, a h_____, linguistic universal, and an evaluation procedure.

IV. Explain the following concepts or theories. (20%)
1. Functional Sentence Perspective
2. Cohesion
3. LAD
4. Case Grammar

255

V. Match each term in Column A with one relevant item in Column B. (10%)

A	B
(1) N. Trubetzkoy	a. situational context
(2) J. Firbas	b. prosodic phonology
(3) B. Malinowski	c. definition of the phoneme
(4) J. R. Firth	d. Systemic-functional grammar
(5) M. A. K. Halliday	e. Communicative dynamism
(6) F. de Saussure	f. X-bar theory
(7) V. Mathesius	g. langue and parole
(8) Noam Chomsky	h. leader of the Prague School
(9) Boas and Sapir	i. Behaviorism
(10) Bloomfield	j. American Structuralism

VI. Essay questions. (20%)
1. What is the essence of Functional Sentence Perspective?
2. What is the Prague School best known for?

参考答案

I.
1. B 2. A 3. C 4. A 5. A 6. A 7. B 8. D 9. C 10. C

II.
1. F 2. F 3. T 4. T 5. F 6. F 7. T 8. T 9. T 10. F

III.
1. synchronic   2. phonetics   3. J. R. Firth
4. systemic   5. sociologically   6. distribution
7. Bloomfieldian   8. Descriptivism   9. innateness
10. hypothesis-maker

IV.
1. FSP: It stands for Functional Sentence Perspective. It is a theory of linguistic analysis which refers to an analysis of utterances (or texts) in terms of the information they contain.
2. Cohesion: The Cohesion shows whether a certain tagmeme is dominating other tagmemes or is dominated by others.
3. LAD: LAD, that is Language Acquisition Device, is posited by Chomsky in the 1960s as a device effectively present in the minds of children by which a grammar of their native language is constructed.
4. Case Grammar: It is an approach that stresses the relationship of elements in a sentence. It is a type of generative grammar developed by C. J. Fillmore in the late 1960s.

V.
(1) c   (2) e   (3) a   (4) b   (5) d   (6) g   (7) h   (8) f   (9) j   (10) i

VI.
1. Functional Sentence Perspective (FSP) is a theory of linguistic analysis which refers to

Chapter 12
Theories and Schools of Modern Linguistics

an analysis of utterances in terms of the information they contain. The principle is that the role of each utterance part is evaluated for its semantic contribution to the whole. A sentence contains a point of departure and a goal of discourse. The former is called Theme, and the latter, Rheme. FSP is to describe how information is distributed in sentence. FSP deals particularly with the effect of the distribution of known information and new information I discourse.

2. The Prague School is best known and remembered for its contribution to phonology and the distinction between phonetics and phonology. Following Saussure's distinction between langue an parole, Trubetzkoy argued that phonetics belonged to parole whereas phonology belonged to langue. On this basis he developed the notion of *phoneme* as an abstract unit of the sound system as distinct from the sounds actually produced. A phoneme may be defined as distinct from the sum of the differential functions. Sounds may be phonemes in so far as they can serve to distinguish meaning.

Further Practice

I. Fill in each of the following blanks with (an) appropriate word(s).

1. Modern linguistics began from the Swiss linguist Ferdinand de _____.
2. Saussure believed that language is a system of _____.
3. Saussure's ideas on the arbitrary nature of sign, on the relational nature of linguistic units, on the distinction of _____ and _____ and of synchronic and diachronic linguistics, etc. pushed linguistics into a brand new stage.
4. The Prague School practiced a special style of synchronic linguistics, and its most important contribution to linguistics is that it sees language in terms of _____.
5. According to FSP, a sentence contains a point of _____ and a goal of _____.
6. According to Malinowski, meaning is not something that exists in sounds, but something that exists in the relations of _____ and their _____.
7. Firth's second important contribution to linguistics is his method of _____ analysis.
8. Harris is generally taken for the man who marked the maturity of American _____ linguistics.
9. Sapir holds that although language and thought are intimately related, they are not to be considered the same. Language is the _____, and thought is the end product: without language, thought is impossible.
10. _____ in linguistics holds that children learn language through a chain of *stimulus-response reinforcement*, and the adult's use of language is also a process of *stimulus-response*.
11. Chomsky believes that language is somewhat innate, and that children are born with what he calls a Language Acquisition _____.
12. Chomsky holds that the basic grammatical _____ and _____ exist in all languages and all human infants are born with knowledge of them.
13. For Pike, a language has its own hierarchical systems independent of meaning. All languages have three interrelated hierarchies: _____, _____ and _____.
14. In Case Grammar developed by Fillmore the _____ is regarded as the most important part of the sentence, and has a number of _____ with various noun phrases. These relationships are called _____.
15. Generative Semantics considers that all sentences are generated from a semantic structure,

which is often expressed in the form of a _____ that is similar to that in philosophy.

II. Mark the following statements with "T" if they are true or "F" if they are false. Provide explanations for the false statements.
1. Most people agree that Saussure's work marked the beginning of modern linguistics.
2. In psychology, Saussure was influenced by the Austrian psychiatrist S. Freud.
3. Saussure was the first to notice the diversities of language.
4. All linguistics in the twentieth century are Saussurean linguistics.
5. The point of departure is called Theme; the goal of discourse is called the Rheme.
6. Language may use different syntactic structures, but the order of ideas remain basically the same.
7. FSP deals particularly with the effect of the distribution of known (or given) information and new information in discourse.
8. Saussure was the first Professor of General Linguistics in Great Britain. The majority of university teachers of linguistics in Britain were trained under him.
9. London School stressed the importance of context of situation and the system aspect of language.
10. According to Malinowski, the real linguistic data are the complete utterances in actual uses of language.
11. Malinowski's concept of *linguistic environment* and *meaning as functions* in the context of situation provided useful background for further development of linguistics carried out by Halliday.
12. Firth defined the context of situation as including the entire cultural setting of speech and the personal history of the participants rather than as simply the context of human activity going on at the moment.
13. It is an important and admirable part of the Prague School tradition to believe that different types of linguistic description may be appropriate for different purposes.
14. TG method can not only describe the surface structure of a sentence, but also interpret the internal grammatical relationships within a sentence, getting closer to the truth of language than IC analysis.
15. The defect of a finite state grammar, as Chomsky sees, lies in that it is inappropriate to explain the complexities of the human cognitive system.
16. Phrase-structure rules formalize some of the traditional insights of constituent structure analysis.
17. One of the problems with transformational rules is that they cannot generate passive sentences.
18. A generative grammar is used to describe one language, i.e. English, because each language has its own system.
19. Halliday's interpersonal function is realized by Mood and Modality which refer to our experience of process.
20. Structuralism is based on the assumption that grammatical categories should be defined not in terms of meaning but in terms of distribution.

III. Mark the choice that best completes the statement.
1. Which book became the most important source of Saussure's ideas and of his influence upon succeeding generations of linguists?

Chapter 12
Theories and Schools of Modern Linguistics

   A. *Course in General Linguistics*.
   B. *Coral Gardens and Their Magic*.
   C. *Handbook of American Indian Languages*.
   D. *Language*.
2. Saussure's ideas were developed along three lines: linguistics, sociology and _____.
   A. psychology   B. methodology   C. natural science   D. semiotics
3. According to Saussure, the _____ is the central fact of language.
   A. symbol   B. choice   C. system   D. sign
4. Firth was influenced by _____.
   A. Sausssure   B. Malinowski   C. Halliday   D. Sapir
5. The most important aspect of Malinowski's theory is concerned with _____.
   A. system   B. communication
   C. the functioning of language   D. grammar
6. Firth pointed out that in actual speech, it is not phonemes that make up the paradigmatic relations, but _____.
   A. morpheme   B. purpose of communication
   C. phonematic units   D. communicative competence
7. _____ is regarded as one of the most distinguished linguists in the post-Bloomfieldian era.
   A. Harris   B. Halliday   C. Firth   D. Boas

IV. Match the theories in Column A with those scholars in Column B

A	B
(1) Language is one of the *social facts*, which are radically distinct from individual psychological acts.	a. Halliday
(2) A phoneme may be defined as the sum of the differential functions.	b. Trubetzkoy
(3) Language is to be regarded as a mode of action, rather than as a counterpart of thought.	c. Sapir
(4) Language is a means of doing things and of making others do things. It is a means of acting and living.	d. Saussure
(5) Systemic-Functional Grammar	e. Firth
(6) He defines language as *a purely human and non-instinctive method of communicating ideas, emotions and desires by means of a system of voluntarily produced symbols*.	f. Malinowski
(7) Linguistics is a branch of psychology, and specifically of the positivistic brand of psychology known as behaviourism.	g. Chomsky
(8) Transformational-Generative Grammar	h. Boas
(9) The distance between the speaker and hearer, two separate nervous systems, is bridged up by sound waves.	i. Bloomfield

V. Answer the following questions as comprehensively as possible, giving examples if necessary.
1. What are the three important notions that mark the Prague School?

2. What is special about Systemic-Functional linguistics?
3. Please adopt at least one of the theories in modern linguistics to analyze the following sentences. What kind of attitude do you have toward this linguistic phenomenon?

   The old men and women left the room.
   Bill sold the invisible men's hat.
   They don't smoke and drink.
   I saw her duck.
   The chicken is too hot to eat.
   This is my small son's cot.
   I said I would see you on Tuesday.
   Students hate annoying professors.
   Sue adores men who love women who don't smoke.
   They hit the man with a cane.
   I want more expensive clothes.

4. Give a brief account of X-bar theory.

参考答案

I.
1. Saussure
2. signs
3. langue, parole
4. function
5. departure; discourse
6. sounds; environment
7. prosodic
8. descriptive
9. means
10. Behaviorism
11. Device
12. relations and categories
13. phonological; grammatical; referential
14. verb; relationships; Cases
15. proposition

II.
1. T 2. T
3. F. Saussure was the first to notice the complexities of language.
4. T 5. T 6. T 7. T
8. F. Firth, the first Professor of General Linguistics in Great Britain. The majority of university teachers of linguistics in Britain were trained under Firth and their work reflected his ideas.
9. T 10. T
11. F. Malinowski's concept of *linguistic environment* and *meaning as functions* in the context of situation provided useful background for further development of linguistics carried out by Firth.
12. T
13. F. It is an important and admirable part of the London School tradition to believe that different types of linguistic description may be appropriate for different purposes.
14. T 15. T 16. T
17. F. On the contrary, transformational rules are too powerful. An ordinary sentence can

Chapter 12
Theories and Schools of Modern Linguistics

be transformed at will, negated, passivized, with certain elements added or deleted, without restrictions. This problem becomes worse when dealing with some English verbs which don't have passive structures.
18. F. A generative grammar is not limited to particular languages, but to reveal the unity of particular grammars and universal grammars. It does not describe one language as an end, but as a means to explore the universal rules in the hope of revealing human cognitive systems and the essential nature of human beings.
19. F. Interpersonal function embodies all uses of language to express social and personal relations. This includes the various ways the speaker enters a speech situation and performs a speech act.
20. T

III.
1. A 2. A 3. D 4. B 5. C 6. C 7. A

IV.
(1) d (2) b (3) f (4) e (5) a (6) c (7) i (8) g (9) i

V.
1. Of the many ideas developed in Prague School, three points are of special importance. First, it was stressed that the synchronic study of language is fully justified as it can draw on complete and controllable material for investigation but no rigid theoretical barrier is erected to separate diachronic study. Second, there was emphasis on the systemic character of language, elements are held to be in functional contrast or opposition. Third, language was looked on as functional in another sense, that is, as a tool performing a number of essential functions or tasks for the community using it.
2. Halliday's Systemic Functional Grammar is different from other linguistic theories in the following aspects. Firstly, it attaches great importance to the sociological aspects of language. Secondly, it views language as a form of doing rather than a form of knowing. Thirdly, it gives a relatively high priority to description of the characteristics of particular languages and particular varieties of languages. Fourthly, it explains a number of aspects of language in terms of clines. Fifthly, it seeks verification of its hypothesis by means of observation from texts and by means of statistical techniques. Lastly, it has as its central category the category of the system
3. All these sentences are ambiguous. In IC analysis, Immediate Constituents are constituents immediately, directly, below the level of a construction.

    Immediate constituent analysis can be defined as the analysis of a sentence in terms of its immediate constituents—word groups (or phrases), which are in turn analyzed into the immediate constituents of their own, and the process goes on until the ultimate constituents are reached. Through IC analysis, the internal structure of a sentence may be demonstrated clearly, and ambiguities, if any, will be revealed. Its problems:

    First, at the beginning, some advocators insisted on binary divisions. But this is not always possible.

    Second, constructions with discontinuous constituents will pose technical problems for tree diagrams in IC analysis.

    The most serious problem is that there are structural ambiguities which cannot be revealed by IC analysis.

    Ambiguity can be analysed in other ways.

In factual, explanatory prose, ambiguity is considered an error in reasoning or diction; in literary prose or poetry, it often functions to increase the richness and subtlety of language and to imbue it with a complexity that expands the literal meaning of the original statement. William Empson's *Seven Types of Ambiguity* (1930; rev. ed. 1953) remains a full and useful treatment of the subject.

4. X-bar theory is a component of linguistic theory which attempts to identify syntactic features presumably common to all those human languages that fit in presupposed framework. It claims that among their phrasal categories, all those languages share certain structural similarities, including one known as the *X-bar*, which does not appear in traditional, for inter alia natural English language, phrase structure rules. X-bar theory was first proposed by Chomsky (1970) and further developed by Jackendoff (1977). The letter X is used to signify an arbitrary lexical category; when analyzing a specific utterance, specific categories are assigned. Thus, the X may become an N for noun, a V for verb, an A for adjective, or a P for preposition.

The term X-bar is derived from the notation representing this new structure. Certain structures are represented by $\overline{X}$ (an X with an overbar). Because this is difficult to typeset, this is often written as X', using the prime symbol. In English, however, this is still read as *X bar*. The notation XP stands for X Phrase, and is equivalent to X-bar-bar (X with a double overbar), written X'', usually read aloud as X double bar.

综 合 测 试

Comprehensive Test

One

I. Mark the choice that best completes the statement.

1. The _____ nature of language is a sign of sophistication and it makes it possible for language to have an unlimited source of expressions.
   A. recursive   B. creative
   C. arbitrary   D. culturally transmissible

2. _____ is interested in the system of sounds of a particular language; it aims to discover how speech sounds in a language form patterns and how these sounds are used to convey meaning in linguistic communication.
   A. Phonetics   B. Articulatory phonetics
   C. Phonology   D. Auditory phonetics

3. _____ manifest various grammatical relations or grammatical categories such as number, tense, degree and case.
   A. Roots   B. Stems
   C. Derivational affixes   D. Inflectional affixes

4. As a major component of the study of language, _____ consists of a set of abstract rules that allow words to be combined with other words to form grammatical sentences.
   A. morphology   B. concord   C. formalism   D. syntax

5. The two words *petrol* and *gasoline* are _____.
   A. dialectal synonyms
   B. stylistic synonyms
   C. synonyms that differ in their emotive meaning
   D. collocative synonyms

6. Language acquisition is concerned with language development in _____.
   A. human beings   B. animals
   C. both human beings and animals   D. none of these

7. As the term suggests, psycholinguistics is viewed as the intersection of _____.
   A. psychology and phonology   B. psychology and linguistics
   C. linguistics and biology   D. psychology and biology

8. Language is _____ in that communicating by speaking or writing is a purposeful act.
   A. instrumental   B. social
   C. conventional   D. useful

9. In general, linguistic change in _____ of a language is more noticeable than that in other systems of the grammar.
   A. the sound system   B. the vocabulary
   C. the syntax   D. the sound system and the vocabulary

10. *Retire* is a _____.
    A. compound word   B. free morpheme with a prefix *re-*
    C. morpheme word   D. bound morpheme with a prefix *re-*

11. In *John gave Mary a book*, *give* is a _____-place predicate.
    A. one   B. two   C. three   D. four
12. The two English sounds [l] and [r] are _____.
    A. stops   B. fricatives   C. affricates   D. liquids
13. Language can be used to refer to contexts not present in the immediate situation of the speaker. This is what _____ means.
    A. arbitrariness   B. creativity   C. duality   D. displacement
14. _____ plays the performative function.
    A. *Hello, do you hear me?*
    B. *You'd better go to the clinic.*
    C. *Can't you see people are dying?*
    D. *What a blessing!*
15. A particular register often distinguishes itself from other registers by all of these EXCEPT _____.
    A. having a number of distinctive words
    B. using words or phrases in a particular way
    C. having a very different accent
    D. having special grammatical constructions

II. Fill in each of the following blanks with an appropriate word. The first letter of the word is already given.

1. Chomsky defines c_____ as the ideal user's knowledge of the rules of his language.
2. The short vowels are also l_____ vowels.
3. M_____ is the basic unit in the study of morphology.
4. A clause that takes a subject and a finite verb, and at the same time stands structurally alone is known as a f_____ clause.
5. S_____ can be simply defined as the study of meaning.
6. Halliday proposes a theory of m_____ of language, that is, language has ideational, interpersonal and textual functions.
7. Different languages have a similar level of complexity and detail and reflect general abstract properties of the common linguistic system called the Universal G_____.
8. The fact that the constituent parts of a complex word have little potential for rearrangement shows that the unit of word has the identification of s_____.
9. Sociolinguistics is the sub-discipline of linguistics that studies language in s_____ contexts.
10. In Saussure's view, language is a system of signs, each of which consists of two parts: s_____ and s_____. And the relationship between these two parts is a _____.
11. When two words are c_____ antonyms, one always presupposes the other.
12. The vocal cords are brought momentarily together to create the g_____ obstruction, such as the English sound [h].
13. A few English roots may have both free and bound v_____.
14. Foreign language learners will subconsciously use their L1 knowledge in learning the foreign language and this is called language t_____.
15. A_____ is the concept proposed by Hymes to refer to a learner's ability to use correct forms of language in a specific socio-cultural context.

III. Mark the following statements with "T" if they are true or "F" if they are false. Provide explanations for the false statements.

1. A study of the features of the English used in Shakespeare's time would be a diachronic study.
2. The transcription of sounds with letter-symbols together with the diacritics is called narrow transcription.
3. The central element in a simple sentence, or in each clause, is the infinite verb.

4. How a compound is written is simply a matter of convention, and convention should be respected in this case.
5. Meaning is central to the study of communication.
6. Language learning and use are determined by the intervention of biological, cognitive, psychosocial, and environmental factors.
7. The study of the relationship between meaning and perception belongs to the study of psycho-semantics.
8. Social variation of language is the most discernible and definable.
9. As a general rule, language change is universal, continuous, and to a considerable degree, regular and systematic.
10. From the early days of the 20th century, the dominant tradition of linguistic study was that linguists should study language as it is and language should be studied as it is.
11. The deep structure of *the love of God* is *God loves everybody*.
12. There is no absolute synonymy.
13. Aptitude test tries to discover the learner's general level of language mastery.
14. Metalingual function of language enables us to see the charm of human language.
15. Lexemes generally appear in dictionaries as those entries.

IV. Match each term in Column A with one relevant item in Column B.

1.

A	B
(1) arbitrariness	a. Its advantage lies in the great productive power our language is endowed with.
(2) duality	b. We can use language to produce new meanings.
(3) creativity	c. It partially explains why language is creative by nature.
(4) displacement	d. A name is given to a new entity at random.
	e. The sounds in languages are secondary units and words are primary units.
	f. We can use language to review history.
	g. This feature makes it difficult for us to memorize new words, because we do not know the internal relationship between the form and the meaning of the word.

2.

A	B
(1) lexeme	a. [p]
(2) phoneme	b. /p^h/
(3) word	c. -ly (as the suffix)
(4) sound	d. fat
(5) morpheme	e. writer
	f. /p/
	g. men

V. Explain the following concepts or theories.
1. Narrow transcription
2. Negative transfer
3. Complementary distribution
4. Sequential rules
5. Inflectional affixes
6. Polysemy
7. Pragmatics
8. Illocutionary act
9. Complementary antonymy
10. Diachronic linguistics

VI. Analyze the following with your own linguistic knowledge.
A. Never match *a* with plural forms.
B. People usually do not match *a* with plural forms.

VII. Answer the following questions as comprehensively as possible, giving examples if necessary.
1. Describe with examples the classification of morphemes.
2. Describe major sense relations with examples.
3. What is the relationship between duality and creativity?
4. The following dialogue that took place in an English pub serves as a good example for us to see various aspects of language functions. Explain the concept of language functions (such as informative, emotive, conative, and interpersonal) with examples taken form the dialogue.

   Bill: *How did it go?*
   Mike: *Oh, fantastic! I took some really good photographs. I am sure I will win the competition.*
   Lily: *Well, you'd better buy us all a drink, then.*
   Mike: *Yes, what would you all like? (He went to the barman) I'd like four pints of best bitter.*
   Barman: *Excuse me, sir, how old are you?*
   Mike: *Sixteen, why?*
   Barman: *I think you know why.*

5. What is the distinction between Chomsky's competence and Hymes' communicative competence?

参考答案

I.
1. A 2. C 3. D 4. D 5. A 6. A 7. B 8. A 9. D 10. B 11. C
12. D 13. D 14. B 15. C

II.
1. competence   2. lax   3. Morpheme   4. finite
5. Semantics   6. metafunctions 7. Grammar   8. stability
9. social   10. signified; signifier; arbitrary 11. converse 12. glottal
13. variants   14. transfer   15. Appropriateness

III.
1. F. It should be a synchronic study.
2. T
3. F. The central element in a simple sentence, or in each clause, is the finite verb.
4. T 5. T 6. T
7. F. what the relationship between meaning and perception is belongs to the study of pragmatics.
8. F. Regional variation of language is the most discernible and definable.
9. T 10. T

11. F. The deep structure of *the love of God* is *God loves somebody* and *somebody loves God*.
12. T
13. F. Aptitude test tries to find how good the testee is in learning language.
14. F. Metalingual function enables us to talk about the language itself.
15. F. Lexemes have to appear in different grammatical context, because they are seen as abstract units underlying the smallest units in the lexical system of a language.

IV.
1. (1) d; g   (2) c; e; a   (3) b   (4) f
2. (1) d   (2) b; f   (3) d;e; g   (4) a; b   (5) d; c; g

V.
1. Narrow transcription refers to a way to transcribe speech sounds with letter-symbols together with the diacritics. For instance, [ɫ] is used to indicate dark [l]. This way is required and used by the phoneticians in their study of speech sounds. With the help of the diacritics they can faithfully represent as much of the fine details as it is necessary for their purpose.
2. When learners subconsciously use their L1 knowledge in learning a second language, transfer occurs. Transfer can be positive or negative. It is apparent that for any two languages, similar patterns exist alongside different patterns in their grammatical and other systems. Presumably, positive transfer occurs when an L1 pattern is identical with, or similar to, a target language pattern. Conversely, negative transfer occurs when an L1 pattern is different from the counterpart pattern of the target language. Negative transfer, known as interference, was once believed to be the major source of difficulties experienced and errors made by L2 learner on the ground that where differences existed between L1 and L2, the learner's L1 knowledge would interfere with the second language.
3. When two speech sounds never occur in the same environments and they don't distinguish meaning, these two sounds are said to be in complementary distribution. They are usually two allophones of the same phoneme; for example, [p] and [pʰ] are just two allophones of the phoneme /p/ which are in complementary distribution.
4. The rules that govern the combination of sounds in particular language are called sequential rules, for example, in English, if a word begins with a [l] or a [r], and then the next sound must be a vowel.
5. Inflectional affixes manifest various grammatical relations or grammatical categories such as number, tense, degree and case.
6. When one word has more than one meaning, we call this polysemy. For instance, the English word *table* has at least seven meanings.
7. Pragmatics can be defined in various ways. A general definition is that it is the study of how speakers of a language use sentences to effect successful communication. As the process of communication is essentially a process of conveying meaning in a certain context, pragmatics can also be regarded as a kind of meaning study.
8. An illocutionary act is the act of expressing the speaker's intention; it is the act performed in saying something.
9. Complementary antonymy is a kind of antonymy. The members of a pair in this type are complementary to each other. Words that belong to complementary antonymy are alive: dead, male; female, etc.
10. Diachronic linguistics is the study of language through the course of its history. For example, the study of English pronunciation change through the course of history is a research of diachronic linguistics.

VI.
"Never match *a* with plural forms" is a piece of English grammar. The first sentence presents

it in a prescriptive command, while the second presents the grammar in a descriptive statement. To be prescriptive is to prescribe how language ought to be, and to be descriptive is simply to describe what language is objectively. The nature of linguistics as a science determines its preoccupation with description instead of prescription. Prescription is also important in some particular fields, e.g. in second language learning and in the process of standardizing a dialect in a particular region or country.

VII.

1. Morphemes can be classified as follows:
   (1) morpheme: the smallest meaningful unit of language.
   (2) Free morphemes and bound morphemes: free morphemes are independent units of meaning which can be used freely all by themselves, such as, *help*, *table*, *room* etc. Bound morphemes can not be used by themselves, but must be combined with other morphemes to form words that can be used independently. Bound morphemes include two types: roots and affixes.
   (3) Affixes are of two types: inflectional and derivational. According to its position in the new word, affixes are divided into two kinds: prefixes and suffixes.
2. Major sense relations include:
   (1) Synonymy refers to the sameness or close similarity of meaning, for example, the relationship between the two words *autumn* and *fall*.
   (2) Polysemy refers to the same word may have more than one meaning. Take the word *table* for example: it has at least seven meanings.
   (3) Homonymy refers to the phenomenon that words having different meanings have the same form, i. e., different words are identical in sounds or spelling or both, such as the relationship between *rain/reign* and *bow v.* / *bow n*.
   (4) Hyponymy refers to the sense relation between a more general, more inclusive word and a more specific word, for instance, *flower/rose*, *tulip*, *carnation*...
   (5) Antonymy is used for oppositeness of meaning; words that are opposite in meaning are antonyms, such as *hot/cold*, *alive/dead*.
3. Duality and creativity are two design features of language. Duality is the property of having two levels of structures, such that units of the primary level are composed of elements of the secondary level and each of the two levels has its own principles of organization. By creativity we mean language is resourceful because of its duality and its recursiveness. The creativity of language partly originates from its duality, namely, because of duality the speaker is able to combine the basic linguistic units to form an infinite set of sentences, most of which are never before produced or heard.
4. Language has some practical functions. Jacobson established a framework of language functions and classified them into the following categories: referential (to convey message and information), poetic (to indulge in language for its own sake), emotive (to persuade and influence others through commands and entreaties), phatic (to establish communion with others) and Metalingual function (to clear up intentions, words and meanings). Other linguists such as Halliday, Austin and Searle proposed theories that classify functions in other ways. Despite of the different terminology they have used to name functions, they more or less share the same opinion: language is not merely an instrument to inform. It can do things as well. The analysis here follows the terms used by most of the linguists. The are informative, emotive, performative, etc. as those used in the textbook. You may analyze the following dialogue this way:

   Bill: *How did it go?* (informative, asking for information)
   Mike: *Oh, fantastic*! (emotive, expressing feelings) *I took some really good photographs. I am sure I will win the competition.* (informative and emotive, expressing attitude of certainty)

Lily: Well, you'd better buy us all a drink, then. (performative, making a request)

Mike: Yes, what would you all like? (informative) (*He went to the barman*) I'd like four pints of best bitter. (performative, making a request)

Barman: Excuse me, sir, (phatic) *how old are you*? (informative as it appears to be, but performative in fact, refusing the request)

Mike: Sixteen, why? (informative)

Barman: I think you know why.

5. Noam Chomsky's competence refers to grammatical knowledge of the ideal language users and has nothing to do with the actual use of language in concrete situations. Although Chomsky's *rule-governed creativity* aptly describes a child's mushrooming grammar at the age of 3 or 4, it did not, according to Hymes, account sufficiently for the social and functional rules of language. Hymes' communicative competence, then, is that aspect of competence that enables the speakers to convey and interpret messages and to negotiate meanings interpersonally within specific contexts. Communicative competence is relative, not absolute, and depends on the cooperation of all the participants involved. Communicative competence includes not only the ability to form correct sentence but to use them at appropriate times. The basic idea of communicative competence is the ability to use language appropriately, both receptively and productively, in real situations. Communicative competence can be defined, in terms of three components. The first is grammatical competence, which involves the accurate use of words and structures. The second is sociolinguistic competence. It enables the learner to know to speak properly according to the social context. The third is called strategic competence, the ability to overcome potential communication problems in interaction.

Two

I. Mark the choice that best completes the statement.

1. The _____ nature of language explains the symbolic nature of language: words are just symbols; they are associated with objects, actions, ideas, etc. by convention.
   A. duality   B. arbitrary   C. productive   D. displacement

2. _____ are pitch variations, which are caused by the differing rates of vibration of the vocal cords.
   A. Stresses   B. Voicings   C. Tones   D. Intonations

3. *-ish* in the word *boyish* is _____.
   A. a free morpheme   B. a root
   C. a stem   D. an affix

4. The sentence *John likes linguistics, but Mary is interested in history* is a _____.
   A. simple sentence   B. coordinate sentence
   C. complex sentence   D. clause

5. _____ is NOT a design feature of language.
   A. Arbitrariness   B. Creativity
   C. Communicability   D. Duality

6. Once the notion of context was taken into consideration, semantics spilled over into _____.
   A. semantics   B. pragmatics   C. morphology   D. syntax

7. _____ can be divided into inflectional and derivational ones.
   A. Roots   B. Words   C. Affixes   D. Stems

8. _____ does not have anything to do with Halliday or his theory.
   A. Systemic theory   B. Ideational function
   C. Universal Grammar   D. Thematic analysis

9. Among the six processes proposed by Halliday, _____ process is concerned with the representation of inner experience.

A. material   B. verbal   C. mental   D. relational
10. The idea that the meaning of a sentence depends on the meanings of the constituent words and the way they are combined is usually known as _____.
   A. projection theory
   B. integrating rule
   C. principle of compositionality
   D. semantic theory
11. Among the following items, _____ is not related to a process in reading.
   A. eye movement   B. the perceptual span
   C. the immediacy assumption   D. understanding
12. That language may determine our thinking patterns is _____.
   A. Sapir-Whorf Hypothesis
   B. Chomsky's Language Innateness
   C. Grice's Non-Conventionality
   D. Corders Interlanguage
13. The following are words used to describe conventional forms of meter and sound EXCEPT _____.
   A. sonnet   B. quatrains   C. synecdoche   D. couplets
14. When analyzing dramatic language, we may look at the language in terms of the following EXCEPT _____.
   A. free indirect speech   B. turn quantity and length
   C. exchange sequence   D. production errors
15. Item _____ will be listed in a Situational syllabus.
   A. making apologies   B. quantity
   C. subjunctive mood   D. at the railway station

II. Fill in each of the following blanks with an appropriate word. The first letter of the word is already given.
1. D_____ features refer to the defining properties of human language that distinguish it from any animal system of communication.
2. A_____ phonetics studies the sounds from the speakers point of view, i.e., how a speaker uses his organs to produce the sounds.
3. Bound morphemes contain two types: roots and a _____.
4. Words and phrases are organized according to the s_____ categories they belong to.
5. S_____ is concerned with the inherent meaning of the linguistic form.
6. As the process of communication is essentially a process of conveying meaning in a certain context, pragmatics can also be regarded as a kind of m_____ study.
7. The p_____ function of language can extend to the control of reality as on some magical or religious occasions.
8. M_____ is a branch of linguistics which studies the internal structure of words and the rules by which words are formed.
9. P_____ is the study of language in relation to the mind.
10. For every sentence we have two levels of structure: the d_____ structure and s_____ structure. The former may be defined as the abstract representation of the syntactic properties of a construction. The latter is the final stage in the syntactic derivation of a construction.
11. In the aspect sense relation, when a word is a hyponym of itself, it is called an a_____.
12. The c_____ view to errors is that an error may serve as a negative stimulus which reinforces bad habits, so it should not be allowed to occur.
13. Firth regarded l_____ as a social process, as a means of social life, rather than simply as a set of agreed-upon semiotics and signals.
14. In terms of m_____ of articulation, [p] and [b] can be classified into the category of

stops.
15. A major theory in pragmatics is the theory of c_____ i_____, proposed by Grice.

III. Mark the following statements with "T" if they are true or "F" if they are false. Provide explanations for the false statements.

1. Modern linguistics is mostly descriptive.
2. Of the two media of language, writing is more basic than speech.
3. *-er* in the word *bigger* is an inflectional affix.
4. The relationship between the embedded clause and its matrix clause is one of a part to a whole.
5. The two words *knight* and *night* are homographs.
6. Even without considering the knowledge, linguistic communication still can be satisfactorily accounted for in a pragmatic sense.
7. The Old English is simply unintelligible like a foreign language, so nothing in the Modern English originates from it.
8. Consciously or unconsciously, people's social backgrounds exert a shaping influence on their choice of linguistic features that are appropriate to their social identities.
9. Language is merely a system of communication.
10. Language came into existence by ancient people imitating the sounds of the animal calls in the wild environment they lived.
11. CAI aims at seeing educational problems on the part of the teacher.
12. The meaning of a word is an analyzable whole.
13. Linguists are concerned with only those sounds that are produced by the human speech organs in so far as they have a role to play in linguistic communication.
14. When two different word forms are identical in every way except for one letter which occurs in the same place in the sequence, the two words are said to form a minimal pair.
15. Vibration of the vocal cords is the criterion that distinguishes vowels from consonants.

IV. Match each term in Column A with one relevant item in Column B.

A	B
(1) variable word	a. seldom
(2) invariable word	b. follow
(3) grammatical word	c. or
(4) lexical word	d. though
	e. the
	f. boy
	g. redundantly
	h. why

V. Explain the following concepts or theories with one or two examples.

1. argument
2. general linguistics
3. reference
4. syntactic category
5. derivational affixes
6. context
7. converse antonymy
8. bilingual
9. co-hyponym

10. applied linguistics

VI. Fill in the brackets, giving examples in the square brackets.

word ⎰ monomorphemic word = (1) morphemes [2]
⎱ polymorphemic word ⎰ compound word [3]
⎱ other word ⎰ root [4] in word [5]
(6) ⎨ prefix [para]
⎩ suffix [7]
(8)

VII. Answer the following questions as comprehensively as possible, giving examples if necessary.

1. Distinguish the following cases of ambiguity by tree diagrams.
 sentence a: *The boy saw the man with the telescope.*
 sentence b: *The magician touched the child with the wand.*
2. What are vocal folds? How do they work in pronouncing the voiceless sound, voiced sound and the glottal stop?
3. Employ examples to present the differences between broad transcription and narrow transcription.
4. What is linguistic context and what is situational context of a text? Give an example to illustrate them.
5. What does Chomsky mean by Language Acquisition Device (LAD)?
6. In what way is the human language different from animal communication system?

参考答案

I.
1. B 2. C 3. D 4. B 5. C 6. B 7. C 8. C 9. C 10. C
11. D 12. A 13. C 14. A 15. D

II.
1. Design   2. Articulatory   3. affixes   4. Syntactic
5. Sense   6. meaning   7. performative   8. Morphology
9. Psycholinguistics 10. deep; surface   11. auto-hyponym   12. structuralist
13. language   14. manner   15. conversational implicature

III.
1. T
2. F. Of the two media of language, speech is more basic than writing
3. T 4. T
5. F. The two words *knight* and *night* are homophones.
6. F. Without the knowledge of context, linguistic communication can not be satisfactorily accounted for in a pragmatic sense.
7. F. Many of the most basic terms in the English language originate form the Old English.
8. T
9. F. Language can be seen as a system of communication but it is not only a system of communication. Four design features of human language distinguish it from any other animal communication system.
10. F. The saying mentioned is one theory of the origin of language-bow-wow theory. We still have some more theories about the origin of human language.
11. T
12. F. The meaning of a word is not an analyzable whole. It may be seen as a complex of different semantic features.
13. T
14. F. The difference does not lie in one letter, but in one sound segment. Sometimes two letters make one sound, such as *ck* in the word *stock* do.

15. F. Although all the vowels have the feature of voicing, some consonants also do. Voicing cannot be used to differentiate vowels and consonants.

IV.
(1) b; f (2) a; c; d; e; h (3) c; d; e; h (4) a; b; f; g

V.
1. An argument is a term which refers to some entity about which a statement is being made. In the sentence *Helen is a girl*, *Helen* is the argument.
2. The study of language as a whole is often called general linguistics. This deals with the basic concepts, theories, descriptions, models and methods applicable in any linguistic study, in contrast to those branches of study which relate linguistics to the research of other areas.
3. Reference means what a linguistic form refers to in the real, physical world; it deals with the relationship between the linguistic element and the non-linguistic world of experience.
4. Constituents that can be substituted for one another without loss of grammaticality belong to the same syntactic category.
5. Derivational affixes are added to an existing form to create a word, *-ate* in the word *tolerate*.
6. The notion of context is essential to the pragmatic study of language. It is generally considered as constituted by the knowledge shared by the speaker and the hearer. The shared knowledge is on two types: the knowledge of the language they use, and the knowledge about the world, including the general knowledge about the world and the specific knowledge about the situation which linguistic communication is taking place.
7. Converse antonymy is a special type of antonymy in that the members of a pair do not constitute a positive-negative opposition. They show the reversal of a relationship between two entities, like words *doctor* and *patient*.
8. When a person knows or uses two languages, we say that he/she is a bilingual or a bilingual person. For example, if one speaks Chinese and English, we say that he is a bilingual person.
9. Hyponyms that share one superordinate are called cohyponyms. For example, *cat* and *dog* share one superordinate *animal*, so they are cohyponyms.
10. Applied linguistics is a term covering several linguistic subjects as well as certain interdisciplinary areas that use linguistic methods, like psycholinguistics, computational linguistics, sociolinguistics, etc. to study the nature of language teaching.

VI.
(1) free   [2] dog   [3] hotdog   [4] nation
[5] international   (6) affix   [7] -ise   (8) infix

VII.
1. Sentence a:
   Meaning one *the boy used a telescope to see the man* can be shown by the following tree diagram:

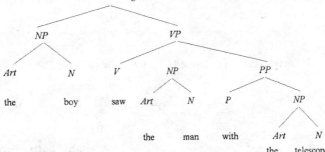

   Meaning two *the boy saw a man who had a telescope in his possession* can be shown by the following tree diagram:

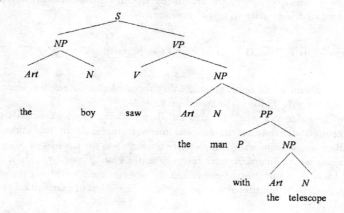

Sentence b:
Meaning One *the magician used a wand to touch the child* can be shown by the following tree diagram:

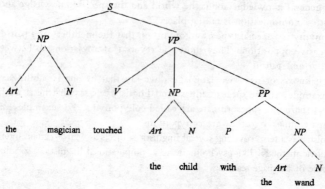

Meaning Two *the magician touched a child who had a wand in his or her possession* can be shown by the following tree diagram:

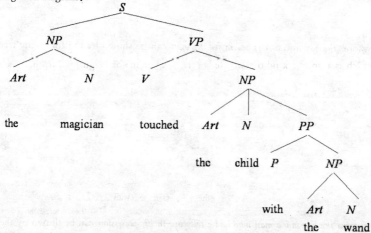

2. The larynx contains two pairs of structures, the vocal folds and ventricular folds. The vocal folds lie horizontally below the latter and their front ends are joined together at the back of Adam's apple. When the vocal folds are apart, the air can pass through easily and the sound produced is said to be voiceless. When they are closed together, the airstream causes them to vibrate against each other and the resultant sound is said to be voiced. When they are totally closed, no air can pass between them. The result of this gesture is the glottal stop.
3. Narrow transcription and broad transcription are both methods we use in transcribing sounds. When we use a simple set of symbols in our transcription, it is called a broad transcription, like we use [i] to represent the sound in the word *limp*.

    When we use more specific symbols to show more phonetic detail, it is called a narrow transcription, like we use [p^h] to represent the sound *p* pronounces in word *stop*.
4. The situational context refers to the following features: the relevant participants and the relationship between them, the non-verbal action (such as facial expressions, gestures accompanied) of the participants, the time and place of the event in which the text occurs, etc. Linguistic context refers to the verbal features of a text. The internal relation between components of the text, such as what has been stated before and what will be stated afterwards in the text, is the major concern. Sometimes the stress of intonation is also part of the linguistic context. The following dialogue may illustrate the point here.

    Husband: *I need the car tomorrow. The kids can take the school bus.*
    Wife: *Good. That's very good for the family.*
    Husband: *Nice day.*

    The situational context here contains the following things: (1) the dialogue occurs between a couple. (2) They are not in good terms at the moment, or at least the wife is not happy about her husband using the car which she uses to send the kids to school every day. (3) Maybe she says *Good* in an ironic tone, or strange voice. (4) The husband does not want to start a fight, so he quickly ends the conversation by *Nice day*. (5) The conversation possibly takes place at their home, and in the evening before bedtime. (6) The husband is very likely to be a self-centered person who seldom negotiates family matters with his wife.

    The linguistic context here seems rather interesting. Sentence *I need the car...* offers a perfect linguistic context for the understanding of the next sentence *The kids can take the school bus*. The wife's angry remarks to his decision (being the linguistic context for his wife's response) are presented by the ironic use of *Good* and *very good for the family* which don't go along very well with the surface connection of meaning. However, the husband detects his wife's anger from her use of *good* and with this as the linguistic context; he wants to end the conversation quickly. *Nice day* in fact means *Stop it. I don't want to quarrel with you*.

    The concept of linguistic context and situational context helps us to see the complicated factors that influence the interpretation of language in communication.
5. Chomsky believes that language is somewhat innate, and that children are born with what he calls LAD, which is a unique kind of knowledge that fits them for language learning. He argues the child comes into the world with specific innate endowment, not only with general tendencies or potentialities, but also with knowledge of the nature of the world, and specifically with knowledge of the nature of language. Children are born with knowledge of the basic grammatical relations and categories, and this knowledge is universal.
6. The difference lies in that human language has four design features while any of animal communication systems don't.

Three

I. Mark the choice that best completes the statement.
1. Today, the grammar taught to learners of a language is basically _____.

A. descriptive   B. prescriptive
   C. both A and B   D. neither of the two
2. The clear /l/ and the dark /ɫ/ are _____.
   A. in complementary distribution   B. in free variation
   C. both A and B   D. neither of the two
3. *-ed* in the word *played* is _____.
   A. a free morpheme   B. a root
   C. a derivational affix   D. an inflectional morpheme
4. The _____ function of language is primarily to change the social status of persons.
   A. interpersonal   B. informative
   C. textual   D. performative
5. Whorf believes that speakers of different languages perceive and experience the world differently and that is the notion of _____.
   A. linguistic determinism   B. language determinism
   C. social relativism   D. linguistic relativism
6. What essentially distinguishes semantics from pragmatics is _____.
   A. whether in the study of meaning the context of use is considered
   B. whether it studies the meaning or not
   C. whether it studies how the speakers use language to effect communication
   D. whether it is a branch of linguistics
7. Of all the following examples, _____ is NOT an example of the affix addition.
   A. the addition of *-able* to a verb, such as in *readable*
   B. the addition of *-ment* to a verb, such as in *accomplishment*
   C. the attachment of *-ize* to a noun or adjective, such as in *stabilize*
   D. the addition of *a* or *an* before a noun, such as in *an apple*
8. In English, inflectional affixes are mostly _____.
   A. prefixes   B. suffixes   C. infixes   D. stems
9. That the use of language involves a network of systems of choices is the opinion of _____.
   A. Halliday   B. Saussure   C. Chomsky   D. Firth
10. Of the following _____ does NOT belong to the three sub-types of antonymy.
    A. gradable antonymy   B. converse antonymy
    C. complementary antonymy   D. complete antonymy
11. _____ is NOT included in Firth's famous *Context of Situation* theory.
    A. The non-verbal action of the participants
    B. The properties of the phonematic units
    C. The relevant objects
    D. The effects of the verbal action
12. The phrase *backwash effect* is often used in _____.
    A. systemic functional grammar
    B. error analysis
    C. testing
    D. sociolinguistics
13. We can often find the phrase *immediate constituents* in _____.
    A. transformational generative grammar
    B. systemic functional grammar
    C. traditional grammar
    D. structural grammar
14. The following ideas about language are wrong EXCEPT _____.
    A. Language evolves within specific historical, social and cultural context

B. Language has a form-sound correspondence
C. Language is a means of communication
D. Language is not related to any of the individuals who use it
15. Because _____ can distinguish one phoneme from another, it is a distinctive feature for English obstruents.
   A. voicing   B. nasalization   C. place   D. aspiration

II. Fill in each of the following blanks with an appropriate word. The first letter of the word is already given.
1. The ultimate objective of language is not just to create grammatically well-formed sentences, but to convey m _____.
2. Vibration of the vocal cords results in a quality of speech sounds called "v _____".
3. Those morphemes that can not be used by themselves, but must be combined with other morphemes to form words are called b _____ morphemes.
4. The incorporated, or subordinate, clause is normally called an e _____ clause.
5. The study of sounds is called p _____, and the study of sound patterns is called p _____.
6. Context is generally considered as constituted by the knowledge shared by the s _____ and the hearer.
7. The most widely spread morphological changes in the historical development of English are the loss and addition of a _____.
8. A _____ refers to a way of pronunciation which tells the listener something about the speaker's regional or social background.
9. Inflection is the manifestation of grammatical relationships through the addition of inflectional affixes, such as n _____, p _____ and f _____.
10. One-word utterances sometimes show an overextension or under extension of r _____.
11. In Katz and Postal's proposal stated in "An Integrated Theory of Linguistic Description", the d _____ provides the grammatical classification and semantic information of words.
12. Nasalization rule read: a non-nasalized sound is transformed into a n _____ sound when it appears before a nasalized sound.
13. The process of insertion of a nasal sound to the article *a* when it appears before a word *orange* is known as e _____.
14. The p _____ relation, Saussure originally called Associative, is a relation holding between elements replaceable with each other at a particular place in a structure, or between one element present and the others absent.
15. In Chomsky's linguistic model, the m _____ component is responsible for the correct spelling and pronunciation of the words in the surface structure.

III. Mark the following statements with "T" if they are true or "F" if they are false. Provide explanations for the false statements.
1. Language is not an isolated phenomenon; it is a social activity carried out in a certain social environment by human being.
2. Speech is made up of continuous bursts of sounds.
3. Acoustic phonetics is the study of the production of speech sound.
4. The primary function of the vocal organs is to fulfill the basic biological needs of breathing and eating.
5. The lungs are involved in the production of speech.
6. Even if we think of a sentence as what people actually utter in the course of communication, it is still a sentence.
7. Many words that were popular among Middle English speakers have lost their Modern users. For example, Shakespeare's *Romeo and Juliet* contains such words as *beseem*, *wot* and *gyve*.

8. A lingua franca has to be a native language currently spoken by a particular people.
9. To tell whether a sound is a consonant or not, we should judge its manners of articulation.
10. Semi-vowel and semi-consonant actually refer to the same kind of sound.
11. Two words, or two expressions, which have the same semantic components, will be synonymous to each other.
12. Meaning is extracted from text or speech by relating what is presented to information stored in short-term memory.
13. In English *some books* is a case of number concord.
14. Synchronic linguistics refers to the approach which studies language over various periods of time and at various historical stages.
15. A single phoneme always represents a single morpheme.

IV. Match each term in Column A with one relevant item in Column B.

A	B
(1) Invention	a. smog
(2) Blending	b. Xerox
(3) Abbreviation	c. aeroplane→plane
(4) Acronym	d. brunch
(5) Back-formation	e. WTO
(6) Analogical creation	f. gangling→gangle
(7) Borrowing	g. wrought→worked
	h. laser→lase
	i. bicycle→bike
	j. professor→prof
	k. atom (from Greek)

V. Explain the following concepts or theories.
1. Prescriptive and descriptive
2. Diacritics
3. Bound root
4. Grammatical relations
5. Selectional restrictions
6. Speech act theory
7. Gradable antonymy
8. Standard language
9. Esperanto
10. Equivalence

VI. Fill in each of the following blanks with the original forms of abbreviation items in linguistics, and then put in the corresponding square brackets the specific linguistic field in which the abbreviation forms are used.

1. IC _____ (   )
2. IPA _____ (   )
3. CD _____ (   )
4. RP _____ (   )
5. UG _____ (   )

VII. Answer the following questions as comprehensively as possible, giving examples if necessary.
1. Describe the major ways of word formation with some examples.
2. What do you know about *the minimum free form*?
3. What does syntax study? Give a brief account of the major approaches in the development of syntax.
4. Why do we say that the analysis of a sentence in terms of theme and rheme is functional?
5. It has been observed that women tend to approximate more closely to the standard language than man do. Why do you think this is so?
6. Briefly explain what phonetics and phonology are concerned with and what kind of relationships hold between the two.

参考答案

I.
1. B   2. A   3. D   4. D   5. D   6. A   7. D   8. B   9. A   10. D
11. B   12. C   13. D   14. A   15. A

II.
1. meaning   2. voicing   3. bound
4. embedded   5. phonetics; phonology 6. speaker
7. affix   8. Accent   9. number; person; finiteness
10. reference   11. dictionary   12. nasalized
13. epenthesis   14. paradigmatic   15. morpho-phonemic

III.
1. T   2. T
3. F. Articulatory phonetics is the study of the production of speech sounds.
4. T   5. T
6. F. Because then the sentence is an utterance.
7. T
8. F. A lingua franca may, but does not need to be a native language currently spoken by a particular people.
9. F. To tell whether a sound is a consonant or not, we should judge its manners of articulation and the places of articulation.
10. T   11. T
12. F. Meaning is extracted from text or speech by relating what is presented to information stored in long-term memory.
13. T
14. F. Diachronic linguistics studies language over history.
15. F. A single phoneme may represent a single morpheme, but they are not identical. The phoneme /z/ in [gəuz] (goes) represents the third-person singular present tense morpheme, but /z/ occurs very often when it has nothing to do with this specific morpheme, for example, when /z/ occurs in [reiz] (raise).

IV.
1. b   2. a, d   3. c, i, j   4. e   5. f, h   6. g   7. k

V.
1. If a linguistic study describes and analyzes the language people actually use, it is said to be descriptive; if it aims to lay down rules for "correct" behavior, i.e. to tell people what they should say and what they should not say, it is said to be prescriptive.

2. As some speech sounds produced differ only in some detailed aspects, the IPA provides its users with a set of symbols called diacritics, which can be added to the letter-symbols to make finer distinctions than the letters alone make possible.
3. A bound root is often seen as part of a word; it can never stand by itself although it bears clear, definite meaning; it must be combined with an affix to form a word.
4. Our linguistic knowledge includes an awareness of a distinction between the structural and logical functional relations of constituents called grammatical relations.
5. Whether a sentence is semantically meaningful is governed by rules called selectional restrictions, i.e., constraints on what lexical items can go with what others.
6. Speech act theory is an important theory in the pragmatic study of language. It was originated with the British philosopher John Austin in the late 50's of the 20th century. It is a philosophical explanation of the nature of linguistic communication. It aims to answer the question *What do we do when using a language?*
7. Gradable antonymy refers to the gradable oppositeness of meaning, because there are often intermediate forms between two gradable antonyms such as *love- like-dislike-hate*.
8. The standard language is a superposed, socially prestigious dialect of language. It is the language employed by the government and the judiciary system, used by the mass media, and taught in educational institutions, including school settings where the language is taught as a foreign or second language.
9. Esperanto is an artificial language, thought to be the most successful Interlingua of international understanding. Esperanto consists of a very simple phonetic-phonological, morphological, and syntactic structure.
10. The logical connective equivalence, also called biconditional and symbolized as ↔, is a conjunction of two implications. That is, $p \equiv q$ equals $(p \rightarrow q)$ & $(q \rightarrow p)$. It corresponds to the English expression *if and only if ... then*, which is sometimes written as *iff ... then*. The condition for the composite proposition to be true is that if and only if both constituent propositions are of the same truth value, whether true or false.

VI.
1. Immediate Constituent; syntax
2. International Phonetic Association / International Phonetic Alphabet; phonology
3. Communicative Dynamism; syntax
4. Received Pronunciation; phonology
5. Universal Grammar; syntax

VII.
1. The major ways of word formation are as follows:
   (1) Compounding is the combination of two or sometimes more than two words to create new words, such as, *girlfriend* and *overtake*.
   (2) Acronyms are words formed by the initials of several words. For example, *radar* is formed by *radio detecting and ranging*.
   (3) Blends are words composed of parts of more than one words. For example, *brunch* is formed by *breakfast* and *lunch*, while *smog* is formed by *smoke* and *fog*.
   (4) Back-formations are composed by removing what is mistakenly considered to be affixes.
   (5) Abbreviations or clippings are shortened forms of words.
   (6) Borrowings are words borrowed from other languages.
2. *The minimum free form* was first suggested by Leonard Bloomfield. He advocated treating sentence as *the maximum free form* and word *the minimum free form*, the latter being the smallest unit that can constitute, by itself, a complete utterance. For example, expressions like *Hi*, *Hello*, etc, may extend a whole and complete meaning. But, there are opponents who argue that not all word-like units would satisfy this criterion, as the articles *a* and *the* in English could

not stand by themselves.
3. Syntax refers to the study of the rules governing the way words are combined to form sentences in a language, or simply, the study of the formation of sentences. There are many opinions of various schools toward syntactic study. One example is the traditional approach. Traditionally a sentence is seen as a sequence of words. The traditional approach to syntax is the study of words, such as the classification of words in terms of parts of speech, the identification of functions of words in terms of subject, predicate, etc. These parts of speech and functions are sometimes called categories, like number, gender, case, tense and aspect, etc. (Then you may list the structural approach and generative approach to syntax afterwards)
4. The analysis of a sentence in terms of theme and rheme is functional in the sense that this approach is concerned with the semantic side of constituents of a sentence. It is information oriented as it makes the distinction between the known and the new, the more important and the less important. Contrary to the analysis in terms of subject and predicate, theme and rheme approach does not look at a sentence in the perspective of the formalism, which prescribes that the subject should be in the nominative form in languages with case distinctions, and the form of the predicate verb should be in agreement with the subject in certain categories.
5. The phenomenon is generally explained by the low social status of women in the society. Perhaps, by speaking in a more standard variety and not choosing the vulgar forms, women feel they should be given due respect.
6. Phonetics is mainly concerned with the study of sounds while phonology the study of sound patterns. Phoneticians describe how speech sounds are produced by speech organs, classifying them into vowels and consonants. They devised sets of symbols that can be used for transcribing sounds in language, the phonetic transcription. Phonetics also studies how sounds are transmitted and received, but those two points are not within the considerations of linguistic studies here. Phonology is concerned with the linguistic patterning of sounds in human languages, with its primary aim being to discover the principles that govern the way sounds are organized in languages, and to explain the variations that occur. Unlike phonetics which studies all possible speech sounds, phonology only studies the way speakers of a language systematically use a selection of these sounds in order to express meaning. Unlike phonetics which describes the different variations of a sound when it is pronounced, phonology is more interested in the patterning of such sounds and the rules that underlie such variations. Phonology analyzes and determines an individual language's phonological structure, i.e. which sound units are used and how they pattern. Then the properties of different sound systems are compared so that hypotheses can be developed about the rules underlying the use of sounds.

Four

I. Mark the choice that best completes the statement.
1. Language acquisition is concerned with language development in _____.
   A. human beings B. animals
   C. both human beings and animals D. none of these
2. In language acquisition, what is actually acquired by young children is _____ that are fundamental to the grammaticality of speech.
   A. some words and expressions B. all the rules in language
   C. words and sentences D. some general rules
3. _____ phonetics is the study of the physical properties of the sounds produced in speech.
   A. Articulatory B. Acoustic
   C. Auditory D. Audio-lingual
4. Distinctive features in phonology are similar to _____ in semantics.
   A. semantic features B. immediate constituents
   C. identical features D. linguistic components

5. Syntactic deep structure was developed to _____.
   A. explain relations between sentences with the same meaning
   B. explain a single sentence with more than one meaning
   C. explain relations between sentences with different meaning
   D. both A and B
6. In general, linguistic change in _____ of a language is the more noticeable than that in other systems of the grammar.
   A. the sound system
   B. the vocabulary
   C. the syntax
   D. the sound system and the vocabulary
7. Although English has borrowed most heavily from French, other languages have also made contributions. For example, *tea*, *typhoon*, and *silk* are from _____, and *seminar*, *noodle* and *poodle* are from _____.
   A. China; German   B. Hindi; German
   C. China; Hindi   D. Turkish; China
8. _____ does NOT belong to semantic changes.
   A. Broadening   B. Borrowing
   C. Folk etymology   D. Class shift
9. The meaning of a sentence is abstract and de-contextualized, while the meaning of an utterance _____.
   A. is context-independent   B. is concrete and context-dependent
   C. is the sum total of its components D. never remains stable
10. Obstruction between the back of the tongue and the velar area results in the pronunciation of _____.
    A. [k] and [g]   B. [k] and [n]
    C. [g] and [h]   D. [h] and [k]
11. We can understand and produce an infinitely large number of sentences including sentences we never heard before, because language is _____.
    A. creative   B. arbitrary
    C. innate   D. rule-governed
12. The two words suite and sweet are _____.
    A. hyponyms   B. relational antonyms
    C. homographs   D. homophones
13. According to _____ rule, the word *sign* should be pronounced as [sain].
    A. deletion   B. sequential
    C. assimilation   D. Suprasegmental
14. The labiodental sounds in the following are _____.
    A. [p] and [b]   B. [f] and [v]
    C. [θ] and [ð]   D. [k] and [g]
15. _____ represents the deep structure Q Mary pres be pleased SOME REASON.
    A. *For some reason Mary is pleased.*
    B. *Mary is pleased for some reason.*
    C. *Why is Mary pleased?*
    D. *Why Mary is pleased?*

II. Fill in each of the following blanks with an appropriate word. The first letter of the word is already given.

1. Once the notion of c_____ was taken into consideration, semantics spilled over

into pragmatics
2. A sentence is a grammatical concept, and the meaning of a sentence is often studied as the abstract, intrinsic property of the sentence itself in terms of a p_____.
3. The history of English lexical expansion is one that is characterized with heavy b_____ and word formation.
4. G_____ are sometimes called *semivowels*.
5. Words that are close in meaning are called s_____.
6. IPA is the short form for both International Phonetic A_____ and International Phonetic A_____.
7. F_____ e_____ refers to a change in form of a word or phrase, resulting from an incorrect popular notion of the origin or meaning of the term or from the influence of more familiar terms mistakenly taken to be analogous.
8. In Halliday's idea, the three metafunctions of language: ideational, interpersonal and textual are related to three grammatical systems: t_____, m_____ and t_____.
9. Besides the inter-speaker differences in speech, there are i_____ differences associated with the speech situation: who is speaking to whom about what under what circumstances for what purpose.
10. Language is v_____ because the primary medium is sound for all languages, no matter how developed their writing systems are.
11. P_____ is concerned with investigating the psychological reality of linguistic structures.
12. SEMANTIC FEATURES of a word may be used to explain s_____ r_____.
13. C_____ vowels are established to be a set of arbitrary reference points on an auditory basis, so that a given vowel could be described in terms of its r_____ to them.
14. If two sounds occurring in the same environment do not contrast, that is, the substitution of one for the other does not produce a different word form, but merely a different pronunciation of the same word, then the two sounds are in f_____ v_____.
15. The fact that the English word *strike* is pronounced as *sutoraiki* after it was borrowed by the Japanese is a case of a_____.

III. Mark the following statements with "T" if they are true or "F" if they are false. Provide explanations for the false statements.

1. Language is not an isolated phenomenon; it is a social activity carried out in a certain social environment by human beings.
2. A phoneme is not further analyzable.
3. A phoneme is the basic unit in the study of phonetics.
4. a. *The man beat the child*.
   b. *The child was beaten by the man*.
   In the above two sentences the logical subject is the same NP *the man*.
5. Just like the sentences, all the utterances are complete in terms of syntax.
6. The examples of semantic narrowing include *wife*, *girl*, *fowl* and *bird*.
7. Bilingualism refers to a linguistic situation in which two very different varieties of language are used either by an individual or by a group of speakers, such as the inhabitants of a particular region or nation.
8. *Lexeme* is an academic name for *word*.
9. Nouns, adverbs, and adjectives belong to function words.
10. All monomorphemic words are free morphemes, and polymorphemic words are called compounds.
11. Linguistic communications are usually presented to us in the form of written text or speech. While the process of comprehension appears to be similar in both cases, some of the initial stages of processing differ.

12. Behaviourism in linguistics holds that children learn language through a chain of *stimulus-response reinforcement*.
13. The word *coward* is made up of a root morpheme and a derivational prefix
14. The unexploded plosive [k°] as in the word *act* is a different phoneme from the exploded plosive [k] as in the word *ask*.
15. What speech act theory is most concerned with is the illocutionary acts, because it attempts to account for the ways by which speakers can mean more than what way.

IV. Match each term in Column A with one relevant item in Column B.

A	B
(1) ideational function	a. actor
(2) textual function	b. goal
(3) interpersonal function	c. reference
	d. cohesion
	e. mood system
	f. transitivity system
	g. theme
	h. modal subject

V. Explain the following concepts or theories.
1. Synchronic and diachronic
2. Langue and parole
3. Complementary distribution
4. Locutionary act, illocutionary act and perlocutionary act
5. Semantic broadening
6. A lingua franca
7. Grammatical marker
8. LAN
9. Displacement

VI. Analyze the following with your own linguistic knowledge.
1. Analyze and present the phrase structure components and phrase structure rules of the sentence *The man drew a picture*.

VII. Answer the following questions as comprehensively as possible, giving examples if necessary.
1. Distinguish the following cases of ambiguity with tree diagrams.
   a: *They said she would go yesterday*.
   b: *Dick decided on the boat*.
2. What are the three metafunctions proposed by Halliday?
3. What is the relationship between superordinate and hyponym in hyponymy?
4. How is Dictionary Word different from our daily understanding of a word?
5. How do semantics and pragmatics differ in their approach to the study of meaning?

参考答案

I.
1. A 2. D 3. B 4. A 5. D 6. D 7. A 8. B 9. B 10. A
11. A 12. D 13. A 14. B 15. C

Comprehensive Test

II.
1. context
2. predication
3. borrowing
4. Glides
5. Synonyms
6. Alphabet; Association
7. Folk; etymology
8. transitivity; mood; theme
9. intra-speaker
10. vocal
11. Psycholinguistics
12. sense; relations
13. Cardinal; relation
14. free; variation
15. addition

III.
1. T
2. F. A phoneme is further analyzable because it consists of a set of simultaneous distinctive features.
3. F. A phoneme is the basic unit in the study of phonology.
4. T
5. F. Some utterances are not complete in terms of syntax, and some can not even be restored to complete sentences.
6. F. *Bird* is an example of semantic broadening.
7. F. It is not two very different varieties of language, but two standard languages.
8. F. *Lexeme* is the abstract unit underlying the smallest unit in the lexical system of a language, which appears in different grammatical context. While *word* refers to the common factor underlying a set of forms, a unit of vocabulary, a lexical item or a lexeme. They are not the same item.
9. F. Nouns, adverbs, adjectives belong to content words.
10. F. All monomorphemic words are free morphemes, and polymorphemic words which consist wholly of free morphemes are called compounds.
11. T   12. T
13. F. The word is made up of a root morpheme and a derivational suffix.
14. F. They are the same phoneme, but in free variation.
15. T.

IV.
(1) a; b; f   (2) g; c; d   (3) e; h

V.
1. Language exists in time and changes through time. The description of a language at some point in time is a synchronic study; the description of a language as it changes through time is a diachronic study.
2. Langue refers to the abstract linguistic system shared by all the members of a speech community, and parole refers to the realization of langue in actual use. Langue is the set of conventions and rules which language users al have to abide by, and parole is the concrete use of the conventions and the application of the rules.
3. Two allophones of the same phoneme never contrast each other and they occur in different environments. Thus they are said to be in complementary distribution, such as, [p] and [p^h].
4. A locutionary act is the act of uttering words, phrases, clauses. It is the act of conveying literal meaning by means of syntax, lexicon and phonology. An illocutionary act is the act of expressing the speaker's intention; it is the act performed in saying something. A perlocutionary act is the act performed by or resulting from saying something; it is the consequence, or the change brought about by the utterance; it is the act performed by saying something.
5. Semantic broadening refers to the process in which the meaning of a word becomes more general or inclusive than its historically earlier denotation. An example of semantic broadening is the modern use of the word *dog*. In its Old English and Middle English forms, the word had a narrower meaning and was used for a hunting breed only. While today *dog* is used to encompass all breeds of canine animals.

6. A lingua franca is a variety of language that serves as a medium of communication among groups of people for diverse linguistic backgrounds. For this reason, a lingua franca must be an agreed-upon *common tongue* used by people thrown in social contact for various purposes.
7. Grammatical marker is also called syntactic marker, it is used to mark the detailed part of speech of a word. The { } in the dictionary serves as a grammatical maker indicating the grammatical classification like adjective or noun, etc, of the given words
8. LAN is a term to refer to local area networks. The networks are established by computers linked together by cables in a classroom, a lab or a building.
9. Displacement means that human languages enable their users to symbolize objects, events and concepts which are not present (in time and space) at the moment of communication. For example, we can describe things happened yesterday by language because of displacement.

VI.

The phrase structure component and phrase structure rules are as follows.
S→NP + VP
VP→V + NP
NP→Det + N
Det→*the*, *a*
N→*man*, *picture*
V→*drew*
(A tree diagram can also be used to illustrate them.)

VII.

1. Sentence a: *They said she would go yesterday*.

   Meaning One: According to them, she would go yesterday.

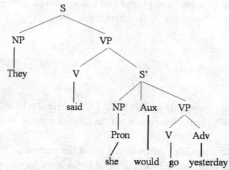

Meaning Two: What they said yesterday is that she would go.

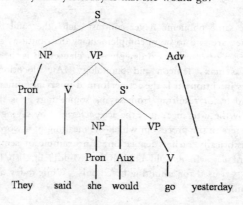

Sentence b: *Dick decided on the boat*.
Meaning One: It was on the boat that Dick finally made the decision.

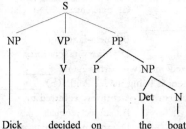

Meaning Two: He decided to buy the boat.

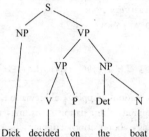

2. Interpersonal function refers to the function of language by which people make sociological use of language to establish and maintain their status in a society. Ideational function refers to the function that language carries to describe the speaker's experience of the real world, including the inner world of his own consciousness. Textual function refers to the function that language has to provide for making links with itself and with features of the situation in which it is used.
3. Hyponymy refers to the relationship of meaning inclusion. The upper term in the sense relation of hyponymy, the class name is called superordinate, and the more specific term is the hyponym. The superordinate and the hyponym have the relation of inclusion. And both the two terms may be missing sometimes. A superordinate may be missing sometimes. In English there is no superordinate for the color terms *red*, *green*, *black*, etc. Hyponyms may also be missing. In contrast to Chinese, there is only one word in English for the different kinds of uncles: 伯伯，叔叔，姑父…
4. Word, also called Lexeme, is a common factor underlying a set of forms in the lexical system of a language. Daily understanding of a word can come in forms of *work*, or *works*, or *worked*, or *working*, but only *work* appears as a dictionary entry word. Dictionary Word is the abstract unit which appears in different grammatical contexts.
5. Generally semantics studies meaning in the language system while pragmatics studies meaning in use. Semantic approaches to word meaning and sentence meaning, regardless what theories they are, all work within the language system. However, pragmatics tries to work out rules that govern speakers and hearers use the language in daily communication.

Five

I. Mark the choice that best completes the statement.
1. When the vocal folds are apart, the air can pass through easily and the sound produced is said to be _____.
   A. voiced   B. the glottal stop   C. voiceless   D. silent
2. _____ proposed the theory of deep and surface structure.

A. Halliday   B. Saussure   C. Chomsky   D. Firth
3. Among the six processes proposed by Halliday, _____ process is known as a process of being.
   A. material   B. mental   C. existential   D. relational
4. Semantic components are _____.
   A. ordinary words   B. meta-language
   C. syntactic markers   D. binary taxonomies
5. A proposition can be analyzed into two parts: A(n) _____ is a term which refers to some entity about which a statement is being made. And a(n) _____ is a term which ascribes some property, or relation, to the entity, or entities, referred to.
   A. subject; predict   B. subject; object
   C. predicate argument   D. argument; predicate
6. *The shooting of the man was terrible* means _____.
   A. The man's shooting skill was very poor
   B. It was terrible that the man was shot
   C. The man was terribly shot
   D. Both a and b
7. *Uglification, UNESCO, smog, TV, gym, typewriter, Xerox* are formed respectively by the ways of _____.
   A. derivation, coinage, back-formation, clipping, abbreviation, blending, and acronym
   B. coinage, back-formation, clipping, abbreviation, blending, acronym, and derivation
   C. derivation, acronym, blending, abbreviation, clipping, back-formation, and coinage
   D. blending, abbreviation, clipping, back-formation, derivation, acronym, and coinage
8. Directives (as they are used in Speech Act Theory) are attempts by the speaker to get the hearer to do something, so _____ is not in this class.
   A. *Open the window!*   B. *You'd better go to the clinic.*
   C. *Your money or your life!*   D. *I fire you!*
9. The two English sounds [l] and [r] are _____.
   A. stops   B. fricatives   C. affricates   D. liquids
10. Language can be used to refer to contexts removed from the immediate situation of the speaker. This is what _____ means.
    A. arbitrariness   B. productivity
    C. duality   D. displacement
11. Interpersonal function enacts _____ relationship.
    A. social   B. experiential   C. status   D. inter-regional
12. The English spelling system has one letter to represent _____.
    A. each phoneme   B. each morpheme
    C. each sound   D. none of the above
13. The sentence *John read the book which I wrote* has undergone _____ type of transformational rules.
    A. an insertion rule
    B. a deletion rule
    C. insertion and movement rules
    D. insertion, deletion and movement rules
14. Of the following pairs of words _____ would be useful in determining whether an English speaker has a British or American accent.
    A. *bird* and *aunt*   B. *fall* and *autumn*
    C. *lift* and *left*   D. *feather* and *honourable*
15. The sound [ʒ] can be described by the properties as listed in _____.
    A. voiced alveolar fricative
    B. voiced post-alveolar fricative

C. voiced post-alveolar affricate
D. voiceless labio-dental fricative

II. **Fill in each of the following blanks with an appropriate word. The first letter of the word is already given.**
1. P_____ are sentences that did not state a fact or describe a state, and are not variable.
2. C_____ is a process of combing two or more words into one lexical unit.
3. Language varieties other than the standard are called nonstandard, or v_____ language.
4. Evidence in support of lateralization for language in the left hemisphere comes from researches in d_____ listening tasks.
5. W_____ is a unit of expression that has universal intuitive recognition by native-speakers, whether it is expressed in spoken or written form.
6. If one studies how a certain sentence comes into being, namely, how words combine to form the sentence, the person is carrying out s_____ studies.
7. Among the six processes proposed by Halliday, v_____ process may be called a process of saying.
8. Among the six processes proposed by Halliday, m_____ process is also known as a process of doing and is concerned with the representation of outer experience.
9. *Pass* and *fail* are c_____ antonyms.
10. The vocal cords are brought momentarily together to create the g_____ obstruction, such as when producing the English sound [h].
11. Van Dijk and Kintsch argue that most stories would follow a certain set patterns which are called m_____.
12. The analysis of the words of a sentence according to parts of speech and the syntactical arrangement of the words in a sentence is called p_____.
13. The tendency to choose the easier form of linguistic unit and gradually phase out the more difficult is called e_____.
14. Conventionally a phoneme is put in s_____ bars while an allophone is put in s_____ brackets.
15. O_____ words seem to be a convenient evidence for the *bow-wow theory* about the origin of language.
16. To find out the distinctive sounds, the customary practice is to try to find m_____ p_____, word forms which differ from each other only by one sound.
17. P_____ c_____ is a term used to refer to language used for establishing an atmosphere or maintaining social contact rather than for exchanging information or ideas.
18. A semantic model of meaning which claimed that meaning is essentially a threefold relationship between linguistic forms, concepts and referents is known as s_____ t_____.
19. A_____, one of the four components of communicative competence proposed by D. H. Hymes, refers to the ability to use correct forms of language in a specific socio-cultural context.
20. In *injustice* and *imperfect*, *in-* and *im-* are supposed to be the a_____ of the same morpheme.

III. **Mark the following statements with "T" if they are true or "F" if they are false. Provide explanations for the false statements.**
1. The idea of doing something while speaking can certainly be broadened to include all the non-conventional acts such as stating, promising, requesting, and suggestion.
2. The Indo-European language family is the first and most widely investigated language family of the world.
3. Obscene, profane and swear words are all taboo words that are to be avoided entirely, or at least avoided in mixed company.

4. Derivational affixes change the word class of the word they attach to.
5. The linguistic branch that studies both morpheme and phoneme is called morphonology.
6. Sentences like the active and the negative are each derived from the same deep structure. The difference between them simply comes from the operation of relevant transformation.
7. Very few adults seem to reach native-like proficiency in all aspects of a second language, particularly in morphology.
8. Transfer can be positive and negative, and negative transfer is also known as interference.
9. Prefixes modify the meaning of the stem, but usually do not change the part of speech of the original word.
10. The pair *doctor* and *patient* are complementary opposites.
11. Chomsky's T. G. grammar has been considered by many people as an insurrection against Bloomfieldian linguistics and behaviorist psychology.
12. Semantics is concerned with principles of forming and understanding correct sentences.
13. Deep structure is the abstract syntactic representation of a sentence, an underlying level of structural organization which specifies all the factors governing the way the sentence should be interpreted.
14. Saussure's notion of parole is to some degree analogous to Chomsky's notion of competence.
15. A syllable consists of three parts: the onset, the peak and the remix.

IV. Match each term in Column A with one relevant item in Column B.

A	B
(1) material process	a. thinking
(2) existential process	b. saying
(3) behavioral process	c. physiological behavior
(4) mental process	d. doing in the physical world
(5) verbal process	e. world of consciousness
(6) relational process	f. happening
	g. having attribute
	h. creating
	i. *I feel cold.*
	j. *On the hill is his hut.*
	k. symbolizing

V. Explain the following concepts or theories with one or two examples.
1. language transfer
2. connotation
3. entailment
4. descriptive study
5. dialect
6. the critical age hypothesis
7. Creole
8. Grimm's law
9. semantic change
10. Cooperative Principle

VI. Analyze the following with your own linguistic knowledge.

Use semantic knowledge to analyze this sentence *John killed Bill but Bill didn't die*.

VII. Answer the following questions as comprehensively as possible, giving examples if necessary.

1. What are the so-called *design features* of language?
2. What are the major phonological theories used to distinguish phonemes of a language?
3. Why do we say that language is arbitrary?
4. How can we identify new information in speech?
5. Discuss some causes that lead to the systematic occurrence of errors in second language acquisition.
6. Do you agree that pragmatics is to explain how we mean more than we say?

参考答案

I.
1. C 2. C 3. C 4. B 5. D 6. D 7. C 8. D 9. D 10. D
11. A 12. D 13. D 14. A 15. B

II.
1. Performatives   2. compound   3. vernacular   4. dichotic
5. Word   6. syntactic   7. verbal   8. material
9. complementary   10. glottal   11. macrostructure   12. parsing
13. economy   14. slash, square   15. Onomatopoeic   16. minimal, pairs
17. phatic, communion 18. semantic, triangle 19. Appropriateness 20. allomorphs

III.
1. T 2. T 3. T
4. F. Derivational affixes might or might not change the word class of the word they attach to.
5. T. 6. T.
7. F. It's not in morphology, but in phonology.
8. T 9. T
10. F. The pair doctor and *patient* are converse opposites.
11. T.
12. F. Semantics is not concerned with the principles of forming and understanding correct sentences. It is the syntax that is about principles of forming and understanding correct sentences.
13. T.
14. F. Parole is somewhat like performance.
15. F. It consists of the onset, the peak and the coda.

IV.
(1) d; f; h   (2) j   (3) c   (4) a; e; i   (5) b   (6) g; k

V.
1. No matter whether they learn the target language consciously or subconsciously, learners have come to the task of acquiring a second language with their L1 knowledge. Naturally, learners will subconsciously use their L1 knowledge in learning a second language. This is known as language transfer.
2. Philosophers use connotation to mean the properties of the entity a word denotes. In semantics, connotation is what is communicated by virtue of what language refers to. For example, in certain context, *It is cold here* has the connotation of letting someone close the window.
3. Entailment is a relationship between two or more sentences. If knowing that one sentence is true

gives us certain knowledge of the truth of the second sentence, then the first sentence entails the second. Sentence *His sister has gone to China* entails that *he has a sister*.
4. Descriptive study refers to the study of language in which the rules to which the members of a language community actually conform are just described. For example the utterance *people usually do not add an 'a' before an uncountable noun*. belongs to the descriptive study.
5. Dialect is a linguistic system that is tied to a specific region in such a way that the regional distribution of the system does not overlap with an area covered by another such system. For example, we have Dalian dialect and Shangdong dialect in China.
6. The critical age hypothesis refers to a period in one's life extending from about age two to puberty, during which the human brain is most ready to acquire a particular language and language learning can proceed easily, swiftly and without explicit instruction.
7. A Creole language is originally a pidgin that has become established as a native language in some speech community. That is, when a pidgin comes to be adopted by a population as its primary language, and children learn it as their first language, then the pidgin language is called a Creole.
8. Grimm found a series of consonant shifts that occurred in the history of the Germanic languages including English, Dutch, German, Swedish and Danish. The following are the three sets of consonant shifts that Grimm discovered:

    a. b——p
       d——t
       g——k
    b. p——f
       k——x (>h)
    c. bh——b
       dh——d
       gh——g

9. Semantic shift is a process of semantic change in which a word loses its former meaning and acquires a new, sometimes related, meaning. An example of semantic shift is the word *silly*. Quite surprisingly, a *silly* person was a happy person in Old English and a naive person in Middle English, but has become a foolish person in Modern English.
10. In making conversation, the participants must first of all be willing to cooperate, and this general principle is called the Cooperative Principle. It goes as follows: make your conversational contribution such as required at the stage at which it occurs by the accepted purpose of direction of the talk exchange in which you are engaged. To be more specific, there are four maxims under this general principle: the maxim of quantity, the maxim of quality, the maxim of relation, and the maxim of manner.

VI.

This sentence is a self-contradictory sentence.

The semantic components of *kill* include *die*, but we have another expression of *not die* in this sentence which is contradictory to *die*. So we say that this sentence is a self-contradictory sentence.

VII.

1. Design features refer to the defining properties of human language that distinguish it from any animal system of communication. There are four major design features. The four design features are as follows:
   (1) arbitrariness: Arbitrariness refers to the fact that the forms of linguistic signs bear no natural relationship to their meaning. A good example is the fact that different sounds are used to refer to the same object in different languages. Language is arbitrary by nature, but it is not entirely arbitrary. e.g. There are words in every language that imitate natural sounds and some compound words are also not entirely arbitrary.
   (2) creativity: By creativity we mean language is resourceful because of its duality and its

repulsiveness. Creativity is unique to human language. Most animal communication systems appear to be highly restricted with respect to the number of different signals that their users can send and receive.
  (3) duality: By duality is meant the property of having two levels of structures, such that units of the primary level are composed of elements of the secondary level and each of the two levels has its own principles of organization.
  (4) displacement: Displacement means that human languages enable their users to symbolize objects, events and concepts which are not present (in time and space) at the moment of communication.
2. Minimal pairs are word forms which differ from each other only by one sound. For example, in English, *pin* and *bin*, *pin* and *pen* are each a minimal pair. If the sounds, which make the difference in the minimal pair, can distinguish meaning in the language, they should be assigned to different phonemes.
  Complementary distribution refers to the situation in which two sounds never occur in the same environment. When two sounds are in complementary distribution, they may just two allophones of the same phoneme, such as the dark and clear / l / in the words like *love* and *small*.
3. Arbitrariness refers to the fact that the forms of linguistic signs bear no natural relationship to their meanings. But in real life situation, language is not completely arbitrary.
  At the sound level, the onomatopoetic word is not arbitrarily coined; it is formed by imitating the sounds in nature.
  At the sentential level, the words are not arbitrarily arranged, in certain places we should fill in certain words. For example, to fill in the slot of subject, we should not use verbs or adjectives but simply nouns.
  So language is to some extent arbitrary.
4. The new information is generally located in the Rheme. Of course, high pitch and key also reveals where the new information is.
5. The interference of mother (negative transfer) used to be the only explanation for errors. However, it is now believed to be inadequate. It is more reasonable to say that the learner knows some rules of language but applies them in the wrong place. Thus overgeneralization may be another cause.
6. Absolutely right. As pragmatics studies how people use language in communication, it naturally looks at how people use the language in *abnormal* ways, that is, with some implications.

Six

I. Mark the following statements with "T" if they are true or "F" if they are false. Provide explanations for the false statements.
1. The word *hour* contains a diphthong and a pure vowel.
2. The sound /p/ in the word *expensive* is pronounced as a voiceless consonant.
3. Halliday's linguistic potential is similar to the notions of *parole* and *performance*.
4. It is one of the cardinal principles of modern linguistics that spoken language is more basic than written language.
5. A stem is any morpheme or combination of morphemes to which an affix can be added.
6. *Happiness is colder than me* is a grammatical but unacceptable sentence.
7. The relation between form and meaning in human language is natural.
8. Broad transcription represents phonemes of a language whereas narrow transcription denotes its particular allophones.
9. Derivation is the manifestation of grammatical relationships.
10. /u/ is a mid-high front rounded vowel.
11. By *displacement* we mean that language can refer to contexts removed from the immediate situations of the speaker.

12. Greek does not belong to Indo-European Language Family.
13. *After taking the right turn at the intersection...* is a case of lexical ambiguity.
14. Cultural transmission refers to the fact that the details of the linguistic system must be learned anew by each speaker.
15. NP may consist of NP + (S).
16. *Plural* is a morpheme.
17. The voiced dental fricative is /z/.
18. Allophones are described in phonetic terms.
19. Allomorphs which share the common meaning should occur in parallel formations.
20. In the following pair of sentences, Sentence b presupposes Sentence a.
    a. *John managed to finish in time.*
    b. *John tried to finish in time.*

II. Fill in each of the following blanks with (an) appropriate word(s).
1. Predication analysis is to break down predications into their constituents: _____ and _____.
2. One of the design features termed as _____ means that human languages enable their users to symbolize objects, events and concepts which are not present (in time and space) at the moment of communication.
3. The five *associative meanings* categorized by Leech are: _____, social, _____, reflected and collocative.
4. Of the three branches of phonetics, the _____ phonetics studies sounds from the speaker's point of view; the _____ phonetics looks at sounds from the hearer's point of view; the _____ phonetics studies the way sounds travel by looking at sound waves.
5. It is generally agreed that linguistics should include at least five parameters, namely, phonologic, _____, syntactic, semantic and _____.

III. Mark the choice that best completes the statement.
1. Of the following words, the sound [l] in _____ is a clear one.
   A. *tell* B. *quilt* C. *leaf* D. *peel*
2. Of the following pairs _____ is in complementary distribution.
   A. [l] as in [leik] and [m] as in [meik]
   B. [l] as in [liːf] and [f] as in [tef]
   C. [l] as in [liːd] and [r] as in [riːd]
   D. none of the above
3. Of the following pairs _____ doesn't form a minimal pair.
   A. *pill* and *till* B. *dill* and *gill*
   C. *gale* and *gale* D. *beat* and *pea*
4. If three consonants should cluster together at the beginning of a word, the first phoneme must be _____.
   A. /s/ B. /t/ C. /l/ D. /p/
5. [k] is a voiceless _____.
   A. alveolar stop B. velar stop
   C. post-alveolar plosive D. velar fricative
6. [z] is a _____.
   A. voiced approximant B. post-alveolar affricate
   C. voiced alveolar fricative D. voiced alveolar affricate
7. [j] is a _____.
   A. glottal fricative B. palatal approximant
   C. alveolar approximant D. palatal fricative
8. [ə] is a _____ vowel.

    A. low back lax unrounded   B. central front unrounded
    C. central lax unrounded   D. high front tense unrounded

9. The one that does not fall into the property of *alveolar* is _____.
    A. [m]   B. [t]   C. [n]   D. [r]

10. / l / and / r / function as a minimal pair in _____.
    A. lead and read   B. led and red   C. peel and pear   D. both A and B

IV. Match the phonetic features in Column B with the correspondent phonetic alphabets in Column A.

A	B
(1) [k]	a. velar
(2) [θ]	b. nasal
(3) [s]	c. dental
(4) [b]	d. fricative
(5) [l]	e. voiced
(6) [t]	f. voiceless
(7) [m]	g. bilabial
(8) [h]	h. alveolar
	i. plosive
	j. glottal

V. Specify the following pairs according to the sense relation.
    a. *hit / miss (a target)*   b. *own / belong to*   c. *lesson / lessen*
    d. *rich / poor*   e. *squeak / creak*   f. *tap / faucet*
    g. *above / below*   h. *the morning star / the evening star*
    i. *saw / hacksaw*   j. *sow (to scatter seeds) / sow (female adult pig)*
    (1) complementary antonyms _____
    (2) synonyms _____
    (3) relational opposites _____
    (4) gradable antonyms _____
    (5) homonyms _____
    (6) hyponymy _____

VII. Answer the following questions as comprehensively as possible, giving examples if necessary.
1. Comment on the sentence *She was already half dead then.* in terms of sense relations.
2. What does the following logical form stand for in English? (where j = Jane, b = Bill, c = Carol, L = like:) L (j, b) & ~ L (j, c)
3. What category/categories of CP does the following exchange violate?
    A: *Are you going to use your laptop this evening?*
    B: *I haven't finished my assignment yet.*
4. Do you think the idea that the subject of a sentence is the person or thing that does the action is acceptable?
5. Is it correct to say that every one (even a radio news announcer) speaks a dialect?

参考答案

I.
1. T   2. F   3. F   4. T   5. T   6. T   7. F   8. T   9. F   10. F

11. T 12. F 13. T 14. T 15. T 16. T 17. F 18. T 19. T
20. T

II.

1. arguments; predicate 2. displacement 3. connotative; affective
4. articulatory; auditory; acoustic 5. morphologic; pragmatic

III.

1. C 2. D 3. D 4. A 5. B 6. C 7. B 8. C 9. A 10. D

IV.

(1) a; f; i (2) c; d; f (3) f; h (4) e; g; i
(5) h (6) f; h; i (7) b; e; g (8) d; f; j

V.

(1) a (2) e; f; h (3) b; g (4) d (5) c; j (6) i

VI.

1. In theory *dead* and *alive* belong to the category of complementary antonyms. A person can be said to be either dead or alive, but never, a little dead, or more dead. However, figuratively, a person can be said to be *half dead*. *He is more dead than alive*, *etc*. But in terms of sense relations, *dead* and *alive* are not gradable antonyms.
2. Jane likes Bill and Jane doesn't like Carol.
3. It violates the Maxim of Relation *Be relevant*. Apparently B's response to the question is not relevant as B refuses to make what he says relevant to A's preceding question. B understands A's question as a request (possibly A's going to borrow his laptop) and he doesn't want to lend it to A for some reason. In order not to be impolite, he gives his reason as *I am using it tonight, because I haven't finished my assignment yet*. If we take the exchange as the following, then we will not have problems in making them relevant.
    A: *Are you using your laptop tonight? If you are not, I want to borrow it.*
    B: *Sorry, I can't lend you, for I am using it to finish it my assignment.*
4. The idea is not acceptable. Although quite some subjects of the sentences are the persons or the things that perform the action, still a lot of subjects don't. The following examples can prove this point.
    a. *It is him that the letter is directed to.*
    b. *There are many tables and chairs in the room.*
    c. *The inflectional affixes are conditioned by non-semantic linguistic factors.*
    d. *The boy was chased by a dog.*
    None of the subjects in the sentences above perform the action.
5. Yes. Strictly speaking, everyone speaks a certain dialect. Dialect refers to all variations arising from differences among users, namely, the space, the temporal factor and the social distance. The moment a person speaks, no matter whether he speaks the standard language (which is a dialect too), or non-standard language, he inevitably speaks a certain regional dialect, temporal dialect and social dialect. His speech carries a certain accent, remarkable features of his time and social status.

Seven

I. Mark the following statements with "T" if they are true or "F" if they are false. Provide explanations for the false statements.

1. Sonorants are always voiced.

2. [ʃ] is a palatal approximant.
3. English obstruents can be distinguished by voicing.
4. By creativity we mean language is resourceful because of its duality and its recursiveness.
5. A stem may contain a root and a derivational suffix.
6. Derivational affixes very often add a minute or delicate grammatical meaning to the stem.
7. In the production of consonants at least three articulators are involved.
8. [u] is a high back lax rounded vowel.
9. When allophones are in complementary distribution, they never occur in the same context.
10. A word, rather than a morpheme, is a grammatical unit.
11. Thematic meaning is what is communicated through association with another sense of the same expression.
12. In English *some books* is a case of number concord.
13. Parole is the actual phenomena or data of utterances.
14. Italian is not a member of the Indo-European Language Family.
15. If the air is stopped in the oral cavity but the soft palate is down so that it can go out through the nasal cavity, the sound produced is an oral stop.
16. All the allomorphs should have common meaning.
17. Linguistics is generally defined as the scientific study of a particular language.
18. Some sentences may comply perfectly with the grammar rules of the language, but they may not be semantically meaningful.
19. Any language can be a lingua franca.
20. Synchronic linguistics refers to the approach which studies language over various periods of time and at various historical stages.

II. Fill in the following blanks.
1. The design features of language are (1) _____, (2) _____, (3) _____, (4) _____, (5) _____ and (6) _____.
2. The syllable consists of three parts: the (7) _____, the (8) _____, and the (9) _____.
3. The four principles in the linguistic study are (10) _____, (11) _____, (12) _____, and (13) _____.
4. Name five of the *associative meaning* categorized by Leech: (14) _____, (15) _____, (16) _____, (17) _____, (18) _____.
5. Predication analysis is to break down predications into their constituents: (19) _____ and (20) _____.

III. Mark the choice that best completes the statement.
1. _____ means language can be used to refer to contexts removed from the immediate situations of the speaker.
   A. Duality   B. Assimilation
   C. Displacement   D. Context
2. *-less* in *carelessness* is a _____.
   A. stem   B. suffix   C. free root   D. bound root
3. The symbol N indicates a/an _____.
   A. lexical category   B. phrasal category
   C. intermediate category   D. lexical insertion rule
4. Pair _____ belongs to the category of gradable antonyms.
   A. *over/under* B. *weak/strong* C. *open/shut* D. *sell/buy*
5. Promises and offers are characteristic of the group of _____ of illocutionary acts.
   A. representatives   B. declaratives
   C. commissives   D. expressives

6. Speakers of particular social groups, such as teenagers, criminals, soldiers, or pop-groups, have their *in-group* language called _____.
   A. taboo B. jargon C. pidgin D. dialect
7. The clear / l / and the dark /ɫ/ are _____.
   A. in complementary distribution
   B. in free variation
   C. both a and b
   D. neither of the two
8. The two English sounds [l] and [r] are _____.
   A. stops B. fricatives C. affricates D. liquids
9. When three consonants cluster together at the beginning of a word, the first phoneme must be _____.
   A. /s/ B. /t/ C. /l/ D. /p/
10. _____ belongs to the closed-class words.
    A. *Can* B. *Table* C. *Go* D. *By means of*
11. _____ suffixes do not change the word class of the word they attach to.
    A. Derivational B. Morphological
    C. Invariable D. Inflectional
12. In order to refer collectively to the items in a sentence which substitute for other item of constructions, we should regard _____ as a separate word class.
    A. auxiliaries B. particles C. determiners D. pro-form
13. The word _____ belongs to the category of postdeterminers.
    A. *several* B. *double* C. *this* D. *the*
14. The plural morpheme can be expressed in the form of { − s ∼ − z∼ − iz ∼ − ai ∼ − iː ∼ − n}and _____.
    A. { ∼ − ∅ } B. { ∼ − is }
    C. { ∼ − iːs } D. { ∼ − iʃ }
15. The word *positron* is an example of _____.
    A. invention B. abbreviation C. blending D. acronym
16. _____ refers to an abnormal type of word-formation where a shorter word is by deleting an imagined affix from a longer form already in the language.
    A. Analogical creation B. Acronym
    C. Abbreviation D. Back-formation
17. The process of word formation by shifting the word class to change the meaning of a word is called _____.
    A. broadening B. meaning shift
    C. conversion D. narrowing
18. The constraints on words in a paradigmatic relation, different from those in a syntagmatic relation, are _____ only.
    A. semantic B. lexical C. syntactic D. sequential
19. _____ are pitch variations, which are caused by the different rates of vibration of the vocal cords.
    A. Stresses B. Liaisons C. Intonations D. Tones
20. The following factors contribute to the formation of new pronunciation except _____.
    A. loss of sound B. addition
    C. assimilation D. gliding

Comprehensive Test

IV. Match the proper description from the list under Column B with the underlined part of each word under Column A. Notice some under A may have more than one description under B.

A	B
1. deafen	a. free form
2. boyish	b. bound root
3. conceive	c. inflectional suffix
4. impenetrable	d. derivational suffix
5. vibration	e. inflectional prefix
6. Indo-European	f. derivational prefix
7. underline	g. inflectional infix
8. input	h. derivational infix
9. sit-in	i. stem
10. involved	j. none of the above

V. **Specify the following pairs according to the sense relation.**
1. date (a kind of fruit) / date (a particular day) _____
2. homely / domestic _____
3. narrow / wide _____
4. sea / see _____
5. host / guest _____
6. brother / sister _____
7. guilty / innocent _____
8. tool / ax _____
9. lift / elevator _____
10. odd / even _____

VI. **Answer the following questions.**
1. Define ALLOPHONE with an example.
2. What is assimilation?
3. What is the criterion used in IC analysis?
4. SEMANTIC FEATURES or SEMANTIC COMPONENTS of a word may be used to better account for sense relations. Use examples to support this idea.
5. BLENDING, ABBREVIATION and ACRONYMY are the ways by which people have used to create new words and expressions. How do they differ from one another? Use examples to help you to distinguish them.
6. In some dialects of English the following words have different vowels as is shown by the phonetic transcriptions:

A	B	C
bite [bʌjt]	bide [bajd]	die [daj]
rice [rʌjs]	rise [rajz]	by [baj]
ripe [rʌjp]	bribe [brajb]	sigh [saj]
wife [wʌjf]	wives [wajvz]	rye [raj]

a. How may the classes of sounds that end the words in columns A and B be characterized?

b. How do the words in column C differ from those in columns A and B?
c. Are [ʌj] and [aj] in complementary distribution? Give your reasons.
d. If [ʌj] and [aj] are allophones of one phoneme, should they be derived from /ʌj/ or /aj/?

7. How many methods can you use to identify a phoneme?
8. What is the difference between concord and government in syntactic analysis?

参考答案

I.
1. T 2. F 3. T 4. T 5. T 6. F 7. F 8. T 9. T 10. F
11. F 12. T 13. T 14. F 15. F 16. T 17. F 18. T 19. T 20. F

II.
(1) arbitrariness   (2) duality   (3) productivity   (4) displacement
(5) cultural transmission (6) interchangeability (7) onset   (8) peak
(9) coda   (10) exhaustiveness   (11) consistency   (12) economy
(13) objectivity   (14) connotative   (15) social   (16) affective meaning
(17) reflected   (18) collocative   (19) arguments   (20) predicate

III.
1. C 2. B 3. A 4. B 5. C 6. B 7. A 8. D 9. A 10. C
11. D 12. D 13. A 14. A 15. C 16. D 17. C 18. C 19. D 20. D

IV.
1. d 2. a 3. b 4. f 5. b 6. f 7. j 8. a 9. a 10. c

V.
1. homonymy   2. synonymy   3. gradable antonymy
4. homophones   5. converse antonymy   6. co-hyponyms
7. complementary antonymy   8. hyponymy   9. synonymy
10. complementary antonymy

VI.
1. Variants of a phoneme are called allophones of the same phoneme. Allophones are to be in complementary distribution because they never occur in the same context. That is to say that [p] always occurs after [s] while [pⁿ] always occurs in other places.
2. Assimilation refers to the change of a sound as result of the influence of an adjacent sound, which is more specifically called *contact* or *contiguous* assimilation. Assimilation is often used synonymously with coarticulation. Similarly, there are two possibilities of assimilation: if a following sound is influencing a preceding sound, we call it regressive assimilation; (such as: since [sins], sink [siŋk]) the converse process, in which a preceding sound is influencing a following sound, is known as progressive assimilation.
3. The criterion used is substitutability: whether a sequence of words can be substituted for a single word and the structure remains the same. In the case of *Poor John ran away*, *poor John* can be replaced by John, ran away by ran in terms of structure. Both are about somebody doing something. In the terminology of Saussure, we can say *poor John* and *John*, and *ran away* and *ran*, are each in a paradigmatic relation. They are identical syntactically speaking.
4. It is claimed that by showing the semantic components of a word in this way, we may better account for sense relation. Two words, or two expressions, which have the same semantic components, will be synonymous with each other. For example, bachelor and unmarried man

are both said to have the components of HUMAN, ADULT, MALE AND UNMARRIED, so they are synonymous with each other. Words which have a contrasting component, on the other hand, are antonyms, such as man and woman, boy and girl, give and take. Words which have all the semantic components of another are hyponyms of the latter, e.g. boy and girl are hyponyms of child since they have all the semantic components of the other, namely, HUMAN and -ADULT.

5. These three types of word formation help people to make words shorter, for the sake of economy. However they differ in various ways. **Blending** is a relatively complex form of compounding, in which *two roots* are blended by joining the initial part of the first root and the final part of the second root, or by joining the initial parts of the two roots. For example, transistor = transfer + resister. Acronym is made up from *the first letters* of the name of an organization, which has a heavily modified headword. For example, UNESCO. **Abbreviation** (also called clipping) is a way by which a new word is created by cutting the *final, or the initial part, or both the initial and final parts* of a word. For instance, ad for advertisement, plane for aeroplane, flu for influenza.

6. a. In column A, the words end in voiceless consonants, while in column B the words end in voiced consonants.
   b. In column C, the words end in vowels.
   c. Yes, [ʌj] only occur when the final consonants is voiceless, while [aj] occurs when the final consonants are voiced or vowels.
   d. [ʌj] is derived from [aj] because it only occurs when the consonant following it is voiceless while [aj] occurs elsewhere.

7. Minimal pairs, complementary distribution, free variation, phonetic similarity and pattern congruity

8. Concord means a is in agreement with b, while government means a controls b.

Eight

I. **Mark the following statements with "T" if they are true or "F" if they are false. Provide explanations for the false statements.**

1. Each language contains two systems rather than one, a system of sound and a system of meaning.
2. Morphemes are regarded as abstract constructs in the system of sound.
3. The critical age hypothesis unfolds the fact that the human brain is specially equipped for language acquisition.
4. A root is not always a free form.
5. The left brain does better in pattern-matching tasks and in recognizing faces.
6. The hard roof of mouth is called hard palate.
7. Descriptive linguists are concerned with how languages work, not with how they can be improved.
8. [n] is one of syllabic consonants.
9. In the transformation of the sentence *He doesn't sleep well*, do-support transformation comes first.
10. Derivation is the manifestation of grammatical relationships between morphemes in a word.
11. [æ] is a mid-low back unrounded vowel.
12. *Kids* and *children* are synonyms despite their stylistic difference.
13. All lexems are word-lexemes.
14. *The turkey is ready to eat now* is a case of lexical ambiguity.
15. Cultural transmission refers to the fact that the details of the linguistic system must be learned anew by each speaker.
16. Allophones are described in phonetic terms.

17. Certain vowels in English change their pronunciation depending on whether or not they are stressed.
18. Chomsky took the phrase as his basic syntactic unit.
19. A tree diagram used in generative transformational grammar is another way of presenting phrase structure rules.
20. The phonetic symbol for the velar nasal is [m].

II. Mark the choice that best completes the statement.

1. Manners of articulation and places of articulation are closely related to the production of _____.
    A. words   B. vowels   C. consonants   D. segments
2. _____ is the place of articulation made with two pieces of vocal folds pushed towards each other.
    A. Uvular   B. Pharyngeal   C. Glottal   D. Velar
3. The word *boy* is a _____ word.
    A. closed-class   B. grammatical   C. variable   D. lexeme
4. The word *haircut* is a / an _____ compound, while *baby-sit* is a / an _____ compound.
    A. adjective, verb   B. verb, noun
    C. noun, verb   D. verb, adjective
5. Study syntax from the aspect of Immediate Constituent is the concern of _____ approach.
    A. traditional   B. structural   C. generative   D. functional
6. In one sentence we should employ the correct sentence order like Subject + Predicate + Object. It belongs to the _____ study of the sentence.
    A. semantic   B. syntagmatic   C. paradigmatic   D. traditional
7. We can use _____ to present two different meanings of the same phrase *the love of mother*.
    A. IC analysis   B. deep structure
    C. projection rules   D. semantic description
8. _____ does not belong to the functional study of language.
    A. tones and their meanings   B. cohesion in texts.
    C. context   D. universality in linguistics
9. Psycholinguistics may concern with the following entities EXCEPT _____.
    A. reading comprehension   B. storage
    C. sentence production   D. textual organization
10. If you constantly repeat something to others when not necessary, you have violated the maxim of _____.
    A. manner   B. quality   C. quantity   D. relation
11. In the poetic analysis the relationship between the ending words *love* and *prove* in each line is that of _____.
    A. alliteration   B. consonance   C. assonance   D. rhyme
12. The concept competence originally comes from _____. It refers to the grammatical knowledge of the ideal language user.
    A. Saussure   B. Chomsky   C. Halliday   D. Firth
13. Selecting participants, evaluation are the work required in _____.
    A. teaching   B. learning
    C. syllabus designing   D. evaluating
14. The following linguists have all discussed about linguistic systems in their studies EXCEPT _____.
    A. Halliday   B. Grice   C. Firth   D. Saussure
15. Among the following scholars, _____ belongs to the London School.
    A. Sapir   B. Bloomfield   C. Firth   D. Boas

Comprehensive Test

III. Write the phonetic symbol for each of the following described sounds.
1. voiceless affricate _____
2. velar nasal _____
3. palatal semivowel _____
4. voiced labiodental fricative _____
5. voiced lateral _____
6. voiced retroflex _____
7. voiceless bilabial stop _____
8. voiceless palatal sibilant _____
9. high back tense rounded vowel _____
10. mid front lax unrounded vowel _____

IV. Give two possible meanings for each of the following sentences.
1. I saw the dark blue sea.
2. She loves her cat more her husband.
3. I didn't call because she was ill.
4. Could this be the invisible man's hair tonic?
5. The governor is a dirty street fighter.
6. The police stopped fighting after dark.

V. Describe the sense relation between each pair.
1. tongue (organ in the mouth), tongue (language)
2. mark (indication), mark (unit of German currency)
3. fair, fare
4. older, elder
5. ear (organ of hearing), ear (part of wheat, corn)
6. effective, efficient
7. farther, father
8. power (strength), power (influential state)

VI. Classify the items in Column A by putting in Column B the number that stands for the category. Note that one word in Column A may belong to more than one category at the same time.

A	B
1. follow	a. variable words
2. to (infinitive marker)	b. invariable word
3. the	c. open classed word
4. rose (n.)	d. closed classed word
5. since	e. grammatical word
6. *up* as in *do up*	f. lexical word
7. *has* as in *He has come*.	g. particle
8. *has* as in *He has two pens*.	h. determiner
9. there	i. auxiliary
10. several	j. pro-word

VII. Complete the following statements with appropriate terms.
1. _____ refers to the abstract linguistic system shared by all the members of a speech community and _____ refers to the actualized language.
2. _____ is the study of the rules governing the ways words, word groups and phrased are combined to form sentences in a language.
3. _____ is the typological classification of languages according to how the sounds and sound features of language are organized into phmological systems.
4. To find the distinctive sounds, the customary practice is to try to find _____-word forms

which differ from each other only by one sound.
5. _____ is proposed by J. Austin (1962) and J. Searle (1969).
6. Transformational rules are those rules which relate or transform _____ of a sentence into _____.
7. In his Handbook of phonetics, Henry Sweet made a distinction between _____ and _____.
8. _____ is the place of articulation made with the tongue tip of blade and the alveolar ridge.
9. The constituent parts of a complex word have little potential for rearrangement shows that *word* has the property of _____.
10. The fact that we can put various words in the bracket in the sentence ( ) *ate the cake.* belongs to the _____ study of syntax.
11. When we are reading an article, the information we get from the former text results in the _____ context effects.
12. If you tell someone the time instead of the price that is inquired by the person, you violate the maxim of _____.
13. The line *and palm to palm is holy palmer's kiss* in a poem is in _____ foot.
14. In _____ translation, we use computers to do the translation work.
15. The *minimal pairs* test shows that the word _____ simply refers to a *unit of explicit sound contrast*.

VIII. Answer the following questions.
1. What would language be like if it had not the properties of arbitrariness and duality?
2. How does utterance meaning differ from sentence meaning?
3. The following dialogue happens in the real life situation between two friends. Use your knowledge of pragmatics to analyze it.
   Mary: They say that pretty girls usually die early.
   Tom: You do not have to worry about that.
4. How do we distinguish English consonants from each other?

参考答案

I.
1. F 2. F 3. T 4. T 5. T 6. T 7. T 8. T 9. T 10. F
11. T 12. T 13. T 14. F 15. T 16. F 17. T 18. F 19. T 20. F

II.
1. C 2. C 3. C 4. C 5. B 6. B 7. B 8. D 9. D 10. A
11. D 12. B 13. C 14. B 15. C

III.
1. [tʃ]   2. [ŋ]   3. [j]   4. [v]   5. [l]
6. [r]   7. [p]   8. [ʃ], [s], [tʃ]   9. [uː]   10. [e]

IV.
1. The blue sea is in darkness. The color of the sea is blue dark.
2. She loves her cat more than she loves her husband.
   She loves her cat more than her husband loves her cat.
3. I didn't call her because she was ill.
   I called her not because she was ill.
4. Could this be the hair tonic for the invisible man?
   Could this be the man's hair tonic which is invisible?

综合测试
Comprehensive Test

5. The governor is a street fighter who is also very dirty.
   The governor is a fighter on the dirty street.
6. The police stopped others from fighting after dark.
   The police no longer fought after dark.

V.
1. polysemy   2. hyponymy   3. homonymy   4. synonymy
5. homonymy   6. synonymy   7. homonymy   8. Polysemy

VI.
1. a, c, f   2. g, b, d, e   3. h, b, d, e   4. a, c, f   5. b, d, e
6. g, b, d, e   7. i, a, c, f   8. a, c, f   9. j, b, d, f   10. h, b, d, f

VII.
1. langue, parole
2. Syntax
3. phototypology
4. minimal pairs.
5. Speech Act Theory
6. deep structures, surface structures
7. narrow romic, broad romic (transcription)
8. Alveolar
9. stability
10. structural, paradigmatic
11. specific
12. relation
13. iambic
14. machine
15. phoneme

VIII.
1. Arbitrariness means that the forms of linguistic signs bear no natural relationships to their meaning. For instance, we cannot explain why the flower rose is called in English pronounced [rəuz] and spelt *rose* but not something else. Duality refers to the property of having two levels of structures, such that units of the primary level are composed of elements of secondary level and each of the two levels has its own principles of organization.

   Arbitrariness of language makes it potentially creative, that is, a newly invented sign can be used to refer to a new meaning. Sometimes literary works or news reports have invented words to name some new ideas or products. Duality makes language productive, for limited number of units at primary level may form numerous ways of combination to form different units at secondary level. For instance, tens of thousands of words are formed out of a small set of sounds, and out of the huge number of words there can be endless number of sentences and in turn can form unlimited number of texts.

   It is hard to imagine how human beings communicate if both features were not there. One thing for sure is that *language* is no longer a language. It might be called an animal communication system.

2. Utterance meaning, also called speaker's meaning or contextual meaning, is what the speaker uses to mean other than conceptual meaning of the sentence. It differs from the kinds of meaning in semantics in that its interpretation depends more on who the speaker of sentence is, who the hearer is, when and where it is used. In a word, it depends more on the context. The following example can help to explain this point clearly.

   A good day for a picnic uttered by someone on a picnic trip when the weather was nasty definitely means the opposite to the sentence meaning of *A good day for a picnic*.

3. In this dialogue, there is a conversational implicature in Tom's utterance. Actually, Tom wants to deliver the message that Mary is not pretty at all.

   In our conversation, we usually follow the Cooperative Principle, which contains four maxims. The four maxims are the maxim of quality, the maxim of quantity, the maxim of relation and the maxim of manner.

   In the above dialogue, the maxim of relation is violated, for Tom's utterance dose not seem to be related to Mary's. However, knowing that Tom must mean something related to her utterance, Mary can delude that Tom reveals the idea that she is not pretty at all.

From the above example, we learn that we can delude the conversational implicature on the basis of Cooperative Principle when the speaker expresses something indirectly.

4. In English, consonants are pinned down by their places of articulation, manners of articulation and the voicing.

The actual relationship between the articulators and thus the way in which the air passes through certain parts of the vocal tract are referred to as manners of articulation. There are several basic ways in which articulation can be accomplished: the articulators may close off the oral tract for an instant or a relatively long period; they may narrow the space considerably; or they may simply modify the shape of the tract by approaching each other.

And where in the vocal tract there approximation, narrowing, or the obstruction of air is called places of articulation. Consonants may be produced at practically any place between the lips and the vocal folds. There are eleven places of articulations distinguished on the IPA chart.

When the places and manners of articulation are set, for most cases there are two sounds pinned down. For example, the *stop* and *bilabial* can pin down two sounds /b/ and /p/. If we want to further distinguish these two sounds, we should employ the factor of voicing. /b/ has the feature of voiced and /p/ has the feature of voiceless.

So, by places and manners of articulation and sometimes an additional *voicing*, we can distinguish the consonants in English.

Nine

I. **Mark the following statements with "T" if they are true or "F" if they are false. Provide explanations for the false statements.**

1. The creativity of language originates from duality because duality the speaker is able to combine the basic linguistic units to form an infinite set of sentences.
2. The performative function of language is primarily to maintain the social status of persons.
3. Phonetics studies the rules governing the structure, distribution, and sequencing of speech sounds and shape of the syllable.
4. Psycholinguistics investigates the interrelation of language and brain, in processing and producing utterances and in language acquisition, biological foundations of language, the relationship between language and cognition, etc.
5. Informative function is also called ideational function in the framework of functional grammar.
6. In the production of consonants at least two articulators are involved.
7. [s, f, w, j, uː] are continuants but [h] is not.
8. A stem is any morpheme or combination of morphemes to which an affix can be added.
9. The two principal types of relations which Saussure identified are syntagmatic and paradigmatic relations. Paradigmatic relation is the relation between one item and others in a sequence, or between elements which are all present.
10. Sometimes a superordinate may be a superordinate to itself; a hyponym may be a hyponym of itself.
11. If a proposition p is true, then its negation $\sim p$ is false. And if p is false, then $\sim p$ is true.
12. External evaluation, which checks whether and to what degree the program has taught what it meant to teach.
13. There are cases in which one does not need a conventional procedure to produce a performative.
14. The presence of a conversational implicature relies on a number of factors: the conventional meaning of words, the CP, the linguistic and situational contexts, etc. So if any of them changes, the implicature will not change.
15. DACTYLIC is a metrical foot of three syllables, the first of which is long or accented and the next

two short or unaccented, as in *MER-rily* or *LOV-er boy*, or from Byron's *The Bride of Abydos*, KNOW ye the | LAND where the | CY-press and | MYR-tle

16. At the beginning of a story, we should be able to predict that narrative reference to everything in the fiction except items generally assumed by everyone in our culture must be new, and hence should display indefinite reference.
17. The categories used by novelists to represent the thoughts of their characters are not the same as those used to represent a speech.
18. Content validity refers to the extent to which the test adequately covers the syllabus area to be treated. There are also construct validity, empirical validity and face validity.
19. When the language structures or skills are further divided into individual points phonology, syntax and lexis, it is called a discrete point test.
20. The London School is best known and remembered for its contribution to phonology and the distinction between phonetics and phonology.

II. Fill in each of the following blanks with an appropriate word.

1. By _____ is meant the property of having two levels of structures, such that units of the primary level are composed of elements of the secondary level and each of the two levels has its own principles of organization.
2. _____ function is concerned with interaction between the addresser and addressee in the discourse situation and the addresser's attitude toward what he speaks or writes about.
3. _____ is made with the back of the tongue and the soft palate.
4. The principle of _____ creation can account for the co-existence of two forms, regular and irregular, in the conjugation of some English verbs.
5. An _____ construction is one whose distribution is functionally equivalent, or approaching equivalence, to one of its constituents, which serves as the centre, or head of the whole.
6. According to Chomsky, a grammar is said to have two systems: a rule system and a principle system. The rule system has four components: _____, syntax, phonetic form component, logical form component.
7. Predicate _____, also called predicate calculus, studies the internal structure of simple proposition.
8. _____ psycholinguists are concerned above all with making inferences about the content of the human mind.
9. _____ refers to using the name of part of an object to talk about the whole thing, and vice versa.
10. There is plenty of evidence to show the widespread influence of the mother tongue. A systematic study of evidence of the sort is called _____ analysis.

III. Mark the choice that best completes the statement.

1. If we focus on the speech sounds produced by the speech organs by identifying and classifying the individual sounds, then this is the domain of _____.
   A. phonology   B. acoustic phonetics
   C. articulatory phonetics D. auditory phonetics
2. _____ proposes a theory of metafunctions of language.
   A. Chomsky   B. Saussure   C. Jacobson   D. Halliday
3. _____ is concerned with the internal organization of words.
   A. Morphology B. Syntax   C. Semantics   D. Phonology
4. _____ is not the term used to classify the English consonants in terms of manners of articulation.
   A. Approximant   B. Lateral
   C. Plosive   D. Bilabial
5. The sounds in _____ are alveolars.

A. [f] and [v] B. [t] and [d]
   C. [ʃ] and [ʒ] D. [k] and [g]
6. The sound with the features "bilabial nasal" is _____.
   A. [j] B. [t] C. [m] D. [ŋ]
7. The word _____ is not a compound.
   A. *sunflower* B. *friendship* C. *moonwalk* D. *miniskirt*
8. *Bridge* is an English word, but when it refers to a type of card game, the meaning is borrowed from an Italian word. This process of borrowing is termed as _____.
   A. loanblending   B. loanshift
   C. loan translation   D. loan-word
9. _____ first suggested treating sentence as *the maximum free form* and word *the minimum free form*.
   A. Bloomfield B. Quirk C. Whorf D. F. de Saussure
10. In the words *maps*, *dogs*, *watches*, *mice* and *sheep*, each of /s/, /z/, /iz/, /ai/ and /iː/ is a (an) _____ of the plural form.
    A. allomorph   B. allophone
    C. similar phoneme   D. counter phoneme
11. _____ is an unmarked word.
    A. Bad B. Low C. Old D. Short
12. To some extent, the difference between gradable and complementary antonyms can be compared to the traditional logical distinction between _____ and _____.
    A. denotation, connotation
    B. contrary, contradictory
    C. partially different, totally different
    D. totally different, partially different
13. Among the following pairs of words, _____ can be called converse opposites.
    A. *old / young*   B. *alive / dead*
    C. *male / female*   D. *doctor / patient*
14. _____ observed that in a primitive culture the meaning of a word greatly depended upon its occurrence in a given context, or rather, upon a real language situation in life
    A. Bronislaw Malinovski   B. John P. Firth
    C. Franz Boas   D. Edward Sapir
15. The first major theory in the study of language in use was proposed by a philosopher _____.
    A. William B. Chomsky C. Austin D. Grice
16. The hearer's shutting the window is the _____ act of the utterance *It is cold in here*.
    A. illocutionary   B. perlocutionary
    C. locutionary   D. none of the above
17. All the following people make revision on Grice's CP and its maxims except _____.
    A. Wilson B. Levinson C. Horn D. Austin
18. The presence of a conversational implicature relies on a number of factors: the conventional meaning of words used, the CP, the linguistic and situational contexts, etc... So if any of them changes, the implicature will also change or even be cancelled. This fact shows the _____ of implicature.
    A. calculability   B. cancellability
    C. non-detachability   D. non-conventionality
19. _____ is concerned with exploiting relationships between documents to improve the efficiency and effectiveness of retrieval strategies.
    A. Content analysis   B. Evaluation
    C. Efficiency degree   D. Information structure
20. _____ is an error caused by negative transfer.

A. *goed*   B. *comed*
C. *foots*   D. *He tomorrow come*.

IV. Match the proper description from the list under Column B with the underlined part of each word under Column A. Notice some under A may have more than one description under B.

A	B
1. short<u>en</u>	a. free form
2. book<u>ish</u>	b. bound root
3. re<u>ceive</u>	c. inflectional suffix
4. <u>im</u>patient	d. derivational suffix
5. <u>Bio</u>logy	e. inflectional prefix
6. <u>Pre</u>pare	f. derivational prefix
7. <u>under</u>take	g. inflectional infix
8. <u>out</u>put	h. derivational infix
9. cut-<u>in</u>	i. stem
10. involve<u>s</u>	j. none of the above

V. Analyze the following observations on language, drawn from the works of various writers and scholars, and try to relate each quotation to one of the modern linguistic theories.

A. Language is the dress of thought. [From *Lives of the English Poets*: *Cowley*, by Samuel Johnson]
B. I (Samuel Johnson) am always sorry when any language is lost, because languages are the pedigree of nations. [From *Tour to the Hebrides*, by James Boswell]
C. A language is a dialect with an army and a navy. [attributed to Max Weinrich]
D. *To God I speak Spanish, to women Italian, to men French, and to my horse - German* [attributed to Emperor Charles V]
E. *Language is fossil poetry* [From *Essays*: *Nominalist and Realist*, by Ralph Waldo Emerson]

参考答案

I
1. T   2. F maintain → change   3. F Phonetics → phonology
4. F brain → mind   5. T   6. T
7. F   8. F. an inflectional affix   9. F. Syntagmatic
10. T   11. T   12. F internal
13. T   14. F not → also   15. T
16. T   17. T not → exactly   18. T
19. T   20. F Prague

II.
1. duality   2. Interpersonal   3. Velar   4. analogical   5. endocentric
6. lexicon   7. logic   8. Cognitive   9. Synecdoche   10. contrastive

III.
1. C   2. D   3. A   4. D   5. B   6. C   7. B   8. B   9. A   10. B
11. C   12. B   13. D   14. A   15. C   16. B   17. D   18. B   19. D   20. D

IV.
1. d   2. a   3. b   4. f   5. b   6. f   7. j   8. a   9. a   10. c

V.

A. Language, culture and thought. Human beings do not live in the objective world alone, nor alone in the world of social activity as ordinarily understood, but are very much at the mercy of the particular language which has become the medium of expression for their society. It is quite an illusion to imagine that one adjusts to reality essentially without the use of language and that language is merely an incidental means of solving specific problems of communication or reflection. The fact of the matter is that the *real world* is to a large extent unconsciously built upon the language habits of the group. No two languages are ever sufficiently similar to be considered as representing the same social reality. The worlds in which different societies live are distinct worlds, not merely the same world with different labels attached... We see and hear and otherwise experience very largely as we do because the language habits of our community predispose certain choices of interpretation. (Sapir 1958 [1929], p. 69)

B. Multilingualism, varieties of language

C. Dialect and language. It is one of the most frequently used aphorisms in the discussion of the distinction between dialect and language. It points out the influence that political conditions can have over a community's perception of the status of a language or dialect. The aphorism is often incorrectly attributed to the Yiddish linguist Max Weinreich, who published but did not coin it.

D. Register, code-switching. This assertion of multilingual expertise (attributed to Charles V, king of Spain and Holy Roman Emperor, 1500-58) suggests that already in the king's time languages were seen in some quarters as having utilitarian purposes.

E. Etymology, tropes. The etymologist finds the deadest word to have been once a brilliant picture. Language is fossil poetry. As the limestone of the continent consists of infinite masses of the shells of animalcules, so language is made up of images, or tropes, which now, in their secondary use, have long ceased to remind us of their poetic origin.

Ten

I. Mark the following statements with "T" if they are true or "F" if they are false

1. If we are not fully aware of the nature and mechanism of our language, we will be ignorant of what constitutes our essential humanity.
2. A phoneme is the smallest unit of sound and cannot be further analyzed.
3. Anthropological linguistics refers to the approach which studies language over various periods of time and at various historical stages.
4. The features that define our human languages can be called distinctive features.
5. The stimulus-response model provides the point of departure for behaviorist research.
6. Voice is a grammatical category of verbs which expresses the subjective attitude of the speaker towards the state of affairs described by the utterance.
7. "The ideal user's knowledge of the rules of his language" defined by Chomsky is communicative competence.
8. AUTHORIAL STYLE looks closely at how linguistic choices help to construct textual meaning. When we examine it, we will need to examine linguistic choices which are intrinsically connected with meaning and effect on the reader.

9. Phonetic similarity means that the allophones of a phoneme must bear some phonetic resemblance.
10. Slips of the tongue or pen made by either foreign language learners or native speakers are generally referred to as lapses.
11. A lingua franca has to be a native language currently spoken by a particular people.
12. Manner of Articulation is the only way by which we tell whether a sound is a consonant or not.
13. Noun phrases, verb phrases and prepositional phrases usually form endocentric constructions.
14. Embedding is the means by which one clause is included in the main clause in syntactic subordination.
15. Meaning is extracted from text or speech by relating what is presented to information stored in short-term memory.
16. In English some books is a case of number concord.
17. The belief that speakers of different languages perceive and experience the world differently is the notion of language relativism.
18. A single phoneme always represents a single morpheme.
19. Blending is a form of compounding, in which a new word is created by cutting the final part, initial part or cutting both the initial and the final of a word.
20. Parole is the term used by Saussure to refer to utterances.

II. Fill in each of the following blanks with an appropriate word with the hint of the initial letter (Write complete word forms on your answer sheet).

1. The r_____ theory is a theory of meaning which relates the meaning of a word to the real world.
2. R_____ is the term used in linguistics to describe the relationship between a particular style of language and its context of use.
3. V_____ is made with the back of the tongue and the soft palate. An example in English is [k] as in *cat*.
4. Evidence in support of lateralization for language in the left hemisphere of the brain comes from researches in d_____ listening tasks.
5. A major theory in p_____ is the theory of conversational implicature, proposed by Grice.
6. In the aspect of sense relation, when a word is a hyponym of itself, it is called an a_____.
7. Bound morphemes contain two types: roots and a_____.
8. The p_____ function of language can extend to the control of reality as on some magical or religious occasions.
9. Foreign language learners will subconsciously use their L1 knowledge in learning the foreign language and this is called language t_____.
10. When two words are c_____ antonyms, one always presupposes the other.

III. Mark the choice that best completes the statement

1. _____ function constructs a model of experience and logical relations.
   A. Interpersonal   B. Textual   C. Metalingual   D. Ideational

2. _____ is not the term used to classify the English consonants in terms of manner of articulation.
   A. Approximant   B. Lateral   C. Plosive   D. Bilabial
3. In the following word _____, the articulation of bilabial is not manifested.
   A. pet   B. met   C. how   D. web
4. Triphthongal glides in English can be heard in the word _____.
   A. tide   B. toy   C. how   D. wire
5. In the words *maps*, *dogs*, *watches*, *mice* and *sheep*, each of /s/, /z/, /iz/, /ai/ and /iː/ is a(an) _____ of the plural form.
   A. allomorph
   C. similar phoneme
   B. allophone
   D. counter phoneme
6. In the word *international*, *national* is _____.
   A. a suffix   B. a root   C. a stem   D. a prefix
7. The agent of the sentence *Sam was hit by a truck running behind a car* is _____.
   A. a car   B. Sam   C. a truck   D. none of the above
8. The following statements are in accordance with Halliday's opinions on language EXCEPT _____.
   A. The use of language involves a network of systems of choices
   B. Language is never used as a mere mirror of reflected thought
   C. Language is a system of abstract forms and signs
   D. Language functions as a piece of human behavior
9. Componential Analysis is a way proposed by the _____ semanticists to analyze the word meaning.
   A. structural   B. cognitive   C. behavioral   D. functional
10. Of the following pairs of words, _____ belongs to the type of complementary antonyms.
    A. employer/employee
    C. rich/poor
    B. captive/free
    D. fast/slow
11. The following are factors that help to produce near synonyms EXCEPT _____.
    A. conceptual difference
    C. dialectal difference
    B. stylistic difference
    D. connotative difference
12. The research purposes of sociolinguistics include all the following EXCEPT _____.
    A. to generalize the societal rules that explain and constrain language behavior
    B. to discover the relationship between speakers' social status and their phonological variations
    C. to determine the symbolic value of language varieties for their speakers
    D. to draw inferences about the relationship between register and kinds of change in language
13. The presence of a conversational implicature relies on all the following factors EXCEPT _____.
    A. the Principle of Manner
    B. the conventional meaning of words used
    C. the CP
    D. the linguistic and situational contexts
14. The following statement "There is a mixture of the tiger and the ape in the character of a Frenchman" is an example of _____.
    A. metonymy   B. synecdoche

C. antonomasia　　　　　　　D. personification
15. The utility of the corpus is increased when it has been _____.
　　A. encoded　　　B. sorted　　　C. annotated　　　D. programmed
16. To know how much a learner has mastered the content of a particular course, a teacher should set up _____ test.
　　A. an aptitude　　　　　　　　B. an achievement
　　C. a diagnostic　　　　　　　　D. a proficiency
17. The opinion that "Errors show that the learner has not changed his mother tongue habits into desired habits of the new language" is very likely to be held by _____.
　　A. structuralists
　　B. functional grammarians
　　C. transformational-generative grammarians
　　D. formalists
18. Which of the following findings concerning basic processes in reading is NOT true?
　　A. The reader is believed to carry out the processes required to understand each word and its relationship to previous words in the sentence as soon as that word is encountered.
　　B. The reader's eyes move across a page of text smoothly.
　　C. The perceptual span encompasses fewer letters to the left of fixation but more to the right.
　　D. The perceptual span covers almost 20 letters.
19. Firth did not regard language as _____.
　　A. a social process
　　B. a set of agreed-upon semiotics and signals
　　C. a means of doing things and making others do things
　　D. a means of social life
20. MOOD and MODALITY in Systemic Functional Grammar help to realize _____ function.
　　A. ideational　　　B. textual　　　C. interpersonal　　　D. metalingual
21. In a syllable, a vowel often serves as _____.
　　A. Peak or Nucleus　　B. Onset　　C. Coda　　D. stress
22. In terms of the meaning expressed by words, they can be classified into _____.
　　A. grammatical words and lexical words
　　B. content words and lexical words
　　C. grammatical words and function words
　　D. full words and empty words
23. Poly-morphemic words other than compounds may be divided into _____.
　　A. roots and affixes
　　B. bound morphemes and free morphemes
　　C. free morphemes
　　D. roots and free morphemes
24. _____ can best describe the following group of words:
　　fry→fried, Sunday + school→Sunday school
　　A. inflection and compound　　　B. compound and derivation
　　C. inflection and derivation　　　D. derivation and blending
25. In English, CASE is a special form of the noun which frequently corresponds to a

combination of preposition and noun, and it is realized in all the following channels EXCEPT _____.
   A. inflection   B. following a preposition
   C. word order   D. following an adjective
26. Which of the following is NOT included in G. Leech's seven types of meaning?
   A. Connotative meaning   B. Referential meaning
   C. Contextual meaning   D. Affective meaning
27. _____ studies the internal structure of simple propositions.
   A. Predicate calculus   B. Propositional calculus
   C. Sentential calculus   D. Truth value
28. Sapir-Whorf Hypothesis, also called as Linguistic determinism, has alternatively been referred to as _____.
   A. Linguistic resemblance   B. Linguistic relativity
   C. Linguistic universality   D. Linguistic rationality
29. Four categories of Maxims in Grice's Cooperative Principle include all the following EXCEPT _____.
   A. MANNER   B. RELATION
   C. CANCELLABILITY   D. QUANTITY
30. The following are MT research methods EXCEPT _____.
   A. The linguistic approach
   B. The interlingual approach
   C. The transfer approach
   D. The corpus-based
31. The sense relation which holds the pair of words here—there is _____.
   A. homonymy   B. complementary antonymy
   C. gradable antonymy   D. converse antonymy
32. The sense relation which holds the pair of words before—after is _____.
   A. homonymy   B. complementary antonymy
   C. gradable antonymy   D. converse antonymy
33. The sense relation which holds the pair of words sweet-suite is _____.
   A. homonymy   B. complementary antonymy
   C. gradable antonymy   D. synonymy
34. The sense relation which holds the pair of words richer-poorer is _____.
   A. homonymy   B. complementary antonymy
   C. gradable antonymy   D. converse antonymy
35. The sense relation which holds the pair of words morning star-evening star is _____.
   A. synonymy   B. hyponymy
   C. gradable antonymy   D. homonymy
36. The sense relation which holds the pair of words potato chips-junk food is _____.
   A. synonymy   B. hyponymy
   C. homonymy   D. converse antonymy
37. In plain English CAUSE(x, (~HAVE (x, y))) means _____.
   A. x gives y x B. x does not have y
   C. x causes y not to have x D. x causes x not to have y
38. The connective implication corresponds to the English _____.
   A. "if…then"   B. "if and only if…"

  C. "and"   D. "or"
39. Cognitive linguists look at the sentence *I fell into a depression* as a case of _____ metaphors.
  A. ontological   B. structural   C. orientational   D. vertical
40. Pair _____ falls into the syntagmatic association.
  A. pen - write   B. black - white
  C. judge - guard   D. farm - harm

IV. Answer the following questions briefly

1. Use your linguistic knowledge of sense relations to explain what makes the following humorous. (10 points)
 a. Question: Why was Six afraid?
   Answer: Because Seven Eight Nine.
 b. Education kills by degrees.
2. What design feature/s of language does each of the following language phenomena show? Explain briefly why you think so. (20 points)
 a. cir → encircle or circular
 b. 我感冒了 = I have a cold / I caught a cold. (English)
      = Hargab baa ku haya. (Somali)
      = Tá slaghdán ort. (Irish)
      = 나는 감기에 걸렸다. (Korean)
 c. 小虎：妈妈，我昨晚梦见你带我去迪斯尼乐园了。
 d. As captain of the plane, Helen took her place in the henpit and started the engine.
3. Specify what type/branch of linguistic study will most likely deal with each of the following research questions. (10 points)
 A. Which lexeme has the highest frequency on the data?
 B. What factors have brought new words into our daily use of the language?
 C. Is it possible to use this device to recognize the kidnapper's voice among thousands of calls you get every day?
 D. What are the drawbacks of using logical forms to translate a complex sentence?
 E. What are the differences between real-world tasks and pedagogical tasks?
 F. Does the universal quantifier presuppose the existence of an entity named by the argument?
 G. What factors will cancel the presence of a conversational implicature?
 H. How does language represent the way human beings perceive and conceptualize the world?
 I. Is *touchable* in the word *untouchable* a stem or a root with a suffix?
 J. In what kind of context the production of a sound will be influenced by a neighboring sound?

V. Answer the following essay questions (40 points)

1. Use the underlined sentences in the following dialogue as examples to explain the functions of language. (10 points)
Tom: I've got an extra ticket for the opera on Saturday. Do you know anyone who might like to go?
Mary: Not offhand. But I'll ask around.
Tom: Well, thanks.

Mary: Hey, come to think of it, I'm free! I'd love to go.
Tom: Great! Do you mind driving?
Mary: Not at all. Pick you up at seven?

2. Use your knowledge of morphology to invent a brand name for a pet shampoo which will be marketed in English speaking countries. Explain your reasons. (10 points)
3. In the English speaking world, there is variation in the use of "-ing" in words such as *morning*, and *laughing*. The variants are [iŋ]—the standard variant—and [in], a non-standard variant. The following table shows the results of a study which investigated whether the **sex of addresser** had an effect on which variant was used by two informants when they greeted people with "Morning, or Good morning".

Variant used	Male addresser	Female addresser
[iŋ]	26%	72%
[in]	74%	26%

How would you account for these findings? (20 points)

参考答案

I
1. T 2. F 3. F 4. F 5. T 6. F 7. F 8. F 9. T 10. T
11. F 12. F 13. F 14. T 15. F 16. T 17. F 18. F 19. F 20. T

II.
1. referential 2. Register 3. Velar 4. dichotic 5. pragmatics 6. auto-hyponym
7. affixes 8. performative 9. transfer 10. converse

III.
1. D 2. D 3. C 4. D 5. A 6. C 7. C 8. C 9. A 10. B 11. D 12. D
13. A 14. B 15. C 16. B 17. A 18. B 19. B 20. C 21. A 22. A 23. A
24. A 25. D 26. B 27. A 28. B 29. A 30. D 31. B 32. C 33. A 34. C
35. A 36. B 37. D 38. A 39. C 40. A

IV.
1. Homonymy and polysemy are often the source of humor. The word *Eight* is a homophone for *ate*. The phrase *by degrees* is polysemous.
2. a. Duality
   b. Arbitrariness and Duality
   c. Displacement
   d. Creativity
3. A. computational linguistics   B. sociolinguistics   C. computational linguistics
   D. semantics   E. applied linguistics   F. semantics
   G. pragmatics   H. cognitive linguistics   I. applied linguistics
   J. phonology

V.
1. The functions of language concerned here: informative, performative, emotive and phatic. (Note one piece of language may play more than one functions)

A: <u>I've got an extra ticket for the opera on Saturday. Do you know anyone who might like to go?</u> (informative and performative)
B: Not offhand. But I'll ask around.
A: <u>Well then, thanks.</u> (phatic)
B: <u>Hey, come to think of it, I'm free! I'd love to go.</u> (emotive and informative)
A: <u>Great!</u> (emotive) <u>Do you mind driving?</u> (performative)
B: Not at all. Pick you up at seven?

2. This is an open question. Any application of word formation, such as derivation, clipping, blending, compounding, abbreviation, in creating a brand name will do. A further explanation of the motivation will definitely add to the score.

3. Some social factors are believed to influence our language behavior in a social context. Among these factors, some major ones include 1) class; 2) gender; 3) age; 4) ethnic identity; 5) education background, etc. The results of the investigation show how the factor of gender has an impact on the linguistic behaviors of the informants (the person who greeted others). Interestingly, the females used the standard variant to greet others while the males used the non-standard variant. It seems that women wanted to establish a better social identity for themselves before others but males did not care that much. This fact shows that it is women's place in society that makes them linguistically behave in that way. These findings prove there is correlation of language and society.

References

Aitchison, J. 2000. *The Articulate Mammal: An Introduction to Psycholinguistics*. Beijing: Foreign Language Teaching and Research Press.

Alexander, L. G. 2000. *New Concept English: Practice and Progress* (Book 1). (4th ed). Beijing: Foreign Language Teaching and Research Press.

Aronoff, M. & J. Rees-Miller. 2001. *The Handbook of Linguistics*. Beijing: Foreign Language Teaching and Research Press.

Aronoff, M. & K. Fudeman. 2005. *What Is Morphology*? Oxford: Blackwell.

Biber, D. and S. Conrad. (eds.). 1998. *Corpus linguistics*, Beijing: Foreign Language Teaching and Research Press.

Brown, J. D. & T. Hudson. 2002. *Criterion-referenced Language Testing*. Cambridge: Cambridge University Press

Carroll, D. 2000. *Psychology of Language*. Beijing: Foreign Language Teaching and Research Press.

Cook, V. 2000. *Chomsky's Universal Grammar: An Introduction*. Beijing: Foreign Language Teaching and Research Press.

Cook, V. 2000. *Linguistics and Second Language Acquisition*. Beijing: Foreign Language Teaching and Research Press & Macmillan Publishers Ltd.

Ellis, R. 2000. *Second Language Acquisition*. Shanghai: Shanghai Foreign Language Education Press.

Finegan, E. 2005. *Language: Its Structure and Use*. Beijing: Peking University Press.

Fromkin & Rodman. 1993. *An Introduction to Language*. Fort Worth: Harcourt Brace College Publishers.

Garman, M. 2002. *Psycholinguistics*. Beijing: Peking University Press.

Goodluck, H. 2000. *Language Acquisition: A Linguistic Introduction*. Beijing: Foreign Language Teaching and Research Press & Blackwell Publishers Ltd.

Hadumpd, B. 2000. *Routledge Dictionary of Language and Linguistics*. Beijing: Foreign Language Teaching and Research Press.

Hudson, G. 2005. *Essential Introductory Linguistics*. Beijing: Peking University Press.

Hughes, H. 2003. *Testing for Language Teachers*. (2nd ed). Cambridge: Cambridge University Press.

Larsen-Freeman, D. 2000. *Techniques and Principles in Language Teaching*. Oxford: Oxford University Press.

Larsen-Freeman, D. & M. H. Long. 2000. *An Introduction to Second Language Acquisition Research*. Beijing: Foreign Language Teaching and Research Press.

Li, G. 2000. *A New English Course: Student's Book*. Shanghai: Foreign Language Education Press.

McNamara, T. 2000. *Language Testing*. Oxford: Oxford University Press.

Poole, S. 2000. *An Introduction to Linguistics*. Beijing: Foreign Language Teaching and Research Press.

Radford, A. & M. Atkinson. (eds.). 2000. *Linguistics: An Introduction*. Beijing: Foreign Language Teaching and Research Press.

Richards J. C. & T. S. Rodgers. 2001. *Approaches and Methods in Language Teaching*. Cambridge: Cambridge University Press.